GRAPEVINE

Anthony Rose switched careers after winning the *Observer*/Peter Dominic New Wine Writer Award in 1985. The following year he joined the *Independent* as its wine correspondent. He is the current Glenfiddich Drink Writer of the Year and won the Wine Guild of the United Kingdom's Wine Columnist of the Year Award in 1988, 1989 and 1993 as well as its trophy in 1993. He has judged wine competitions in Australia, South Africa, France, New Zealand and the United States as well as the UK and contributes to *Decanter, Wine, Wine & Spirit* and *L'Officiel des Grands Vins*. He has also contributed to the *Oxford Companion to Wine*, the *Harrods Book of Wine* and sundry other publications.

A former deputy editor of *Wine* and editor of *Wine & Spirit*, **Tim Atkin** is the wine correspondent of the *Observer*. He also writes regularly for *Esquire, Wine* and *Saveur*. He won the Glenfiddich Drink Writer of the Year Award in 1988, 1990 and 1993 and was the Wine Guild of the United Kingdom's Wine Columnist of the Year in 1991, 1992 and 1994. In 1994, he was the first recipient of the Wines of France Award. He has contributed to a number of books on wine as well as publishing two of his own – *Chardonnay* and *Vins de Pays d'Oc*. He is a regular member of *Wine* magazine's tasting panels and has judged wines in the UK, France and Australia.

Reviews of the 1994 Edition

'Objective, contentious and helpful, Rose and Atkin give praise where it is due, but also dish out some pithily devastating criticisms'

Off-Licence News

'It's worth buying *Grapevine* just for the detailed critique of each store's buying policy and personnel, which leaves one or two well-aimed dents in immaculate reputations. Wonderfully judgmental'

Scotland on Sunday

'Articulate and opinionated' *Sunday Express*

'The breadth of selection is impressive and the comments on each wine succinct'

Financial Times

'Accurate, up-to-the-minute, stylishly written and, though aimed at the consumer, makes useful and easy reading for people in the hospitality industry who wish to take the pulse of the market'

Caterer & Hotelkeeper

'A brilliant value book, this one is for the serious armchair shopping-spree planner. Study this, and your supermarket trolley need hardly touch the floor!'

Hampstead & Highgate Express

Grapevine

The Complete
Wine Buyer's Handbook
1995 Edition

Anthony Rose and Tim Atkin

HEADLINE

To Hazel Rose and Ron Atkin, two people we can count on
to follow our recommendations

First published in paperback in 1994
by HEADLINE BOOK PUBLISHING

10 9 8 7 6 5 4 3 2 1

ISBN 0 7472 4700 5

Typeset by Avon Dataset Ltd., Bidford-on-Avon, B50 4JH

Printed and bound in Great Britain by
Cox and Wyman Ltd, Reading, Berks

HEADLINE BOOK PUBLISHING
A division of Hodder Headline PLC
338 Euston Road
London NW1 3BH

CONTENTS

ACKNOWLEDGEMENTS

Like its predecessor, this completely new edition of *Grapevine* could not have been written without the help of a large number of indulgent wine buyers and PR people, who organised extensive bespoke tastings, checked the answers to our irritable flow of questions and faxes and submitted themselves for interview and interrogation.

Our thanks to the following people in Britain: At Asda: Nick Dymoke-Marr, Philip Clive and Juliet White; at Budgens: Annie Todd and Tony Finnerty; at the Co-op: Master of Wine Arabella Woodrow; at Davisons: Michael Davies; at Fuller's: Roger Higgs; at Somerfield: Angela Mount; at Greenalls Cellars: Nader Haghighi and Kevin Nicholls; at Kwik Save: Master of Wine Angela Muir and Deborah Williams; at Majestic Wine Warehouses: Debbie Worton, Tony Mason and Sarah 'Stonky' Wykes; at Marks & Spencer: Jane Kay, Viv Jawett and Chris Murphy; at Morrison's: Stuart Purdie; at Oddbins: Katie MacAulay, Karen Wise, John Ratcliffe and Steve Daniel; at Safeway: Master of Wine Liz Robertson and Elizabeth Oldham; at Sainsbury's: Diane Lamb, Faith Gauld and Mark Kermode; at Spar: Master of Wine Philippa Carr and Liz Aked; at Tesco: Janet Lee, Chris Bourne and Stephen Clarke; at Thresher, Wine Rack and Bottoms Up: Master of Wine Jo Standen, Gilda Witte, Jayne Bridges, Kim Tidy, Julian Twaites and John Woodriffe; at Unwins: Bill Rolfe and Jim Wilson; at Victoria Wine: Thomas Woolrych, Nicola Harvey and Rosemary Neal; and at Waitrose (John Lewis): Jane Turner and Masters of Wine Julian Brind and David Gill.

And for help with our cross-Channel chapter: At Auchan: Yves Rouet; at Bar à Vins: Luc Gille; at Calais Wine & Beer: Marco Attard, Neil Cotton, Simon Delannoy and Jerôme Castledine; at Le Chais: Vincent Théret; at Continent: Olivier Beaufils and Pascal Pilon; at EastEnders: the incomparable Dave West; at The Grape Shop: Martin Brown and Katrina Thom; at La Maison du Vin: Master of Wine Richard Harvey and Chris Bullimore; at Mammouth: Patrick

Novak; at Perardel: Franck Boutard and Monique Janot; at Pidou: Francis Pille and Denis Letailleur; and at The Wine Society: Julie Stock.

At Headline, our thanks are due to Ian Marshall, who again edited the book at a gallop, Alan Brooke, who had the confidence to sign us up for a second year; and to Janet Ravenscroft, who copy edited the original manuscript. Thanks, too, to our proof reader Fiona Wild. Back in Colliers Wood, Lyn Parry held the book together in the last week. Lastly, a big thank you to our agents Fiona Lindsay and Linda Shanks at Limelight Management.

It goes without saying that none of the above bears any responsibility for the opinions, comments and tasting notes which follow. Just as well, really.

HOW TO USE GRAPEVINE

Our marks need to be looked at in the context of the accompanying tasting note and the way wine changes and develops in bottle – for better or worse. Scores are not immutable or definitive. Every wine has its own intrinsic qualities and, by definition, our comments are subjective. With two palates to consider each wine, we hope to eliminate some of our individual prejudices. Nevertheless, just because we like something, it doesn't mean you have to, and vice versa. If tastes were uniform, we might as well pour a few samples into a computer, give you the print-out and go home.

Wines are divided into four price brackets in the UK:
Under £3
£3–5
£5–8
Over £8

and four in France:
Under 20 francs
20–30 francs
30–50 francs
Over 50 francs

Where a wine costs over £8 or 50 francs, we try to give a further indication of its price in the note. There is, after all, a big difference between something which retails at £8.49 and something which weighs in at £30.

We have made every effort to ensure that the wines we list are available, although some may be out of stock. Prices may also vary. By tasting in a concentrated three-month period, we aim to be as up-to-date as possible.

Grapevine's symbols

The symbols and numbers used in *Grapevine* work as follows:

QUALITY:
20 Nirvana
19 The suburbs of Nirvana
18 Truly outstanding
17 World-class
16 Excellent
15 Very good
14 Good everyday drinking
13 Everyday drinking
12 Drinkable (occasionally with a peg over your nose)
11 Almost drinkable
10 Almost undrinkable
9 and below   Faulty or plain disgusting

VALUE FOR MONEY:
£££   Superb value
££   Good value
£   Fair value
0   Poor value

Unlike other guides, we score on quality as well as value for money. Hence it is perfectly possible for a wine to score 17 and £ or 14 and £££. Wines scoring 17 or more appear in bold for ease of reference. We also rate wines according to sweetness (for whites, sparkling wines and rosés) and weight (for reds and fortifieds), as well as drinkability:

SWEETNESS (WHITES AND ROSÉS):
1 Bone dry
2 Dry
3 Off-dry
4 Medium dry
5 Medium sweet
6 Sweet
7 Very sweet
8 Exceptionally sweet
9 Time to call the dentist

FB   Full-bodied
MB   Medium-bodied
LB   Light-bodied

DRINKABILITY:

♪   Drink now

         Drink now or keep

♮   Past it

STAR RATINGS:
Each of the chains in this guide is given a star rating out of five. These range from half a star, represented as (*), to four and a half, or ****(*). This year, no one achieved the full five star rating.

How we taste
We taste later and more thoroughly than any other guide. All the wines listed in this book were sampled between June and September 1994. At every outlet we look at the top ten best-selling wines as well as a representative range from the chain's main list. In every case, this includes wines under £5, as well as more expensive fare.

We also visit and interview every retailer in person, whether it be in France or the UK. It goes without saying that we are both independent judges. We do not write for, work for or accept advertising or funding from retailers. Above all else, we are consumers and journalists.

Another special feature of *Grapevine* is that we include wines we don't like, as well as those we do. We believe that a critic's job is to criticise constructively, pointing out the bad as well as the good. Apart from providing a few laughs, this has a positive result: several wines that we trashed in last year's guide have not reappeared in 1995. Farewell, BB Club Brut.

We try not to overdo it, though. Many of the poorest wines we taste are not listed. We see it as our role to throw out some of the truly awful bottles. Where we've left them in, they tend to be popular wines, top ten best sellers or things with an undeservedly inflated reputation.

We aim not to go over the top in our descriptions or succumb to the curse of the wayward tendril of the vine. We try to give you enough information to make the wine sound interesting – or not, on occasion. But more than that, we have no desire to dictate what you should enjoy. Happy drinking.

INTRODUCTION

We've never had it so good, mark II

We began the 1994 edition of *Grapevine* with a solid pat on the back for the British wine industry. No other country, we argued, offered consumers as wide or as interesting a selection of wines. Well, the encouraging news is that it's still true. The range offered by British supermarkets, off-licences and wine merchants remains second to none. We reckon that's worth another pat on the back.

In fact, things are arguably even more diverse than a year ago. Just when we thought there were no more winemaking countries to discover, we've seen the arrival of good things from Uruguay, Argentina, Slovenia, Slovakia and the Czech Republic to set alongside the classics of the New and Old Worlds. What will they come up with next? Latvia? Uganda? Uzbekhistan?

A substantial chunk of the research for this book was carried out in supermarkets along the veteran-packed northern French coast. As the rain tipped down and commemorative D-Day traffic first-geared its way towards the nearest bar, we consoled ourselves with the thought that, however fractious and tired we were, we wouldn't have to taste hypermarket wine for another 12 months. Next time you're in a Continent, Prix Gros or Casino take a good look at the range of wines. If that doesn't make you feel lucky, nothing will.

Takeover time

Despite our general optimism, events in the high street over the last few years have not necessarily served the cause of diversity. In 1992, the Thresher Group pounced on Peter Dominic and killed off the name. In 1993, Victoria Wine did the same to Augustus Barnett. This year, both supergroups have consolidated their positions. Victoria Wine swallowed the last of Augustus Barnett, creating a new retail pyramid with a Wine Rack-style chain called Victoria Wine Cellars at its apex. And Thresher put increased brawn behind Bottoms Up, its by-the-case operation, and developed the convenience store format.

The emergence of these powerful supergroups has negative as well as positive aspects. On the one hand, their buying muscle squeezes the more old-fashioned independent chains such as Unwins and Davisons. But, on the other, it helps the high street to staunch the flow of customers to the supermarkets and gives them a run for their money.

Supermarket or down-market?

For the time being, however, that flow goes on. The supermarkets continue to dominate the take-home market. And as we saw with Tesco's summer 1994 takeover of the Scottish chain William Low, the four big groups (Sainsbury's, Tesco, Asda and Argyll) are determined to increase their share of the retail pie.

There is nothing necessarily wrong with this, although the Big Four have once again used cheap prices as their primary offensive weapon. Some might argue that this is fine and dandy for the consumer. But if the result is a rash of cheap and nasty wines, not to mention off-licence closures, redundancies and nothing to plough back into the business, no one is really better off in the long run.

We have seen a continuation of last year's downward trend, aggravated by discounters such as Netto, Aldi and Kwik Save paring prices to the bone and by the threat of cross-Channel shopping. This, in turn, has prompted supermarkets such as Asda and Budgens to concentrate more effort on their own discount outlets, respectively Dales and Penny Market.

Few retailers have resisted the pressure to shift more wine. Indeed, this year has seen more hype and salesmanship than ever before: £1.99 promotions, wine fairs, customer mail-outs, multibuys, wine linked with food, and all manner of price-cutting.

The value thing

As a general rule, the more you pay for wine, the more interesting it gets. This is particularly true in the £3–8 bracket. Tax, VAT and the retailer's margin account for such a large chunk of the cost of a cheap bottle that by the time you've deducted them, you're not leaving much for the wine if you spend less than £3. There are good wines out there at under £3 – indeed, many of them are included in this book – but you've got to be increasingly selective.

Nevertheless, the average price of a bottle of wine in Britain is stuck in the £2.99 quicksand. To sell more expensive wine, a retailer needs to get people excited about a product. In theory, this is where the independent wine merchant comes in.

Due to lack of space, the expansion of our cross-Channel section and the excessive demands already placed on our sleep patterns, we don't cover the independents in *Grapevine*. But we think it's worth mentioning that no one in the high street can match the best specialists for service, special offers, in-depth knowledge and range.

Some come close, though. And in view of the general down-market trend, it is encouraging to see not only Oddbins but the likes of Thresher, Wine Rack, Majestic, Waitrose, Victoria Wine and Bottoms Up encouraging people to try new wines and to trade up from the bargain basement.

The cross-Channel conundrum

This year has witnessed the rise and rise of the Calais buying spree. Cross-Channel shopping applies to beer more than wine, but the phenomenon has become so well-established since the first edition of *Grapevine* was launched in November 1993 that we have developed the cross-Channel section into a substantial part of the book, rather than leaving it as an afterthought.

It is significant that the big boys have followed the pioneers across the English Channel. Sainsbury's has set up stall and Tesco's new venture is going to open soon. Such groups do not open stores lightly. So unless the Chancellor suddenly does an uncharacteristic about turn, it looks as though cross-Channel shopping is here to stay (see our cross-Channel chapter for further details). Time to load up your transit van.

Window dressing and the fine wine graveyard

As we've already said, the ranges stocked by the major half dozen retailers are impressive. But the full line-up of wines doesn't always filter down into the smaller stores.

Most supermarkets and off-licences are 'segmented' according to size and location. Some include a handful of fine wines in top stores as a way of window-dressing. This makes it difficult to say that a certain wine is stocked by a particular store. We applaud retailers, such as Morrison's, who carry the full range in every branch. It makes life simpler for customers (and for us).

At the same time, we sympathise with an organisation at the

opposite extreme, such as the Co-op. Despite their best intentions, it is often impossible for stores to carry more than a basic range, either because of size or logistical headaches.

Things are improving, however. With the general trend towards dismantling fine wine sections (those wooden wine racks are too intimidating for most people), there should be more space on the shelf for wines in the vital £3–8 range.

Gold medal syndrome

We've also noticed a certain amount of duplication between retailers. Part of the problem has to do with competitions like the International Wine Challenge. When wines win gold medals, buyers scramble to get them on their lists. Because if they don't, their bosses ask questions when they walk into a rival store and find it there. The practice of 'cherry-picking' golds and silvers gives rise to identikit wine ranges, and in the long run reduces drinker's choice. In this respect, we applaud the likes of Waitrose and Oddbins, whose ranges reflect a bolder, more individual approach to wine buying.

Scattergun wine buying

A related problem customers face is choosing from similar styles of wine. We found this last year at Thresher, which stocked a bewildering number of Alsace wines and New Zealand Sauvignons. Thresher claims it's listened to criticism and this is by and large true. All the same, however patriotic it might be, we still think that 30 English wines on the list is overdoing it. Even Oddbins has sprayed the scattergun from time to time. We applaud the chain's pioneering work in Chile, but couldn't it cut out a few of the Sauvignons and Chardonnays?

Whither the New World?

Are we starting to see a change in the New World pecking order, brought about in part by higher prices from Australia and New Zealand? Certainly there's been something of a shift in attitude towards South Africa and Chile.

It's an indication of how quickly political events have moved that last year we considered excluding Cape wines. South Africa has always had the potential to be the new Australia, producing two and half times the yield of the New World market leader. But it's been the skunk of the world for so long, that it's going to take a while before it achieves Australia's range of styles and prices.

Nevertheless, in 1994, South Africa established itself as a winemaking country capable of providing flavoursome, value-for-money wines, with its highly developed white wine technology on the one hand and its distinctive, near-native Pinotage on the other. For the time being, it's still polarised between cheap, fruity whites and the more expensive estate wines. Good value, attractive wines from the likes of Backsberg, Fairview and Danie de Wet are beginning to point the way.

After a whole heap of misplaced enthusiasm a few years ago, Chile is at last beginning to come good, responding to the UK market with some intensely flavoured, well-priced whites and improving Bordeaux-style reds. We have yet to see evidence of widespread quality winemaking and diversity of style, but producers such as Santa Carolina, Caliterra, Casablanca and Cono Sur have made a promising start. Let's hope Chile can keep the prices reasonable.

California is still the New World's great underperformer. It has the potential to make better wines than any of its competitors in the £5–8 bracket and the fluent command of bullshit to sell them. But what do we get over here? Gallo, Gallo and more Gallo. Oddbins has done a good deal to show what California can do, and there have been isolated sightings of good value from the likes of Corbett Canyon at Victoria Wine, but we'd like to see California making a real push in the UK over the next year.

Eastern Europe
If South Africa is the snoozing giant of the New World, Eastern Europe is its counterpart in the northern hemisphere. Here, too, things are at last beginning to stir. And once again the status quo is changing.

After a long spell at the top of the mound, Bulgaria has been challenged and, we feel, overtaken by Hungary, at least as far as white wines are concerned. Part of the Hungarian success is due to flying winemakers, mostly from Australia and New Zealand. Harnessing good raw material to their own technological blandwagon, they continue to produce popular styles of clean, fruity wines at attractive prices.

Elsewhere in the east, Slovakia and the Czech Republic have emerged as surprising sources of drinkable wine. Moldova has yet to fulfil its undoubted potential, despite the arrival of Australian giant Penfolds. Good wines are the exception rather than the Moldovan rule. The same, give or take the Aussies, is true of Romania, another country with massive potential.

Is it rash to predict that world-class wines will emerge from the former Eastern Bloc by the end of the century? We think not. But problems of consistency continue to dog Eastern European wines. It would be a tragedy if a growing reputation came unstuck for lack of proper funding, equipment and knowledge.

The British wine trade is divided into two camps on the issue. Despite misgivings on the part of important players such as Tesco, Oddbins and the Co-op, others, such as Safeway, Waitrose and Sainsbury's, are prepared to commit themselves to Eastern Europe via flying winemaker projects and in-depth relationships with local wineries. Fingers crossed . . .

The natives are friendly

Despite their unfamiliar and often hard-to-pronounce names, indigenous grapes are increasingly entering the high street frame. It's partly because they're cheap of course, but, long-term, they could help to bring some excitement to a market obsessed with a clutch of fashionable varieties. We feel Chardonnay and Cabernet Sauvignon mania has gone far enough. Give us more Torrontes, more Kekfrankos, more Periquita, please.

The resurgence of indigenous grapes is apparent not just in Eastern Europe, but in the south of France, where there is a burgeoning interest in Mediterranean varieties, and in Italy, Spain and Portugal too. The joint ventures between Australia's Mitchelton and Bodegas y Bebidas in Spain, Geoff Merrill and GIV in Italy, and Peter Bright's work in Portugal have all helped to focus attention on unfamiliar flavours. For which, many thanks.

Star turns for 1995

One of the surprises of the year was the large number of excellent Muscadets we came across. Could this be the start of a renaissance? Still in France, we had some wonderful Chablis. And the Languedoc-Roussillon again demonstrated why it is the most exciting, up-and-coming wine region in the world.

We have also noticed an improvement in the quality of Italian reds – and whites – in the middle price bracket. Italy has always been good at designer packaging, but now the wines are living up to their advance billing. Have Italian producers finally seen reality?

Australia has reacted to criticisms of overoaking and begun to lighten up its styles. Australian Chardonnays with the words 'unoaked' or 'unwooded' on the label must give the oak chip industry a few restless nights.

Last year we saw a few good things from Spain. And we're pleased to report that the number has increased hugely. Rioja provides some truly excellent value wines, such as those from Campillo, Berberana and Martinez Bujanda. Navarra has started to challenge its more famous neighbour, and Raimat in Catalonia is also showing a return to form.

The revelation has been the whites, however. Solana (one of our wines of the year) typifies this new breed of modern, but distinctively Spanish white. We were delighted to find half a dozen really enjoyable Iberian whites on supermarket and high street shelves.

Must improve
And who are we going to dump on this year? Ready? Well, the biggest single disappointment has been the quality, or rather lack of it, of Beaujolais. Since it went up in price a few years ago, with no corresponding increase in quality, Beaujolais has provided very poor value for money.

Apparently, people still buy the stuff, but we wonder how much longer this can go on. There are good wines made in the region – the likes of Pierre Savoye and Château de Thivin prove that – but too many of the Beaujolais we see here taste thin and joyless. Whatever happened to the uncomplicated, juicy Gamays we used to love?

Claret under £4 has once again been a terrible disappointment. Red Burgundy, too, failed to stack up, even at the £10 level. We are not surprised to see Alsace in decline either (it's plummeted from 220,000 to 120,000 cases in a year), since, with a few exceptions, it rarely seems to deliver value for money. Vin de Pays des Côtes de Gascogne is, sadly, more hit-and-miss than a simple, technological white ought to be.

Bulgaria is in a mess. For some reason, it seems to think we like drinking coarse wines infused with cheap American oak chips. The 'young vatted' style, which favours fruit over barrel and bottle ageing, is a possible solution. But the problem is that not all young wines, particularly the more rustic styles, take to being drunk young. Bulgaria needs to get its act together fast.

The ubiquitous chip

We have found ourselves this year starting to refer to wines as oaked or unoaked. Oak, like tannin or alcohol, seems to have become an integral feature of the style and taste of wine. If the wine can take the oak, fine, but where it's just a cosmetic end in itself, we'd like to see it toned down or turned into garden furniture.

And there's not just oaked and unoaked wine, but good oak and bad oak too. The flavour of oak has become so popular that too many producers continue to douse the cheapest wine in the cheapest oak chips in an effort to hide the wine's humble origins behind a smokescreen of vanilla and coconut.

The flavour of oak, while still immensely popular, is under scrutiny in the high street. It is significant that one supermarket has hedged its bets by selling an Oak-aged Claret because of customer demand, and, at the same time, an 'Unwooded Australian Chardonnay'. Meanwhile another supermarket has specially asked its Spanish red supplier to take out a few oak chips. Is the era of chips with everything drawing to a close? We hope so.

Corkiness

And just to finish on an upbeat note, let's talk about mould. We've hardly done a tasting for *Grapevine* this year without coming across two or more corked bottles. On more than one occasion, we have had two, and once, three corked bottles of the same wine.

What are we talking about here? Is a corked wine something with bits floating on the surface? No, corkiness derives from the interaction of the bleaching of the cork with cracks in its surface, producing a substance known as TCA (Trichloranysol), which smells and tastes of mould.

Most people in the wine trade concede that corkiness now affects something like one in every 25 bottles. That's an awful lot of mould. And an awful lot of bottles that people ought to be returning to their local retailer.

But corkiness is not always easy to spot. The taint can be so obvious that the wine reeks of mould, or so faint that it is hard to detect. Even if the wine is obviously corky, and even if you are in a position to return the bottle and ask for your money back, nothing can make up for the disappointment of opening a faulty bottle.

How long before the wine business finds another solution? It's hard to imagine a classed growth claret in a carton or a wine box. The mould-breaking polyurethane stopper, which looks like a cork but doesn't produce off-flavours, is one possible solution. No-fuss screw-caps may not be very pretty, but they are highly effective. Isn't it time a few more producers switched to them, at least for inexpensive wines?

See you next year.

THE 1995 *GRAPEVINE* AWARDS

Wine Retailer of the Year: The Thresher Group
For improving the quality of what we drink in Britain through its three retail chains, Bottoms Up, Wine Rack and Thresher, and for proving that the high street off-licence doesn't have to rely on cigarettes, soft drinks and £1.99 promotions for survival.

Winemaker of the Year: Danie de Wet of De Wetshof Estate
For his commitment to producing world-class Chardonnays in the Cape. As well as being one of South Africa's best winemakers, Danie de Wet has always been committed to good labour practices. For us, he epitomises the spirit, warmth and generosity of the new South Africa.

Most Improved Wine Retailer of the Year: Marks & Spencer
For listening to criticism and effecting a wholesale rethink of its range to include more value-for-money wines and some exceptional dinner party bottles.

Cross-Channel Wine Retailer of the Year: The Grape Shop
For providing excellent service and the best and most cosmopolitan range of wines in the cross-Channel ports, if not the whole of France, and demonstrating that there's life beyond the cash-and-carries of Calais.

GRAPEVINE'S WINES OF THE YEAR

As we did in the first edition of *Grapevine*, we have selected three cases of the year: red, white and sparkling. These are 36 wines that we think represent characterful, value-for-money drinking. There are plenty of other outstanding wines in the pages that follow, but we picked these particular bottles for their combination of quality and availability. Stockists are listed after each wine.

We have tried to choose a variety of styles. We could have picked 12 red wines entirely from, say, the Languedoc, but we wanted to please readers who like other things, too. For the statistically-minded, the results by country were: Australia (4), Chile (2), England (1), France (8, as well as 9 Champagnes), Hungary (1), Italy (4), Portugal (1), South Africa (3), Spain (2), United States (1). That ought to keep the French happy.

Apart from the sparkling wines, none of our wines costs more than £8. Indeed, the majority retail at under £5 and one scraped in under the £3 barrier. Most score 17 for quality and £££ for value for money. Where they score slightly less, it tends to be because they are inexpensive. A wine which gets 15 and £££ and sits on the shelf at £2.99 is arguably worthy of greater recognition than a £20 claret or red Burgundy.

WHITE WINES OF THE YEAR CASE

1993 Sainsbury's Frascati Secco Superiore, Geoff Merrill
£££ / 1 / ▐   16/20
A distinctive blend of Malvasia del Lazio and Malvasia di Candia
with 50 per cent Trebbiano for ballast. This weighty, rich, Roman
white with its spicy stem ginger character almost restores your
faith in Frascati.
Stockist: Sainsbury's (including Calais)

Chais Cuxac Chardonnay, Vin de Pays d'Oc
£££ / 2 / ▐   16/20
From one of France's best co-operatives, this oak-aged Chardonnay
is made by Serge Dubois in a toffee and buttered toast mould with
fresh acidity for balance. One of the Languedoc's outstanding
Chardonnays.
Stockist: Morrison's

1993 Solana White, Ribeiro
£££ / 2 / ▐   17/20
The offspring of a timely liaison between Australia's Mitchelton
Wines and Spain's Bodegas y Bebidas. Winemakers Don Lewis and
Francisco Diaz Ubero have used indigenous north-western Spanish
grapes, Torrontes and Treixadura, to produce a brilliant,
characterful white. A zesty, lemon and lime-like, modern white
with some Australian fruit richness and plenty of Spanish
personality. Long may the partnership flourish.
Stockists: Morrison's; Oddbins

1992 Stellenzicht Noble Late Harvest Weisser Riesling, half-
bottle
£££ / 7 / ►   17/20
Stunning value for money at under £4 for a half-bottle, this is a
raisiny dessert wine with lots of crystallised citrus fruit freshness
and zip. We never suspected the Cape could produce things like
this. Made in limited quantities, so hurry, hurry, hurry.
Stockists: Victoria Wine; Oddbins

1994 Houghton Wildflower Ridge Chenin Blanc, Western Australia

£££ / 2 / ▌   17/20

From Hardy's Western Australian operation, this is a hugely aromatic Chenin Blanc with masses of cassis, grapefruit and tropical fruit flavours and a hint of smokiness from partial oak-ageing. It's nice to see an interesting white made from something other than Chardonnay and Semillon from Australia.

Stockist: Waitrose

1993 Domaine de la Rénaudie, Sauvignon de Touraine

£££ / 2 / ▌   17/20

A subtle, nettley Sauvignon Blanc with crisp, restrained gooseberry flavours and a minerally edge more commonly associated with Sancerre than more lowly Sauvignon de Touraine. Made at an 18-hectare property in St-Aignan-sur-Cher from 20-year-old vines, it's incredible value at under £5.

Stockist: Oddbins

1992 Mâcon Igé, Les Roches Blanches, Les Vignerons d'Igé

£££ / 2 / ▌   17/20

A ripe, almost unctuous, unoaked white Mâcon-Villages with plenty of buttery, peachy, intense fruit flavours and enough acidity for balance. One of the best white Burgundies around, especially at under a fiver. It's encouraging to see a wine of this quality emerging from a co-operative in the Mâconnais.

Stockist: Fuller's

1994 Casablanca Sauvignon Blanc, Lontue Valley

£££ / 2 / ▌   17/20

One of the best Sauvignon Blancs in Chile, which, at under £5, is now selling at a realistic price. An intense apple and citrus fruit flavoured dry white with super concentration, heading more towards New Zealand than the Loire Valley in style.

Stockist: Oddbins

1993 Danie de Wet Grey Label Chardonnay, Robertson

£££ / 2 / ▌   17/20

The bear-like Danie de Wet was one of our star winemakers last year, and he's done it again in 1995. Trained at Geisenheim in Germany, he has become South Africa's leading Chardonnay

specialist, making subtle, understated wines of freshness, elegance and, above all, excellent value for money. Partially barrel-fermented, this is a citrus and vanilla-scented stunner with beautiful balance and intensity of flavour.
Stockist: Sainsbury's (including Calais)

1992 Château Carsin, Bordeaux Blanc
£££ / 2 / ▬-   17/20
Mandy Jones is an Aussie who's worked in Portugal, Chile and Australia as well as Bordeaux. At Château Carsin, she specialises in white wines, experimenting with combinations of oaks, yeasts and grape varieties. The 1992 is the best Carsin to date, blending 20 per cent Sauvignon Blanc and 80 per cent Semillon in an elegant, toasty Graves-style white with a touch of Australian-style tropical fruit. Bordeaux could do with a few more Mandies. The equally excellent 1993 should be available by Christmas 1994.
Stockists: Sainsbury's; Waitrose

1993 Chapel Hill Riesling, Eden Valley
£££ / 2 / ▮   17/20
Made by Pam Dunsford, one of a growing band of women winemakers in Australia, this superb, cool climate Eden Valley Riesling has nothing to do with the Hungarian wine of the same name. Highly aromatic, fresh and zesty – definitely one of Australia's most delicate Rieslings.
Stockist: Bottoms Up

Pellegrino Superiore Secco Marsala
£££ / 2 / ▮   17/20
A large part of the pleasure of this Sicilian fortified wine is its astonishing amber-gold colour. But the aroma and flavours in the bottle live up to the advance billing: caramel fudge and orange peel with attractively balanced fruit sweetness and a dry, almondy finish. Who said Marsala was just for cooking?
Stockist: Victoria Wine

RED WINES OF THE YEAR CASE

1993 Safeway Hungarian Merlot, Szolo-Bor, Villány
£££ / MB / ▌   16/20
Safeway apparently paid good money to the designers of the truly ghastly Jane Austen meets Brides of Dracula label adorning this stunning Eastern European red. It certainly deserves better: a soft, finely textured Merlot with blackberry fruit and a hint of pepper. Like its whites, Hungary's reds are speeding away from the competition.
Stockist: Safeway

1992 Château de Belesta, Côtes du Roussillon Villages
£££ / MB / ▌   16/20
Surprisingly, this comes from large-volume supplier Les Vignerons Catalans. It's an equal blend of Syrah, Grenache and Carignan with intensely peppery aromas, vibrant young fruit and an elegance rarely found in cheap Roussillon reds. More like a Crozes-Hermitage or St Joseph than a Roussillon.
Stockist: Safeway

1992 Monastère de Trignan, Coteaux du Languedoc
£££ / FB / ▌   17/20
Wow! A great follow-up to the wonderful 1991, and they've still managed to keep it under £4. Super-aromatic, old vine Syrah from the Languedoc, using the carbonic maceration technique to maximise fruit flavours and keep the texture smooth. A massively spicy, rosemary and thyme-infused red. All that's missing is the parsley.
Stockist: Majestic

1990 Château La Voulte-Gasparets, Corbières
£££ / FB / ►   17/20
Consistently among the best producers in the Languedoc-Roussillon, this estate makes wines to blow your socks and shoes off. Super concentration and masses of spicy, garrigue-scented fruit with a chunkiness that promises further development.
Stockist: Sainsbury's

1988 Rioja Crianza Campillo
£££ / MB / ▌   17/20
An outstanding bargain from Bodegas Campillo, one of the

youngest and best wineries in the Rioja region. The peculiarity here is that Campillo uses only Tempranillo grapes in its red wines, instead of the more usual blend of varieties. The result is a gamey, mature Rioja with sumptuous oak integration adding spicy complexity. As good as many a Gran Reserva, but at a fraction of the price.
Stockists: Asda; Oddbins

1991 Il Caberno, Giordano
£££ / MB / 🍷   17/20
One of M&S's best recent finds, with a handsome package that belies its price tag. The wine is pretty special too, blending Piedmontese Nebbiolo with 15 per cent Cabernet Sauvignon. (In the circumstances, we wondered whether 'Il Nebbiolo' might not have been a more appropriate name.) An intriguing, approachable wine with finely judged oak and none of the traditional Nebbiolo hardness.
Stockist: Marks & Spencer

1992 Rosemount Estate Shiraz, South-East Australia
£££ / MB / 🍷   16/20
Rosemount Estate made its name with its Chardonnays, but its Shiraz can be equally good, if not better. This is a dense, but supple, highly aromatic red with masses of peppery, spicy fruit. Blended from vineyards in South Australia as well as Rosemount's native New South Wales, it's a great introduction to the joys of a grape which does brilliantly Down Under.
Stockist: Sainsbury's

1991 Backsberg Cabernet Sauvignon, Paarl
£££ / MB / 🐌   17/20
The 160-hectare Backsberg estate is best known for its elegant Chardonnays. But this excellent red, made from recently planted South African clones of Cabernet Sauvignon, is equally exciting in its own way. Halfway to an Australian Coonawarra Cabernet in style, it's an elegant tobacco, mint and blackcurrant-like wine with balance and ageing potential.
Stockist: Waitrose

1992 McWilliams Mount Pleasant Cabernet Sauvignon
£££ / MB / 🐌   17/20
McWilliams is one of the most underrated family wineries in

Australia, concentrating on substance rather than publicity. Part of the reason is that, until recently, its reputation was based almost entirely on fortified wines. Now it's adopted a more dynamic approach to table wine production, we should start to see a few more stunners like this. From irrigated vineyards in the New South Wales district of Riverina, this is an intense, concentrated berry fruit Cabernet Sauvignon with perfectly judged American oak. Like most of McWilliams' wines, this one will age well in bottle.
Stockist: Oddbins

1990 Cappello di Prete, Vino da Tavola del Salento, Candido
£££ / FB / ❶   17/20
A mature, southern blend from Italy's Mediterranean heel, full of savoury, raisin and tobacco fruitiness and delightfully fresh acidity. At just over £5, this is one of the best value Italian reds on the market. About time we caught onto what's happening in Italy.
Stockist: Bottoms Up

1993 Cono Sur Pinot Noir Reserve
£££ / MB / ❶   17/20
Made by American winemaker Ed Flaherty at the Concha y Toro owned Cono Sur Chimbarongo Estate winery in the Rapel region of Chile, this second release is the best Pinot Noir we've come across so far from South America. It even rivals the likes of Saintsbury and Acacia in California, except on price, where, remarkably, it's under £6. A rich, chocolatey, nicely oaked Pinot Noir with voluptuous loganberry and raspberry fruit flavours.
Stockists: Fuller's; Oddbins

1989 Cartuxa, Evora
£££ / FB / ➡   17/20
A structured, old-fashioned blend of Periquita, Moreto, Aragones and Trincadeira from the flatlands of southern Portugal's Alentejo region. With its tarry, peppery fruit and raisiny sweetness, this is the Iberian Peninsula's answer to first-rate Cahors.
Stockists: Thresher Wine Shops; Wine Rack; Bottoms Up

FIZZ OF THE YEAR CASE

Michel Genet Blanc de Blancs Brut, Chouilly
£££ / 2 / 🍾   17/20
A 100 per cent Chardonnay fizz with a malty, Ovaltine-like bouquet
and considerable finesse. A bargain at under 100 francs.
Stockist: The Grape Shop

1988 Vintage Champagne St Gall, Premier Cru Brut
£££ / 2 / 🍾   17/20
This is the Champagne to go for at M&S, even though it tips the
scales at around £18. Superbly aromatic, with intense Pinot Noir
character and toasty richness. Classy stuff.
Stockist: Marks & Spencer

Champagne Herbert-Beaufort, Carte d'Or Brut Grand Cru
£££ / 2 / 🍾   17/20
A grand cru grower's Champagne from family-owned vineyards in
and around the aptly named village of Bouzy, showing lots of
rugged individuality. It's a big, honest mouthful of Champagne,
made mainly from Pinot Noir grapes.
Stockist: Tesco

Heritage Brut
£££ / 2 / 🍾   16/20
Made by English-based Australian John Worontschak, this is one
of the few drinkable sparkling wines made in England. Elegant
and dry with Champagne-like toastiness and bottle-age. Surprise
your Glyndebourne friends with this one.
Stockists: Victoria Wine; Safeway

Drappier Carte d'Or Brut NV Champagne
£££ / 2 / 🍾   17/20
Almost entirely made from Pinot Noir, this young, but well-
balanced Champagne shows the classically creamy, red-fruit
character of the Aube district. Intensely fruity and stylish with
considerable elegance and length.
Stockists: Thresher; Bottoms Up; Wine Rack

Veuve Clicquot Yellow Label Champagne NV Brut
£££ / 2 / ▌   17/20

Veuve Clicquot Yellow Label is consistently among the best Grande Marque Champagnes. It's a rich blend of 56 per cent Pinot Noir, 28 per cent Chardonnay and 16 per cent Pinot Meunier. Although still on the young side, it's full-bodied and possessed of considerable finesse.
Stockists: widely available

Waitrose Brut NV, Blanc de Noirs
£££ / 2 / ▌   17/20

This was one of *Grapevine*'s sparkling wines of the year in 1994 and it's done it again. Made entirely from Pinot Noir grown in the Aube region of Champagne near Les Riceys, it's ripe, malty, forward fizz with charming strawberry fruitiness. We defy you to dislike it.
Stockist: Waitrose

Oeil de Perdrix NV, Léonce d'Albe
£££ / 2 / ▌   17/20

Oeil de Perdrix is French for partridge eye – a reference to the wine's delicate pinkish colour, rather than a weird food and wine combination. This is a finely crafted, well-balanced Champagne with excellent Pinot Noir fruit and depth of flavour.
Stockist: Majestic

Sainsbury's Blanc de Noirs Champagne, NV
£££ / 2 / ▌   17/20

A fine blend of 80 per cent Pinot Noir and 20 per cent Pinot Meunier from patrician merchant, Bruno Paillard. A malty, Ovaltine-like fizz with style and finesse.
Stockist: Sainsbury's

Champagne Albert Etienne Brut Rosé
£££ / 1 / ▌   17/20

With its attractive onion-skin colour, this is an elegantly dry rosé Champagne with delicate red fruits flavours and considerable finesse. When Champagne comes up with this sort of quality at around £13, it's hard to beat.
Stockist: Safeway

Scharffenberger Mendocino NV Brut
£££ / 2 / ▌   17/20

The Pinot Noir component of this superb, toasty California fizz has been increased from 60 to 70 per cent, making the wine even more enjoyable than it was last year. There may be better Californian sparkling wines, but none can match Scharffenberger for value for money. At just under £9, this elegant fizz is one of the New World's great bargains.

Stockist: Asda

1991 Green Point
£££ / 2 / ▌   17/20

This successful Yarra Valley winery has produced a brilliant successor to the 1990, which was also one of *Grapevine*'s wines of the year in 1994. The Pinot Noir content has been increased, and Pinot Meunier has been added to the blend for the first time. Otherwise, this follows on nicely from the previous vintage, showing considerable toasty complexity and finesse. Parent company Moët et Chandon must be delighted to see Dr Tony Jordan maintaining Green Point's high standards.

Stockists: Fuller's; Majestic; Oddbins; Sainsbury's; Unwins; Victoria Wine; Waitrose

ASDA ***(*)

Head Office: Asda House, Southbank, Great Wilson Street, Leeds, LS11 5AD

Telephone: 0532 435435

Number of branches: 203 including seven Dales

Credit cards accepted: Access, Visa

Hours of opening: Monday to Saturday 9.00am to 8.00pm; Sunday 10.00am to 5.00pm

By-the-case sales: Yes

Glass loan: Yes

Home delivery: No

Clubs: No

Discounts: On cases and mixed cases

In-store tastings: Yes, in selected stores

Top ten best-selling wines: Liebfraumilch; Lambrusco Bianco La Vigna; Lambrusco Bianco; Lambrusco Rosso La Vigna; Valencia Red; Côtes du Roussillon; Claret; Cape Red Wine Box; Asda Hock; Asda Cape White

Range: GOOD: Southern France, Germany, Italy, Australia, Chile
AVERAGE: Spain, Portugal, Eastern Europe, Loire, New Zealand, Burgundy, Bordeaux, Champagne and sparkling wines, Chile, California
POOR: ALSACE, BEAUJOLAIS

We nearly lost one of the wine trade's great double acts this year. The wisecracking, stripey-shirted Nick Dymoke-Marr was strongly rumoured to be on his way to a new job, leaving mountain biking action man Philip Clive to run the Asda wine department alone. But the rumours proved groundless: a cause for celebration here at *Grapevine*. Asda tastings wouldn't have been the same without him.

As well as being an enormously amiable duo, Clive and Dymoke-Marr are a very effective buying unit. They have been working together for nearly four years now and, in that time, have turned Asda's range into one of the best and leanest around. In the past, Asda was known for its innovative labels more than its wines. These days the stuff in the bottles regularly lives up to its advance billing.

A third of the 350-strong wine range has changed in the last year, but the overall number remains the same. 'If we want to add something new,' says Dymoke-Marr, 'something else has to give.' Recent areas of expansion include California, Italy, South Africa, Spain, sparkling wines and Chile.

Occasional indulgences still feature on the Asda list – especially from Australia, Italy and Germany – but as a rule, the buyers stick to sub-£5 fare. Only five per cent of sales are over a fiver, so they'd be foolish to do otherwise. This doesn't mean they have to buy bland wines. The selections from Italy, Chile and the South of France prove that characterful things exist at the lower end of the market. 'We're looking for commercial wines that are still typical of their region,' says Clive.

The Asda top ten is still dominated by Lieb and Lambrusco, but even here there are encouraging signs. The two Cape bag-in-box wines are the first New World wines to break into the best sellers. And the Côtes du Roussillon red has followed on the heels of last year's enjoyable St Chinian, showing that Asda customers appreciate what's happening in the South of France.

Asda has what the marketing bods call a good 'geographical spread'. There are nearly 200 stores stretching from Elgin to St Austell, with the majority in Lancashire and Yorkshire. Although northern based, with a significant 26 supermarkets in Scotland, the acquisition six years ago of 60-odd Gateway stores gave Asda a presence in Birmingham, London and Bristol, too.

Philip Clive thinks the Scottish stores are an important part of the business, especially given Tesco's recent purchase of William Low. 'Scottish customers are very loyal and they remember that Asda was the first English supermarket to set up in a lot of Scottish towns. We're seen as the pioneers.'

A third of Asda's range also finds its way into Dales, its two-year-old discount stores. Dales' seven outlets in the Midlands and the North have their own wine buyer, Neil Austin, who makes a few special purchases too small to go into the full Asda estate. But by and large, he sticks to the core Asda range. You wonder what Dales' customers make of some of the space commodore labels adorning Asda's own-label wines. At least they can be sure that the wines will taste all right – not always the case in discount stores, where orange Lambrusco several years past its sell-by-date is worryingly commonplace.

The growth of discounters has affected attitudes at Asda. 'We've offered more £1.99 deals than in the past,' says Clive. 'But we try to avoid buying just on price. We look for things that are enjoyable to drink.' Prices across the range are keener this year than last. It is a source of pride to Asda that it can compete with and even beat Kwik Save on some lines.

Pricing is vital to a new in-store concept known at Asda as the Sauna Project. This was still on test in a couple of stores as we went to press, but will be in 180 supermarkets by mid-1995. Sauna sounds like a new health club at Asda House, but in practice it's a detailed strategy to increase wine sales in Asda stores by offering, among other things, key lines at affordable prices. The aim, says Dymoke-Marr, is to be 'the cheapest one-stop shop'.

When Asda carried out some research among its customers, it found that only seven per cent of them bought wine. Dymoke-Marr: 'Wine is a monster opportunity and we've found that 80 per cent of our sales at £1.99 are incremental business. It's vital to get people to make that first purchase. And to do that you need people in store who are salesmen rather than just shelf-stackers.'

This is where the second plank of the Sauna Project comes in. Asda ran a successful training scheme last year for its employees. some 214 of them took the Wine & Spirit Association's Certificate course, and only 11 failed. 'There's a real sense of pride in the drinks departments now,' adds Dymoke-Marr, 'and it's paying off in extra business.'

Another thing which emerged from customer research was that the wine shelves were difficult to understand, especially for those adventurous souls who wanted to try something different. The solution, Asda is convinced, is to group wines together by taste and price rather than country of origin.

'The groupings are more logical,' says Clive, 'with all the dry wines together, all the medium sweet wines together, and so on. We've trialled it in a couple of stores and we're convinced it's the way forward. Customers are buying wines they've never tried before. We've introduced clear graphics and simpler descriptions to help people find their way around.'

In keeping with the more customer-helpful approach, Asda has dispensed with racks for its more expensive wines, which put people off, and replaced them with a bookshelf-come-lectern. There are also wooden barrels in the wine departments for the first time to give the places a more human feel and 'slow down the Frascati drinkers'.

The general idea, says Clive, is to provide tastings and advice and to tempt non-wine drinkers into the department. 'Asda has five million shoppers a week, so the potential is enormous. Three years ago, we had a lot of problems as a chain, but now we're on a roll.'

White

Under £3

FRANCE

Asda Vin de Pays des Côtes de Gascogne
£ / 2 / 1   13/20
A light, fresh, appley Gascon white from the ubiquitous Yves Grassa, with a tart finish.

1993 Le Pigoulet, Vin de Pays de Gers
££ / 2 / 1   14/20
Made by Yves Grassa's great rivals at the Plaimont co-operative, this is a more honeyed, grapefruity style, showing good zesty balance.

Asda Côtes de Duras Sauvignon Blanc
£££ / 2 / 1   15/20
The best of Asda's cheap French whites, showing good, nettle and apple varietal character and some boiled-sweet fruitiness.

GERMANY

Liebfraumilch, St Ursula, QbA
£ / 5 / 🍾   13/20
Clean, sweet, grapefruity Lieb slightly lacking in aromatherapy.

Hock, Augustus Weinkellerei
0 / 4 / 🍾   10/20
'Refreshing medium white', says the optimistic back label. Well,
it is white, and on the sweet side of off-dry, but lovers of cheap
German wine may find the battery-acid finish a bit rasping.

1993 Asda Niersteiner Spiegelberg Kabinett
£££ / 3 / 🍾   15/20
Floral, grapey, sweet pea-like Müller-Thurgau with fresh balanced
acidity and none of the cloying sweetness you often find on
German wines at this price.

1993 Deidesheimer Hofstück Kabinett
£ / 5 / 🍾   13/20
Another Müller-Thurgau-based white from the St Ursula co-
operative at Bingen in the Rheinhessen. A step up from
Liebfraumilch, but still showing too much sugar for our
palates.

HUNGARY

1993 Hungarian Muscat, Dunavar, St Ursula
££ / 3 / 🍾   14/20
A soft, spicy, medium dry white, bottled by the modern St Ursula
winery, which tastes more like a Gewürztraminer than a Muscat.
Perhaps that's why we enjoyed it.

1993 Hungarian Chardonnay Private Reserve, Mecsekalji
££ / 2 / 🍾   14/20
A cool-fermented, unoaked Chardonnay in an uncomplicatedly
peachy, boiled-sweets mould. Pleasant drinking at the price.

1993 Hungarian Pinot Blanc
£ / 2 / 🍾   13/20
The unusual Hallowe'en style label is more interesting than this

faintly bitter Eastern European wine. At under £3, it's an affordable party quaffer.

ITALY

Lambrusco Bianco La Vigna, 5% Volume
£ / 6 / 📖   11/20
Grapey sweetness and a rather tart green apple character are the distinguishing features of this partially fermented, low-in-alcohol fizzy white.

Lambrusco Amabile dell'Emilia
£ / 6 / 📖   ·   13/20
With eight per cent alcohol, this is more of a wine than the previous confection, with frothy grape and lemon zest fruit. Fine if you like this sort of thing.

Asda Sicilian Bianco
£££ / 2 / 📖   15/20
A wonderfully individual Sicilian dry white made from the native Catarratto and Grecanico grapes blended with Trebbiano by the Curatolo brothers in Marsala. It's distinctly Mediterranean in style with hints of resin and lime and a tangy, crisp finish. Remarkable value.

SOUTH AFRICA

Clearsprings Cape White
££ / 3 / 📖   14/20
From the reliable Simonsvlei co-operative, this is an off-dry, grapefruity Chenin Blanc made with pleasantly fresh, apple and pear fruitiness and the mass market in mind.

SPAIN

Asda Valencia Medium Dry White
££ / 4 / 📖   13/20
Made from the Merseguera grape, this is a baked, medium dry, marmaladey white from the Spanish Levante.

£3–5

AUSTRALIA

1993 Asda South-Eastern Australia Semillon/Chardonnay
££ / 2 / 🍾   14/20

From Château Yaldara based in South Australia's Barossa Valley, this is a light, fresh, pineapple and vanilla flavoured, dry blend with nice Semillon character to the fore.

1993 Mitchelton Unoaked Marsanne
£££ / 2 / 🍾   17/20

Even better than the excellent 1992, this distinctive white is one of the few wines in the New World produced from the Rhône Valley's Marsanne grape. Rich, honeysuckle and melon aromas add complexity to this beautifully balanced, unoaked classic made by Don Lewis, Mitchelton's talented winemaker.

1993 Asda South Australia Chardonnay
£££ / 2 / 🍾   15/20

From Angove's, who also make Stone's Ginger Wine in Australia, this is partially barrel-aged Chardonnay with restrained citrus fruit spice, fresh acidity and a savoury, almost marmitey note.

Barramundi South-Eastern Australia Semillon/Chardonnay
0 / 3 / 🍾   11/20

Made, apparently, from a blend of trophy-winning Semillon and oak-matured Chardonnay', this is a light, sweetened up Aussie white with formula oak character. Would the offending trophy please own up.

CHILE

1992 Asda Chilean Sauvignon Blanc
££ / 2 / 🍾   14/20

A wine that tickled our palates last year, but which is getting on in age. The fruit is starting to fade, but there's still enough smoky, gooseberry flavour for enjoyment. Look out for the 1993.

1992 Rowanbrook Chardonnay Reserve
££ / 2 / ▌   15/20
Crisp, fresh, zesty Chilean Chardonnay from the modern Canepa winery, which has spent eight months in French oak to add another vanilla-flavoured layer of complexity. Nicely balanced stuff.

FRANCE

1993 Domaine St François Sauvignon Blanc, Vin de Pays d'Oc
£££ / 2 / ▌   16/20
This is the product of a joint venture between honorary Australian flying winemaker, Hugh Ryman, and the Foncalieu co-operative, showing Ryman at his value-for-money best. Zesty, grapefruity Sauvignon Blanc with textured weight and balance.

1993 Fortant de France Sauvignon Blanc, Vin de Pays d'Oc
££ / 3 / ▌   14/20
Sweeter, softer and more commercial than the Hugh Ryman wine, and also 60 pence dearer on the shelf, this is made in a New World style and plays down the grape's grassy overtones.

1993 Château Fondarzac, Entre-Deux-Mers
££ / 2 / ▌   15/20
If the previous two wines are modern in style, this is a more old-fashioned contrast, but no less interesting for that. A ripe, rich, herby and appealingly rustic Bordeaux blend from producer, Claude Barthe.

1992 Muscadet de Sèvre-et-Maine Sur Lie, Domaine Bossard
£££ / 1 / ▌   16/20
Another characterful French white, this time made by leading organic winemaker Guy Bossard. A lees-y, toasty, honeyed, yet bone-dry Muscadet which has fattened nicely over the past year. Long may the bugs leave him alone.

Asda Chardonnay, Vin de Pays d'Oc
££ / 2 / ▌   14/20
A fresh, fruity, unoaked Chardonnay from Fortant de France in the Languedoc with elegant peach and grapefruit flavours. A wee bit lean, perhaps.

1993 Asda White Burgundy
£ / 2 / ▮   13/20

From Côte Chalonnaise *négociant*, Antonin Rodet, this is an undistinguished white Burgundy rounded out by a light touch of oak. We'd like to see more fruit on wines like this, especially at a fiver a go.

GERMANY

1992 Asda Mainzer Domherr Spätlese
££ / 5 / ▮   14/20

Perfumed, spicy German sweetie with lychee-like flavours and pleasant citrus freshness. Good value at just over £3.

1991 Wiltinger Braunfels Riesling Kabinett, Van Volxem
££ / 3 / ▮   15/20

A refreshingly zesty Saar Riesling with tangy, sweet and sour fruit balancing on a knife edge of steely acidity.

ITALY

1993 Asda Frascati Superiore
££ / 2 / ▮   14/20

From the Swiss Schenk group, this dry Roman white has some characterful, nutty fruit and a bitter Italianate twist.

1993 Soave Classico 'Corte Olive', Lenotti
£££ / 2 / ▮   16/20

Blended by flying winemaker, Gaetane Carron, this is a super-rich, hoppy Soave with lots of Italian depth and freshness. Soave for readers of *Loaded* magazine.

1993 Orvieto Classico, Cardeto, Orvieto Co-operative
££ / 2 / ▮   14/20

From the largest producer of Orvieto Classico, this is a selection of what the co-operative regards as its best wines made from a blend of the native Procanico, Verdello and Grechetto grapes. A nutty Umbrian dry white with bracing acidity.

1993 Pinot Grigio Ca' Pradai, Bidoli, Grave del Friuli
££ / 2 / ▌   14/20

A fat, smoky, modern white jointly made by Bidoli Arrigo and French winemaker Gaetane Carron during a productive vintage in Italy. Good value at under £3.50.

SOUTH AFRICA

1993 Van Loveren Sauvignon Blanc
0 / 2 / ▌   12/20

A dilute Cape Sauvignon Blanc from the Robertson region with negligible varietal character. We hope the 1994 is an improvement.

1994 Fairview Estate Gewürztraminer
££ / 3 / ▌   15/20

Winemaker Charles Back is one of the most innovative producers in South Africa, creating a variety of interesting styles to suit overseas markets. This is a light, elegant, attractively priced Gewürztraminer with a touch of rose petal, which has replaced two Alsace wines on the Asda list.

1993 Van Loveren 'Spes Bona' Chardonnay
£ / 2 / ▌   13/20

Rather like the Sauvignon Blanc, this barrel-fermented Chardonnay lacks varietal character and focus.

UNITED STATES

1992 Dunnewood North Coast Chardonnay
££ / 2 / ▌   15/20

A blend of West Coast wines from the Napa, Sonoma and Mendocino regions, which proves that California can deliver at under £4.50 when it tries. Toasty oak and fresh citrus fruit flavours make this a highly appealing style.

£5-8

AUSTRALIA

1993 Goundrey Langton Chardonnay
£££ / 2 / ▌ 17/20

Goundrey have done it again. The 1992 Chardonnay was one of *Grapevine*'s wines of the year last year, and this delicately oaked, intensely fruity, cool climate Mount Barker white is as good, if not better. It's crept over £5, but it's still one of the best-value New World Chardonnays on the market.

1992 St Hilary Chardonnay
££ / 2 / ▌ 16/20

A very different style of Australian Chardonnay made by the giant Orlando winery from grapes grown in the Padthaway region of South Australia. Ripe tropical fruit and toasty, butterscotch oak make this a substantial mouthful of wine.

FRANCE

1993 Domaine des Deux Roches, St Véran
£££ / 2 / ▬ 17/20

Domaine des Deux Roches is one of the top estates in the Mâconnais region of southern Burgundy, producing both oaked and unoaked styles of Chardonnay. The oak here is beautifully judged adding complexity to the flavoursome, grapefruity characters of the *appellation*. This is as good as a top Pouilly-Fuissé and quite a bit cheaper.

GERMANY

1992 Graacher Himmelreich Riesling Kabinett, Reichsgraf von Kesselstatt
££ / 3 / ▬ 16/20

Thanks to the influence of forward-looking manager, Annegret Reh-Gartner, von Kesselstatt is one of the best distributed of Germany's top estates. This is classic Mosel Riesling with intense cassis-like aromas, Cox's apple fruit and a hint of that petrolly complexity that makes the region so exciting. Every bit as good now as it was last year.

1992 Niersteiner Pettenthal Riesling Auslese, von Metternich
£££ / 7 / ⊯-   17/20
From one of the top estates in the Rheinhessen, this ripe, concentrated Riesling is highly aromatic with a mixture of grapefruit and mango flavours and a deliciously zesty tang. It's honeyed and sweet, but perfectly balanced.

SOUTH AFRICA

Clearsprings Cape White, Medium, Simonsvlei Co-operative, 3 litre box
£ / 3 / ⬦   13/20
From the reliable Simonsvlei co-operative, this is a medium-dry, peardroppy Chenin Blanc in a three-litre bag-in-box designed for the sweet of tooth. A top ten best seller at Asda.

Red

Under £3

BULGARIA

Burgas Country Red Cabernet Merlot
£££ / MB / ⬦   14/20
Brambly, fresh, modern Bulgarian red in the young vatted style pioneered by Safeway and widely imitated ever since.

1990 Bulgarian Reserve Cabernet Sauvignon, Oriachovitza
££ / FB / ⬦   15/20
An Australian-inspired, full-bodied red with lots of sweet American oak and tannic fruit. Bulgaria's attempt at a Penfold's red.

FRANCE

Asda Cabernet Sauvignon, Vin de Pays d'Oc
££ / MB / ▌   14/20
From the Limoux co-operative best known for its sparkling
Blanquette de Limoux and barrel-fermented Chardonnays, this is a
juicy, unoaked, cool climate Cabernet Sauvignon with fresh acidity.

Asda Merlot, Vin de Pays d'Oc
£££ / MB / ▌   15/20
A soft, grassy, youthful Merlot with chocolatey fruit and a slightly
dry finish from the South of France's Fortant de France operation.
Better than most cheap clarets.

1992 Domaine de Barjac, Vin de Pays du Gard
£ / LB / ▌   13/20
A peculiar, organic animal from the South of France, tasting like a
cross between a plummy California Zinfandel and a light, spicy
Eastern European red. Weird, man.

Asda St Chinian
£££ / MB / ▌   15/20
Another winner from the South of France, made in a soft, peppery,
carbonic maceration style by the reliable Val d'Orbieu producers
group. Huge colour and aroma and bags of juicy, winter warming
fruit.

Asda Claret
£ / MB / ▌   13/20
Light, easy-drinking, basic red Bordeaux from *négociant* Yvon Mau.
Like last year, we were put off by some green tannins in the back
of the mouth.

HUNGARY

1993 Asda Hungarian Cabernet Sauvignon, Villány Co-operative
£££ / MB / ▌   14/20
In the 1994 edition of *Grapevine*, we asked for more fruit on this
co-operative's Cabernet Sauvignon. Not only has the consultant
winemaker obliged with a supple, minty style, but Asda has also

repackaged the wine with a brilliant folk art label.

ITALY

Lambrusco di Modena Rosso
0 / LB / ▌   10/20
Tart, sweet, partially fermented Ribena-like red with bubbles in it.

1993 Riva Sangiovese di Romagna
£££ / MB / ▌   15/20
A fresh, savoury, unoaked barbecue red made in Emilia Romagna
by French winemaker Gaetane Carron. Chocolate and cherry fruit
with an Italian twist. Brilliant value at under £2.50, and looks good
on the dinner table, too.

1993 Montepulciano d'Abruzzo, Cantina Tollo
£££ / MB / ▌   15/20
Another super-value Italian red in a classy bottle made in the soft
carbonic maceration style to smooth the rustic edges of the
Montepulciano grape. Still on the meaty, farmyardy side.

Asda Sicilian Rosso
££ / MB / ▌   13/20
Baked, raisiny fruit, Mediterranean style with pronounced
sweetness.

MOROCCO

Domaine Mellil Moroccan Red
0 / FB / ▌   11/20
Thick, alcoholic, baked North African red. This should have a
fatwa put on it.

PORTUGAL

1991 Asda Douro Red
££ / MB / ▌   14/20
From Mateus Rosé producer, Sogrape, this is a full-bodied, pepper
and plum Portuguese red from the steeply-terraced Port wine
region of the Douro Valley. Robust, tobaccoey quaffing stuff.

ROMANIA

Romanian Country Red Pinot Noir/Merlot
£ / MB / 🥄   12/20
As with last year's Feteasca Neagra/Cabernet Sauvignon blend, this jammy Romanian red is a little shy about its birth year. We're still offering a weekend in Bucharest to anyone who can enlighten us. Third prize . . .

SOUTH AFRICA

Clearsprings Cape Red
££ / MB / 🥄   14/20
Like the Cape Red in the popular winebox format, this mellow blend of Cinsault, Grenache and Pinotage is a soft, strawberry glugger with a little bit of oak character to help it on its way down.

SPAIN

Asda Valencia Red, Vicente Gandia
££ / MB / 🥄   13/20
A sweetish, commercial Valencian blend of Bobal and Monastrell with lots of soft, plummy fruit. A top ten best seller at Asda.

1989 Asda León, Vina da Mesa
0 / FB / 🥄   12/20
Asda has moved on from the surprisingly voluminous 1986 vintage to the 1989. We're not sure what happened in 1987 and 1988, but the more recent vintage is less enjoyable. Rustic, deeply coloured, mouth-puckering red.

£3–5

AUSTRALIA

1992 Asda South Eastern Australia Shiraz/Cabernet
££ / MB / 🥄   14/20
From Château Yaldara in the Barossa Valley, this blend has moved on to a new vintage, but the song remains pretty much the same,

with a ragbag of leather, mint and coffee undertones and pleasant strawberry fruitiness. An easy-drinking wine.

1990 Asda South Australia Cabernet Sauvignon
££ / FB / ▮   14/20
A year down the track, this Cabernet Sauvignon is disappearing into a siding. It retains some minty fruit and sweet vanilla oak, but the wine's starting to dry out.

1992 Penfolds Bin 35 Shiraz/Cabernet, South Australia
££ / FB / ▮   15/20
A typically exuberant Penfolds blend with charred American oak and berry fruit. Let's hope they can keep the price under £5 during this period of pressure on grape prices in Australia.

Barramundi South Eastern Australia Shiraz/Merlot
0 / LB / ▮   10/20

Almost a parody of an Australian red wine. A mishmash of unripe and stewed blackcurrant fruit with some oak character thrown in for good – or bad – measure.

CHILE

1993 Asda Chilean Cabernet/Merlot
££ / MB / ▮   15/20
More tannic than last year's stunning Cabernet/Merlot blend, with masses of deeply coloured blackcurrant fruit and a little bit of stalky greenness, but still one of the best-value Chilean reds on the market.

1991 Rowanbrook Reserve Cabernet Sauvignon
£££ / MB / ▮   16/20
From the ultra-modern Canepa winery, this is a French-oak aged red, exclusive to Asda. Last year we accused the 1990 of taking itself a little too seriously, but this year we've been won over by the fleshy, supple, blackcurrant and vanilla oak concentration.

FRANCE

Asda Beaujolais
£ / LB / ▌   13/20
Light, Beaujolais Nouveau-style Gamay from the Celliers des
Samsons umbrella co-operative with a banana and strawberry
character. Doesn't hang around long.

1992 Beaujolais Villages, Domaine des Ronze
£ / MB / ▌   14/20
There's more cherry fruit and plumskin weight on this blend of
village Beaujolais with a touch of pepper and distinct Gamay fruit.

Asda Red Burgundy
£ / MB / ▌   13/20
A basic, coarsely oaked red Burgundy from Côte Chalonnaise
négociant, Antonin Rodet. The Pinot Noir fruit is as shy and retiring
as it was last year.

1992 Château de la Ramière, Côtes du Rhône
£ / MB / ▌   14/20
Nicely aromatic Grenache-based southern Rhône quaffer, showing
the dilution of a watery vintage.

1992 Pinot Noir, Vin de Pays de l'Aude, Oak-aged
££ / MB / ▌   15/20
Having mastered Burgundy's white grape, Chardonnay, to the
extent that its best examples are auctioned annually for exceedingly
high prices, the Limoux co-operative apppears to be turning its
attention to the Côte d'Or's trickier red variety, the Pinot Noir.
This is a pretty good first attempt with cherryish, tutti-fruity
characters and nicely handled oak. We thought it was impossible
to find drinkable Pinot Noir in France at under £4, but this wine
has changed our minds.

Asda Fitou
£££ / FB / ▌   16/20
Ten years ago, Fitou was one of the most fashionable wines in
Britain. Then it lost its way, somewhere up in the Corbières. Now
it's back at its value-for-money best, if this example from the go-
ahead Mont Tauch co-operative is anything to go by. A peppery,

aromatic, southern French stunner. How do they turn out stuff like this at £3.29?

1992 Château de Cabriac, Corbières
£££ / FB / ▶   15/20
A blend of the Mediterranean's leading quality red grape varieties, Syrah, Mourvèdre and Grenache, from an estate in the Corbières. Lighter than the incredibly concentrated 1991, but this herb-infused, characterful southern red is still great value. It finishes on the dry side.

1993 Mas Segala Côtes du Roussillon Villages
£££ / FB / ▶-   16/20
From an estate owned by Charles Faisant, national sales manager of the Foncalieu co-operative, this big, chunky blend of mainly Grenache, Carignan and Syrah, aged in oak barrels, is in need of at least three years in bottle to reach its peak.

ITALY

1992 Chianti Colli Senesi
£££ / MB / ▶   15/20
To promote this wine, Asda are offering it in a three-litre bottle at Christmas. If it's made of the same heavy-duty, designer glass as the 75cl version, you'll need a forklift truck to get it off the shelf and an Arnold Schwarzenegger to pour it for you. The wine itself is pretty muscular too, with characterful, robust fruit and fresh acidity. A bargain at under £3.50.

1990 Chianti Classico Quercia al Poggio
£££ / MB / ▶   17/20
Made by one of Italy's top winemakers, Maurizio Castelli, this is a real step up with beautifully balanced, savoury, concentrated fruit and stylish, cedary French oak. From one of Tuscany's best recent vintages, the wine is drinking well now but will continue to age gracefully in bottle. A smart wine in a smart bottle.

1991 Cirò Rosso Classico Librandi
££ / FB / ▶   15/20
An idiosyncratic blend of Montepulciano and Sangiovese grapes

from Calabria in the foot of southern Italy. A big, alcoholic, aromatically minty red which has come over all old-fashioned in the last 12 months. Oaky, chocolatey and rich.

PORTUGAL

1990 Asda Bairrada
0 / FB / ⸮   12/20
Portuguese reds often age well, but this one has gone all sweaty and rustic on us.

SOUTH AFRICA

1992 Fairview Estate Shiraz
£ / FB / ➥   14/20
A massively minty Cape red from Charles Back's jamboree bag of styles, showing chewy, leathery tannins and lots of blackberry fruit concentration. Distinctly firm, robust stuff, which may come round over the next year.

SPAIN

1990 Asda Rioja, Faustino Bulecia
£ / MB / 🍷   13/20
An aromatic, pleasantly oaked crianza Rioja with soft, strawberry fruit and a dry, old-fashioned finish.

1988 Rioja Crianza Campillo
£££ / MB / 🍷   17/20
An outstanding bargain from Bodegas Campillo, one of the youngest and best wineries in the Rioja region. The peculiarity here is that Campillo uses only Tempranillo grapes in its red wines, instead of the more usual blend of varieties. The result is a gamey, mature Rioja with sumptuous oak integration adding spicy complexity. As good as many a Gran Reserva, but at a fraction of the price.

£5–8

AUSTRALIA

1989 Goundrey Windy Hill Cabernet Sauvignon
£££ / MB / 🍷   17/20

The 1988 vintage of this wine replaced Château Margaux'
Pavillon Rouge in the Asda wine range. Wine buyer Nick
Dymoke-Marr's decision is vindicated by this equally fine
follow-up vintage from Mount Barker winery, Goundrey.
An elegant, cigar-box red in the Pauillac mould, which
disproves French jibes about one-dimensional Australian
wines.

FRANCE

1993 Fleurie Domaine Verpoix
££ / MB / 🍷   15/20

Fleurie is one of the most popular of the Beaujolais crus, as much
for its appealing name as its wines. This is a rustic, traditional
Gamay with plenty of strawberry fruit, but not much of the charm
we associate with Fleurie.

1991 Château de Parenchère, Bordeaux Supérieur
££ / MB / ↦   15/20

Like the 1990 vintage, this modern, coffee bean style claret is on
the chewy side, and needs time to soften.

1990 Château Balac, Cru Bourgeois, Haut-Médoc
££ / MB / ↦   15/20

This is a classic Bordeaux blend of 40 per cent Cabernet Sauvignon,
30 per cent Cabernet Franc and 30 per cent Merlot from a property
just outside Pauillac, owned by Anjou producer Luc Touchais.
Good concentration of plump, fleshy fruit, aged in oak, from a
great vintage.

ITALY

1990 Montescudaio Rosso delle Miniere Sorbaiano
£££ / FB / ➧—   16/20
Wine buyer Nick Dymoke-Marr describes this oak-aged blend of
Sangiovese and Cabernet as 'my indulgence for the year'. A smoky-
oak, concentrated, rich supertuscan with considerable tannins from
a small DOC in the north-west of Tuscany near Livorno. Indulge
yourself with Dymoke-Marr's choice.

1988 Barolo Bricco Boschis, Cavalotto
£££ / FB / ➧—   16/20
From a single vineyard owned by the Cavalotto family below the
hamlet of La Morra, this is a tannic, characterful, game and truffle-
like Barolo made in a traditional style, but showing more Nebbiolo
fruit sweetness than many old-fashioned Piedmontese reds.

SOUTH AFRICA

Clearsprings Cape Red, 3 Litre Box
££ / MB / ▌   14/20
Although this Asda top ten boxed red is deliberately commercial,
we rather enjoyed its strawberry sweetness and South African
backbone. A good party red for people to pour all over their feet.

Rosé

£3–5

SOUTH AFRICA

1994 Fairview Estate Dry Rosé
£££ / 3 / ▌   15/20
A day-glo rosé made entirely from Beaujolais' Gamay grape in the
Paarl region of South Africa. Winemaker Charles Back starts off
with clear grape juice, and according to Asda's Nick Dymoke-Marr,
'lobs bunches of Gamay into it'. The result is a ripe, fruity,
redcurrant-like pink with a little bit of sweetness.

Sparkling

£3–5

FRANCE

Varichon et Clerc Sparkling Chardonnay

£££ / 2 / ▌   16/20

This is smartly packaged French sparkling wine in expensive-looking black and gold. Good, toasty maturity for a young fizz with nicely balanced, appley fruit and attractive elegance. Something of a surprise.

Blanquette Méthode Ancestrale

£ / 5 / ▌   14/20

A light, naturally sweet fizz made from the Mauzac grape variety, this resembles a cross between Moscato d'Asti and cider. So it should appeal to lovers of both – or neither.

ITALY

Asda Asti Spumante

£ / 6 / ▌   13/20

Fragrant, grapey, cloying Italian DOCG fizz.

SPAIN

Asda Cava

£ / 3 / ▌   13/20

Good package, shame about the rather earthy bubbles inside.

Over £8

FRANCE

Asda Champagne NV Brut

£ / 2 / ▌   14/20

A young, slightly unripe, own-label Champagne from the giant Marne et Champagne group.

UNITED STATES

Scharffenberger Mendocino NV Brut
£££ / 2 / ▌   17/20
The Pinot Noir component of this superb, toasty California
fizz has been increased from 60 to 70 per cent, making the
wine even more enjoyable than it was last year. There may
be better Californian sparkling wines made at Iron Horse
and Roederer Estates, but neither can match Scharffenberger
for value for money. At just under £9, this elegant fizz is
one of the New World's great bargains.

Fortified

£5-8

FRANCE

Muscat de Rivesaltes, Château de Blanes
0 / 7 / ▌   13/20
Not one of the great fortified southern French Muscats. Tealeafy,
alcoholic and rather bitter.

BUDGENS *(*)

Head Office: Budgens Stores Limited, Stonefield Way, Ruislip, Middlesex, HA4 0JR

Telephone: 081 422 9511

Number of branches: 98, of which nine are Penny Market

Credit cards accepted: Visa, Access, Switch

Hours of opening: Monday to Friday 8.30am to 8pm; Saturday 8.00am to 8.00pm; Sunday 9am to 6pm

By-the-case sales: At peak trading times of the year only

Glass loan: No

Home delivery: No

Clubs: No

Discounts: Discounts on case sales

In-store tastings: Yes

Top ten best-selling wines: Budgens Vin de Table Red; Budgens Vin de Table White; Budgens Claret; Vin de Pays de l'Ardèche; Blanc de Blancs Special Cuvée; Budgens Liebfraumilch; Budgens Lambrusco Bianco; Budgens Vino Bianco; Budgens Vino Rosso; Bulgarian Country Wine.

Range: GOOD: Regional France, sparkling wine and Champagne
AVERAGE: Portugal, South Africa, Bordeaux, Loire, Italy, Spain, Eastern Europe, Sherry, Australia, Alsace
POOR: California, Burgundy, Germany

Before this year's tasting in central London, the last we'd seen of Budgens' wine buyer Tony Finnerty was his back, disappearing towards the Tropic of Ruislip. After our brief encounter, he slipped away to Ireland to welcome Jack Charlton and the lads home from the World Cup – a rare excursion for a man with the burden of

Budgens' wine department on his slim shoulders.

Finnerty has been travelling a lot more this year, with two trips to Germany, two to France and one to Spain. But as the man in charge of fortified wines, spirits, fags, fizz and table wines, he can't afford to stray too far from base camp. 'If I went to Australia, I'd probably come back to find the whole place in flames,' he says.

So has the Lone Ranger found a sidekick? 'Still no Tonto,' reflects Finnerty ruefully, 'only the company horse.' Working single-handedly, he continues to update and expand the Budgens range. The line-up has grown from 250 to 300 wines in the last year, with 150 the minimum offering in smaller stores. Size doesn't always correspond to the class of catchment area, however. As Finnerty admits, some of the smallest stores are in the best potential locations.

The number of Budgens stores is set to increase by four, from the current tally of 89, over the coming months. But the main thrust of the company's investment is Budgens' discount arm, Penny Market. Budgens' customers are still fixated on under £3 wines. So much so, in fact, that Penny Market, which stocks around 30 table and fortified wines, is due to expand its empire to 40 stores over the next two years.

As you might imagine, Liebfraumilch and Lambrusco still feature strongly at Budgens. A case of 'ere we go, 'ere we go, 'ere we go again. But there has been activity in other areas, too. Last year one of Tony Finnerty's objectives was to get more New World wines into the range. Jacob's Creek is, not surprisingly, a big seller, but there are other things as well, including Australia's Orlando RF range and Lindemans Rouge Homme, New Zealand's benchmark Montana Cabernet Sauvignon, and the fine Backsberg Chardonnay from South Africa. At the same time, Finnerty has taken on California's Gallo 'because they came out with a cheque book'.

As well as installing more New World wines, Finnerty has spent time on the more traditional areas of France, Italy, Spain and Eastern Europe. The South of France remains a good-value option at Budgens with new listings from the Val d'Orbieu giant and an interesting white made from the Terret grape by flying winemaker Jacques Lurton. The Grüner Veltliner from Austria is better than ever, and Finnerty has craftily snapped up a graceful, mature Gran Reserva Rioja for under £5.

Another success he can take credit for is the introduction of the 'cut-price special'. Every two weeks, a brochure is delivered to local homes with, among other things, suggestions for food and wine combinations. 'We've been trying to sell better wines by giving a "deep cut" on promotional wines. As a result, sales volume has shot up by 30 per cent more than the company's overall sales.' Finnerty has also introduced 'single bottle pick', a scheme allowing customers to order from the fine wine section, even if the wine isn't available on the shelf.

Given the constraints of the business, a relatively small number of stores and the downmarket leanings of his customers, he continues to do a fair job. But the challenge remains considerable. He has made a stab at jazzing up the German and Eastern European wines, but there is still work to do in other areas of the range. The Lone Ranger could do with a Tonto, not just the company horse, to help him infuse the range with excitement. Hi, ho Silver.

White

Under £3

FRANCE

1992 Bordeaux Blanc, Bouey & Fils
0 / 2 / 1   11/20
Basic grapefruity Bordeaux dry white marred by a musty touch of cork.

HUNGARY

1993 Nagyrede Blanc, Hungarian Country White (50cl), Szoloskert Co-operative
££ / 2 / 1   14/20
Perfumed Muscat-style Hungarian white in an attractive, slimline Italianate designer bottle made from the native Hárslevelü and Zenit grape varieties.

ITALY

Tocai del Veneto, Vino da Tavola, Zonin
0 / 2 / ❷   11/20
Very basic north-eastern Italian white. Bland, faintly pongy stuff.

£3–5

AUSTRALIA

1993 Hardy's RR, Medium Dry White
£ / 4 / ❷   14/20
RR stands not for rest and recreation, but for Rhine Riesling. We preferred the new vintage to last year's soupy performance. Still a touch cloying, but showing some nice lime peel fragrance and fresher acidity.

AUSTRIA

1993 Grüner Veltliner, Winzerhaus
£££ / 2 / ❷   16/20
The eccentric author of the definitive *Wines of Austria* thinks that Grüner Veltliner smells of lentils and bayleaves. These weren't the first aromas that struck us, but we were very impressed all the same by this fresh, smoky, green bean-like white. It reminded us of a toned down New Zealand Sauvignon Blanc.

FRANCE

1993 Sancerre, Les Chasseignes, Foussier Père et Fils
£ / 2 / ❷   14/20
Like all Sancerre, this is hardly cheap. The *appellation* can be worth the premium, but not for this rather dilute effort.

1993 Geminian Vin de Pays d'Oc, Grenache
££ / 2 / ❷   14/20
This is produced at the Cuxac co-operative for the sprawling Val d'Orbieu group. Talented winemaker Serge Dubois makes the most of a normally dull grape variety with this refreshingly crisp Mediterranean dry white.

Vin de Pays des Côtes de Thau, Jacques Lurton
££ / 2 / 🍾   14/20

French flying winemaker Jacques Lurton made this Terret-based blend from grapes grown on the shores of the picturesque Etang de Thau near Sète. A modern banana and lemon peel quaffer.

GERMANY

1992 Schmitt Vom Schmitt, Pinot Blanc, Gustav Adolf Schmitt
£ / 3 / 🍾   13/20

Quite fat for a German wine, but showing some pleasant off-dry grapiness on the palate. A wine that doesn't quite live up to its stylish label.

1991 Baden Gewürztraminer Reserve, Badischer Winzer-keller
££ / 3 / 🍾   15/20

A nice smoky Gewürztraminer from one of the warmer German regions across the border from Alsace, showing good acidity and balance and an attractive spice and marzipan fruitiness.

1992 Schmitt Vom Schmitt Niersteiner Spätlese, Gustav Adolf Schmitt
£ / 4 / 🍾   13/20

We expected a bit more excitement from a so-called late harvest Spätlese. This is a step up from basic Liebfraumilch, but what isn't.

Over £5

FRANCE

Château le Gardera Blanc, Cordier
£ / 1 / 🍾   14/20

Soft, waxy, old-style Bordeaux white from a go-ahead *négociant*. Austere and a little long in the tooth.

Red

Under £3

HUNGARY

1993 Hungarian Country Red (50cl), Szoloskert Co-operative
££ / LB / ▌   14/20
This blend of the indigenous Eastern European Kekfrankos and
Zweigelt varieties is so light, it's almost a rosé. But don't let the
colour put you off. The wine has some character and soft
strawberry fragrance with fresh acidity and a nip of tannin.

ITALY

Merlot del Veneto, Vino da Tavola
££ / MB / ▌   14/20
A grassy, fruity Italian red with a fresh bitter-cherry twist. Decent
house red material.

SPAIN

Castillo de Betera, Valencia, Cherubino Valsangiacomo
0 / MB / ▐   9/20
Souped up with a dry bitter finish, probably best injected
intravenously for a quicker fix.

£3–5

AUSTRALIA

1993 Brown Brothers Tarrango
£ / MB / ▌   13/20
Tarrango? As we found out last year, it is neither a marsupial, an
after shave, nor the latest dance craze. In fact, Tarrango is a rare
crossing of Touriga Nacional and Sultana grapes from Victoria.
We enjoyed the Beaujolais-like 1992 considerably more than this
rooty, unripe effort.

FRANCE

1993 Chinon, Les Bernières, Marcel Martin
£ / MB / 🍾   13/20

There's plenty of pencil shaving Cabernet Franc character on the nose here, but rasping acidity and overly herbaceous fruit detract from the enjoyment.

1992 Côtes de Saint-Mont, Tuilerie du Bosc, Plaimont
£ / FB / ➥   13/20

The Plaimont co-operative is capable of better things than this tannic, overoaked and somewhat joyless blend of Tannat and Cabernet Sauvignon. May soften in time.

1993 Geminian, Merlot, Vin de Pays d'Oc
££ / MB / 🍾   14/20

Full, plummy vibrant and chewy southern red from the excellent Cave de Cuxac and winemaker Serge Dubois. Good cheap plonk.

1993 Geminian Cabernet Sauvignon, Vin de Pays d'Oc
££ / FB / 🍾   14/20

As you'd expect from the Cabernet Sauvignon grape, this is a mite more austere than the Merlot, and may need a little more time to round out.

1992 Château Caudeval, Fronton, Alain Pradier
0 / FB / 🍾   11/20

Hard and charmless, like Joan Collins, but also unyielding.

Costières de Nîmes, Domaines Viticoles
££ / MB / 🍾   14/20

An old-style raisiny Grenache-based red from the Languedoc/Provence border with a year or two under its waistline.

GERMANY

1993 Dornfelder Niersteiner Klostergarten, Weingut Hermannshof
££ / MB / 🍾   14/20

Germany's chilly climate isn't best suited to red wine production, but this soft, sweet and juicy curiosity might surprise you.

SPAIN

1988 Marqués de Caro, Tinto Reserva
0 / MB / 🍷   12/20
Cosmetic oak and confected fruit make this a rather coarse and
undistinguished Spanish red.

1981 Gran Condal, Gran Reserva
£££ / MB / 🍷   16/20
For £1.50 more, you could line yourself up with a bottle of this
venerable 13-year-old Rioja with delicate wild strawberry fruit and
well-judged coconutty oak.

UNITED STATES

1992 Sutter Home Merlot
£ / MB / 🍷   13/20
Famous for its sickly, so-called white Zinfandel, Sutter Home has
apparently branched out. A confected, green pepper style
California red.

Rosé

£3-5

FRANCE

Côtes de Provence Rosé, Billette
0 / 2 / 🍷   12/20
Made by Listel, the company responsible for some of France's
least distinguished rosés, this is a hard, earthy pink in a skittle
bottle. It hasn't travelled well.

Sparkling

£3–5

AUSTRALIA

Flinders Creek Brut, Savage Wines
££ / 2 / ❧   14/20
A Chardonnay/Pinot Noir blend from a New South Wales co-operative. Lemony, inexpensive fizz made using the cuve close or tank method.

Flinders Creek Brut Rosé
££ / 3 / ❧   15/20
From the same co-operative, this is a quaffable strawberry cup fizz with more delicacy than many an Australian sparkler.

CO-OP **

Head Office: CWS National Retail Buying, PO Box 53, New Century House, Manchester, M60 4ES

Telephone: 061 834 1212

Number of branches: 2,500

Credit cards accepted: All major credit cards

Hours of opening: Varies from store to store. Mainly 8.00am to 8.00pm Monday to Saturday

By-the-case sales: In selected superstores

Glass loan: In selected superstores

Home delivery: Arranged at local level

Clubs: Offers to Co-op members

Discounts: Occasionally on large orders

In-store tastings: At least once a month in superstores

Top ten best-selling wines: Co-op Liebfraumilch; Co-op Lambrusco Bianco; Co-op Laski Rizling; Co-op Claret; Co-op Vin de Pays des Côtes Catalanes Red; Co-op Hock; Co-op La Mancha Red; Co-op Valencia Red; Co-op Vin de Table Red; Co-op Vin de Table White

Range: GOOD: Germany

AVERAGE: Eastern Europe, Australia, Loire, regional France, sparkling, England, Beaujolais, Bordeaux, Italy, Portugal, Spain, United States

POOR: Burgundy, South Africa, New Zealand, Chile, South Africa

When we tasted Co-op's range for the 1995 edition of *Grapevine*, Arabella Woodrow, the Co-op's wine development manager, confessed that 'the range is not as big as it might be'. She told us: 'We're currently looking at a programme to expand the number of wines in our bigger stores. Ideally, we'll have them by the end of the year.' We hope she's right, but we couldn't help feeling a slight sense of déjà vu.

Last year we got rather excited about some of the new additions to the Co-op range, like South Africa's Thelema Mountain and California's Shafer. We said we were worried they might not filter through to Co-op stores as quickly as they should, but some of them simply failed to arrive.

All part of the charm of the good old Co-op? Perhaps. But the nebulous identity of the sprawling Co-op movement can create problems when it comes to putting together a coherent wine range. 'It's a question of logistics,' says Woodrow. 'If we're only putting the wines in our top ten stores, we can't ship five pallet loads.'

She produces a thick ring-bound book, containing the core range each of the 2,500 licensed Co-op stores is expected to stock, depending on size of store. Co-ops vary in size from tiny neighbourhood convenience stores to gigantic Co-op superstores like the one in Aberdeen. So you begin to get an idea what a logistical headache it must be to get more than the basic range onto crowded store shelves.

To make matters worse, the structure of the Co-op is split into Co-op Wholesale Stores (CWS) and Co-op Retail Stores (CRS). Arabella Woodrow and co-buyer Paul Bastard buy for over half the shops in the Co-op movement. While CWS stores must stock the range Woodrow and Bastard buy, the more independent CRS branches are free to shop around. As Woodrow says, 'We're never certain what will be in a CRS, but at least we know what's in our stores.' A relief for them no doubt, but less so perhaps for customers looking for a Co-op wine recommended in the press.

Co-op's core range of own-label wines represents around one-third of the wines in the range, but accounts for nearly 50 per cent of sales. Not surprisingly, these are the cheapies. Liebfraumilch, Lambrusco and Lutomer Laski Rizling are the top three, while the rest of the top ten is equally predictable. Having said that, the quality of the basic wines has improved since last year with a core of clean, fresh fruity flavours predominating.

Apart from Lambrusco, Co-op bottles its entire top ten itself, helping to keep costs to a minimum and pare prices to the bone. In all, 1.3 million cases of wines and spirits go through Co-op's bottling plant each year, although this may change in the future now that the bottling plant has been sold off.

This year Co-op has concentrated on the New World, with the object of introducing interesting wines from a spread of different countries and expanding its customers' choice. According to Arabella Woodrow, 'Australia has been very successful, way above anything we've ever seen before,' as Co-op customers discover the exuberant delights of its clean, sun-drenched fruit flavours. South Africa is set to take off, but has lagged behind because, with commendable, politically correct restraint on the Co-op's part, Woodrow got the green light to stock Cape wines only this time last year.

In Europe, the Co-op has expanded its German range considerably with some good-value wines at Kabinett level. Given its left leanings and the fact that over 80 per cent of the Co-op's wine sales are under £3 a bottle, Eastern Europe would appear to be ideal territory for co-operative exploration. But the range here is surprisingly disappointing.

For similar reasons to Tesco, Woodrow is cautious about Eastern Europe. 'We've taken the softly, softly approach to Eastern Europe. You've got to watch it very, very closely, since there are a lot of exciting things, but also a lot of variability. You've virtually got to isolate the vat you want, but we don't have the resources.' This is a shame because, as we see at Safeway and Waitrose, Eastern Europe may be a challenge, but it's far from terra non grata.

It's been a stable year overall for the Co-op wine department. Sales, according to Woodrow, are up on last year, despite the twin threats of the discounters and cross-Channel shopping. Part of the increased sales volume comes from £1.99 promotions. 'If you put something on at £1.99, customers are screaming for it,' says Woodrow, reflecting a feeling that the whole sector is more price-led than it was a year ago.

We wish Arabella Woodrow and Paul Bastard good luck with their plans to extend the range. It's already beginning to take on a more balanced, better quality look. Now the challenge is really on.

White

Under £3

CROATIA

Lutomer Laski Rizling
££ / 4 / ▮   13/20
The only Croatian wine we've knowingly tasted this year, this is a
clean medium-sweet white with an attractive label and some
pleasant blackcurrant-leaf fruitiness.

FRANCE

Co-op Vin de Pays des Côtes de Gascogne, Grassa
0 / 3 / ▮   11/20
Pretty thin, tired stuff from Yves Grassa, the man who pioneered
Vin de Pays des Côtes de Gascogne. We've come across one or
two good Grassa wines this year, but it pays to be selective.

GERMANY

Co-op Liebfraumilch, Pfalz
£ / 5 / ▮   12/20
A slightly tart finish put us off this otherwise respectable, popular
German sweetie.

Co-op Hock
££ / 5 / ▮   13/20
Floral, fruity, fresh Hock with Müller-Thurgau grapeyness and good
balance. One of the better bargain-basement German whites on
the market.

ITALY

Lazio Bianco, Pallavicini
££ / 2 / ▮   15/20
A fresh, dry, lemon and lime-like white from Gazza country, showing
plenty of Italian character. Unlike some examples, this wine was freshly
bottled, so is at its best. Guaranteed not to belch at dinner parties.

Co-op Lambrusco Bianco
££ / 6 / ▌   13/20

From the partially fermented school of Lambrusco, this five per cent alcohol fizzy white is clean, fruity and sherbetty.

SPAIN

Co-op Valle de Monterrey, Vino de la Tierra
££ / 2 / ▌   13/20

From the Casta Verde in Spain's temperate Galicia region, this is a decent, if neutral, clean dry white with a touch of appley sweetness.

UNITED STATES

Co-op California Colombard, Bronco
££ / 2 / ▌   13/20

Drier and better balanced than most Californians at the same price, this is a clean, affordable introduction to West Coast whites.

£3–5

ARGENTINA

1993 Etchart Torrontes
££ / 2 / ▌   15/20

Torrontes is one of the most interesting South American aromatic grape varieties, and this example from top producer Etchart shows the grape at its zesty, floral best. Refreshingly clean and well-balanced, like a cross between fragrant Muscat and spicy Gewürztraminer.

AUSTRALIA

1992 Butterfly Ridge Colombard/Chardonnay, Angoves
££ / 2 / ▌   14/20

A distinctive Australian blend whose richness, and toasty, honeyed characters reminded us of the Semillon grape. An interesting alternative to straight Chardonnay.

1993 Hardy's Nottage Hill Chardonnay
£ / 3 / ▌   13/20

Rather obvious, sweet white from Down Under. Half a glass would be more than enough.

CHILE

1993 Peteroa Sauvignon Blanc, Canepa
££ / 2 / ▌   14/20

One of a large number of supermarket whites made at the Canepa winery near Santiago, true to the cool-fermentation recipe. This is a fresh, grapefruity Sauvignon Blanc with zippy acidity.

1993 Santa Carolina Chardonnay, Los Toros Vineyard
££ / 2 / ▌   14/20

Thirty per cent of this wine was aged in American oak barrels, which accounts for its pungently spicy char. The oak is prominent, but there's plenty of good, underlying citrus fruit intensity for balance. Good value at under £4.

FRANCE

Co-op Vin de Table White, 1 Litre
£ / 4 / ▌   11/20

An aromatically challenged, medium sweet white apparently from the south-west of France.

1993 Vin de Pays d'Oc Marsanne, Val D'Orbieu
££ / 2 / ▌   15/20

A welcome new listing at the Co-op, this is a characterful, rustic dry white made from the grape of the northern Rhône, Marsanne, by the giant Val d'Orbieu operation. A full-bodied white with subtle fruit flavours.

1993 Vin de Pays d'Oc Viognier, Val d'Orbieu
£££ / 2 / ▌   16/20

This wine is available in more limited quantities than the Marsanne, which is a shame, as it's every bit as good. Made from the fashionable grape of Condrieu, it's a highly aromatic white, with crisp, nicely balanced apricot flavours and none of the cloying fatness you often get with Viognier.

1993 Château Pierrousselle Blanc, Entre-Deux-Mers
£ / 2 / ▌   13/20

We've had more aromatic white Bordeaux than this Semillon/ Sauvignon Blanc blend, but on the palate there's plenty of carbon dioxide zip and light, lemony fruit with a peppery note.

1993 Vin de Pays d'Oc Chardonnay, Fleur du Moulin
££ / 2 / ▌   15/20

Spicy, fruity, lightly oaked white from the Domaines Virginie set-up near Béziers in the Languedoc. This is one of the better-balanced Virginie Chardonnays, and an excellent drink at the price.

1991 Bourgogne Blanc Chardonnay, Jules Vignon
££ / 2 / ▌   15/20

Jules Vignon is code for Labouré-Roi, the Nuits-St-Georges-based *négociant* which supplies several supermarkets with their house Burgundies. A well-made, buttery, fresh Chardonnay with a delicate touch of oak spice.

1990 Monbazillac, Domaine du Haut-Rauly, Pierre Alard, half-bottle
£££ / 7 / ▌   16/20

Surprisingly good for a Monbazillac, an *appellation* whose sweet wines rarely send you skipping down the street. But in a great dessert wine year like 1990, when there was plenty of noble rot, or botrytis, character in the vineyards, the wines gained an extra dimension of honeyed richness. This is unctuously sweet with fine lemon peel freshness for balance. A good Sauternes substitute.

GERMANY

St Ursula Galerie Pinot Blanc
££ / 2 / ▌   14/20

A smoky, pear-like Pinot Blanc which reminded us of a lighter style of Alsace white. Fragrant and fruity with crisp acidity.

1992 Forster Schnepfenpflug Riesling Kabinett
££ / 3 / ▌   16/20

A fresh, modern German white with floral, rose petal aromas, off-dry lime and peach fruitiness and classically mouth-watering Riesling acidity.

1990 Co-op Spätlese, Pfalz
£ / 5 / ▌   13/20
Made entirely from the Ortega grape, the offspring of Müller-Thurgau's union with the Wagnerian-sounding Siegerrebe grape, this is a sweet grapefruit and pineapple cocktail of a Rheinpfalz white.

1992 Graacher Himmelreich Spätlese, Adolf Huesgen
££ / 4 / ▌   14/20
A good, but not great, Mosel Riesling with fresh appley intensity and a slightly austere aftertaste.

HUNGARY

1993 Gyöngyös Hungarian Chardonnay, Hugh Ryman
0 / 2 / ▌   12/20
Sweet, flat and lacking in freshness, a wine which has its ups and downs owing to rather primitive cellar technology. When it's good, it's very good, but when it's bad . . .

1993 Gyöngyös Estate Sauvignon Blanc, Hugh Ryman
££ / 2 / ▌   15/20
This is the best Sauvignon Blanc we've encountered from the pioneering Gyöngyös Estate. Made in a mini-New Zealand style, it's a zesty, aromatic dry white with citrus fruit sweetness and acidity. A caveat: we have noticed inconsistency between Gyöngyös bottlings.

ITALY

Co-op Orvieto Secco
££ / 2 / ▌   14/20
Fresh, dry, pleasantly nutty blend of Trebbiano, Malvasia and Grechetto from the Umbria region.

NEW ZEALAND

1993 Forest Flower Dry White, Villa Maria
££ / 3 / ▌   14/20
A reminder of the New Zealand wine industry's Germanic origins, Müller-Thurgau is still far and away New Zealand's most widely

planted grape variety, even if the Kiwis try to keep quiet about it. This is a fruity, off-dry Gisborne white which needs to be as fresh as possible for maximum enjoyment. We look forward to the 1994.

1993 Nobilo White Cloud, Gisborne

£ / 3 / ▌   14/20

Along with Montana and Cloudy Bay, this consistent blend of Müller-Thurgau and Sauvignon Blanc is one of New Zealand's most successful exports. A massively commercial, fruity, off-dry white with a pleasant edge of greenness to slice through the sugar.

1993 Montana Sauvignon Blanc

£££ / 2 / ▌   16/20

A wine that never lets you down. Montana's hugely successful Sauvignon Blanc has been selling at under a fiver for as long as we can remember, so it's hardly surprising to see it among the top ten best-selling wines in the UK. A textbook elderflower and asparagus style with lively acidity and rounded, tropical fruit.

SOUTH AFRICA

1994 Goiya Kgeisje Sauvignon/Chardonnay, Vredendal Co-operative

£ / 2 / ▌   13/20

The great selling point of this northern Cape white is that it's the first wine to appear on UK shelves in any given vintage. In marketing terms, this makes it South Africa's answer to Beaujolais Nouveau. We enjoyed this fresh, green bean-style white blend a little more in 1993.

£5–8

FRANCE

1993 Sancerre, Domaine Rimbault

££ / 2 / ▌   16/20

One of the few wines over £5 at the Co-op, this is a characterful, flinty, crisp Sancerre from a single domaine. A wine that doesn't need to flex its muscles to win you over.

1993 Chablis, Les Vignerons de Chablis
££ / 2 / ﹏   16/20
How does the La Chablisienne co-operative do it? We haven't had
a bad wine from the co-operative which dominates the Chablis
region in 1994. This unoaked Chardonnay is still tight at the
moment, but it has good underlying minerally intensity and will
provide excellent drinking throughout 1995.

GERMANY

**1990 Bernkasteler Badstube Riesling Kabinett, von
Kesselstatt**
££ / 3 / 🍷   16/20
Classic Mosel Riesling from the consistently excellent von Kesselstatt
estate, showing dry, lime and Granny Smith apple fruit and a hint of
the keroseney character of mature, Mosel Valley Riesling.

Red

Under £3

FRANCE

Co-op Claret
££ / LB / 🍷   13/20
Light, fresh, grassy claret bottled by the Co-op in Manchester. It's
still on the young side, but there's some pleasant cherryish
fruitiness too.

Co-op Vin de Pays des Côtes Catalanes
0 / MB / 🍷   11/20
Baked rustic, Roussillon quaffer from vineyards close to the
Pyrenees. The sort of red the Midi doesn't need to make any more.

GERMANY

1993 Nussdorfer Bischofskreuz Rotwein
££ / LB / 🍷   14/20
A vibrant, deeply coloured German red, made principally from

the Dornfelder grape. Soft, cherry fruit reminiscent of Beaujolais, but far better value at under £3.

HUNGARY

1992 Chapel Hill Hungarian Cabernet Sauvignon
£££ / MB / 🍷   15/20
Another brilliant-value red, this time from the Balaton Boglar co-operative, one of Aussie flying winemaker Kym Milne's many global outposts. Lots of fresh, sweet, blackcurranty fruit with a twist of Hungarian pepperiness. Bring on the goulash.

ITALY

1992 Co-op Montepulciano d'Abruzzo
££ / MB / 🍷   13/20
This is a basic, rustic, bitter-cherry and chocolate style Italian quaffer. Bring on the pizza.

SPAIN

Co-op La Mancha Red
£ / MB / 🍷   12/20
The faint sweetness on this central Spanish plonk offsets the robust tannins on the aftertaste, but can't quite conceal its Sancho Panza origins.

Co-op Valencia Red
£ / MB / 🍷   12/20
Sancho Panza Mark 2.

UNITED STATES

Co-op California Ruby Cabernet
££ / FB / 🍷   14/20
Ruby Cabernet is a crossing of Carignan and Cabernet Sauvignon grapes by the University of California at Davis, a clever way of combining quantity with quality. This is a big, tannic, cassis-like red with lots of sweet fruit and a chewy finish.

£3-5

AUSTRALIA

1993 Co-op Jacaranda Hill Shiraz/Cabernet
£ / MB / ᳚   13/20

A pleasant, if obvious, minty Australian blend at a good price. Our only complaint is that the wine's a little short on flavour.

1991 Peter Lehmann Vine Vale Shiraz
£ / MB / ᳚   14/20

Lashings of sweet, coconutty American oak and mint from a man they call the bear of Barossa. Subtle it isn't, but this robust, Barossa Valley Shiraz shows what Australia is all about. A wine which appeals to the heart, or somewhere further south, rather than the head.

1993 Brown Brothers Tarrango
£ / MB / ᳚   13/20

Tarrango? As we found out last year, it is neither a marsupial, an aftershave, nor the latest dance craze. In fact, Tarrango is a rare crossing of Touriga Nacional and Sultana grapes from Victoria. We enjoyed the Beaujolais-like 1992 considerably more than this rooty, unripe effort.

BULGARIA

1990 Lovico Suhindol Merlot Reserve
£ / MB / ᳚   13/20

A case of Bulgaria meets old-style Rioja with lots of charry, Bourbon whiskey oak and tobaccoey, blackcurrant fruit. The parts are greater than their sum.

CHILE

1992 Santa Carolina Merlot
££ / MB / ᳚   14/20

From the Santa Rosa vineyard in the Maipo Valley near Santiago, this is a light, aromatic, grassy Chilean Merlot made by leading winemaker, Ignacio Recabarren. Needs food.

FRANCE

Co-op Vin de Table Red, 1 Litre
££ / MB / 🍷   13/20
Deeply coloured, softly textured southern French quaffer with robust dry tannins and a hint of orange peel. Good party red.

1992 Vin de Pays d'Oc, Merlot, Domaine St Julien
££ / MB / 🍷   15/20
Excellent-value, mini-Pauillac style red with coffee bean oak, plump, grassy Merlot fruit and tannic bite. A deceptively serious wine from Jacques Lurton, *Grapevine*'s 1994 winemaker of the year.

1993 Château Pierrousselle Rouge, Michel Lafon
£ / MB / 🍷   13/20
Plummy, solid claret which needs slightly more time to soften. The previous vintage was a little softer, but this is still decent value red Bordeaux at under £4.

1992 Co-op Côtes du Rhône Villages, Domaine de Hauterive
£ / MB / 🍷   14/20
Traditional Grenache-based, southern Rhône red with peppery, sweet fruit, firm backbone and some astringency. A shade pricey.

ITALY

1992 Gaierhof Teroldego Rotaliano
££ / MB / 🍷   14/20
From Trentino in the Alpine foothills of northern Italy, this is a light, juicy quaffer, made from the local Teroldego grape. Its soft, aromatic impact is immediate enough, but it doesn't hang around.

PORTUGAL

1990 Co-op Douro Tinto, Sogrape
££ / MB / 🍷   15/20
A wine which proves that Douro reds don't have to be a dustbin for surplus Port grapes. Made by the go-ahead Sogrape group, this is a mature, modern red with smooth, ripe fruit and a distinctively Portuguese undertone.

SPAIN

1990 Pozuelo Tinto, Bodegas Castaño
££ / MB / 🍷   15/20
A good-value Spanish tinto from vineyards west of Alicante, showing plenty of sweet pepper and American oak spice, supported by an attractive, if robust, fruitiness. A wine that needs strongly flavoured food.

UNITED STATES

1991 Monterrey Classic Pinot Noir
£ / LB / 🍷   13/20
An ageing, slightly vegetal West Coast attempt at a red Burgundy, which has lost some of its immediacy and fruit.

£5–8

FRANCE

1992 Morgon Les Charmes, Domaine Brisson
££ / MB / ⬥   16/20
Gérard Brisson makes some of the most ageworthy reds in Beaujolais. This well-structured Gamay is a strapping, concentrated red from one of the best crus in the region and should develop like a red Burgundy as it ages. One of the best Beaujolais we've come across this year.

Sparkling

£3–5

SPAIN

Co-op Cava Brut, Codorniu
££ / 2 / 🍷   15/20
The Chardonnay component in this sparkling Spanish white gives it some attractive lemony freshness, setting it apart from many of the run-of-the-windmill, bog-standard cavas on the market.

£5–8

AUSTRALIA

Seaview Brut
££ / 2 / ▌   **15/20**
Back on form after a couple of indifferent years, this is a fresh,
toasty fizz with appealing tropical fruit ripeness.

Over £8

FRANCE

Veuve Honorain Champagne Blanc de Noirs Brut
££ / 3 / ▌   **15/20**
Made from Pinot Noir and Pinot Meunier grapes grown in the
Aube region of Champagne, this is a young, fruity fizz with
pronounced sweetness and an appealing strawberry-cup character.

DAVISONS **(*)

Head Office: Davisons Wine Merchants, 7 Aberdeen Road, Croydon, Surrey, CR0 1EQ

Telephone: 081 681 3222

Number of branches: 76

Credit cards accepted: Access, Visa

Hours of opening: Monday to Saturday from 10.00am to 2.00pm and 5.00pm to 10.00pm. Sunday 12pm to 2.00pm and 7.00pm to 9.00pm

By-the-case sales: Yes

Glass loan: Free

Home delivery: Free in local area

Clubs: No

Discounts: Eight-and-a-half per cent on mixed or unmixed cases

In-store tastings: Yes, occasionally

Top ten best-selling wines: Pampette Blanc Dry; Jacob's Creek Semillon/ Chardonnay; Pampette Blanc Medium; Pampette Rouge; Cape Cellars Sauvignon Blanc; Muscadet de Sèvre-et-Maine; Hardy's Nottage Hill Chardonnay; Frascati Secco, Superiore Ambra; Terras d'el Rei Tinto; Hardy's Nottage Hill Cabernet Sauvignon

Range: GOOD: Bordeaux, Burgundy, Australia, regional France, Port
AVERAGE: Loire, New Zealand, South Africa, Rhône, Italy, Eastern Europe, Germany, Chile, Champagne and sparkling wines, Spain, Portugal
POOR: United States

It was one of the sadder moments of the summer. The closing down sale was in its final few days and a handful of bargain-hunting customers were picking their way through the entrails of Master Cellar.

Managing director Michael Davies was trying to take an unsentimental view of the closure of Davisons' prime wine warehouse site in Croydon. 'The store just wasn't washing its face,' he said, 'but when you look at the number of people who've come in here to buy wine over the last week, you wonder where they've been for the last year.'

With the scent of blood in the air, the store's turnover jumped from £3,000 to £20,000 a week. But it was all too late. After ten years as Davisons' flagship outlet, the Master Cellar has disappeared.

It is a sign of the times that the site will be converted to a pub or wine-oriented brasserie. 'I'm very sad to be going down that route, but it's very, very difficult out there. I'm not convinced that we're coming out of the recession as far as our wine shops are concerned. We're down on down.'

Mr Davies is one of the more bullish British retailers, so when he tells you things are bad, they must be very bad indeed. But he hasn't given up just yet. He was about to open a new branch when we visited in the late summer of 1994 and remains a great wine enthusiast. Nevertheless, he concedes that 'We're putting all our spare cash into freehold pubs at the moment. I have to think of the business in 50 years' time.'

This is quite a turnaround, as well as a tacit admission of failure. When Michael Davies took over the company in 1975, a hundred years after his great-grandfather John Thomas Davies founded a prosperous chain of Victorian pubs, Davisons had already started to concentrate on the off-licence side of its business. Michael Davies accelerated the process.

Davisons exchanged its central London locations for out-of-town sites and expanded in line with the UK wine boom. To this day, most of Davisons' 76 stores are in hydrangea-belt locations on the fringes of the capital. Davies says that in the late 1970s and early 1980s, family-owned chains such as Davisons and Unwins were in the forefront of high street change. 'The brewery off-licences were awful and we were the people who began to give customers what they wanted.'

Things are rather different in the mid-1990s. First Peter Dominic was gobbled up by Thresher, then Augustus Barnett by Victoria Wine. Both are now more exciting as a result. The supermarkets, too, have developed stronger wine ranges and cross-Channel shopping has become the latest bane of the British retail scene.

'Unless you're very good at what you do,' says Davies, 'you simply won't survive in today's climate.'

So what's the future for an operation like Davisons? It has several things in its favour: an experienced wine buyer, loyal, generally well-informed staff and traditional strengths in Bordeaux, Burgundy and Port. Not that Davisons is a stick-in-the-mud business. Indeed, it has embraced the New World with considerable enthusiasm. This is reflected in Davisons' top ten, which contains three Australian and one South African wine, and in the sales figures – nearly 20 per cent of Davisons' business is Australian. 'It's what I drink at home,' says Davies.

Davisons' dependence on France is not as marked as it was. Ten years ago, 55 per cent of its sales were French, compared with 38 per cent today. 'We've seen huge changes in a decade,' says Davies. Davisons made its reputation as a claret and Burgundy specialist, but this side of the business appears to be in decline. Michael Davies' attempt to launch a claret club this year foundered due to lack of customer interest.

But as well as the company's undoubted strengths, there are countervailing weaknesses. The shop logo still looks like a bad German wine label, with heavy Gothic script on a dark background. And the 400-strong wine range is not as exciting as it could be. The basic Pampette wines are dull and even the Australian list is brand-led.

The other thing that worried us this year was that several wines appeared to be approaching or past their sell-by-date. Things that were fading last year are still around, due to poor stock rotation, or simply a decline in sales.

Michael Davies has a lot of work on his desk, so maybe he doesn't spend as much time updating the range as he should. New finds this year have come from Romania, southern France and the New World, but old favourites need to be reassessed from time to time, too. This applies to expensive Burgundies and clarets as much as to Pampette Blanc and Don Gulias Tinto.

In response to questions about the future of Davisons, Davies lifts his hands in frustration. 'You name it,' he says 'we're doing it: delivery, glasses, advice and very good managers.' This is true enough, but if Davisons is to survive as a viable off-licence chain, it needs to upgrade its shops and provide more excitement on the shop floor. Otherwise, Master Cellar may not be the last closure.

White

Under £3

FRANCE

Pampette Blanc Dry
0 / 2 / 🍾   11/20
Davisons has been buying this tart green apple white for over a
decade, so presumably somebody must be drinking it. You could
do a lot better for £2.99.

£3–5

AUSTRALIA

1993 Jacob's Creek Semillon/Chardonnay
££ / 3 / 🍾   15/20
One of Britain's most popular wine brands, selling nearly as many
bottles as the much-advertised Piat d'Or. When you consider that
Jacob's Creek retails at £4.29 in such a price-conscious country,
that's quite an achievement. This is thoroughly enjoyable stuff
with restrained tropical fruit sweetness, fresh acidity and a splinter
or two. Long may this level of quality and value continue.

1993 Hardy's Nottage Hill Chardonnay
£ / 3 / 🍾   14/20
För fans of plump oak-steered Aussie Chardonnay. Subtlety is not
Hardy's Chardy's strong card.

FRANCE

1992 Muscadet de Sèvre-et-Maine, Pierre Millot
£ / 1 / 🍾   13/20
This pleasant, if basic, Muscadet is getting on a bit, so watch out
for the 1993.

1992 Sauvignon Trois Mouline, Vin de Pays d'Oc
£ / 2 / 🍾   14/20
One year on, this unusual wine has lost a little of its edge, but

retains an appealing, waxy richness.

1993 Chardonnay, James Herrick, Vin de Pays d'Oc
££ / 1 / 🍾   15/20
The second vintage from Englishman James Herrick's impressive
New World style vineyards near Narbonne. This is more elegant
and restrained than the 1992 with deftly handled oak and a lime-
like streak of acidity.

1992 Sauvignon de Touraine, Domaine des Sablons
£ / 1 / 🍾   13/20
Basic, nettley stuff with a rasp of austere acidity. You can see why
so many wine drinkers buy Montana Sauvignon Blanc.

ITALY

1993 Frascati Secco Superiore, Ambra
££ / 2 / 🍾   14/20
One of the best-selling brands in the country, blended by importers
Enotria. If you like decent Frascati, this nutty, nicely balanced white
is a good buy.

1992 Nuragus di Cagliari, Sardinia, Dolia
£ / 1 / 🍾   14/20
From the Dolianova co-operative in Sardinia, this is a ripe apple
and pear style dry white which has filled out in the last 12 months.

NEW ZEALAND

1992 Hawkes Bay Estate Sauvignon Blanc
£ / 2 / 🍾   14/20
A wine of two halves. The aromatics have been given the red card,
but there's still some nice zesty, melon and elderflower fruit on
the pitch. We'd like to see the new vintage here.

SOUTH AFRICA

1993 Cape Cellars Sauvignon Blanc, KWV
£ / 2 / 🍾   13/20
A smoky, rather undistinguished Cape white in which pre-
fermentation grape handling has left a bitter edge.

£5-8

AUSTRALIA

1993 Penfolds Organic Sauvignon/Chardonnay, Clare Valley
£££ / 2 / ⚑   16/20
Cynics might question the Penfolds leviathan's long-term commitment
to the organic cause, but there's no denying the success of this
European-style, cool climate blend of Sauvignon Blanc and
Chardonnay with its polished oak handling and citrus-like elegance.

1992 Wyndham Estate Chardonnay Bin 222
£ / 3 / ⚑   13/20
The sort of old-fashioned, smoky-bacon, oak and tropical fruit
cocktail that seems to be going out of style, but it might appeal to
Australian Chardonnay neophytes.

FRANCE

1985 Château Filhot, Sauternes, half-bottle
£ / 4 / ⚑   14/20
1985 was not one of the greatest Sauternes vintages, owing to a
lack of the magic botrytis mould that turns grapes to a honey and
apricot elixir. A candied, lightly fruity dessert wine.

ITALY

1992 Avignonesi Bianco, Sauvignon/Chardonnay
£ / 2 / ⚑   14/20
Another white wine which has suffered a bit over the last year.
The Sauvignon Blanc component in this experimental Tuscan blend
has turned blowsy and bitter with age.

NEW ZEALAND

1993 Nautilus Sauvignon Blanc
£ / 2 / ⚑   15/20
Made by Yalumba, one of Australia's few remaining family giants,
this has all the aromatic, sweet pea intensity and green bean flavour
you'd expect from a New Zealand Sauvignon Blanc. On the pricey
side though.

Over £8

FRANCE

1991 M de Malle Graves
0 / 2 / ❷   14/20
Fattish, dry white from Château de Malle, a producer better known
for its unctuously sweet Sauternes. A wine that's seen better days.

1991 Saint Romain Jean Germain
££ / 2 / ❷   16/20
Saint Romain, situated in the hills behind the better-known
Burgundy village of Meursault, tends to produce racier wines than
its neighbour. A modern white Burgundy with nutty intensity and
subtle oak.

1989 Meursault Les Cloux, Domaine Javillier
0 / 2 / ❷   13/20
Rather like Ridley Scott's *Alien*, the oak has taken over the wine
here. Fine if you like charred toast.

1990 St Aubin Premier Cru, Domaine Morey
£££ / 2 / ❷   17/20
**St Aubin is another of the Côte d'Or's lesser villages, but in
vintages like 1990, it can rival Burgundy's best. An elegant,
zesty Chardonnay with a fresh, citrus-fruit finish and good
concentration.**

1989 Chassagne Montrachet Premier Cru, Les Chaumées, Domaine Morey
£ / 2 / ❷   16/20
On the pricey side at over £25, but this is a strapping, mature
white Burgundy with plenty of toasty oak. A wine that needs full-
flavoured food.

1985 Château Rieussec, Sauternes
£ / 5 / ❷   15/20
Owned by the aristocratic Baron de Rothschild, Château Rieussec
can be among Sauternes' leading properties. We have enjoyed the
1988 and 1989 in our time, but this opulent, honeycomb and peach
style sticky is two lemons short of a fruit bowl.

GERMANY

1992 Oppenheimer Sackträger Silvaner Kabinett Halbtrocken, Guntrum
£ / 3 / ⌷   14/20

Floral, weighty, off-dry white with Alsace pretensions. On the dear side at just under £9, especially given the availability of fine German wines at half the price.

1989 Bernkasteler Lay Riesling Kabinett, S.A. Prum
££ / 2 / ⌷   15/20

All the component parts of a top Mosel Riesling are here: kerosene, lime and Granny Smith apple. But the wine hasn't quite gelled yet. The tart finish may soften in time, but don't bet your house on it.

Red

Under £3

SPAIN

Don Gulias Tinto
0 / MB / ⌷   11/20

Oak-flavoured Don Darias tastealike with an acidic, astringent finish.

Toro, Moralinos Tinto
0 / FB / ⌷   8/20

There's only one good producer we know of in the western Spanish *denominación* of Toro, and this isn't it. Volatility, overextraction and bitterness make it a photo finish between wine faults.

£3–5

FRANCE

1992 Cabernet Sauvignon, Vin de Pays des Côtes de Thongue, Domaine St Martin
£ / MB / 🍷   14/20
From the Domaine de l'Arjolle in the tiny Languedoc vin de pays *appellation* of Côtes de Thongue, a modern, green pepper Cabernet Sauvignon with nicely judged oak. Finishes on the dry side.

1992 Syrah, Vin de Pays d'Oc, Domaine Causse
£ / MB / 🍷   13/20
Domaine Causse is made by the Béziers-based, forward-looking Domaines Virginie. This is typical, soft sweetly drinkable stuff. A little short on indigenous character, perhaps.

1993 Cabernet/Syrah, Vin de Pays d'Oc, Domaine de Montpezat
££ / MB / 🍷   15/20
Another Virginie red, this time showing a bit more depth of character and robust tannin.

ITALY

1992 Merlot del Veneto, Via Nova
£ / LB / 🍷   13/20
From the Cantina Bartolomeo Breganze, a light, pleasantly balanced Merlot with a nip of acidity.

PORTUGAL

1992 Terras d'el Rei Tinto
££ / FB / 🍷   14/20
Good to see this raisiny, robust red from the Reguengos co-operative in Davisons top ten best sellers. A wine with real Portuguese personality.

£5–8

AUSTRALIA

1992 Parrot's Hill Barossa Valley Cabernet Sauvignon
0 / MB / 🍷   13/20

Light, minty red from Australian giant BRL-Hardy. Overpriced for a rather simple style.

1990 Penfolds Coonawarra Cabernet Sauvignon
££ / FB / ➡   16/20

Masses of colour, concentrated fruit and sweet sawdusty American oak give this the stamp of Penfolds, but there's some balancing Coonawarra elegance too. Poor person's Bin 707.

1991 Craigmoor Mudgee Shiraz
££ / MB / 🍷   15/20

Mudgee is a New South Wales *appellation* with big ambitions. We found the bouquet a little composty, but enjoyed the smoothness and balance on the palate.

1991 Jamieson's Run Coonawarra
££ / MB / 🍷   16/20

A Shiraz-based brand which over the years has cleaned up on the Australian wine show circuit. Minty, blackberry fruit elegance, plenty of oak and Coonawarra freshness.

FRANCE

1992 Beaujolais-Villages, Château Vierres, Georges Duboeuf
0 / MB / 🍷   13/20

Georges Duboeuf on an off-day. Light, dull Beaujolais-Villages. Sorry, Georges, you can't win 'em all.

1990 Château Mendoce, Côtes de Bourg
££ / MB / 🍷   15/20

A Davisons' stalwart. Softish Merlot-based claret with chocolatey richness and fine-grained tannins from the right bank of the Gironde Estuary.

1988 Château de Belcier, Côtes de Castillon
££ / FB / ☞   15/20
Intense, savoury oak aromas with a core of juicy Merlot fruit and
good backbone. Needs time for the oak to soften.

ITALY

1991 Vina Peperino, Vino da Tavola, Teruzzi & Puthod
££ / MB / ☞   16/20
A designer-led Tuscan Sangiovese in a heavy-duty bottle with a
neo-Bayeux tapestry label. Modern, oaky supertuscan with sweet
cherry and pepper fruitiness. Would grace any dinner party table.

Over £8

AUSTRALIA

1991 E & E Black Pepper Shiraz
£ / FB / ☞   15/20
A no-holds-barred old-fashioned leathery Shiraz. Masses of alcohol,
oak and tannin lurk behind the elegant Italian-style bottle.

FRANCE

1990 Châteauneuf-du-Pape, Domaine Font de Michelle
££ / FB / ☞   16/20
A muscular follow-up to the excellent 1988 vintage, with classic
heady aromas and knee-trembling alcohol. Put this away for five
years and then approach with a large stick.

1989 Santenay Clos Rousseau, Domaine Morey
0 / MB / ☝   14/20
A wine with some delicate Pinot Noir flavours struggling to get
past the oak barrel staves.

1988 Chambolle-Musigny, Domaine Machard de Gramont
££ / MB / ☞   16/20
Leafy, sweet, old-fashioned red Burgundy with pleasant rusticity
and lots of gamey, mature fruit.

1989 Savigny-lès-Beaune, Les Guettes, Domaine Pavelot
£££ / MB / ▌   17/20
The pick of Davisons' extensive red Burgundy range,
showing all the seductive fruit of one of the best vintages of
the last decade. A wine to enjoy in its youth.

1989 Gevrey-Chambertin, Domaine Burguet
££ / MB / ▌   16/20
Turd-like aromas (and believe it or not that's one of the best things
about red Burgundy) and genuine Pinot Noir fruit. A wine that
builds on the palate.

1986 Château Beau Site, St Estèphe
£££ / MB / ➤   17/20
Serious claret from a seriously tannic vintage, just beginning
to show its class after a long hibernation. Concentrated, rich
fruit and well-integrated oak make this a wine to savour in
good company.

1986 Château Les Hauts Conseillants, Lalande de Pomerol
££ / MB / ▌   16/20
A good mini-Pomerol from a satellite appellation. Nice mellow,
malty Merlot fruit showing a fair bit of dry tannin, but plenty of
concentration.

1988 Château Tour de Malle, Graves
£ / MB / ▌   15/20
Lightish, elegant Graves with a touch of green pepper fruit and
pleasant oak, drinking well now.

1986 Château Maucaillou, Moulis
££ / MB / ➤   16/20
Classy stuff from Moulis in the Médoc. Rich, intense Cabernet
Sauvignon dominated fruit with nicely evolved tannins.

FULLER'S ***(*)

Head Office: Fuller, Smith & Turner plc, Griffin Brewery, Chiswick Lane South, London, W4 2QB

Telephone: 081 994 3691

Number of branches: 62

Credit cards accepted: Visa, Access

Hours of opening: Monday to Saturday 9.30am to 10.00pm; Sunday 12pm to 3pm and 7pm to 9pm.

By-the-case sales: Yes

Glass loan: With deposit of 50 pence per glass

Home delivery: Free locally

Clubs: No

Discounts: One free bottle with every unmixed case

In-store tastings: Every Saturday in all stores

Top ten best-selling wines: 1993 Le Gascony Blanc, Vin de Pays des Côtes de Gascogne; 1990 Bulgarian Cabernet Sauvignon Reserve, Oriachovitza; Liebfraumilch Egbert; 1993 Le Gascony Rouge, Vin de Pays des Côtes de Gascogne; Lambrusco Bianco, Zonin; 1993 Nottage Hill Chardonnay; 1993 Côtes de Duras, Berticot Sauvignon Blanc; 1992 Nottage Hill Cabernet Sauvignon; 1993 Penfolds Bin 21; 1993 Oxford Landing Chardonnay

Range: GOOD: Red Bordeaux, Australia, New Zealand, Italy, Rhône, Loire, Spain, Burgundy

AVERAGE: Champagne and sparkling wines, regional France, Germany, United States, Chile, South Africa

POOR: Portugal, Eastern Europe

As bouncers fly round ears in the contest for the hearts, minds and wallets of high street wine shoppers, the key to the survival of a small independent chain such as Fuller's is to keep both eyes fixed on the retail ball. In this respect, Fuller's is better placed than some of its competitors. Unlike, say, Unwins, it has the helmet, pads and gloves of a family brewery business to protect it.

For Fuller's new wine buyer Roger Higgs, it must be reassuring to know that there are all those comforting London brick pubs somewhere in the background. When times get tough, he can always slip into the George and Vulture to wash down his cheese and pickle sandwich with a skinful of Chiswick Bitter. And with 200 pubs in the Fuller's estate, it also gives him a chance to improve on the large format Liebfraumilch on offer behind the bar.

The 62 Fuller, Smith & Turner high street stores may be a useful shop window for London Pride, Chiswick Bitter, Fuller's Summer Ale and ESB, but Higgs knows that they have to pay their way in the cut-throat world of the high street. For this to happen, he's aware that he needs to put his stamp on a range whose quality and range was drifting towards a sandbank last year.

At the same tine, he can't afford to alienate existing customers. 'There's a lot of customer loyalty,' says Higgs. 'You can't just blow the whole range out of the water. We have people who've been buying at Fuller's for a very long time.'

Higgs is a cheerful, skateboarding northerner, who was recruited from Oddbins in March 1994 when Fuller's previous buyer, Alastair Llewellyn-Smith, left for Harrods. As we mentioned last year, Llewellyn-Smith had himself been in the job for a relatively short time, during which he set about expanding the range. But now it's over to Higgs. Given Oddbins' success in the high street, it was a smart move by Fuller's director, Mark Dally, to choose him. He has rapidly made use of his buying and managerial experience at the Griffin Brewery.

Higgs was brought up in Manchester and got a student job in an Oddbins store, before managing shops in Manchester and Knutsford. He was then recruited to the Oddbins buying team in London. 'When I came here, my whole life had been Oddbins,' he says. 'I was in a state of shock when I left.'

Although Higgs is, in a sense, Oddbins man incarnate, he is well aware of the dangers of trying to turn Fuller's into just another Oddbins. But it's only natural that he should bring with him a handful of excellent Oddbins wines such as Australia's Wirra Wirra, Chile's Cono Sur and Spain's Vega de Moriz (Casa de la Viña). Good wines don't stop being good wines, just because you move somewhere else. 'Some wines I said no to because they're at Oddbins. Others are just so good that I said so what,' says Higgs. All in all about 15 of the 100 new wines he's bought this year are Oddbins lines.

Higgs began by looking at the range and by dumping 60 wines from the 575-strong list. In the main, these were things that weren't moving quickly enough through the stores. He also set about improving blends such as the Gascon white to a fruitier, more palatable style. An important longer-term aim is to work on improving store managers' knowledge of the range with more information and promotions. Whereas in the past in-store tastings used to be intermittent events, now they are held weekly in all stores.

In the few months since Roger Higgs' arrival, it was already evident during this year's tasting that he was going to do more than tinker with the range. Out had gone the quirky Greek wines and a few others. And in had come a better range, particularly from the classic French regions of Bordeaux, Burgundy and the Rhône as well as regional France, Australia and New Zealand.

With four Australian wines in Fuller's top ten (and only a single Lieb and Lambrusco), Fuller's customers had already discovered the exuberant fruit flavours of the New World. Higgs complains that there were too many obvious brands in the range from Australia. He has already made a big dent in the New World with more distinctive Australian wines, but as Australian prices creep higher, he has plans to increase the range of wines from Chile and South Africa too.

Fortunately for Higgs, he has been given a hand by the general upturn in the market. Fuller's stores suffered in 1993, but things improved in 1994, with turnover up ten per cent as we went to press. Because of the poor results in 1993, Fuller's called a halt to its planned store refits, but it's taken the gold, burgundy and black paint out again and opened two new stores, with another three about to come on-stream.

The success of Fuller's off-licence business depends on two things. The first is Higgs' ability to enthuse his shop managers and to get a few more good wines on the shelf. The second is the brewery's long-term commitment to an increasingly competitive trade. Good luck, Roger, let's hope the next round's on you.

White

Under £3

FRANCE

1993 Chardonnay, Vin de Pays du Jardin de la France, Bahuaud
£ / 2 / 🍶   13/20
A nettley Loire Chardonnay with a crisp acidity reminiscent of the Chenin Blanc grape.

GERMANY

Liebfraumilch, Johannes Egbert
££ / 5 / 🍶   13/20
One of the better Liebfraumilchs on the market, with fresh, aromatic power and soft, grapey fruit. An almost elegant Lieb, if that's not a contradiction in terms.

ITALY

Lambrusco Bianco, Zonin
£ / 6 / 🍶   11/20
This is clean and fizzy. That's two redeeming features. We struggled to find a third.

PORTUGAL

JP Branco, Vinho de Mesa
£ / 2 / 🍶   13/20
An aromatic blend of the native Fernão Pires and Muscat grapes from southern Portugal. Pleasant orange peel zest and a rustic edge.

£3–5

AUSTRALIA

1993 Hardy's Nottage Hill Chardonnay
£ / 3 / ▌   13/20

Rather obvious, sweet white from Down Under. Half a glass would be more than enough.

1993 Oxford Landing Chardonnay
££ / 2 / ▌   16/20

Fresher and better balanced than the 1992 vintage, with flavours of ripe peaches and a well-handled touch of oak for balance.

1993 Leeton Downs Semillon, Riverina
££ / 2 / ▌   14/20

A warm climate Semillon from the irrigated Riverina region, showing restrained oak character and lemon curd fruitiness. Only the strident aftertaste lets you down.

1993 Rothbury Estate Chardonnay/Semillon
££ / 2 / ▌   15/20

More elegant and restrained than many of Rothbury's full-blooded whites, but none the less enjoyable for that. An intense peach and pineapple blend with fruit from Cowra, Mudgee, Hunter Valley and Griffith (all wine regions in New South Wales), and a smidgeon of oak.

FRANCE

1993 Le Gascony Blanc, Vin de Pays des Côtes de Gascogne
££ / 2 / ▌   14/20

A vast improvement on last year's charmless effort, thanks to the addition of more Colombard by Fuller's new wine buyer, Roger Higgs. Soft, fresh tangy white with pleasant grapey fruit. One of the better Gascon whites on the market.

1993 Berticot Sauvignon Blanc, Côtes de Duras
££ / 2 / ▌   15/20

Clean, modern, lemon zest-like Sauvignon from south-western France with a refreshing prickle. Good value at under £3.50.

1992 Mâcon Igé, Les Roches Blanches, Les Vignerons d'Igé
£££ / 2 / ▌   17/20
A ripe, almost unctuous, unoaked white Mâcon-Villages with
plenty of buttery, peachy, intense fruit flavours and enough
acidity for balance. One of the best white Burgundies
around, especially at under a fiver. It's encouraging to see a
wine of this quality emerging from a co-operative in the
Mâconnais.

1993 Mâcon-Villages, Charles Viénot
£££ / 2 / ▌   17/20
This is the sort of thing Burgundy needs to produce if it's
going to win back wine drinkers from the blandishments
of New World Chardonnay. A fresh, focused modern-style
white with well-handled oak and lots of citrus fruit
character. More please.

1993 Vin de Pays d'Oc Sauvignon Blanc, Jacques Lurton
££ / 2 / ▌   15/20
Pungent, New Zealand style Sauvignon Blanc with aromas of green
bean and tinned pea, rounded out by a touch of fruit sweetness.
Jacques Lurton, *Grapevine*'s winemaker of the year in 1994,
seemingly does this kind of thing in his sleep.

1993 La Serre Chardonnay, Vin de Pays d'Oc
£ / 2 / ▌   14/20
A well-crafted, tangy southern French Chardonnay with a touch
of oak character and pleasant honeyed fruit.

1993 Chardonnay, James Herrick, Vin de Pays d'Oc
££ / 1 / ▌   15/20
The second vintage from Englishman James Herrick's impressive
New World style vineyards near Narbonne. This is more elegant
and restrained than the 1992, with deftly handled oak and a lime-
like streak of acidity.

NEW ZEALAND

1992 Hawkes Bay Estate Sauvignon Blanc
£ / 2 / ▌   14/20
A wine of two halves. The aromatics have been given the red card,

but there's still some nice zesty, melon and elderflower fruit on the pitch. We'd like to see the new vintage here.

£5–8

AUSTRALIA

1993 Rowan Chardonnay, Victoria
££ / 2 / 🍾   16/20
From St Huberts, one of the top names in Victoria's Yarra Valley, this is an elegant Chardonnay with some aromatic mint character and tropical, passion fruit flavours.

1993 Rothbury Estate Chardonnay, Hunter Valley
£ / 2 / 🍾   15/20
Forward, mouth-filling stuff with rich, barley-sugared fruit and well-judged oak, kept fresh by a prickle of carbon dioxide and nice citrusy acidity. A little pricey perhaps.

1992 Rockford Eden Valley Riesling
£ / 3 / 🍾   15/20
Winemaker Rocky O'Callaghan disdains subtlety in wine. What he's after are big, ripe flavours with lots of alcohol. The formula appears to find favour with wine buffs, for whom Rocky is a cult figure. This rich, toasty Riesling has roughly double the alcohol content of a Mosel white. You have been warned.

FRANCE

1992 Chablis, Domaine de Vauroux
££ / 2 / 🍾   15/20
A fresh, modern unoaked, fruity style of Chardonnay with some appealing Chablis character and full-bodied weight.

1992 Montagny Premier Cru, Denis Philibert
£££ / 2 / 🍾   17/20
Montagny in the Côte Chalonnaise tends to produce rather rustic styles of white Burgundy. But this is a stylishly toasty Chardonnay from an excellent vintage. Rich and honeyed with remarkable depth of flavour for

the *appellation* and crisp, balancing acidity. Nice one, Denis.

1993 Viognier, Vin de Pays d'Oc, Domaine des Salices, Jacques Lurton
££ / 2 / ❚   15/20
One of the better Viogniers produced in the Languedoc, where the grape is developing into a fashion item. Opulently peachy fruit and smoky oak make this an appealing wine. Low-yielding Viognier is never cheap, but this is comparatively good value at just under £6.

NEW ZEALAND

1993 Dashwood Sauvignon Blanc, Marlborough
££ / 2 / ❚   16/20
Dashwood is the second label of Marlborough-based winery, Vavasour, but you'd never guess it from this pungent, elderflower-style Sauvignon Blanc. Good for the vintage, and drier than many of its competitors.

SOUTH AFRICA

1993 Dieu Donné Chardonnay, Franschhoek
££ / 2 / ❚   16/20
The 1992 wooded Chardonnay won all sorts of accolades last year. This deceptively elegant 1993, made by François Malherbe, is not quite in the same class, but it's still one of South Africa's best Chardonnays.

UNITED STATES

1992 Konocti Chardonnay, Napa Valley
0 / 2 / ❚   11/20
The Napa Valley prides itself on being the premium winemaking region in California. But if it keeps turning out things like this coarsely oaked, alcoholic and confected Chardonnay, it ought to consider switching to potato farming.

Over £8

AUSTRALIA

1992 Wirra Wirra Chardonnay, South Australia
£ / 2 / ♪   15/20
The price of this ultra-toasty Chardonnay has crept up in recent
vintages, owing to its popularity as much as anything. It's a no-
holds-barred vanilla fudge and butterscotch white with more
elegance that you'd expect.

1993 Tasmanian Wine Company Chardonnay
££ / 2 / ♪   16/20
The second label from Andrew Pirie's pioneering Tasmanian
winery, Piper's Brook, which produces one of Australia's top
Chardonnays in a Burgundian style. By way of a contrast, the
emphasis of this unoaked white is on crisp, cool climate fruit,
almost bordering on Sauvignon Blanc territory.

FRANCE

1992 Chablis Premier Cru, Montmains, Domaine de Vauroux
£££ / 2 / ⌐   18/20
From one of the best of Chablis' 40 premier cru vineyards
(although only a dozen appear regularly on labels), this is
a powerful, young, highly concentrated Chablis made in a
traditional style, which needs time to emerge from its tight
chrysalis of fruit.

1990 Coteaux de Saumur, Château Hureau, Vatan
£££ / 5 / ⌐   17/20
A Loire Chenin Blanc showing enormous concentration of
honeyed botrytis and toasty fruit. This is a rarity for lovers
of sweet, ripe Chenin Blanc. In a vintage like 1990, the grape
comes into its own, with enough zesty acidity to slice
through the sweetness.

NEW ZEALAND

1992 Goldwater Marlborough Chardonnay

£ / 2 / ❚   15/20

The Goldwaters live in an idyllic setting on Auckland Bay's Waiheke Island, where they make some of New Zealand's best red wines. Their Chardonnay, on the other hand, comes from contract vineyards in Marlborough. It's decent enough, but we found the oak too heavy for the delicate cool climate fruit.

1993 Hunter's Sauvignon Blanc, Marlborough

£££ / 2 / �   17/20

This is the best New Zealand Sauvignon from the difficult 1993 vintage, confirming Hunter's standing as one of the New World's finest wineries. Fabulously aromatic with tropical flavours of passion fruit and melon, cut by elegant grapefruity acidity. Watch out, Cloudy Bay, there's a Hunter about.

1993 Kumeu River Chardonnay

£ / 2 / ❚   16/20

An oddball Chardonnay made by Kiwi Master of Wine Michael Brajkovich, whose family vineyards are entirely based around subtropical Auckland. He takes Burgundian techniques to the limit in this hefty, butterscotch and fudge-like Chardonnay, which is still tightly furled. We're not sure if it will develop into something as good as a Grand Cru Chablis or fall apart. At £14 a bottle, only gamblers need apply.

SPAIN

1992 Augustus Chardonnay, Penedès, Puig & Roca

££ / 2 / ➤   16/20

Made by José Puig, who, as well as developing an unusual corkscrew called the Puigpull, used to work for Miguel Torres, this is an intriguing British début. Drawing on his international experience, Puig has produced a show-winning style of Chardonnay with big, pineappley flavours and lots of nutty oak. It's no pseudo-Meursault, but an individual, concentrated wine in its own right. One of the best Chardonnays in Spain.

UNITED STATES

1992 Crichton Hall Chardonnay, Napa Valley
0 / 3 / 🌓   14/20
Sweet, alcoholic and oaky, this is a Napa Valley Chardonnay made
by an Englishman. Alright if you love butterscotch and toast, but
it's hardly good value at £10 a shot.

Red

Under £3

FRANCE

1993 De Belfont Cuvée Speciale, Vin de Pays de l'Aude
££ / MB / 🌓   14/20
A blend of 80 per cent Portan, the new designer Languedoc grape,
and 20 per cent Merlot, from fortified Muscat de Rivesaltes
specialists, Domaine Cazes. Good plummy stuff in a Gamay-meets-
north-Italian-Dolcetto mould.

1992 Cabernet Sauvignon, Coteaux de Bessille, Jules Boyer
£ / MB / 🌓   13/20
With its attractive, pink sunset label, this raisiny southern French
quaffer tastes more like a Grenache than a Cabernet Sauvignon.

PORTUGAL

JP Tinto, Vinho de Mesa
£ / LB / 🌓   13/20
A fresh, cherried southern Portuguese red made mainly from the
native Periquita grape. Decent at the price.

SPAIN

1993 Rioja Casa del Marqués Sin Crianza
£ / MB / 🌓   12/20
This young, commercial Rioja is pleasant sawdusty stuff. We
felt that the barrel had been brought to this light, mushroomy red

rather than the other way round.

1993 Casa de la Viña, Valdepeñas
£££ / MB / ▌   15/20
This is one wine buyer Roger Higgs prepared earlier. With its juicy,
strawberry-like Cencibel fruit and nip of tannin, it's a ringer for
Oddbins's Vega de Moriz.

£3–5

AUSTRALIA

1992 Nottage Hill Cabernet Sauvignon
0 / FB / ▌   13/20
Coarse, obvious minty red with hefty tannins from the sprawling
BRL-Hardy operation.

1993 Leeton Downs Shiraz/Grenache Riverina
£ / MB / ▌   13/20
If you get tired of drinking London Pride ale (admittedly an unlikely
prospect), this basic, slightly minty, dilute Australian red is also
available in Fuller's pubs. One to wash down the pork scratchings.

1992 Penfolds Bin 2, Shiraz/Mourvèdre
££ / FB / ➡   15/20
The least appreciated of Penfolds' less expensive red wines, this
is a sweetly oaked, minty, blackberryish blend of Rhône and
Provence grapes.

1992 Berri Estates Cabernet Sauvignon, South Australia
££ / MB / ▌   15/20
Since the huge Riverland co-operative, Berri-Renmano, teamed up
with family company Hardy's, its wines have lightened in style.
And thank heavens for that. This pleasantly oaked red is what
Australians call a fruit-driven style. You can sort of see what they
mean.

BULGARIA

1990 Bulgarian Reserve Cabernet Sauvignon, Oriachovitza
££ / FB / 🌡   15/20
An Australian-inspired, full-bodied red with lots of sweet American
oak and tannic fruit. Bulgaria's attempt at a Penfolds' red.

CHILE

1993 Torconal Cabernet/Merlot
£ / MB / 🌡   13/20
A weedy, stalky Bordeaux blend from Chile. There's some elegant
blackcurrant fruit in there somewhere, but it's hard to get at behind
the sharp acidity.

1993 Cono Sur Cabernet Sauvignon
££ / MB / 🌡   15/20
This is a more interesting Chilean red from Cono Sur at
Chimbarongo, with the same elegance but better balance and riper
blackcurrant fruit.

FRANCE

1990 Côtes du Ventoux Syrah, Domaine Castellas
££ / FB / 🌡   15/20
Seriously chunky stuff from the hills of Provence. A traditionally
vinified, robust Syrah with punchy fruit.

1993 Le Gascony Rouge, Vin de Pays des Côtes de Gascogne
£ / LB / 🌡   13/20
A light, somewhat stalky red from the Plaimont co-operative in
Gascony. At least it's clean and fresh with some pleasantly juicy
fruit.

1993 Vin de Pays d'Oc Grenache, Fortant de France
££ / FB / 🌡   15/20
This is one of the few Fortant de France wines whose flavours live
up to the marketing hype: a juicy, spicy, alcoholic red made from
old Grenache vines. If Skalli can do such good things with
indigenous varieties, perhaps it should concentrate on the best of
the Languedoc's raw materials.

1991 Château Roquenagade, Corbières

£££ / FB / ▬▬   **16/20**

From Frédéric Juvet's Languedoc estate, this Syrah-based Corbières is a stunner. Hugely aromatic and spicy with masses of deeply coloured, chunky fruit and a considerable degree of finesse.

ITALY

1992 Montepulciano d'Abruzzo, Citra

££ / MB / ▮   **15/20**

A modern-style Italian red with fresh, savoury fruit, a nip of acidity and robust, dry tannins.

1992 Teroldego Rotaliano, Ca Donini

£ / LB / ▮   **13/20**

Decent, soft, north Italian red made from the native Teroldego grape. Grapeskin aromas and plummy, Beaujolais-like fruit of no great depth.

SPAIN

1990 Rioja Faustino Rivero Ulecia Crianza

£££ / MB / ▮   **16/20**

A modern Tempranillo-dominated Rioja with the emphasis on fruit, rather than barrel-and bottle-ageing. Soft, lightly oaked stuff with an attractively gamey character.

£5–8

AUSTRALIA

1992 Rothbury Estate Shiraz, South Eastern Australia

££ / FB / ▬▬   **16/20**

Further proof of the lighter styles emerging from Rothbury's Hunter Valley base. This is almost like a northern Rhône Syrah, although the American oak gives away its Australian origins. Elegant and refreshing now, but the wine should age for another five years.

1992 Rowan Cabernet/Merlot, Victoria
££ / MB / ⌐   16/20
From the St Hubert's estate in the Yarra Valley, this is a soft, sparingly oaked Bordeaux-style blend with intense berry fruit and vivid concentration.

1992 Rockford Dry Country Grenache
££ / FB / ⌐   16/20
A super-rich, heartwarming red from traditionalist Rocky O'Callaghan, this alcoholic, beefy Barossa Valley Grenache is an old-fashioned classic. One-dimensional perhaps, but what a dimension.

1992 Château Reynella Basket Pressed Shiraz, McLaren Vale, South Australia
££ / FB / ⌐   16/20
No shortage of mint and spicy American oak here. If that sounds a little confected, it shouldn't do, because there's plenty of big, rich, chocolatey Shiraz in there too. Even Rocky O'Callaghan, who makes the original Basket Press Shiraz, would enjoy this one.

1992 Château Reynella Cabernet/Merlot, McLaren Vale
££ / MB / ▮   16/20
Restrained by the standards of warm McLaren Vale, this combines green pepper cool climate fruit and ripe blackcurrant flavours in an attractive package.

CHILE

1993 Cono Sur Pinot Noir Reserve
£££ / MB / ▮   17/20
Made by American winemaker Ed Flaherty at the Concha y Toro owned Cono Sur Chimbarongo Estate winery in the Rapel region, this second release is the best Pinot Noir we've come across so far from South America. It even rivals the likes of Saintsbury and Acacia in California, except on price, where, remarkably, it's under £6. A rich, chocolatey, nicely oaked Pinot Noir with voluptuous loganberry and raspberry fruit flavours.

1992 Cono Sur Cabernet Sauvignon Reserve
£££ / MB / ▌   17/20

Another outstanding red from Ed Flaherty at Cono Sur, only this time we're in Bordeaux rather than Burgundy country. Unusually for Chile, the fruit is soft, supple and ripe and the oak is beautifully integrated. Let's hope Cono Sur keeps the price below £6 for the 1993.

FRANCE

1990 Domaine de Sours, Bordeaux
£ / MB / ▌   13/20

The second wine from an estate in the Entre-Deux-Mers that ought to be concentrating on its Grand Vin instead of syphoning off the dregs into a subsidiary label. Basic, chewy, overpriced stuff.

1992 Santenay, Clos Genet, Denis Philibert
££ / MB / ▌   16/20

From a two-man *négociant* company in Beaune, this is a characterful Pinot Noir with lots of concentration and farmyardy rusticity. A lot of red Burgundy for £8.

1992 Côtes du Rhône, Jean-Luc Colombo
££ / FB / ▌   16/20

Proust lookalike Jean-Luc Colombo is the most sought-after winemaker in southern France, employed as a consultant from Cornas in the northern Rhône to Côtes du Roussillon Villages near Perpignan. He tends to go for new oak and supple, seductive fruit, and this wine, made from declassified Cornas, is no exception. It takes over from Guigal as the best Côtes du Rhône around, albeit at nearly £6.

1992 Crozes-Hermitage, Bernard Chave
££ / MB / ▌   16/20

Perfumed, peppery Syrah, which reminded us more of a St Joseph than a Crozes. Showing good concentration for the vintage, which wasn't anything special, but still on the light side.

1991 Vin de Pays de l'Aude Cabernet Sauvignon, Domaine de Roquenagade
££ / FB / ↦   16/20
If Mas de Daumas Gassac is the Lafite of the Languedoc, this is its Sassicaia. A supercharged, heftily oaked, macho Cabernet Sauvignon, which may take five years to come round. Concentrated, tannic, tealeafy stuff. Come in American wine guru, Robert Parker, this one's for you.

ITALY

1989 Chianti Classico Riserva, Villa Antinori
££ / MB / 🌡   16/20
When he was working through the existing Fuller's range, wine buyer Roger Higgs was pleasantly surprised that this mature, typically Tuscan red tasted so good. Antinori is one of those large volume producers who still pulls out the stops from time to time. We enjoyed it too.

SOUTH AFRICA

1992 Saxenburg Merlot, Stellenbosch
£££ / MB / ↦   16/20
Many Cape reds are dry, rooty and still struggling to find a post-apartheid identity. But this concentrated, juicy Merlot, with its fresh spicy fruit and elegant oak should serve as an example to all.

1992 Dieu Donné Cabernet Sauvignon, Franschhoek
££ / MB / 🌡   15/20
Not quite God-given, but this supple, refreshing Cabernet Sauvignon, with its pronounced oak influence, should appeal to catholic tastes.

SPAIN

1987 Señorio de Nava, Ribera del Duero
£££ / FB / ↦   16/20
Spain's most famous red wine, Vega Sicilia, comes from the Ribera del Duero region north of Madrid. This aged Tinto Fino (Tempranillo) has something of the same character, with lots of colour, sweet vanilla oak and seriously chunky blackberry fruit.

Now into its stride, and, apparently, getting younger. They could probably sell this to crumblies in California.

Over £8

AUSTRALIA

1991 Rockford Basket Press Shiraz
£££ / FB / ➼   17/20
Imitators may come and go, but this is the original Basket Press Shiraz, made by bearded cult figure Rocky O'Callaghan from low-yielding Barossa Valley wines. The basket press in question is more than a marketing slogan - it actually exists. Like Rocky himself, this wine is larger than life: a massively rich, dense, chewy, alcoholic gob of Shiraz with plenty of what Australians like to call 'grunt'.

FRANCE

1990 Château Lynch Moussas, Pauillac
£ / FB / ➼   15/20
Categorised as a fifth growth in the 1855 classification of Bordeaux, this is a modern, exceedingly oaky Pauillac, trying to do a Mouton-Rothschild, but falling a bit short of its ambitions.

1988 Château Gazin, Pomerol
£££ / MB / ➼   18/20
One of those occasions when it's worth parting with £14 to secure a bottle of really exceptional wine. An elegantly poised, Merlot-dominated Right Bank claret with voluptuous, plump fruit and nicely judged vanilla oak. A focused wine that will age gracefully for another decade or more.

1991 Gevrey Chambertin, Premier Cru, Les Champeaux, Vieilles Vignes, Phillippe Naddef
£ / MB / ➊   15/20
Very young, very concentrated and very difficult to enjoy at the moment. It's also very tannic – like a cross between a Syrah and a Grenache – but the wine may come round in time. Hand over £20 and the answer will reveal itself.

1990 Côte Rôtie, Gilles Barge

£££ / FB / ◗━ 18/20

Gilles Barge is President of the growers' association in Côte Rôtie, the aptly named roasted slope of the northern Rhône. 1990 was a difficult drought year in the region but Barge came up with a concentrated, but elegant, classic crushed pepper red. Go on, spoil yourself. It's only £14.

NEW ZEALAND

1992 Waimarama Estate, Hawkes Bay Cabernet/Merlot

£££ / MB / ◗━ 17/20

One of the few southern hemisphere reds to have achieved the concentration and elegance of a First Growth claret, this is New Zealand's answer to Mouton-Rothschild. Masses of supple fruit and toasty oak with a fresh acidity that promises good things for the future. The best red we've tasted from New Zealand in this vintage. Yours for only £11.

UNITED STATES

1992 Saintsbury Garnet Pinot Noir, Carneros

£ / MB / ◗ 15/20

As its name suggests, Garnet is the lightest of the three Pinot Noirs produced at this world-famous Napa Valley winery. It's also the easiest to drink, so it's a pity it's not a bit cheaper. Pleasant, sweetly oaked Pinot.

1991 Crichton Hall Merlot, Napa Valley

££ / MB / ◗━ 16/20

More enjoyable than the same producer's rather overblown Chardonnay, this is a tobaccoey, oak-influenced Merlot with fine tannins and juicy, berry fruit flavours.

Sparkling

Over £8

AUSTRALIA

1991 Green Point
£££ / 2 / 🍷   17/20
This successful Yarra Valley winery has produced a brilliant
successor to the 1990, which was one of *Grapevine*'s wines
of the year in 1994. The Pinot Noir content has been
increased, and Pinot Meunier has been added to the blend
for the first time. Otherwise, this follows on nicely from
the previous vintage, showing considerable toasty
complexity and finesse. Parent company Champagne house
Moët et Chandon must be happy to see Dr Tony Jordan
maintaining Green Point's high standards.

FRANCE

Champagne Brossault NV
£ / 3 / 🍷   14/20
Crisp, young, fruity Champagne which relies on dosage sweetness
to soften its green edge.

Champagne Brossault Rosé NV
£ / 3 / 🍷   14/20
Ditto, except it's pink.

GREENALLS CELLARS **
(INCLUDING WINE CELLARS,
BERKLEY WINES AND CELLAR 5)

Head Office: Greenalls Cellars Ltd, PO Box 3, Loushers Lane, Warrington, Cheshire, WA4 6RY

Telephone: 0925 444555

Number of branches: 477 including 27 Berkley Wines

Credit cards accepted: Access, Visa, Delta, Switch

Hours of opening: Monday to Saturday 10.00am to 10.00pm; Sunday 12.00pm to 2.00pm and 7.00pm to 10.00pm

By-the-case sales: Yes

Glass loan: Yes

Home delivery: Yes

Clubs: Under discussion for Berkley Wines and Wine Cellar

Discounts: Party planning, sale or return offers and quantity discounts up to 15 per cent on wine

In-store tastings: Yes, especially in the new Wine Cellar stores

Top ten best-selling wines: Liebfraumilch; Lambrusco; Moët & Chandon NV Champagne; Bulgarian Cabernet Sauvignon; Hock Tafelwein; Santa Maria Medium Dry; Niersteiner Gutes Domtal; Coldridge Semillon/Chardonnay; Hungarian Cabernet Sauvignon; Paul Humbrieres NV Champagne

Range: GOOD: Bordeaux, Australia
AVERAGE: Southern France, South Africa, Spain, New Zealand, Chile, Italy
POOR: California, Burgundy, Germany, Eastern Europe

By his own confident admission, Nader Haghighi is an ambitious cove. You might never have heard of him, but he's very anxious that you should. An Iranian who worked his way up from assistant shop manager level to operations director at Thresher, Haghighi moved to Cellar 5 (as it was then) in April 1994 and immediately set about changing the place with customary gusto.

The first thing to go was the name Cellar 5. From now on, Cellar 5 will be one of only three, or possibly four, Greenalls Cellars brands. Cellar 5 is owned by ex-brewing company Greenall Whitley, so the new corporate identity makes sense. The three new types of store (in descending order of specialisation) are Wine Cellars, Berkley Wines and, in the all-purpose off-licence slot, Cellar 5. Haghighi is also considering a fourth, food-and-drink-style store.

If you think this all sounds a bit like the Thresher/Wine Rack/ Bottoms Up set-up, you'd have a point. But Haghighi is adamant that he's trying to do something different at Greenalls Cellars. 'I got to a point at Thresher where I wanted a bigger challenge and was seeking to make a bigger impact on the market. The Thresher brands are very different to what I have in mind, with different things to offer the consumer and a different feel.' As we said, Haghighi doesn't lack self-belief.

Greenalls Cellars could provide him with just the challenge he needs. With 477 stores to its name, it's the third biggest off-licence group in Britain behind the Thresher trio and Victoria Wine. But it's never been quite as influential as it should.

History is part of the reason. The current set-up is an amalgam of three different companies. Drew Wine Cellars, Cellar 5 and Blayneys, which joined forces through a process of acquisition between 1985 and 1991. Melding the various elements of the business into a coherent whole has taken several years. If only Haghighi had been with the company then ...

Despite his arrival, the chain has had its share of problems this year. Wine buyer Gerard Barnes left to go to Sainsbury's and, when we tasted in mid-summer, no successor had been appointed. It was not until late August that Haghighi announced the signing of David Vaughan from Boutinot Prince and Geoff Hewitt, an in-house move from Greenalls Services. Both are untried performers on the wider retail stage.

What is certain is that they've got a lot of work to be getting on with. We felt last year that Cellar 5 was beginning to put together the core of an interesting range; 12 months on, there's been a certain loss of focus. There are good things from France, Australia and Chile, but plenty of dull stuff has crept in under the wire too. Eastern Europe, Spain and Germany have provided some particularly uninspiring wines.

The job in prospect at Greenalls Cellars is not easy. Indeed, more than one big name buyer turned it down when he realised the size of the task. Haghighi, characteristically, is undaunted. 'We're number three in the UK at the moment, but I don't expect to stay that way for very long.'

How's he going to do it? Well, the range is set to expand from 250 wines to between 450 in branches of Cellar 5 and Berkley Wines and to 600 in Wine Cellars. The staff are currently undergoing 'development at all levels', presumably in dawn-till-dusk training camps somewhere in the countryside around Warrington. And a new, improved corporate look is expected very soon.

For the time being, all of Greenalls Cellars' branches are in the North and Midlands. 'The furthest south we go is Warwickshire,' says Haghighi, 'but we're looking to expand. I want to get national coverage.' This revelation prompted a front-page headline in the trade paper *Off-Licence News*: 'Segmented Cellar 5 looks south.'

Haghighi is 'keeping his options open', but according to which rumour you believe, is variously interested in Oddbins, Davisons and Unwins. A merger with one of the last two family-owned independent chains is not beyond credibility, even though that would mean yet another period of readjustment at Greenalls.

The problem with big ideas and marketing blather, of course, is that sooner or later people who utter them have to satisfy the accountants. Haghighi is already claiming 'healthy year on year increases', but his vision of what Greenalls Cellars might become has not yet made the transition to reality. Still, if he does even half of the things he's got planned for 1995, it's going to be an interesting year in the high street.

White

Under £3

FRANCE

Côtes de Gascogne Blanc, NV, Yvon Mau
0 / 2 / 1   11/20
Gluey, fruitless Gascon white from Bordeaux *négociant*, Yvon Mau.

GERMANY

1992 Liebfraumilch, St Dominicus
0 / 5 / 🌓   11/20
Floral, dilute, sugary stuff, apparently made from Müller-Thurgau.

HUNGARY

1992 Hungarian Chardonnay, Balaton Boglar
0 / 2 / 🌓   12/20
A green, unoaked Chardonnay with a bit of boiled-sweets character.

ITALY

1992 Trebbiano dell'Emilia, Vino da Tavola
£ / 3 / 🌓   13/20
Off-dry, stewed-apple white from Emilia-Romagna with a coarse finish. Typically neutral Trebbiano.

Lambrusco Bianco, Pascionari
0 / 5 / 🌓   12/20
Gassy, sweet, confected white. Fine if your palate hankers for alcoholic lemonade.

SPAIN

1992 Tres Puentes, La Mancha, Bodegas y Bebidas
0 / 3 / 🌓   12/20
Earthy, basic Spanish white from the vast La Mancha plain with a bit of sweetness to make up for the Airen grape's lack of personality.

Santa Maria, Medium Dry, Valencia
0 / 4 / 🌓   10/20
A barely drinkable, tired, old-fashioned blend of Merseguera and Malvasia. The unacceptable face of Spanish white winemaking.

£3–5

AUSTRALIA

Coldridge Semillon/Chardonnay
0 / 2 / ▮   12/20
A wine which has definitely had more character and fruit in past
vintages. Faintly grubby round the edges.

1993 Penfolds Bin 21 Semillon/Chardonnay
££ / 2 / ▮   14/20
Aromatic, smoky oak and crisp, elegant fruitiness. Another new
wave Australian surfer.

CHILE

1993 Santa Carolina Sauvignon Blanc, Maipo Valley
£££ / 2 / ▮   15/20
Made by Chile's leading white-winemaker, Ignacio Recabarren,
this is a ripe, honeyed, but refreshing style of Sauvignon Blanc,
halfway towards a Semillon.

FRANCE

1992 Chardonnay, Domaine de Lissac, Vin de Pays d'Oc, Hugh Ryman
££ / 2 / ▮   15/20
Toasty oak and rich peachy fruit lifted by zingy acidity. Hugh Ryman
on great form in the Languedoc.

1993 Domaine des Fontanelles, Sauvignon Blanc, Vin de Pays d'Oc, Hugh Ryman
£££ / 2 / ▮   16/20
Another Hugh Ryman star, made at his winery, affectionately
known as The Dump, near Limoux. Elegant, grapefruity Sauvignon
Blanc with good weight and flavour.

GERMANY

1992 Niersteiner Gutes Domtal
£ / 5 / ▌ 13/20

'Specially selected', it says on the label. By whom, we wondered. Actually, if you like this sort of thing, there's some pleasant floral spice and aromatic fruit underneath the sugar.

1992 Oppenheimer Krötenbrunnen Kabinett, Josefinen Kellerei
££ / 4 / ▌ 14/20

A better-balanced, inexpensive German white with floral fragrance and appealing green apple fruit.

ITALY

1993 Chardonnay, Trentino, Ca'vit
££ / 2 / ▌ 14/20

From Italy's alpine north-west, this is an unoaked, well-made Chardonnay with good, fresh acidity and more weight than many of the native whites.

NEW ZEALAND

1993 Timara Dry, Montana
££ / 2 / ▌ 15/20

A blend of Semillon, Müller-Thurgau and Riesling, which tastes surprisingly like a good Kiwi Sauvignon Blanc. This zingy, crisp dry white is the best vintage of Timara we've tasted.

1993 Montana Sauvignon Blanc
£££ / 2 / ▌ 16/20

A wine that never lets you down. Montana's hugely successful Sauvignon Blanc has been selling at under a fiver for as long as we can remember, so it's hardly surprising to see it among the top ten best-selling wines in the UK. Textbook elderflower and asparagus style with lively acidity and rounded tropical fruit.

£5–8

AUSTRALIA

1991 Mitchelton Reserve Chardonnay
£ / 2 / ▮   15/20

Oaky, toasty, full-blown coconut and burnt butter style with a core of elegant, cool climate fruit from Mitchelton in Victoria's Goulburn Valley.

FRANCE

1988 Château des Coulinats, Sainte Croix du Mont
0 / 6 / ▮   10/20

Sweet, coarse sticky white with an unpleasant oiliness. Should be flying the skull and crossbones.

SOUTH AFRICA

1992 Backsberg Chardonnay
£££ / 2 / ▮   16/20

A great follow-up to the hugely enjoyable 1991. A barrel-fermented Cape White with the emphasis on elegant lemon and cinnamon oak flavours.

Red

Under £3

HUNGARY

Hungarian Cabernet Sauvignon, Balaton Boglar
£ / LB / ▮   13/20

Light, fruity, peppermint and cherry style flavours, like a Hungarian Beaujolais.

ITALY

1993 Barbera del Piemonte, Vino da Tavola
££ / MB / 🍾   14/20

Soft, elegant, sweet and savoury Piemontese red with good zip and the typical fresh acidity of the northern Italian Barbera grape.

SPAIN

1993 Casa de la Vigna, Cencibel, Valdepeñas, Bodegas y Bebidas
£££ / MB / 🍾   15/20

One of the new generation of Spanish red wines, with the emphasis on vibrant fruit rather than barrel-ageing. A soft textured red with upfront damson fruitiness.

Montefiel Oaky Red, Vino de la Tierra de Manchuela
0 / MB / 🍾   11/20

A wine that seems to have lost something in translation since last year. The oak appears coarser, the fruit more raisiny and old-fashioned. Perhaps our palates are getting on.

1992 Jumilla, Señorio de Robles Tinto, Bodegas Schenk
£ / LB / 🍾   13/20

Fresh, juicy, decent wine bar plonk from the Valencia-based firm of Schenk.

£3–5

AUSTRALIA

1992 Jacob's Creek Shiraz/Cabernet
££ / MB / 🍾   14/20

Not showing quite as well as the Jacob's Creek whites at the moment, but this is still a pleasantly fruity, oak-influenced introduction to Australian wine with commercial appeal.

1991 Oxford Landing Cabernet/Shiraz, Yalumba
££ / MB / 🍾   14/20

An easy-drinking South Australian red with an elegant, cool climate note and soft, sweetish blackcurrant fruit.

BULGARIA

1989 Bulgarian Merlot, Haskovo Region
0 / MB / ⬥   11/20
Browning at the rim already, this is a dry, old-fashioned Bulgarian relic left over from the communist era. A red that belongs under the bed – or possibly out of the window.

1985 Lyaskovets Reserve Merlot
0 / MB / ⬥   11/20
Another unreconstructed red. They should have left this one in the Gulag cellars.

1989 Bulgarian Cabernet Sauvignon, Sliven
£ / MB / ⬥   13/20
The best of the Greenalls Cellars Bulgarian reds, which isn't saying a great deal. This has some chewy blackberry fruit, but finishes rather dry and rooty. Clearly a purge is required.

CHILE

1988 Santa Carolina Cabernet Sauvignon, Maipo Valley
£ / MB / ⬥   13/20
Winemaker Ignacio Recabarren was just getting into his stride at Santa Carolina in 1988, and has produced considerably more enjoyable things than this greenish, blackcurrant pastille and oak-flavoured red.

FRANCE

1992 Château Ciceron, Corbières
££ / MB / ⬥   15/20
A modern, southern French blend of Grenache, Syrah, Cinsault and Mourvèdre made in a highly aromatic, unoaked, angostura bitters style.

1992 Château Canet, Minervois
£ / MB / ⬥   14/20
Garrigue-scented, soft carbonic maceration style red with firm, almost Italianate acidity.

1990 Château Le Redon, Bordeaux
0 / LB / 🍷   11/20

Pretty feeble stuff, struggling to find an identity. In a vintage like 1990, a château claret really should be better than this weedy example.

1991 La Cuvée des Toques, Beaumes de Venise, Côtes du Rhône Villages
£ / MB / 🍷   13/20

Light on fruit for a Côtes du Rhône Villages, this is a wine dominated by sweet, alcoholic Grenache. We wouldn't take our toque off to this one.

1991 Syrah, Fortant de France
£ / MB / 🍷   13/20

As so often with the Midi *négociant* Skalli Fortant de France, the package promises more than the wine delivers. This is rather tannic and lacks the character one would expect from the Syrah grape.

ITALY

1992 Merlot, Trentino, Ca'vit
££ / LB / 🍷   14/20

A grassy, distinctively northern Italian Merlot with elegant fruit. A good luncheon claret substitute.

NEW ZEALAND

1992 Montana Marlborough Cabernet Sauvignon
££ / MB / 🍷   15/20

Like the same producer's admirable Sauvignon Blanc, this is tremendous value for money at under a fiver. 1992 was the first of two abnormally cool years in New Zealand, and, as a result, the wine is a little leaner than the excellent 1991.

SOUTH AFRICA

1991 Backsberg Pinotage
££ / FB / 🍷   15/20

Backsberg, best known for its good value Chardonnays, also makes a creditable Pinotage, South Africa's claim to an indigenous red-wine style. Sweet raspberry jam with a not unpleasant, faintly rubbery undertone.

SPAIN

1985 Casa de la Vigna Reserva, Cencibel, Valdepeñas, Bodegas y Bebidas
£ / MB / ꕥ   14/20
An old-fashioned, oaky, Rioja-style Spanish red with some sweet, gamey fruit. We preferred the more modern incarnation.

£5–8

AUSTRALIA

1991 Mitchelton Reserve Cabernet Sauvignon
££ / FB / ⬤-   16/20
Winemaker Don Lewis is one of the most underrated performers in Australia, turning out reds and whites to a consistently high standard. This is a rich, concentrated mouthful of vanilla oak and sweet blackcurrant fruit, which should improve with age.

SOUTH AFRICA

1991 Backsberg Klein Babylonstören
0 / FB / ⬤-   13/20
An ambitious, Bordeaux-style blend, which suffers from an all too typical South African rusticity. Rather too green and raw for our liking.

Over £8

AUSTRALIA

1990 Wolf Blass Shiraz, President's Selection
££ / FB / ⬤-   16/20
One of Wolf Blass' winemakers is on record as saying 'no wood, no good'. The company has certainly taken his motto to heart in this dense, massively oaked, minty number. Short on subtlety perhaps, but long on flavour.

1985 Wolf Blass Cabernet Sauvignon, Black Label
££ / FB / 🍷   16/20

This is a bold, beefy flavoursome Aussie Cabernet Sauvignon, proof that the best of the Wolf Blass range age well. Ian Botham drinks Black Label: Wolf Blass Black Label, that is.

FRANCE

1989 Château Monbousquet, St Emilion Grand Cru
£ / MB / 🍷   15/20

Rich, ripe slightly farmyardy Right Bank Merlot-dominated claret from a fine vintage.

1988 Château Haut-Marbuzet, St Estèphe
£ / FB / ↦   15/20

A wine which is highly rated by American wine scorer, Robert Parker, largely, we suspect, because of the punch in the mouth, chocolate and coffee bean oak. Mmm...

SPAIN

1986 Contino, Rioja Reserva
£££ / MB / ↦   17/20

Contino is one of the few single estate Riojas – most are blends from different vineyards. It's also among the handful of consistently great bottles produced in Spain. Sweetly aromatic, this wine is rich in concentrated strawberry-like fruit and savoury American oak flavours. Judging by the superb 1982, a red which still has plenty of life in it.

UNITED STATES

1988 Palmer Vineyards Cabernet Sauvignon
0 / MB / 🍷   13/20

A wine from Great Gatsby country on the north fork of Long Island. You might wonder what they're doing growing red grapes in a place like this, and we'd agree. This rather acid, unripe Cabernet Sauvignon reminded us of an English red. Enough said. Beam it up, Scottie.

Sparkling

£5–8

AUSTRALIA

Blass Brut
0 / 3 / 1   13/20
Rather like the brash, bow-tie wearing self-publicist who owns
the eponymous company, this is long on gas and short on elegance.

Over £8

UNITED STATES

Mumm Cuvée Napa
££ / 2 / 1   15/20
After a couple of dodgy years and several advertising campaigns,
Mumm Cuvée Napa appears to be back on the rails. The fruit quality
is very good, but our reservation is that the wine is being released
so young that it tastes somewhat tart and austere. Tuck it away for
a few months and this one should reward your patience.

KWIK SAVE **(*)

Head Office: Warren Drive, Prestatyn, Clwyd, LL19 7HU

Telephone: 0745 887111

Number of branches: 850 plus

Credit cards accepted: No, but Switch accepted in some stores

Hours of opening: Closed Sunday. Late night opening (until 8pm) on Thursday and Friday

By-the-case sales: No

Glass loan: No

Home delivery: No

Clubs: No

Discounts: No, but the whole range is priced very competitively

In-store tastings: In selected stores

Top ten best-selling wines: Liebfraumilch; Hock; Lambrusco Bianco; Rouge de France; Lambrusco Rosé; Lovico Suhindol Cabernet Sauvignon/Merlot; II Paesano Merlot; Lambrusco Light; Silver Hill Red; Gabbia d'Oro White

Range: GOOD: Italy, regional France, Eastern Europe, Spain
AVERAGE: Bordeaux, Portugal, Australia, South Africa
POOR: Germany, United States, Loire

Australian Chardonnay may not be the first priority on Kwik Save customers' shopping lists, but, lured through the doors of Britain's most dynamic retail operation by the promise of bargain-basement essentials, they come nose to shelf with one of the best-chosen wine ranges in the country.

Kwik Save was the first of the high street discount stores to recognise the benefits of taking wine seriously. Having entrusted Master of Wine and super blender Angela Muir with the job of selecting a decent range, the chain has seen its pioneering move repaid with interest. 'Since we started work on the range just under two years ago,' says Muir, 'sales have roughly doubled, and customers are prepared to spend more on a bottle of wine.'

This is quite an achievement, given that Kwik Saves are basically neighbourhood stores, supplying the community with bathroom tissue, medium sliced bread and vanilla ice cream. For Kwik Save customers, wine is another country. We spotted a couple in one store who had got the top off a litre bottle of Lambrusco before they'd passed the checkout.

Until Angela Muir arrived, everything at Kwik Save was branded in the familiar, deeply dull Piat d'Or, Blue Nun and Black Tower mould. Bidding goodbye to most of Kwik Save's previous suppliers, Muir set out to find good quality wines at the right price. This has meant expanding the range to its current 90 lines, but not frightening the punters too much. 'We're trying to make the unfamiliar more familiar,' says Muir. 'Many of our reds are on the light side, for instance, because not everyone wants a tannic blockbuster.'

There were no own-label wines at all two years ago, but now there's a small selection, dubbed the 'No Frills Range'. Watch out for the first Kwik Save own-label winebox - frill a minute stuff, presumably.

Thanks to Kwik Save's lower than average profit margin, Muir has been able to keep all but three wines under the magic £3 price point. Success has also helped her pass on the advantages of buying direct from the supplier, instead of having to go via middlemen. Some companies refuse to sell to Kwik Save, considering the chain too downmarket. But, as Muir points out, 'They aren't usually in the £2.99 business.'

Muir has continued the job of introducing New World and Eastern European wines, alongside more familiar labels from France, Italy and Germany. Portugal's Leziria, red and white, and, surprisingly perhaps, the Euroblend, Comtesse de Lorancy, have been runaway successes. Eastern Europe has been strengthened with some excellent new-wave Hungarian whites from the flying winemaker duo of Kym Milne and Nick Butler. And not only did the year's supply of Pelican Bay wines from Australia sell out in three months, but customers set off to other shops in search of them.

Muir feels she doesn't need to pander to traditional names if the quality isn't up to scratch. Beaujolais and Côtes du Rhône, for instance, got the chop, because the watery 1993 vintage wasn't good enough. They were replaced with a more imaginative duo of a Grenache/Shiraz vin de pays and an excellent Côtes du Ventoux red. Muscadet, on the other hand, was reprieved, while the New World-orientated southern French group, Domaines Virginie, continues to provide extraordinarily good value.

Despite her best intentions, Muir has so far failed to improve the basic German range, which remains, well, basic. She admits it could do with a nip and tuck and plans to do something about it this year.

German wines notwithstanding, Muir says she likes to think Kwik Save has the best under-£3 range in the country. Moving the chain up half a star in the *Grapevine* hierarchy this year, we are inclined to agree, although it faces very strong competition from Asda and Morrison's in the value-for-money stakes.

Muir's main regret is that Kwik Save doesn't yet have the customer base to enable it to achieve a respectable turnover of wines over £3. Reports from the shop front are that the wines are not shifting as quickly as they might. Muir says that, while Kwik Save has a few ABC1s among its shoppers, 'We never claim to provide special occasion drinking.' Fair enough. But it would be nice to see Kwik Save taking a few more risks. Anyone for Grand Cru Burgundy and fish fingers?

White

Under £3

AUSTRALIA

Pelican Bay Dry White, South-East Australia
£ / 2 / 1   13/20
A commendably inexpensive warm climate Semillon from the under-appreciated McWilliams winery, surprisingly light in alcohol for an Aussie white.

Pelican Bay Medium Dry White, South-East Australia
£ / 3 / 13/20
It might put you off to know that this is a blend of Sultana and Fruity Gordo grapes, but it shouldn't if your tooth is sweetish. Fat and grapey with plenty of fruit.

BULGARIA

1993 Bear Ridge
££ / 2 / 14/20
A real curiosity made in Bulgaria by an Australian winemaker with what to our knowledge is a unique combination of Ugni Blanc, Misket and Welschriesling. The Australian technique shines through in this fresh, aromatic, banana-y white.

CHILE

White Pacific Sauvignon Blanc
£££ / 2 / 15/20
Excellent, refreshingly zingy Sauvignon Blanc from Errázuriz Panquehue (that's 'pan-kay-way') made by airborne Australian Master of Wine Kym Milne. A bargain.

White Pacific Chardonnay/Semillon
£££ / 2 / 16/20
Another Errázuriz Panquehue/Kym Milne partnership, showing lovely ripe peach and melon flavours and fine balance, especially for a wine at such a modest price.

FRANCE

Comtesse de Lorancy, EEC Table Wine
0 / 3 / 12/20
For Comtesse, read Contessa. Most of the grapes for this rather dull Euroblend were grown on the Spanish plain of La Mancha. You can see why they were keen to export them.

Blanc de France, French Table Wine, Selection Cuvée VE 1 Litre
££ / 3 / 🍾   14/20

Cuvée VE, as followers of *Grapevine* will already know, stands for Vite Epargne – Franglais for Kwik Save. Made by the Loire merchant Donatien Bahuaud, this is an all-purpose blend of Ugni Blanc, Gros Plant and anything else that didn't have a home at the time. Pleasantly crisp, off-dry white.

1993 Vin de Pays des Côtes de Gascogne, Cuvée Classique
££ / 2 / 🍾   14/20

Zesty, grapefruity white from D'Artagnan country, produced by the innovative Plaimont co-operative.

1993 Côtes du Ventoux, AC Côtes du Ventoux
£ / 2 / 🍾   13/20

An example of a flying winemaker's wine, in this instance Mark Robertson's, that doesn't quite get off the ground. The raw material of Bourboulenc and Clairette ought to be interesting, but the result tastes flat and a bit heavy, like an overloaded charter to Torremolinos.

1993 Bordeaux Sauvignon, Cuvée VE
££ / 2 / 🍾   14/20

Not quite as good as last year's knockout bargain, but this is still soft, fragrantly grassy Sauvignon Blanc with a dry, herbaceous aftertaste.

1993 Domaine la Gravenne, Vin de Pays d'Oc sur Lie
£££ / 2 / 🍾   15/20

Mauzac is a grape variety which dare not speak its name, even though it is responsible for some pretty decent southern French wines in Limoux and Gaillac. Even here, where it's the core of this crisp, tropically fruity, smooth white from Domaines Virginie, the word Mauzac is nowhere to to seen.

1993 Steep Ridge, Chardonnay/Sauvignon, Vin de Pays d'Oc
£ / 2 / 🍾   13/20

A wine with an Australian name that was bottled in Bordeaux, produced in the Languedoc-Roussillon, and bought by Kwik Save. Who said wine was simple. The combination of Chardonnay and

Sauvignon Blanc sounds better than it tastes – the fatness of the former is not redeemed by the lean acidity of the latter.

GERMANY

1993 Morio Muskat, Qualitätswein, Pfalz
££ / 3 / ▌   14/20
Like the Bordeaux Sauvignon, this isn't as good as it was last year, but we still enjoyed its pleasant honey and marmalade fruit.

1993 Piesporter Michelsberg, Mosel-Saar-Ruwer, K. Linden
££ / 3 / ▌   14/20
The only thing that put us off this dryish, floral Mosel blend was that two tasting samples were mildly corked. We hope you have better luck because the underlying fruit is good.

HUNGARY

1993 Hungarian Country Wine, Balaton Boglar
£ / 2 / ▌   13/20
A tongue-twistingly unusual blend of Muscat, Müller-Thurgau and Kiralyleanyka, made near Lake Balaton by Kym Milne, who clearly has plenty of friends in Hungary. The sweet pea-like aroma of Muscat dominates the trio, and the wine is pleasantly fresh.

1993 Hungarian Chardonnay, Balaton Boglar
0 / 2 / ▌   12/20
Balaton bog-standard Chardonnay with a bitter finish.

ITALY

1993 Soave, Cantina Sociale di Soave
£££ / 1 / ▌   15/20
Textbook Soave with plenty of lemony zip and an almondy bite. Nice to see an Italian co-operative producing wine as good as this, particularly at around £2.70 a bottle.

1993 Frascati Superiore, Villa Pani
£££ / 2 / ▋   15/20
Another first-rate Italian discovery, with a prickle of gas and
excellent buttery weight and flavour. It's unusual to find a drinkable
Frascati under £3.

PORTUGAL

Leziria White, Almeirim
££ / 3 / ▋   14/20
Popular, highly commercial Portuguese light white with a touch
of sweetness and some unashamedly earthy, resinous fruit. Hard
to beat under £2 - which, let's face it, is where Kwik Save scores.

SOUTH AFRICA

1993 Silver Hills White, Stellenbosch
££ / 3 / ▋   14/20
An off-dry Cape blend of Rhine Riesling, Sauvignon Blanc and
Auxerrois. Rich and fat, like many an Afrikaner, but with lively
balancing acidity.

Clearsprings Cape Medium White
£ / 3 / ▋   13/20
Sweetish, faintly cloying white made from the ubiquitous Chenin
Blanc grape known as Steen in South Africa.

SPAIN

Flamenco, Spanish Medium White, Valencia
££ / 3 / ▋   14/20
You wouldn't expect subtlety from a Kwik Save brand name,
and Flamenco doesn't disappoint, but the wine behind the
castanets and twirling skirts is not half bad. It's on the sweet
side, but crunchy Merseguera and Airen fruitiness stop it sticking
to the guitar strings.

£3–5

AUSTRALIA

1993 Angove's Chardonnay, Classic Reserve, South Australia
££ / 2 / ▮   15/20

A step up from last year's charred, overoaked effort. In fact, this was one of our favourite wines at Kwik Save. It's among the few bottles over £3, but it's worth paying the extra pound for a Chardonnay with fresh fruit flavours of melon and pineapple.

Red

Under £3

BULGARIA

Lovico Suhindol, Cabernet Sauvignon/Merlot, Bulgarian Country Wine
££ / MB / ▮   14/20

A popular red with Kwik Save's thrifty customers, which certainly delivers value for money. After years of turning out rather old-fashioned reds, the Bulgarians finally seem to be catching on to fruitier things like this. A sweet plummy red with a touch of tobaccoey oak.

1990 Cabernet Sauvignon, Burgas
££ / MB / ▮   14/20

Nicely integrated toffee-caramel oak and vibrant, modern fruit. Another enjoyable Bulgarian red.

1990 Cabernet Sauvignon Reserve, Oriachovitza
£££ / FB / ▮   15/20

A chip off the Australian block with lashings of coconutty American oak flavour and supple, ripe fruit. If Bulgaria can keep coming up with wines like this, it could do for wine what Hristo Stoichkov has done for football.

CHILE

San Pedro, Chilean Red
£ / LB / ▮   13/20
A light, rather dry, loganberry scented red which appears to have
suffered, like many Chilean wines, from excessive vineyard yields.

FRANCE

Rouge de France, Séléction Cuvée VE
0 / LB / ▮   12/20
Smooth, soft, sweetened red in a Piat d'Or mould.

Vin de Pays de l'Hérault, 1 Litre
££ / MB / ▮   14/20
Big bottle, big value as Kwik Save's customers would have it. A
well-made Languedoc blend of Grenache, Syrah and Merlot
produced by the American-style Skalli Fortant de France operation
in Sète. Juicy, with a fleck of pepper.

1993 Steep Ridge, Grenache/Shiraz, Vin de Pays d'Oc
££ / FB / ▮   14/20
Back at the foot of Steep Ridge, but this time the climb is a more
appealing prospect. It shows to what extent Australia has
influenced things when Frenchmen start calling their Syrah Shiraz.
Aromatic, minty, strawberry fruit.

1993 Château Fontcaude, AC St Chinian
£££ / FB / ▮   15/20
Like most of the reds produced by the New World-influenced
Domaines Virginie, this is in a fruity, drink-me style. But as well as
the appealing fruit, there's some welcome tannin, spice and grip.

Minervois, AC Minervois
£££ / MB / ▮   15/20
Val d'Orbieu is one of the largest wine companies in the world,
producing enormous volumes of southern French reds and whites
to a high quality standard. This rich, supple, peppery red is a classic
example.

1993 Côtes du Ventoux Red, AC Côtes du Ventoux
£££ / FB / ❦   15/20

Proof that southern French co-operatives are beginning to get their act together. Amazing value and an authentic Rhône Valley combination of Grenache, Cinsault and Syrah. Infused with herbs and soft raspberry fruit with a rustic, dry finish.

Claret, AC Bordeaux, Cuvée VE
££ / MB / ❦   15/20

A wine which shows consultant Angela Muir at her exacting best. It's almost impossible to find half-drinkable claret at under £3, but she's done it again with this lush, Merlot-dominated blend.

1993 Merlot Domaine Resclause, Vin de Pays d'Oc
£££ / MB / ❦   16/20

Domaines Virginie firing on all cylinders, producing a wine with the sort of seductive blackberry fruit that should be the envy of Bordeaux at this price.

HUNGARY

1993 Hungarian Merlot, Hungarian Country Wine
££ / LB / ❦   14/20

It says Merlot on the label, but this is in fact a more interesting blend of Bordeaux varieties: Cabernet Franc, Cabernet Sauvignon, and Merlot and the local Kekfrankos grape. Light, bubblegum-style red with plenty of fruit and good acidity.

ITALY

Il Paesano, Merlot del Veneto
0 / MB / ❦   11/20

A peasant indeed.

1993 Arietta, Montepulciano d'Abruzzo
££ / FB / ❦   15/20

With its pseudo-Canaletto label and stylish packaging, this is just the sort of thing to turn people onto Italian reds. Bitter cherry and savoury Italianate fruit on vibrant form.

1993 Valpolicella, Cantina Sociale di Soave
££ / LB / 🍷   14/20

Not quite up to the same co-operative's superlative Soave, but pleasantly banana-like and Beaujoloid nevertheless.

PORTUGAL

Leziria Red, Almeirim
£££ / MB / 🍷   15/20

A value-for-money red that never lets you down. The tannins are softer than last year's more robust version, but there's still plenty of peppery Portuguese character on offer.

SPAIN

Flamenco, Spanish Full Red, Cariñena
££ / MB / 🍷   14/20

Castanets time again. A Garnacha (Grenache)-dominated red with bags of fruit and some gutsy tannins to keep your palate dancing.

Promesa Tinto, Cosecheros y Criadores
£££ / MB / 🍷   16/20

Stunning value from Martinez Bujanda, one of Rioja's most dynamic producers. This is a seductive, strawberry-fruity blend of Cencibel and Tempranillo grapes from the warm plain of La Mancha. The sort of wine that Spain is beginning to produce with encouraging regularity.

Spanish Merlot, Vicente Gandia, Valencia
£ / MB / 🍷   13/20

Spain has so many good native red grape varieties that producing a basic chunky Merlot seems a bit pointless.

UNITED STATES

Maxfield Premium Red, California
0 / MB / 🍷   12/20

Weird, man. This ruby Cabernet-based blend manages to be both sweet and fiercely tannic at the same time. Fine for spliffheads.

£3–5

AUSTRALIA

Angove's Butterfly Ridge, South Australia Cabernet Sauvignon/Shiraz

££ / MB / ▌   14/20

Approachable, commercial Aussie duo with sweet, minty fruit and a hint of Shiraz spice and a soupçon of oak flavour.

Rosé

Under £3

FRANCE

1993 Le Miracle, Côtes du Ventoux Rosé, AC Côtes du Ventoux

£££ / 2 / ▌   15/20

Miracle might be putting it a bit strongly, but this is the best of Mark Robertson's southern French wines. A dry, punchy pink with attractive strawberry and cassis fruit flavours and a nip of tannin.

Sparkling

Under £3

GERMANY

Liebfive, Lightly Sparkling 5% Volume

££ / 5 / ▌   13/20

A creamy, sweet, low-alcohol confection that's fine at the price. Liebfraumilch with bubbles. Mmm...

ITALY

Lambrusco Bianco Light, Partially Fermented Grape Must, 3% Volume

£ / 6 / 🍷   13/20

As close to grape juice as it is to wine, or possibly closer. This is a sickly sweet toffee apple white with restrained alcohol. Lemonade for grown-ups.

£5–8

FRANCE

Champagne Brut, Louis Raymond

£ / 2 / 🍷   13/20

Raymond Revue Bar material.

Fortified

Under £3

SPAIN

Castillo de Liria, Moscatel, Valencia

0 / 8 / 🍷   11/20

Barely a wine. You'd be better off pouring the contents away and replacing with aftershave.

MAJESTIC WINE WAREHOUSES

****

Head Office: Odhams Trading Estate, St Albans Road, Watford, WD2 5RE

Telephone: 0923 816999

Number of branches: 47

Credit cards accepted: Visa, Access, American Express, Switch, Diners

Hours of opening: Monday to Saturday 10am to 8pm; Sunday 10am to 6pm

By-the-case sales: Exclusively, but cases can be mixed

Glass loan: Yes

Home delivery: Free within a five-mile radius of the store

Clubs: No

Discounts: Substantial discounts on unsplit cases of Champagne and selected multi-buys

In-store tastings: Theme tasting weekends, private group tastings and a tasting counter available in all stores at all times

Top ten best-selling wines: Le St Cricq Blanc de Blancs; Blanc de Blancs, Henri Lambert; 1993 Pinot Grigio del Veneto, Pasqua; 1993 Sauvignon de Touraine, Comte d'Ormont, Saget; 1993 Gyöngyös Estate Chardonnay; 1993 Chardonnay, Vin de Pays d'Oc, Bessière; 1993 Mâcon Blanc, Les Chazelles; Le St Cricq Rouge; 1988 Bulgarian Cabernet Sauvignon, Russe; 1990 Domaine Guingal, Cahors

Range: GOOD: Bordeaux, Champagne and sparkling wines, Loire, Burgundy, Germany, regional France, Rhône, Port
AVERAGE: South Africa, California, Australia, Italy, New Zealand, Beaujolais, Alsace, Spain, Portugal, Sherry
POOR: Eastern Europe, Chile

A mission statement which runs 'if it's cheap, we'll buy it', looks as if it should be hanging on the door of Shoprite, Penny Market, SoLo, or any of the other pile-it-high discounters increasingly flogging their cut-price wares around the country.

Hearing it from the mouth of Majestic Wine Warehouses' marketing director, Debbie Worton, is a little surprising, especially given that Majestic has the highest 'till ring' in the high street and, at over £4, probably the highest average bottle sale after Oddbins. But Majestic has built its recent success as much as anything on razor-sharp prices backed by spectacular deals.

Appropriately enough, it was an arch-deal which launched the most recent episode in the Majestic saga. With former Majestic director Tony Mason at the helm, Wizard Wines bought an ailing Majestic for a knock-down £2.5 million in September 1991. The chain was in dire straits then, but after surviving three years of choppy financial seas, Majestic has entered calmer waters.

'It's been a long hard struggle to get back on an even keel,' admits Mason, now Majestic's trading director, 'but this is the first time Majestic's made money in four years.' Less than £500,000 on an annual turnover of £36 million may be a relatively modest crock of gold, but just to see the balance sheet in the black has brought the smiles back at Majestic.

The economy's slow emergence from recession played a part, as did the long hot summer of 1994, in which beer sales went through Majestic's numerous railway arch, cinema and abattoir roofs. But more significant was the fact that Majestic has, in the idiom of the day, gone 'back to basics' – which means 'focusing on buying and trading in good-value products. We've tried to develop a trading culture, going for razor-sharp deals in contrast to the more cautious buying policy of the supermarkets.'

Supermarkets such as Sainsbury's and Tesco – and Bottoms Up rather than Oddbins – are Majestic's strongest competitors. So Majestic needs to distinguish itself in every way it can from the competition. Bringing in good deals is a vital unique selling point (USP in the jargon), because Majestic's traditional customers – typically 40 to 50-year-old men with cash to burn – get bored with the same old wine, week in, week out.

'Our customers spend £75 to £85 a time,' says Debbie Worton. 'They aren't so much young people saddled with huge mortgages or large young families, as people with a higher disposable income to spend on leisure. For them, wine is more than just a commodity. It's a way of life.'

Enter super-deal maker Tony Mason. We were amused this year by Dave West at EastEnders in Calais, who told us that his wine-buying policy was to purchase from people with 'cash-flow problems'. Although he might choose to consult his solicitors about the comparison, there's a touch of the Romford barrow-boy about Tony Mason too, whose finely honed nose for a bargain is one of the sharpest in the wine trade. Who else would have had the nous to plug more than a dozen Majestic wines in thirty seconds of prime time television during a consumer affairs item about cork problems?

Among Tony Mason's more spectacular deals over the past year was a parcel of 5,500 cases of fine wines snapped up from a Jersey company which had overextended itself by buying a vast amount of stock for just two stores. Wines like this don't go into the main list, but are mailed out to customers as part of Majestic's five major promotions during the year. Wines in these cut-price promotions are affectionately titled 'stonkers', going out at 'stonky prices'. If you thought Stonky Price was the name of a South African rugby prop forward, you are now the wiser.

Mason also picked up a couple of vintages of Château de la Jaubertie's top wine, Mirabelle, which, unsaleable at £7.99, looks considerably more interesting on Majestic's concrete floors at £4.99. Three vintages of Domaine de Guingal were sniffed out from the cellars of Château Quattre, a Laurent Perrier-owned Cahors estate, and sold for a knockdown £2.99. Guingal made the Majestic top ten best sellers, as did a parcel of an excellent, fresh, unoaked Chardonnay from the Languedoc: Chardonnay, Vin de Pays d'Oc, Bessière. A delicious red from Tricastin, Domaine Vergobbi, stormed out at £3.99.

Most of these deals are great buys. But, just occasionally, Mason's nose for a bargain leads him up the winery path to the wrong cellar door. This, we suppose, is the price the consumer has to pay.

Mason has continued to plunder the South of France. After a trip to the Languedoc, he returned enthused with a bootful of bargains. 'The South of France represents the best value these days, but we're going through a slightly arid period coming out of recession. The super-deals are not there at the moment,' says Mason, looking momentarily crestfallen at the prospect.

Given the profile of the typical Majestic customer, it's not surprising that 60 per cent of their 700-plus range is French. This may sound like a lot compared with other retailers, but Liebfraumilch, Hock and Lambrusco, so dear to the national palate almost everywhere else in the high street, have slumped from 20 per cent of sales at Majestic a few years back to next to nothing today. Majestic's best sellers include seven French wines, five of them dry whites and two reds.

It's not just the deals that keep Majestic customers coming back for more, however. The regular list contains an impressive range of French classics from Bordeaux, Burgundy and the Rhône with an increasing number of excellent wines from the South of France.

Thanks to Majestic's flexible buying policy, there are also some off-the-wall items such as a Canadian Baco Noir, a white Pinot Noir from northern Italy, and an unusual Pinot Noir/Gamay/Cabernet Franc blend from the little known Cheverny *appellation* in the Loire. The popularity of the New World, as you might expect, continues to grow, with Australia second only to France in sales.

Another of Majestic's USPs is the wine warehouse concept itself, which, apart from concentrating on by-the-case sales, provides car parking, wine tastings, the possibility of browsing freely up and down the airy, well-stocked aisles, and of being served by helpful, enthusiastic staff who know their wines.

When he was at Wizard, Mason moved away from by-the-case sales, claiming that having to spend so much money in one go put off potential customers. Back at Majestic, he's come round to the idea again. 'For someone who wants to buy serious quantities of wine, it allows us to give a level of service which simply cannot be given in a retail scenario.'

Despite the continuing squeeze on the high street off-licence by the big supermarkets, Mason is confident that Majestic has found a niche for itself, which makes it, if not safe, at least relatively sheltered from the buffeting suffered by some of the smaller independent high street chains.

Majestic has added new sites at Worcester, Farnham and Nottingham over the past year to bring the tally of stores to 47. Far from being moribund, Majestic's small but growing empire now extends from Taunton to Stockport with an increasingly strong presence in the Midlands. Perhaps that mission statement should read 'deals for all'.

White

Under £3

FRANCE

1993 Le St Cricq, Blanc de Blancs, Germain Père et Fils
£ / 3 / ▌   12/20
The most interesting thing about this £1.99 apple and aniseed-like quaffer is that it was made in La Mancha and bottled in Bordeaux.

Blanc de Blancs, Henri Lambert
£ / 1 / ▌   13/20
This top ten best seller is one of the longest serving whites at Majestic. It's lemony, quinine-like wine bar white at a good price. Gin and tonic in a bottle for the Sloane set.

1993 Domaine Lanine, Vin de Pays des Côtes de Gascogne, Grassa
£££ / 2 / ▌   14/20
A limited edition Tony Mason special deal, which may be in short supply by the time you read this. All the same, we couldn't resist mentioning what is definitely one of the better Gascon whites around. Grapefruit and lemon zest with some richness derived from the Colombard grape.

1993 Muscat, Vin de Pays des Collines de la Moure, Hugh Ryman, half-bottle
£££ / 6 / ▌   16/20
An elegant, sweetly aromatic, grape- and melon-flavoured curiosity made by Englishman Hugh Ryman from cool climate vineyards in the Languedoc hills.

SPAIN

1993 Santara Dry White, Hugh Ryman
£££ / 2 / ▌   15/20
From Conca de Barbera, a small *denominación* in Catalonia, this is a lemon-fresh blend of the native Macabeu and Parellada grapes. An excellent party white.

£3–5

AUSTRALIA

1993 Penfolds Bin 202 Rhine Riesling
££ / 3 / 🍷   14/20

A fairly recent addition to the Penfolds' range, reflecting the consumer's growing interest in Australian Riesling. Unashamedly commercial, with sweet lime and orange peel fruitiness and crisp acidity.

1993 Church Hill Chardonnay
0 / 2 / 🍷   12/20

Old-style Aussie white from the Mildara stable, showing obvious desiccated coconut and boiled-sweets flavours. Where's the Chardonnay, Bruce?

1993 Penfolds Bin 21, Semillon/Chardonnay, South Australia
£ / 2 / 🍷   15/20

In common with many commercial Australian whites, the 1993 is more restrained than the 1992 vintage. Fresh melon and peachy fruit with a dab of smoky oak and herbal Semillon character. Perfect party and house white. Should be under £5.

CANADA

Stonechurch Vineyards, Vidal/Chardonnay, Niagara
£ / 2 / 🍷   14/20

A curious addition to the Majestic range, made from a blend of the Vidal grape (a crossing of Ugni Blanc and the world-famous hybrid Seibel 4986) and a more glamorous Chardonnay. The former is responsible for a slightly foxy, damp leaf character in the wine's aroma, but there's enough fruit on the palate to make this worth a try.

FRANCE

1993 Sauvignon de Touraine, Comte d'Ormont, Saget
£ / 1 / 🍷   13/20

Clean, fresh, nettley Loire Sauvignon Blanc with a sharp edge. One of Majestic's top ten best sellers.

1993 Chardonnay, Vin de Pays d'Oc, Bessière
£££ / 2 / 🜊   15/20
Tony Mason at his deal-hungry best, snapping up a parcel of crisp, ultra-fresh, unoaked Chardonnay from a co-operative in Béziers. Not surprisingly, it shot straight into Majestic's hit parade.

1993 Mâcon-Villages, Les Chazelles
££ / 2 / 🜊   15/20
A modern, cool-fermented, fruity and forward style of white Burgundy, vinified by Australian winemaker Nigel Sneyd, with the merest hint of rusticity for character.

1993 Muscadet Sur Lie, Cuvée Celtes, Guilbaud
0 / 1 / 🜊   12/20
Apparently, the Asterix-style warrior on the label reminded wine buyer, Tony Mason, of Majestic's information technology director. Perhaps he couldn't think of a better reason for buying it.

1993 Cheverny Blanc, Oisly et Thésée
£ / 1 / 🜊   13/20
An unusual Loire blend of 90 per cent Sauvignon Blanc and 10 per cent Chardonnay from vineyards which have recently been granted (more or less) prestigious *appellation contrôlée* status. A faintly green, nettle and hedgerow white, which was undoubtedly designed with oysters in mind.

1993 Domaine de Sours White
£ / 2 / 🜊   14/20
Ex-Majestic director, Esme Johnstone, whose home is now his castle in the Entre-Deux-Mers region of Bordeaux, didn't make a first wine Château de Sours white in 1993, preferring to put it all into his subsidiary label, Domaine de Sours. This Semillon-based blend is pleasantly oaked, if on the insubstantial side.

1993 Château de la Jaubertie, Bergerac Sec
££ / 2 / 🜊   15/20
Assertive, highly aromatic Bordeaux-style blend from a Bergerac property which has had a long association with Majestic. Not quite as good as last year's release, but you can see why the customers keep coming back for more.

1992 Les Jamelles, Marsanne, Vin de Pays d'Oc
££ / 2 / **]**   15/20
Confronted by this tall, Italian designer bottle, we feared the worst
– a triumph of marketing over content. But how wrong we were.
The wine turned out to be a rich, perfumed, almost exotic southern
French white with waxy, almondy flavours and good acidity.

1992 Montagny Premier Cru, Vignes de la Croix
0 / 2 / **]**   10/20
A deal that went badly wrong.

1992 Château de la Jaubertie, Mirabelle Reserve
££ / 2 / **]**   15/20
A deal that worked. Mirabelle is Château de la Jaubertie's top-of-
the-range white with late-picked super-ripe grapes, treated to oak
fermentation and an £8 price tag. Reduced to £5, this rich, smoky
Sauvignon-based white is well worth the money. Avoid the 1991,
however, which may still be hanging around at Majestic.

1993 Côtes du Ventoux, AC Côtes du Ventoux
£ / 2 / **]**   13/20
An example of a flying winemaker's wine, in this instance Mark
Robertson, that doesn't quite get off the ground. The raw material
of Bourboulenc and Clairette ought to be interesting, but the result
tastes flat and a bit heavy, like an overloaded charter to
Torremolinos.

GERMANY

1992 Cuvée Constantin, Max Ferdinand Richter
££ / 2 / **]**   15/20
Named after Dirk Richter's small son (Constantin, rather than his
daughter, Cuvée, we presume), this is a restrained Mosel Müller-
Thurgau. Pleasantly floral with a green apple bite and a dryness
that's designed for food.

HUNGARY

1993 Gyöngyös Estate Chardonnay, Hugh Ryman
£ / 2 / **]**   13/20
One of the better bottlings of this inconsistent Chardonnay,

with some soft, peachy, honeyed fruit, but a cloying aftertaste.
A wine which has its ups and downs owing to rather primitive
cellar technology. When it's good, it's very good, but when it's
bad...

1993 Gyöngyös Estate Sauvignon Blanc, Hugh Ryman
££ / 2 /   14/20
This is the best Sauvignon Blanc we've encountered from the
pioneering Gyöngyös Estate. Made in a mini-New Zealand style,
it's a zesty, aromatic dry white with citrus fruit sweetness and
acidity. A caveat: we have noticed inconsistency between
Gyöngyös bottlings.

ITALY

1993 Pinot Grigio del Veneto, Pasqua
££ / 2 /   15/20
Yeasty, nutty, peach-like north Italian white with more character
than you often get at this price level. Encouraging to see a wine
like this in Majestic's top ten.

1993 Soave Classico, Tedeschi
££ / 2 /   15/20
Weighty, robust Veneto dry white with a nutty, almondy aftertaste.
If you thought all Soave was neutral and watery, get hold of a
bottle of this one.

1993 Pinot Nero Bianco, Oltrepò Pavese, Bava
££ / 2 /   14/20
A highly unusual Italian wine vinified from Burgundy's red Pinot
Noir grape as a dry white. Retaining some of the strawberry fruit
character of the grape, it's a crisp, delicate curiosity.

1993 Orvieto Abboccato, Antinori
££ / 4 /   15/20
Another individual Italian white, this time made in a medium-dry
style by giant Tuscany-based producer, Antinori. A distinctly
aromatic, beeswax and lime scented white with some attractively
yeasty, almost beer-like characters.

SOUTH AFRICA

1994 Two Oceans Sauvignon Blanc
0 / 2 / ❚   11/20
The two oceans in question are the Atlantic and the Indian. They
could have poured this into either of them and no one would
have cared.

1994 Kiesenhof Chenin Blanc
££ / 2 / ❚   15/20
One of the better inexpensive Cape whites on the market, with
refreshing, grapefruity flavours and a balanced, dry finish.

SPAIN

Fariña Bianco, Semi-Dulce, Bodegas Fariña
0 / 4 / ❚   12/20
Old-style 'Spanish Sauternes' by another name.

UNITED STATES

1991 Electra Orange Muscat, Andrew Quady
£ / 5 / ❚   14/20
Andrew Quady is best known for his sweet fortified wines. But
this ginger, pineapple and nutmeg cocktail is an interesting new
direction. With only four percent alcohol, it's California's answer
to Moscato d'Asti.

£5–8

AUSTRALIA

1993 Preece Chardonnay, Mitchelton
££ / 2 / ❚   15/20
Named after Colin Preece, who was instrumental in creating the
Mitchelton winery in Victoria's Goulburn Valley, this is a fresh,
pleasantly oaked, citrus-fruity Chardonnay from underrated
winemaker Don Lewis. With its postage stamp label, and dark green
bottle, it's a good-looking package too.

1992 Hollick Estate Chardonnay, Coonawarra
££ / 2 / 🍶   16/20
Ian Hollick (known to his friends as Al-co, presumably) is better
known for his Coonawarra reds than his whites. Tropical fruit,
butterscotch oak and a hint of honeyed botrytis make this a
distinctive Chardonnay with a surprising degree of elegance.

1987 Lindemans Botrytis Semillon
££ / 8 / 🍶   15/20
Now that the European Union and Australia's winemakers have
settled their differences over sweet wines, among other things,
we should see many more good-value stickies from Down Under.
This deep, golden, mature Semillon wine oozes honey and barley
sugar sweetness, but has lost the refreshing acidity it once had.

FRANCE

1993 Château de la Jaubertie, Sauvignon Blanc, Bergerac Sec
£££ / 2 / 🍶   16/20
This was made by Charles Martin, maintaining the estate's high
reputation for excellent Sauvignon Blanc. A crisp, assertive, ripe
gooseberry white, combining the best features of the Loire Valley
and New Zealand. The estate has recently been bought from father
Nick by son Hugh Ryman in partnership with Esme Johnstone of
Château de Sours. Watch out for fireworks.

1992 Montagny Premier Cru, La Grande Roche, Louis Latour
££ / 2 / ⌐   16/20
Louis Latour is better known for the quality of his white Burgundies
than his reds. This toasty, modern Côte Chalonnaise white with
its good weight and Chardonnay fruit is a fine example of the
Latour style.

1992 Tokay Pinot Gris, Cave de Ribeauvillé
0 / 3 / 🍶   12/20
Fine if you like ginger ale and baked apples.

1992 Savennières, Clos de Varennes
££ / 1 / ⌐   15/20
Typical Savennières, one of the most steely and long-lived of Loire
dry whites. Pungently nettley, herby stuff with a bracingly austere

finish. Serve with a sandre au beurre blanc, by the banks of the Loire River if possible.

1992 Riesling Grand Cru Wiebelsberg, E. Boeckel

0 / 2 / ▐   **13/20**

Nothing terribly grand about this grand cru Riesling, but then the term doesn't mean much in Alsace, where practically any piece of elevated ground is granted grand cru status. Soft, with sweet and sour cooking apple characters.

1992 Château Thieuley, Cuvée Barrique, Bordeaux

££ / 2 / ►   **16/20**

A modern Bordeaux white blend, which has only just moved into second gear. Showing Graves style, toasty oak, waxy richness and grapefruity flavours in nice balance.

1992 Bourgogne Blanc, Cuvée Georges Faiveley

0 / 2 / ▐   **13/20**

A light, tart, basic white Burgundy with too much oak for its own good and an overinflated price tag.

GERMANY

1992 Trittenheimer Altärchen Riesling Kabinett, Weingut Grans-Fassian

£ / 3 / ►   **15/20**

A little on the expensive side for a Kabinett at nearly £6 a bottle, given what else you can find from Germany at the price. Nevertheless it does show the pure Mosel Riesling character of Granny Smith apples and a hint of kerosene. Crisp and balanced with enough concentration to age.

ITALY

1993 La Prendina Bianco, Vino da Tavola

££ / 2 / ▐   **15/20**

A lightly oaked blend of mainly Trebbiano and Cortese grapes, this is an Italian white with plenty of green olive and baked toffee apple character.

1985 Vin Santo, Ricasoli, 37.5cl
££ / 5 / ▌   15/20
This traditional Tuscan speciality shows the diversity of sweet Italian white wines. It's a rich, fruitcake and orange peel style with a nutty, toffeed aftertaste, designed for dunking cantuccini biscuits.

NEW ZEALAND

1993 Coopers Creek Sauvignon Blanc, Gisborne
£ / 2 / ▌   14/20
Tinned pea and asparagus Sauvignon from Gisborne in New Zealand's North Island. The style sometimes suffers by comparison with Marlborough's more assertive crispness.

1993 Oyster Bay Sauvignon Blanc, Marlborough
££ / 2 / ▌   16/20
From the Delegat stable, this is an appealingly fruity South Island Sauvignon Blanc with elderflower aromas, fresh acidity and rounded tropical fruit sweetness.

1993 Oyster Bay Chardonnay, Marlborough
££ / 2 / ▌   16/20
Another Delegat's white with commendable balance for such a cool vintage. Stylishly oaked, refreshing Chardonnay made to be drunk young.

SOUTH AFRICA

1992 Neil Ellis Chardonnay
££ / 2 / ▌   15/20
From vineyards in the cool, apple-growing territory of Elgin, this is a light, lemony Chardonnay with some vanilla fudge oak produced by Neil Ellis, one of South Africa's most forward-looking winemakers.

UNITED STATES

1991 Pacific Crest Chardonnay
£ / 3 / ▌   15/20
A toasty, Burgundian-style Chardonnay from California with rich, buttery flavours and ripe fruit sweetness.

1992 Kendall-Jackson Chardonnay, Vintners Reserve
0 / 3 / ⬛   13/20
Oaky, souped-up and rather clumsy. A big California Chardonnay
from the winery which pioneered this popular (but not with us)
style.

Over £8

FRANCE

1993 Sancerre Les Roches, Vacheron
££ / 1 / ➤   16/20
A lively, citrus and goosberry-scented Sancerre from one of the
leading producers in the eastern Loire's most famous *appellation*.
Still young and taut, but with enough minerally intensity to stay
the distance.

1992 Chablis Premier Cru Fourchaumes, Adhémar Boudin
£££ / 2 / ➤   17/20
Ignore the dreadfully old-fashioned label, pull the cork and
feast your palate on this superbly rich, super-ripe and
concentrated Chablis. Honeyed fruit is balanced by zesty,
minerally acidity for long life. Longer, probably, than the
grower's dog's: it has a liver complaint thanks to too much
declassified Chablis in its begging bowl.

1992 Chablis, Domaine de Chantemerle, Adhémar Boudin
£££ / 2 / ➤   17/20
An idiosyncratic style from a producer whose cellar
techniques would give an Australian winemaker night-
mares. He warm ferments the wine by leaving the radiators
on in the cellar, then leaves it in battered steel tanks on its
lees for nine months. The result is a rich, complex, rustic
Chablis, to delight traditionalists.

**1990 Gewürztraminer, Grand Cru Hengst, Cave de
Turckheim**
££ / 3 / ➤   16/20
Classic rose petal spice and concentrated but elegantly balanced
Gewürztraminer fruit from Turckheim, one of the best

co-operatives in France. Hengst is clearly a grand cru worthy of
the name.

1986 Château Coutet, Premier Cru Classé, Barsac, half-bottle
0 / 6 / 🍾   14/20
Oaky, macaroon and coconut sweetness with some botrytis
character, but not enough for the vintage. We found this unusually
clumsy for Coutet.

GERMANY

1989 Trittenheimer Apotheke Riesling Auslese, Grans-Fassian
£££ / 5 / 🍾   17/20
**A splendid follow-up to the remarkably long-lived 1983, still
available in some branches of Majestic. A fresh, appley Mosel
with perfect sweet and sour balance, whose petrolly
characteristics will develop over the next decade.**

NEW ZEALAND

1992 Goldwater Marlborough Chardonnay
£ / 2 / 🍾   15/20
The Goldwters live in an idyllic setting on Auckland Bay's Waiheke
Island, where they make some of New Zealand's best red wines.
Their Chardonnay comes from contract vineyards in Marlborough.
It's decent enough, but we found the oak too heavy for the delicate
cool climate fruit.

Red

Under £3

AUSTRALIA

Misty Mooring Red, Angove's
£ / MB / 🍾   13/20
Commercial, soft, light, jammy blend of Grenache, Pinot Noir and
Barbera from Australia's Riverland, lifted by tartaric acidity.

BULGARIA

1988 Bulgarian Cabernet Sauvignon, Russe
££ / MB / 🍷   14/20
A soft, juicy red which tastes considerably younger than a 1988
and as much like a cherryish Pinot Noir as a Cabernet.

FRANCE

Le St Cricq Vin de Table Rouge, Germain Père et Fils
£ / LB / 🍷   12/20
Majestic's riposte to the cross-Channel madness is a rustic, wine
bar plonko from Central Spain, though you'd never guess it from
all those French words on the label.

1990 Cahors, Domaine de Guingal
£££ / FB / 🍷   14/20
A nifty purchase from a Cahors property owned by Champagne
house Laurent Perrier, which found itself with too much stock on
its hands. Majestic was only too pleased to help out by shifting
caseloads of three consecutive vintages. We tasted the dry, chewy,
sage and rosemary scented 1990, but don't be surprised to find
the 1988 or 1989 in store. Great value.

1993 Vin de Pays de Vaucluse, Mark Robertson
££ / MB / 🍷   14/20
Juicy, peppery, Beaujoloid southern red from Kiwi winemaker,
Mark Robertson, with a clod of robust tannin on the finish.

1992 Minervois, Domaine Dougnac
£££ / FB / 🍷   14/20
Spicy, robust, full-throated, traditional Languedoc red with a core
of sweet fruit and lots of firm tannins. A good winter warmer.

£3-5

AUSTRALIA

1991 Angove's Cabernet Sauvignon, South Australia
£ / MB / 🍷   14/20
The owners of the Angove winery suggest that this wine will age

for a decade or more. We think this is overstating the case by about nine years, 51 weeks and six days. It's very much a drink now, mint, blackcurrant and vanilla style.

1992 Penfolds Bin 35 Shiraz/Cabernet, South Australia
££ / FB / ▮   15/20
A typically exuberant Penfolds blend with charred American oak and berry fruit. Let's hope they can keep the price under £5 during this period of pressure on grape prices in Australia.

CHILE

1991 Montenuevo Oak-aged Cabernet Sauvignon, Vinicola Mondragon
£ / MB / ▮   13/20
A slightly green, stalky Chilean Cabernet Sauvignon with the emphasis on cassis fruit rather than oak.

FRANCE

1993 Cheverny Rouge, Oisly et Thésée
££ / LB / ▮   15/20
Like the white Cheverny, this is an unorthodox combination of grapes, in this case Pinot Noir, Gamay and Cabernet Franc. A light, fresh, characterful red with a bit of tannic bite and some juicy, peppery fruit.

1991 Château La Perrière, Bordeaux
£ / MB / ▮   14/20
A Merlot-dominated blend showing soft, forward, green pepper fruitiness and some backbone from a petit château. Not a claret for ageing.

1992 Monastère de Trignan, Coteaux du Languedoc
£££ / FB / ▮   17/20
Wow! A great follow-up to the wonderful 1991, and they've still managed to keep it under £4. Super-aromatic, old vine Syrah from the Languedoc, using the carbonic maceration technique to maximise fruit flavours and keep the texture smooth. A massively spicy, rosemary and thyme-infused red. All that's missing is the parsley.

1990 Coteaux du Tricastin, Domaine Vergobbi
££ / FB / ▌   15/20
A peppery, Grenache-based southern French red that would wipe
the winery floor with many a Côtes du Rhône. Lovely fruit
sweetness and robust layers of tannin.

1992 Château Haut-Lestiac, Bordeaux Supérieur
££ / MB / ▌   15/20
This petit château claret from a fine vintage shows silky Merlot
fruitiness and a touch of ginger spice. Soft, pleasant drinking.

1990 Château Sainte Jeanne, Corbières
£££ / FB / ▌   16/20
Yet another super-value, angostura-spice, garrigue-scented
blockbuster from the Corbières aged in oak barrels. With native
grapes like this around, who needs Cabernet Sauvignon?

1992 Les Jamelles, Mourvèdre, Vin de Pays d'Oc
£££ / FB / ↦   16/20
Mourvèdre is one of the best red grapes planted in Mediterranean
vineyards, which needs lots of sun and sea to ripen fully, reaching
its apogee in Bandol. This is a chunky, tobaccoey example, with
good, ripe balance in an attractive package.

1990 Beaumes-de-Venise, Carte Noire, Côtes du Rhône Villages
£££ / FB / ▌   16/20
Best known for its fortified Muscat de Beaumes de Venise, this
Rhône village produces surprisingly large quantities of red wines
too. This is a specially selected blend from the local co-operative,
combining scented fruit and rich, beefy flavours. As good as many
Châteauneuf-du-Papes.

1990 Côtes du Ventoux, Vidal Fleury
£££ / FB / ▌   16/20
A Provençal blend of Grenache, Syrah, Cinsault and Carignan from
vineyards on the slopes of Mont Ventoux, famous in the cycling
world as one of the toughest obstacles in the Tour de France.
Nothing tough about this mature, richly concentrated, chocolatey
southern red. A southern French stonker.

ITALY

1990 Valpolicella Classico, Tedeschi
££ / MB / ▌   15/20
Leafy, aromatic, smoked-sausage-scented Veronese red from one
of the best producers in the region. Fuller than most commercial
Valpolicellas.

1992 Montepulciano d'Abruzzo, Barone Cornacchia
£££ / MB / ▌   15/20
A wild-eyed country red from mountainous Abruzzi country in
Central Italy. Plenty of colour and fruit concentration, combining
intense flavours of cherry and game with a rasp of tannin and
acidity. Drink with steak tartare.

1986 Notarpanaro Taurino, Rosso del Salento
£££ / FB / ▌   17/20
**A mature, but still lively blend of 85 per cent Negro Amaro
and 15 per cent Malvasia Nera from the heel of southern
Italy. Traditional, spicy, raisiny stuff with a kernel of sweet
fruit and a bite of fresh acidity.**

PORTUGAL

1988 Alentejo Tinto Velho, JM da Fonseca Successores
££ / MB / ▌   15/20
From a winery which still ferments its reds in Ali Baba-style
amphorae, this is a traditional Portuguese blend with a modern
touch supplied by California-trained winemaker, Domingos
Soares Franco. A minty, savoury, essentially old-fashioned
Alentejo red. For people interested in trying something different.
Open, Sesame.

SOUTH AFRICA

1992 Kiesenhof Pinotage
£££ / MB / ▌   15/20
A well-made, baked banana and sweet raspberry Pinotage from
the Douglas Green/Bellingham group. No mistaking the grape
variety here, but drink up.

1991 Millstream Shiraz
£ / MB / ▮   14/20
It may sound Australian, but this wine is a western Cape Shiraz, which tastes uncannily like Pinotage. South African reds often do.

£5–8

AUSTRALIA

1992 Preece Cabernet Sauvignon, Mitchelton
££ / MB / ▮   15/20
Typical Victorian, cool climate eucalyptus aromas from vineyards in the Goulburn Valley. An oaky, concentrated red, which is a bit four-square.

1991 Hollick Estate Coonawarra Red
£££ / MB / ▬   17/20
A distinguished Coonawarra blend of Cabernet Sauvignon and Merlot from one of the smaller, quality-conscious estates in South Australia's finest red wine region. A super-elegant wine with supple, berry flavours, beautifully judged oak and the finesse of a classified claret.

CANADA

1992 Henry of Pelham Baco Noir, Ontario
££ / MB / ▮   15/20
For the benefit of the many ampelography students reading this book (it is, after all, called *Grapevine*), Baco Noir is a crossing of the Cognac grape Folle Blanche with a Riparia hybrid. We can't tell you who Henry of Pelham is, or was, but we liked his unusual wine, with its smoky, toffeed fruit and pronounced new oak. Close your eyes and you could almost be in Burgundy.

FRANCE

1992 Bourgogne Passetoutgrains, Mongeard-Mugneret
£ / LB / ▮   14/20
A wine which the Mongeard family apparently likes to drink at home, perhaps because this bastard style (a blend of Beaujolais'

Gamay with Burgundy's Pinot Noir) is hard to sell at £5.49. Light, pleasant quaffing.

1990 Chinon, Les Garous, Couly-Dutheil
££ / MB / ❶   16/20
Ripe, characteristically grassy Cabernet Franc from a single vineyard in the Touraine *appellation* of Chinon. A full, rich red from a good vintage with none of the hard edges you sometimes find on Chinon.

1992 Bourgogne Rouge, Faiveley
££ / MB / ❶   15/20
Considerably better than the 1991, showing much more of the fruity charm of the Pinot Noir grape and a lot less oak. Mmm...

1992 Juliénas, Joseph Drouhin
£ / MB / ❶   14/20
Beaune-based *négociant* Robert Drouhin is proud of his Beaujolais selection. This souped-up, merchant-style Beaujolais cru has a certain amount of Gamay character, but not enough for our liking at nearly £7.

1990 Vacquéyras, Vidal Fleury
££ / FB / ❶   15/20
A strapping, well-upholstered southern Rhône red made from a traditional blend of 70 per cent Grenache, 20 per cent Syrah and 10 per cent Mourvèdre. A heady, raisiny stonker from a village which was promoted to *appellation contrôlée* status in 1990.

1990 Lirac, Château d'Aqueria
££ / FB / ❶   16/20
A blend of Grenache, Mourvèdre, Cinsault and Carignan from a property best known for its Tavel Rosé. A big, sweet, tobaccoey red with mouth-filling fruit flavours and good length. Another stonker, and we promise that'll be the last one, Sarah.

1991 Côtes du Rhône, Guigal
£ / FB / ❶   14/20
An easy-drinking, southern red with some pepper and oak. Fair enough, but this is a let-down after the excellent Côtes du Rhônes Guigal made in 1988, 1989 and 1990.

ITALY

1988 Recioto della Valpolicella, Tedeschi, half-bottle
££ / FB / ➥-   16/20

Traditionally made from selected Valpolicella grapes left to dry in ventilated barns, this bittersweet, dark chocolatey red from one of the Veneto's best exponents of the style is an acquired taste. The practical half-bottle makes it easy to appreciate without spending a fortune.

NEW ZEALAND

1992 Coopers Creek Huapai Cabernet Merlot, Marlborough
££ / MB / ➥-   16/20

More enjoyable than the 1991, which may still be on the shelves in some branches, this is an elegant, cool climate, Bordeaux-style blend with sweet, cassis fruit and pronounced oak.

SOUTH AFRICA

1989 Meerendal Pinotage
£££ / FB / ➥-   16/20

Cooked bananas and blackcurrant fruitiness make this concentrated, ripe Pinotage from the sprawling Bergkelder group one of the most pleasurable South African reds we've had this year.

1992 Dieu Donné Cabernet Sauvignon, Franschhoek
££ / MB / ▐   15/20

Not quite God-given, but this supple, refreshing Cabernet Sauvignon, with its pronounced oak influence, should appeal to catholic tastes.

1990 Neil Ellis Cabernet Sauvignon, Stellenbosch
£ / MB / ▐   15/20

A wine suffering from green oak flavours. It's still young and tightly wound, with concentrated fruit, so maybe it needs time for the oak to fade into the veldt.

UNITED STATES

1991 Kendall-Jackson Cabernet Sauvignon, Vintners Reserve
0 / MB / **}**   11/20

Overextracted, overoaked, overpriced California Cabernet. We don't understand why anyone would want to buy this kind of thing. We'd rather have Kendal mint cakes, thank you.

Over £8

AUSTRALIA

1990 Lindemans Pyrus, Coonawarra
££ / MB / ⏪   16/20

Lindemans' Bordeaux-style blend of Cabernet Sauvignon, Cabernet Franc, Merlot and Malbec is a rich, concentrated yet elegant Coonawarra red with spicy, berry fruit and mocha-like oak. This wine should age for a decade or more.

1990 Penfolds Coonawarra Cabernet Sauvignon
££ / FB / ⏪   16/20

Masses of colour, concentrated fruit and sweet sawdusty American oak give this the stamp of Penfolds, but there's some balancing Coonawarra elegance too. A poor person's Bin 707.

1990 Penfolds Cabernet Sauvignon Bin 707, South Australia
£££ / FB / ⏪   17/20

If Penfolds' Grange is Australia's answer to the red wines of Hermitage, then this is its riposte to First Growth Pauillac. A blend of Cabernet Sauvignon from selected vineyards in South Australia, this is a tannic, concentrated monster designed for ageing. Come back in the next millennium.

FRANCE

1992 St Aubin Rouge, Premier Cru, Les Combes, Vincent Prunier
££ / MB / ⏪   16/20

From the hills behind Puligny Montrachet in the Côte de Beaune, this is a rich, sweetly oaked Pinot Noir with some attractive strawberry fruit concentration. Only the firm finish betrays its rustic origins.

1987 Château Cantemerle, Haut-Médoc
0 / MB / 🍷   13/20
A fifth growth claret showing herbaceous fruit and a surprising amount of tannin for what was a light vintage in the Médoc. Beginning to dry out.

1990 Vosne-Romanée, Mongeard-Mugneret
£££ / MB / ➡   17/20
To many wine lovers, the village of Vosne-Romanée is the home of the greatest red Burgundies. As well as fabled grands crus such as La Tâche, La Romanée and Echézeaux, Vosne produces some very good village level Pinot Noirs such as this stylish raspberry and loganberry-fruit example. It's not cheap at nearly £16, but a wine like this almost makes you forget about value for money. Warning: this wine can seriously damage your bank balance.

1990 Château de Valois, Pomerol
£ / MB / ▮   15/20
On the firm side for a Right Bank Merlot-dominated wine, this is a chunky, minty claret seemingly built for the long haul. We're not convinced it will get there without a blood transfusion.

SPAIN

1986 Marqués de Murrieta Gran Reserva Ygay
£££ / MB / ➡   17/20
Ygay is the name this world-famous Rioja estate gives to its finest wines. This concentrated red needs a lot of time, but then Murrieta Gran Reservas often do, owing to high acidity and three years' ageing in American oak. It's still austere at the moment, but will continue to evolve for a decade or more. One of the most complex Spanish reds on the market.

Rosé

£3–5

FRANCE

1993 Cante Cigale Rosé de Saignée, Vin de Pays de l'Hérault
£ / 1 / 1   13/20
A southern French blend of Grenache, Cinsault and Syrah with
light raspberry fruit and a dry finish.

£5–8

FRANCE

1992 Chinon Rosé, Couly-Dutheil
£ / 2 / 1   14/20
An unusual wine from one of the leading *négociants* in the Loire
Valley made from the Cabernet Franc grape. Dry and leafy with
delicate cassis fruit.

1992 Sancerre Rosé, Vacheron
££ / 1 / 1   16/20
£8 may sound like an awful lot to pay for a rosé, but this elegant,
bronze-pink Pinot Noir is a delight with strawberry weight and a
degree of complexity.

Sparkling

£3–5

SPAIN

Cava Brut Cristalino NV, Jaume Serra
£ / 2 / 1   13/20
An earthy, lemon peel and yeasty cava with aggressively hard
bubbles.

£5–8

AUSTRALIA

1990 Seppelt Chardonnay Blanc de Blanc Brut
£ / 2 / 🍾   15/20

A creamy, frothy Aussie fizz made entirely from Chardonnay grapes by sparkling wine specialist, Seppelt. Ought to be £1 cheaper.

Taltarni Brut Taché
£ / 3 / 🍾   15/20

A pale, salmon pink fizz from a French producer best known for its red wines. Soft, mouth-filling stuff with pronounced fruit sweetness.

Angas Rosé Brut
£ / 3 / 🍾   14/20

Easy-drinking strawberry-cup fizz, which has lost its value for money edge in the last three years.

Over £8

AUSTRALIA

1991 Green Point
£££ / 2 / 🍾   17/20

This successful Yarra Valley winery has produced a brilliant successor to the 1990, which was one of *Grapevine*'s wines of the year in 1994. The Pinot Noir content has been increased, and Pinot Meunier has been added to the blend for the first time. Otherwise, this follows on nicely from the previous vintage, showing considerable toasty complexity and finesse. Parent company Champagne house Moët et Chandon must be happy to see Dr Tony Jordan maintaining Green Point's high standards.

FRANCE

De Telmont Grande Réserve NV
££ / 3 / 🍾   15/20

De Telmont's non-vintage is one of Majestic's old faithfuls, made in a commercial, fruity style for maximum appeal.

Oeil de Perdrix NV, Leonce d'Albe
££££ / 2 / ▌   17/20
Oeil de Perdrix is French for partridge eye – a reference to
the wine's delicate pinkish colour, rather than a weird food
and wine combination. This is a finely crafted, well-balanced
Champagne with excellent Pinot Noir fruit and depth of
flavour.

Fortified

£5–8

PORTUGAL

Skeffingtons Fine Rich Ruby Port
£ / FB / ▌   14/20
Spirity ruby Port with some liquoricey, pruney flavours and a bite
of tannin. Soft, approachable stuff.

SPAIN

Hidalgo Manzanilla La Gitana
££ / 1 / ▌   16/20
The key to this well-priced Manzanilla Sherry is freshness. At its
best, it's a tangy, savoury, delicate, fortified white with
considerable finesse. Salted almonds time.

MARKS & SPENCER ***

Head Office: 57 Baker Street, London, W1A 1DN

Telephone: 071 268 6155

Number of branches: 300

Credit cards accepted: Marks & Spencer

Hours of opening: Variable

By-the-case sales: Yes

Glass loan: No

Home delivery: Home delivery for a minimum of one case, mixed or unmixed at £3. Free for two cases or more, mainland UK. There is also a new service called Marks & Spencer Wine Cellar which delivers to your home within 48 hours

Clubs: No

Discounts: Twelve bottles for the price of eleven

In-store tastings: Yes

Top ten best-selling wines: White Lambrusco; Oudinot Champagne; Chablis; Italian Chardonnay; Montepulciano d'Abruzzo; Classic Claret; Italian Red (1 Litre); Bulgarian Cabernet Sauvignon, Svischtov; White Burgundy, Cave de Lugny; Vin de Pays des Côtes de Gascogne

Range: GOOD: Champagne and sparkling wines, Burgundy, Bordeaux, Sherry, South Africa, Australia

AVERAGE: Italy, Loire, South of France, New Zealand, Spain, Portugal

POOR: Eastern Europe, Chile

'Quality, value and service worldwide' reads the cover of Marks & Spencer's dark green annual report. Given its occasionally exorbitant profit margins, cynics might quibble with the second of this trio of imposing nouns, but there's no denying the chain's popularity with the punters. Anyone loitering in a city centre branch at lunchtime runs the risk of being trampled to death by ravenous office workers.

The 1994 version of the company overview contained plenty of good news for shareholders. The chain's empire had expanded to 612 stores, stretching from Hong Kong and Canada to Holland and Spain, and profits were up 16 per cent to record levels. That's an awful lot of knickers and chicken tikkas.

It's also an awful lot of wine. M&S makes no secret of being a specialist food retailer, but its 200-strong wine range pulls in the pound notes, too. Any supermarket which can number a £9.99 Champagne, a £6.99 Chablis and a £4.49 white Burgundy among its top ten must be keeping the accountants happy.

M&S's desire to make a profit has not always been to the wine drinker's advantage. Traditionally, new lines were listed on a 'perform or else' basis. Wines which didn't deliver the goods were summarily junked. In other words, caution reigned.

This has resulted in a series of long-term relationships with overseas suppliers. Where the supplier in question is very good (La Chablisienne co-operative springs to mind), this is understandable. But when it's Girelli in Italy, Duboeuf in Beaujolais or St Ursula in Germany, you have to ask why M&S doesn't source its wines from a wider range of producers. The fact that 13 of the company's 200 wines come from one supplier (Girelli) is indicative of an overly cautious buying policy.

To be fair to M&S, the supermarket's customers are a pretty conservative bunch. There's no sign of a New World wine among its best sellers, for example. Indeed, when M&S originally stocked a few Australian wines (ahead of its competitors), they flopped. It's only recently that M&S has given wines from Down Under a second chance.

M&S's cheerful wine buyer, Chris Murphy, is not always given the credit he deserves. Apart from his Australian wines, he was one of the first buyers to spot Domaines Virginie in the South of France, and to realise that South Africa was the coming force in New World winemaking. He also developed a Connoisseur's Selection before other supermarkets. (It wasn't his fault if, once again, M&S's customers failed to appreciate the initiative.)

And yet, despite such high points, the overall wine range was far too safe and predictable. Tasting at M&S was like watching someone clinging to the side of the pool, frightened to swim into the deep end for fear of drowning. 'Uninspired' summed up our feelings in the first edition of *Grapevine*.

But, twelve months on, things are a lot more positive. It's not yet time to crown M&S as the most dynamic force in the high street, but there have been significant improvements since 1993.

Bordeaux, Italy and the cheaper end of the range have all been given a thorough overhaul. And about time, too. In the past, it was almost impossible to find good, inexpensive wines at M&S.

Much of the credit for the new approach belongs to Jane Kay, who works alongside Chris Murphy, and is one of the few British wine buyers to possess an oenology degree. Her Bordeaux education has been particularly useful. She acknowledges that 'a lot of our basic clarets were too austere. We've deliberately gone out to find wines with more fruit, richness and length.'

Even in places where M&S was already comparatively strong, such as Australia and the South of France, there's been plenty of activity. It's good to see punts being taken on a £9 Western Australian Chardonnay like Capel Vale. It's even encouraging, paradoxically, to come across failures such as the Duboeuf Vin de Pays d'Oc Chardonnay. At least someone's taking a few risks.

The Capel Vale is part of a new range of wines at over £8 – a renaissance of sorts for the Connoisseur's Selection. Chris Murphy sees these as 'dinner party wines', or perhaps, this being M&S, TV-dinner wines. There is arguably an element of window-dressing, but the wines are well chosen and fill gaps in the range, especially where red Burgundy is concerned.

All in all, then, this has been a good year for M&S. Some of the duller wines have been thrown out and there is evidence of a greater commitment to everyday, drinkable stuff under £3. Our hunch is that to provide it, the store has taken a more flexible approach to margins.

There are three further initiatives: in-store advisers, new facings in the wine department and a 48-hour delivery service, called Marks & Spencer Wine Cellar. The third of these gives customers access to wines which are not available in store as well as classic M&S lines.

There are still a few weak areas, notably in Eastern Europe and Chile. But M&S has done more than enough to convince us that things have changed for the better. At only 200 wines – owing to the sharp-clawed competition for shelf space – the range is never going to be a match in size for Tesco, Sainsbury's or Thresher. But there's no reason why M&S shouldn't stock a small selection of really good, well-chosen wines. A year ago, that seemed unlikely. Now, who knows . . .

White

Under £3

FRANCE

1993 Côtes de Gascogne, Plaimont
££ / 2 / ▌   14/20
M&S reduced the sweetness on this Gascon blend in 1993. The result is a fresher, zippier Colombard/Ugni Blanc dry white from an impressive, modern co-operative.

ITALY

Cortese del Piemonte, Vino da Tavola, Fratelli Martini
££ / 1 / ▌   15/20
Good to see M&S at last coming up with wines of this quality under £3. From the hills of the Langhe and Monferrato, this is a lime and green olive style white with a crisp, almondy bite.

1993 Italian Chardonnay, Vino da Tavola del Piemonte
££ / 3 / ▌   14/20
It is unusual to find Chardonnay from anywhere under £3 these days, let alone Piemonte, where the labels and bottles usually cost more than a fiver. So well done, M&S, for unearthing this attractive, unoaked Chardonnay with commendable weight.

Lambrusco L, 1 Litre, Girelli
£ / 5 / ▌   13/20
On the neutral side, but clean, refreshingly fruity, and at five per cent alcohol, a light spritzy white.

SPAIN

1993 Conca de Barbera, Hugh Ryman
££ / 3 / 🍾   15/20

Conca de Barbera sounds like an Italian war hero, but in fact it's a little-known *denominación* near Tarragona. Flying winemaker Hugh Ryman has teamed up with Bodegas Concavin to produce an unoaked greengage and gooseberry-like blend of the normally neutral Macabeo and Parellada.

£3–5

AUSTRALIA

Pheasant Gully Colombard, McWilliams
£ / 2 / 🍾   13/20

Floral, aromatic Riverina white, whose bouquet reminded us of a German Müller-Thurgau. An upfront wine which falls away on the palate.

Australian Medium Dry, Lindemans
££ / 4 / ➥   15/20

Don't be fooled by the label. This medium-dry Australian white is a Rhine Riesling by another name. Lindemans are famous for their age-worthy whites, and this toasty, lime-like Riesling from three different regions in south-eastern Australia will develop in bottle.

1993 Rothbury Estate Chardonnay/Semillon
££ / 2 / 🍾   15/20

More elegant and restrained than many of Rothbury's full-blooded whites, but none the less enjoyable for that. An intense peach and pineapple blend with a smidgen of oak from Cowra, Mudgee, Hunter Valley and Griffith, all wine regions in New South Wales.

1993 Hunter Valley Chardonnay/Semillon, Tyrrell
0 / 2 / 🍾   12/20

A disappointingly lean, prematurely-aged blend of Chardonnay and Semillon from one of the Australian wine industry's legendary characters, Murray Tyrrell.

FRANCE

1993 Bordeaux Sauvignon, Yves Pagès
£££ / 2 / 🥄   16/20
The result of a felicitous partnership between Lancashire wine
merchant, Paul Boutinot, and Bordeaux producer Yves Dominique
Pagès. A varietal Sauvignon Blanc with excellent freshness and
weight thanks to a period of ageing on its lees.

1993 Chardonnay Domaine de Mandeville, Vin de Pays d'Oc
££ / 2 / 🥄   15/20
Produced from grapes at Olivier de Mandeville's family estate in
the Aude and bottled by the Cellier des Samsons co-operative in
Burgundy, this has a yeasty, almost savoury, character to add
complexity to an unoaked, fruity Chardonnay.

Duboeuf Chardonnay, Vin de Pays d'Oc
0 / 2 / 🥄   11/20
M&S's wine department challenged 'King of the Beaujolais'
Georges Duboeuf to make a New World style Chardonnay in the
Languedoc-Roussillon. He failed.

1993 Vouvray, Domaine Pouvraie
£ / 4 / 🥄   14/20
Palindromic Vouvray blend from *négociant* Ackerman Laurance,
better known for its sparkling Saumur. Soft pear and apple
sweetness with lively acidity, but lacking a bit of richness.

1993 White Burgundy, Cave de Lugny
££ / 2 / 🥄   15/20
Good unoaked house white Burgundy from a co-operative which
can deliver the goods when it tries.

Jeunes Vignes, La Chablisienne
££ / 1 / 🥄   15/20
An M&S staple from the first-rate La Chablisienne co-operative. As
its name suggests, this is a declassified Chablis made from young
vines not yet entitled to the grown-up *appellation*.

GERMANY

1986 Trittenheimer Apotheke Riesling Spätlese, Franz Reh
£££ / 4 / 🖺   16/20
A wine which is available to mail order customers only, but it's
well worth filling out the order form for this mature, beautifully
balanced, petrolly Mosel Riesling. A palate-watering bargain at
under £5.

1989 Dhroner Hofberger Riesling Kabinett, Franz Reh
£££ / 3 / ⬥   16/20
Also available to mail order customers solely, this is another fine
cider apple and kerosene-like Mosel Riesling from grower Franz
Reh. Another stunner at the price.

HUNGARY

1993 Hungarian Sauvignon Blanc
£ / 2 / 🖺   13/20
Made by Australian winemaker Nick Butler and native Hungarian
Akos Kamocsay at the Nezmely winery near the Danube, this is a
basic, lemony white, not overburdened with Sauvignon Blanc
character.

ITALY

1993 Frascati Superiore, Girelli
£ / 3 / 🖺   13/20
Waxy, almondy, bitter lemon peel Frascati with a customary dose
of sweetness. OK if you like this sort of thing.

1993 Giordani Chardonnay del Piemonte
££ / 2 / 🖺   15/20
Giordani is a welcome newcomer to the M&S suppliers' club,
producing in this case a crisp, cool climate Chardonnay with what
we thought might be a light kiss of oak.

NEW ZEALAND

1993 Kaituna Hills Marlborough Sauvignon Blanc
£££ / 2 / **1**   16/20
This is Montana Sauvignon Blanc travelling under an assumed name, although wine buyer Chris Murphy says the blend is exclusive to M&S. If you like the Montana green bean and elderflower sweetness, as we do, this one's for you.

1993 Kaituna Hills Gisborne Chardonnay
£££ / 2 / **1**   16/20
The Kaituna Hills must be one of the longest mountain ranges in the world, stretching all the way from Marlborough on the South Island to Gisborne on the North. This is an oak-matured, buttered toast Chardonnay with elegance made by Montana winemaker Steve Voysey.

SOUTH AFRICA

Craig Hall Chardonnay/Sauvignon Blanc
£ / 3 / **1**   14/20
A blend which is unusual outside South Africa, but which Cape winemakers seem to favour over the more common Chardonnay/Semillon double act. A slightly confected, honeydew melon and green bean white from Stellenbosch.

1993 Stellenbosch Chardonnay, Vinfruco
£££ / 2 / **1**   16/20
Vinfruco is an export group made up of four quality-minded Cape producers and overseen by star winemaker Neil Ellis. This is an excellent lemon-fresh, partially barrel-fermented style of Chardonnay with some lees-derived complexity.

£5–8

FRANCE

1993 Sancerre, la Charmette, Cave de Sancerre
£ / 2 / **1**   14/20
A basic grassy Sancerre from the local co-op, closer in style to a Sauvignon de Touraine.

1993 Pouilly-Fumé, Vieilles Vignes, Saget
£££ / 1 / ➼   16/20
For the same loot, you get double the flavour and intensity from
this excellent grower's aromatic Pouilly-Fumé. The old vines from
which this wine is produced have endowed it with welcome depth
and concentration. A big improvement on the 1992.

1992 Chablis, La Chablisienne
£££ / 1 / ❱   17/20
**M&S claim to sell more Chablis than anyone else in Britain,
and if the quality of this textbook, creamy dry white is
anything to go by, it's hardly surprising. An unoaked
Chardonnay from the splendid 1992 vintage. Worth buying
by the case.**

1989 Rully Blanc, Les Thivaux, Antonin Rodet
£ / 2 / ❱   14/20
Oaky, peasant fare from Burgundy's Côte Chalonnaise with some
commendable richness. The wine didn't really sing for us.

Over £8

AUSTRALIA

Capel Vale Special Reserve Chardonnay
£££ / 2 / ➼   17/20
**The burnished silver label on this Western Australian
Chardonnay from Dr Peter Pratten's respected Margaret
River Estate is beginning to look a bit tatty, but the wine in
the bottle is a massively concentrated, complex Chardonnay
with surprising elegance. A nimble Sumo.**

FRANCE

1991 Château de Chamirey, Mercurey
0 / 2 / ❱   13/20
Château de Chamirey is one of *négociant* Antonin Rodet's flagship
properties and usually produces some of the best wines in the
Côte Chalonnaise. We found this one overoaked and surprisingly
clumsy.

1990 Meursault, Domaine Boisson Vadot
£ / 2 / ⌟   15/20
An old-fashioned wine from young winemaker Bernard Boisson
Vadot, who in time-sanctioned Burgundian fashion has recently
switched from selling his production to local merchants to bottling
it for his own customers. A fattish, savoury white Burgundy with
some toastiness. Not cheap, but then Meursault seldom is these
days.

Red

Under £3

BULGARIA

1990 Bulgarian Cabernet Sauvignon, Svischtov
££ / MB / ⌟   13/20
One of the few sub-£3 reds on M&S shelves, and a feature of the
chain's top ten. Mature, slightly leathery but smooth, old-fashioned
Cabernet.

FRANCE

**1993 Domaine St Pierre, Vin de Pays de l'Hérault, Domaines
Virginie**
££ / LB / ⌟   14/20
A southern French bramble and bubblegum quaffer from an estate
which was once confiscated in lieu of a gambling debt. No risks
taken here in this soft, Merlot/Syrah/Alicante blend. An
undemanding drink.

ITALY

1993 Montepulciano d'Abruzzo, Girelli
££ / MB / ⌟   14/20
Intensely fruity, young, central Italian red. On the sweet side, but
showing plenty of lively acidity and plummy bite.

1993 Barbera del Piemonte, Vino da Tavola S. Orsola
£££ / MB / ▌   15/20
Like Beaujolais Nouveau for grown-ups, this is a classic pasta-basher
with juicy, cherryish fruit and fresh acidity.

£3-5

AUSTRALIA

Australian Shiraz/Cabernet, McWilliams
£ / MB / ▌   14/20
Mint humbugs in a glass with soft, supple fruit. We found the
wine a bit hollow. A mint with a hole, perhaps.

1991 Lindemans Bin 37 Australian Cabernet Sauvignon
££ / MB / ▌   15/20
Made by the laconic Philip John, Lindemans' senior winemaker,
this is a surefire introduction to Australian Cabernet Sauvignon,
with sweet blackcurrant pastille fruit, silky tannins and toffee-ish
oak.

1992 McLaren Vale Shiraz, Andrew Garrett
0 / FB / ▌   11/20
From Suntory-owned leisure complex cum winery Andrew Garrett,
a bitter, tannic, overwrought red embodying the worst features of
Australian wine and very few of the good ones.

1992 Langhorne Creek Cabernet Sauvignon
££ / MB / ▌   15/20
A minty, well-made Cabernet Sauvignon with pleasant vanilla oak
from Michael Potts' Bleasdale winery in South Australia. It reminded
us more of Cabernet Franc than Sauvignon – like a turbo-charged
Chinon.

FRANCE

1993 Domaine Roche Blanche, Coteaux du Languedoc
££ / MB / ▌   15/20
A fruity, ultra-modern Coteaux du Languedoc red made for
Domaines Virginie by Australian John Weeks and French sidekick,

Pierre de Passendale. The high proportion of Syrah comes through nicely on the bouquet.

1993 Domaine Montrose, Vin de Pays d'Oc
£ / MB / 🌡   14/20

Another Domaines Virginie special, this time with a bit more backbone. We preferred the exuberance of the Roche Blanche to the sterner stuff on offer here.

1993 Château Lacousse, Classic Claret
£ / MB / 🌡   14/20

Château Lacousse is situated in the heart of the Entre-Deux-Mers region, producing good basic, chewy claret from mainly Merlot and Cabernet Sauvignon with a bit of Cabernet Franc. Ought to be 50 pence cheaper.

HUNGARY

1993 Hungarian Cabernet Sauvignon
££ / LB / 🌡   14/20

One of the best labels we've seen from Eastern Europe. The wine is made by Nick Butler from 100 per cent Cabernet Sauvignon, which, in this neck of the woods, has produced a light, cool climate red.

ITALY

Italian Red, 1 Litre, Girelli
£ / MB / 🌡   13/20

Basic Italian quaffer with souped-up, commercial sweetness and dry tannins on the finish.

1992 Valpolicella Classico, Girelli
££ / LB / 🌡   14/20

A perfumed single vineyard Valpolicella from the Fumane Valley, one of Valpolicella Classico's five communes. Nice raspberry and cinnamon fruit with a finish that calls for food.

1991 Chianti Classico, Basilica Cafaggio, Girelli
£ / MB / 🌡   14/20

The Cafaggio estate is situated in the commune of Greve and belongs to the merchant house of Girelli, which has no fewer than 13 out of the 21 Italian wines on the M&S list. This is an old-fashioned Sangiovese-based Chianti with lively acidity.

1991 Il Caberno, Giordano
££ / MB /]   17/20
One of M&S's best recent finds with a handsome package that belies its price tag. The wine is pretty special too, blending Piedmontese Nebbiolo with 15 per cent Cabernet Sauvignon. (In the circumstances, we wondered whether 'Il Nebbiolo' might not have been a more appropriate name.) An intriguing, approachable wine with finely judged oak and none of the traditional Nebbiolo hardness.

PORTUGAL

1989 Dão, Garrafeira, Caves Aliança
£££ / FB / ▬▸   16/20
Caves Aliança is one of the wine world's great traditionalist companies, famous for its long-lived Bairradas and Dãos. Winemaker Dido Mendes trained in California, but still produces wines full of Portuguese character. This is a mature, raisiny red with good spicy, strawberry fruit and well-integrated tannins.

SOUTH AFRICA

1993 Stellenbosch Merlot/Cabernet, Vinfruco
£ / FB /]   14/20
A Vinfruco Cape red blending 80 per cent Merlot from Jan Coetzee's Vriesenhof Estate and 20 per cent Cabernet Sauvignon from Neil Ellis. A robust, aromatic number, which relies on fruit rather than oak for impact. Much better than last year's vintage.

SPAIN

1990 Raimat, Costers del Segre
££ / MB /]   15/20
After a series of difficult vintages, when problems in the cellar dogged this exciting, modern Catalonian winery, things appear to have righted themselves. This is a spicily oaked, mature blend of Cabernet Sauvignon, Tempranillo and Merlot – like a New World/Rioja hybrid.

£5–8

FRANCE

1990 St Emilion, Christian Moueix
£££ / MB / 🖋   16/20
Art collector Christian Moueix loves the label on this savoury, mature, concentrated St Emilion. We think his nose for a good wine is considerably more acute than his eye for a label.

1991 Margaux, Lucien Lurton
£££ / MB / ☞   16/20
This is declassified wine from Margaux second growth, Château Brane Cantenac. It's a bit tight at the moment, but should develop into something special. Elegant Margaux style.

1990 Lirac, Domaine André Méjean
£££ / FB / ☞   16/20
From a producer best known for his Tavel rosés, this is a powerful, sweetly alcoholic, unoaked blend of Grenache, Mourvèdre and Syrah, only available through mail order.

1991 Châteauneuf-du-Pape, Les Couversets, J. Quiot
£ / FB / 🖋   15/20
Jérôme Quiot's Châteauneuf-du-Pape estate is one of the largest in the *appellation*. As well as looking after 86 hectares of vines, he is the President of France's Institut National des Appellations d'Origine. This chunky, partially oak-aged red uses 8 of the 13 permitted Châteauneuf grape varieties, but is dominated by the punch of Grenache.

ITALY

1989 Vino Nobile di Montepulciano, Girelli
£ / MB / 🖋   15/20
From a Tuscan estate owned by a family of Milanese industrialists, this is a fragrant, old-fashioned Vino Nobile with enough red fruit character to convince us that the wine is at its peak. Still, drink up soon.

SPAIN

1985 Marqués del Romeral Gran Reserva, Rioja, AGE
££ / MB / ◗   15/20
Gran Reserva is the name Rioja bestows on what are supposedly its finest wines. This coconutty, venerable blend of Tempranillo, Mazuelo and Graciano was aged for three years in bottle and two in American oak barrels. The result is a mature, old-fashioned Rioja, which is beginning to dry out – like Barbara Cartland.

Over £8

FRANCE

1989 Maranges Premier Cru la Fussière, Antonin Rodet
£ / MB / ◗   14/20
Situated between the villages of Bezize and Sampigny-lès-Maranges, Maranges has only recently been granted *appellation* status. Pleasantly rustic strawberry Pinot Noir and a whiff of the farmyard.

1989 Volnay, Louis Jadot
££ / MB / ➤   16/20
A more structured, oaky red Burgundy from the Côte de Beaune village of Volnay produced by one of Burgundy's leading merchants. Needs time.

1991 Beaune Premier Cru, Clos de la Féguine, Domaine Jacques Prieur
£££ / MB / ➤   18/20
Domaine Jacques Prieur was taken over in the early 1990s by the Côte Chalonnaise-based merchant Antonin Rodet, and has enjoyed improved fortunes ever since. This is highly seductive, elegant Pinot Noir, which should turn a few readers on to the charms of red Burgundy.

1988 Château l'Hospitalet, Pomerol
£££ / MB / ◗   16/20
The second wine of Château Gazin in Pomerol, this is another seductive red – this time from Bordeaux's Right Bank. Smoky oak, coffee bean bouquet and a fleshy core of fruit.

1987 Château Gazin, Pomerol
£££ / MB / ▌   17/20

Don't be put off by the vintage, which was underappreciated on Bordeaux's Right Bank, where the Merlot was picked before the rains. This is a voluptuous, mature claret at the peak of its powers. Well worth the £15 asking price.

1985 Château Grand Mayne, St-Emilion
£ / MB / ▌   15/20

From a vintage such as 1985, you'd expect a 100 per cent Merlot to have a bit more charm than this rather tannic example. Come back next century.

ITALY

1986 Amarone della Valpolicella, Comunali, Carlo Speri
0 / FB / ▌   13/20

Made from grapes traditionally dried on racks in ventilated lofts, this is a hefty, rustic Amarone with characteristic sweet and sour fruit character. A bit pedestrian after all the effort that went into making it.

Sparkling

£3–5

ITALY

Prosecco Brut, Zonin
££ / 3 / ▌   14/20

For a Brut sparkler, this is on the sweet side. All the same, it has a good perfumed, vanilla-pod aroma and attractive apple and pear fizz.

£5–8

AUSTRALIA

1990 Australian Chardonnay, Blanc de Blancs Brut, Seppelt
£ / 2 / ▌   14/20

This is a ripe, foaming Australian Chardonnay with plenty of pineapple fruit, but not much subtlety.

FRANCE

Crémant de Bourgogne, Cave de Lugny
0 / 2 / ❩   13/20
The Cave de Lugny specialises in Champagne-method sparkling
white Burgundies. This beery, slightly austere fizz is not one of
Lugny's greatest hits.

NEW ZEALAND

Blenheim Sparkling Wine, Montana
££ / 2 / ❩   15/20
A ringer for Montana's much appreciated Lindauer sparkling wine,
this is a creamy, mouth-filling blend of Pinot Noir and Chardonnay
with plenty of tangy, young fruit.

SPAIN

Cava, Freixenet
0 / 2 / ❩   13/20
From the people who brought you Cordon Negro, the stuff in a
black satin-sheened bottle, this is an earthy, basic cava of little
distinction. It should be a good £1 cheaper.

Over £8

FRANCE

Oudinot Brut Champagne
£ / 2 / ❩   14/20
A simple, youthfully aggressive Champagne at a reasonable price.

Veuve de Medts, Premier Cru Brut Champagne
££ / 2 / ❩   16/20
A forward, nicely fruity blend of Chardonnay and Pinot Noir from
the Union Champagne co-operative with a bit of toastiness and
soft-textured bubbles.

Champagne Chevalier de Melline, Premier Cru, Blanc de Blancs Brut
£ / 2 / 🍾   15/20
All Chardonnay Champagne from the giant Union Champagne co-operative. Young and fruity, needing time to settle down.

1988 Vintage Champagne Saint Gall, Premier Cru Brut
£££ / 2 / 🍾   17/20
This is the Champagne to go for at M&S, even though it tips the scales at around £18. Superbly aromatic, with intense Pinot Noir character and toasty richness. Classy stuff.

Fortified

£3–5

SPAIN

Pale Dry Sherry, Williams & Humbert
££ / 2 / 🍾   14/20
Good inexpensive Fino Sherry with some typically salty flor characters, good full-bodied fruit and a dry finish.

Medium Sherry, Williams & Humbert
££ / 3 / 🍾   15/20
A sweetish blend of Amontillado and Oloroso with good grilled almonds character and an attractive balance. The vicar's choice.

Rich Cream Sherry, Williams & Humbert
£££ / 8 / 🍾   16/20
The biscuit-tin label hasn't got any better on this Oloroso Sherry sweetened by the addition of sultana-like Pedro Ximenez and Moscatel grapes. But the wine is still rich, raisiny and distinguished with good balancing acidity to prevent it from cloying.

MORRISON'S ***

Head Office: William Morrison Supermarkets Plc, Junction 41 Industrial Estate, Carr Gate, Wakefield, West Yorkshire, WF2 0XF

Telephone: 0924 870000

Number of branches: 73

Credit cards accepted: Access, Visa, Switch, Delta

Hours of opening: Majority 8.30am to 8.00pm weekdays; 8.00am to 6.00pm Saturday; Sunday 10.00am to 4.00pm

By-the-case sales: No reductions

Glass loan: Free in all stores

Home delivery: No

Clubs: No

Discounts: No

In-store tastings: Occasional tastings in selected stores

Top ten best-selling wines: Hock Deutscher Tafelwein; Soveral, Vinho de Mesa; Carreras Dry Red; Gabbia d'Oro Rosso; Morrison's red Rioja; Morrison's Liebfraumilch; 1985 Romanian Cabernet Sauvignon; Morrison's Lambrusco; Gabbia d'Oro Bianco; Merlot del Veneto

Range: GOOD: Regional France, Australia, Champagne, white Bordeaux, Italy
AVERAGE: California, Germany, South Africa, Spain, Portugal, Bulgaria
POOR: Romania, Morocco

Not many people know this, as the immortal Michael Caine might put it, but Morrison's in-store off-licence in Bradford is the largest in Europe. Six thousand square feet of wines, beers and spirits, stacked in an appealingly roomy setting and full of thirsty Yorkshire customers.

Shoppers who never venture north of Hertfordshire may do a double take at the very mention of the supermarket's name, never mind at the fact that it has a range of nearly 470 wines. But canny wine lovers in the North cottoned on to Morrison's well-chosen, value-for-money selection years ago.

'Every time I select a wine,' says buyer Stuart Purdie, 'I say to myself value, value, value.' This echoes the promise of 'low cost bargains' on the supermarket's revolving doors and owner Ken Morrison's personal commitment to competitive prices.

Morrison's sells some of the cheapest wines in the country, offering in several cases good value at astoundingly low prices, but Purdie says he won't stock something just because it's inexpensive. 'I don't see the point of having, say a dirt cheap Australian red, if it doesn't taste good.'

Since Purdie arrived from the now-defunct Peter Dominic chain three years ago, he has presided over the sort of sales increases that keep shareholders – if not speculators – happy. Wine sales have risen by 30 per cent in the last year, against a national increase of three per cent. This is partly down to new stores – nine of them in 1994, with another eight planned for 1995 – but it shows that Morrison's customers like what they see on the shelves.

Purdie says that the store's northern bias influences the sort of wines he buys. There are stores in every major English city except Bristol and London, but the biggest concentration is around Leeds, Bradford, Harrogate and Halifax. 'There is a tendency to drink slightly sweeter wines up here.' But he's still spent 'an awful lot of time recently trying to wean a lot of people off Liebfraumilch and Lambrusco.' It is significant, perhaps, that Morrison's top ten sellers contains a greater number of red wines than most of its competitors.

Changes have not been quite as spectacular as last year, but Purdie has still taken on 80 new wines, mainly from the South of France, Spain, Eastern Europe and the New World. Given that Purdie does all of the buying himself, he does well to travel as much as he does. He was last spotted at the Vinisud fair in Montpellier, signing up some characteristically smart bargains.

The range is pleasingly cosmopolitan, with wines from every corner of the globe, although the emphasis is on sub-£5 fare. The fine wine range is not as exciting as it could be – some of the bottles in the wooden in-store racks are stretching a point – but there's still plenty of interest at shop floor level.

The good thing about Purdie is that he sticks to his own beliefs. He has a good palate for a bargain and enjoys the flexibility of ordering parcels on the spot. 'I can buy up bin ends very quickly,' he says. 'I don't have to go through some complicated command structure and send white-coated quality control teams to the winery before I can buy.'

One of the most praiseworthy aspects of the Morrison's operation is that the entire range is stocked in every one of the 70-odd stores. Several of the major supermarket groups window dress a handful of leading sites, a policy which leads to a certain amount of frustration when customers can't get hold of recommended wines.

They are also pleasant environments in which to buy wine. The 'street concept', in particular, whereby the supermarket is made to look like a series of high street shops, rather than endless rows of neon-lit aisles, is a welcome innovation in retailing.

But the highlight of a Morrison's wine shop is still the regular flow of bargains. There are a number of Italian and French wines under £3 that are a match for anything on a British supermarket shelf. And, with wines like Solana, Santa Carolina Sauvignon Blanc and the 1990 Peter Sichel Margaux, Stuart Purdie has shown that he's not afraid to stock unusual or more expensive wines. Maybe it's time Ken Morrison ventured south of Watford Gap.

White

Under £3

FRANCE

1993 Le Millenaire, Côtes du Roussillon Blanc
££ / 2 / 1   14/20
A typically southern French blend of Grenache Blanc and Macabeu from the Vignerons Catalans co-operative. Waxy, baked, clean and fruity.

1993 Terret, Vin de Pays des Côtes de Thau, Jacques Lurton
££ / 2 / 1   14/20
From the shores of the oyster-rich Bassin de Thau, this is an

unusual dry white made from an undervalued grape variety. A fresh, full, citrusy style with a lively bite.

GERMANY

Hock, F.W. Langguth, Deutscher Tafelwein
£££ / 5 / ▮   14/20
One of the best cheapie German whites we've come across, with fresh, floral, grapey fruit and zippy acidity. We're not surprised that this is Morrison's number one seller.

1993 Liebfraumilch, Zimmermann Graeff
0 / 5 / ▮   12/20
Sweet, unbalanced Liebfraumilch with bitter fruit and tart after taste.

1992 Flonheimer Adelberg Kabinett, Johannes Egberts, Rheinhessen
££ / 3 / ▮   14/20
This floral, grapefruity Müller-Thurgau based, off-dry German white is a pleasant, if dilute, substitute for Liebfraumilch.

ITALY

Gabbia d'Oro Vino Bianco
££ / 2 / ▮   13/20
Neutral, clean, faintly almondy Italian dry white at a bargain basement price.

Lambrusco Bianco dell'Emilia
0 / 6 / ▮   11/20
Sweet, appley, lemonadey white fizz with few redeeming features.

1993 Chardonnay Teresa Rizzi, Vino da Tavola delle Tre Venezie
£££ / 2 / ▮   16/20
An impressive follow-up to last year's brilliant effort from Angela Muir and GIV, the giant Italian wine group. This is a similarly fresh, nutty Chardonnay with citrus fruit intensity.

1993 Pinot Grigio Teresa Rizzi
£££ / 2 / ▌   16/20
An Angela Muir/GIV special, this is one of the best-value Italian whites around. Peachy, fresh fruit with enlivening spritz, and a surprising length of flavour for a wine under £3.

1992 Est! Est!! Est!!! di Montefiascone
£ / 2 / ▌   13/20
Last year, we said that we'd never come across an Est! Est!! Est!!! that lived up to its intriguing brand name. We're still waiting.

MOLDOVA

1993 Moldovan Blanc de Rouge, Cimislia de Moldova
£££ / 2 / ▌   15/20
A curiosity made from Cabernet Sauvignon grapes, vinified like a white wine, a technique Jacques Lurton also employs with some success in the South of France. This aromatic, off-the-wall, cassis-scented white, is almost certainly the first ever Moldovan blanc-de-noirs table wine.

ROMANIA

Romanian Cellarmasters Selection White
0 / 4 / ▌   12/20
A sweetish, baked blend of Chardonnay and the indigenous Feteasca grape. It's rather coarse and tastes a bit like cheap Muscat.

1993 Romanian Chardonnay, Winemaker's Selection
£ / 3 / ▌   13/20
An unoaked Chardonnay produced by Australian winemaker Graham Dixon in a modern, fruity, if neutral style.

£3-5

AUSTRALIA

Woomera Vale Australian White, Yaldara
£ / 3 / ▌   13/20
An aromatic, off-dry Riesling-based Aussie blend with a lime juicy

character. Pleasantly commercial, but a little confected.

1993 Penfolds Bin 21 Semillon/Chardonnay, South-East Australia
££ / 2 / ▌   15/20
In common with many commercial Australian whites, the 1993 is more restrained than the 1992 vintage. Fresh melon and peachy fruit with a dab of smoky oak and herbal Semillon character. Perfect party and house white.

1992 Hanwood Estates Chardonnay, McWilliams
££ / 2 / ▌   15/20
Another toned-down Australian tropical fruit style Chardonnay with a touch of oak, complemented by attractive flavours of melon and grapefruit.

CHILE

1993 Santa Carolina Sauvignon Blanc
££ / 2 / ▌   15/20
A broad, well-balanced Chilean Sauvignon Blanc with a soft-textured, citrus and asparagus fruitiness and none of the grape variety's sharp edges. Surprisingly concentrated for a Chilean white.

ENGLAND

1992 Three Choirs Estate Premium, Medium Dry
££ / 3 / ▌   15/20
Tom Day's Three Choirs is one of the more go-ahead English wineries, and this well-packaged, reasonably priced white is a good introduction to the joys of England's Lilliputian wine industry. Nettley and fresh with a touch of grapefruit and white pepper.

FRANCE

1993 Château St Galier, Graves, Ginestet
££ / 1 / ▌   15/20
An attractive, Semillon-based white Graves at an affordable price. Modern-style, clean, appley freshness with the crispness and aroma of the Sauvignon Blanc adding zip to the waxier Semillon.

Chais Cuxac Chardonnay, Vin de Pays d'Oc
££ / 2 / ▮   16/20

From one of France's best co-operatives, this oak-aged Chardonnay is made by Serge Dubois in a toffee and buttered toast mould with fresh acidity for balance.

1993 Côtes de Gascogne, Domaine de Galoubis, Bordes
£ / 2 / ▮   13/20

A decent Gascon blend of Ugni Blanc, Colombard and Listan from the ubiquitous Hugh Ryman. We've preferred earlier vintages.

1993 Muscadet de Sèvre-et-Maine Sur Lie, La Sablière
££ / 2 / ▮   14/20

A full, fat style of Muscadet with some compensating sur lie bite. At around £3.50, Muscadet is almost good value again.

1993 Bordeaux Sauvignon Blanc
££ / 2 / ▮   15/20

An attractively modern, grapefruity Bordeaux Sauvignon Blanc with good weight and concentration. Bordeaux finally seems to be producing inexpensive white wines worth drinking.

1992 Pinot Blanc, Preiss-Zimmer, Turckheim
££ / 2 / ▮   15/20

A light Alsace Pinot Blanc from the Turckheim co-operative with slightly smoky, spicy fruit and a refreshingly dry finish. A good apéritif white.

Premières Côtes de Bordeaux
££ / 6 / ▮   14/20

A honeycomb-like Bordeaux sticky with some barley sugar sweetness from *négociant* Peter Sichel.

GERMANY

1991 Graacher Himmelreich Kabinett, Weingut Ewald Pfeiffer
££ / 3 / ▮   15/20

A crisp, steely Mosel Riesling with some petrolly complexity at under £4.

1993 Wiltinger Scharzberg Spätlese, Franz Reh
£ / 3 / ▮   13/20
Cheaper and not as balanced as the Graacher Himmelreich, this is
a tart and slightly raw, green apple Mosel white.

HUNGARY

1993 Gyöngyös Estate Sauvignon Blanc
££ / 2 / ▮   14/20
This is the best Sauvignon Blanc we've encountered from the
pioneering Gyöngyös Estate. Made in a mini-New Zealand style, it's a
zesty, aromatic dry white with citrus fruit sweetness and acidity. A
caveat: we have noticed inconsistency between Gyöngyös bottlings.

ITALY

1993 Frascati Superiore Orsola, Fratelli Martini
££ / 2 / ▮   14/20
Nice wine, shame about the naff, frosted glass bottle. A soft,
pleasantly dry, almondy Roman white.

SPAIN

1993 Solana White, Ribeiro
£££ / 2 / ▮   17/20
**The offspring of a timely liaison between Australia's
Mitchelton Wines and Spain's Bodegas y Bebidas.
Winemakers Don Lewis and Francisco Diaz Ubero have used
indigenous north-western Spanish grapes, Torrontes and
Treixadura, to produce a brilliant, characterful white. A
zesty, lemon and lime-like, modern white with some Australian fruit richness. Long may the partnership flourish.**

UNITED STATES

1992 Glen Ellen Chardonnay, Proprietor's Reserve
££ / 3 / ▮   14/20
As you'd expect from one of California's most dynamic wineries,
this is a sweetish, but highly drinkable Chardonnay with buttery,
smoky oak flavours and a touch of residual sweetness for palates
weaned on Coca-Cola.

£5–8

FRANCE

1993 Chablis Domaine de Beauvais, Gérard Tremblay
££ / 2 / ☙   16/20
An old-fashioned, unoaked Chablis with minerally overtones and
good, steely acidity for the long haul.

Red

Under £3

FRANCE

1993 Merlot, Vin de Pays d'Oc, Chantovent Prestige
£ / MB / ⌥   13/20
Soft, sweet, juicy southern red with more green tannin than you'd
expect from a warm climate wine.

Minervois, Cellier La Chouf
£££ / MB / ⌥   14/20
A cheap, but characterful Languedoc *appellation* red with some
classic angostura bitters flavour and robusty, dry fruit. We enjoyed
the wine a little more last year, but it's still stunning value.

1992 Côtes du Roussillon Villages, Vignerons Catalans
££ / MB / ⌥   15/20
A more elegant, peppery southern red, this time from the
Roussillon region in the shadow of the Pyrenees. Another super
value, spicy quaffer.

Coteaux du Languedoc, Tradition, Vignerons de la Carignano
££ / MB / ⌥   14/20
Unusually for France, this red wine is made exclusively from
Grenache, a grape which is usually blended with other varieties,
or siphoned off quietly into southern French rosés. Wine buyer
Stuart Purdie calls this chocolatey, raisiny red 'sex in a glass'. Over
to you, Mrs Purdie.

1992 Corbières Les Fenouillets
£££ / FB / ▮   15/20
The price of this spicy, garrigue-scented Corbières red has gone
up 50 pence or so, but it's still remarkable value at under £3. One
of a series of southern French bargains chez Morrison's.

1992 Peyres Nobles, Corbières
££ / MB / ▮   14/20
An awful lot of wine for under £3. Full-bodied, soft, spicy,
chocolatey Corbières with a slightly rustic dry finish.

1993 Côtes du Rhône Prestige, Cellier des Dauphins
0 / MB / ▮   12/20
Prestige is overstating the case.

ITALY

Gabbia d'Oro, Vino Rosso
0 / MB / ▮   11/20
They should rename this sweet, soupy Italian red blend Piato d'Oro.

1993 Merlot Grave del Friuli, Pasqua
0 / LB / ▮   12/20
Stalky green, north-east Italian Merlot with rasping acidity.
Presumably this one sells on price.

MOLDOVA

1993 Moldovan Merlot, Cimislia de Moldova
£££ / MB / ▮   15/20
Pleasant, fruity, upfront blackcurrant pastille style Merlot from
travelling Frenchman, Jacques Lurton, who has done so much to
drag Moldovan winemaking into the twentieth century.

MOROCCO

Moroccan Red
0 / FB / ▮   11/20
Thick, alcoholic, baked North African red. This should have a *fatwa*
put on it.

PORTUGAL

Soveral, Vinho de Mesa, Real Companhia do Norte de Portugal
£ / FB / ▌   12/20

A dry, unyielding, old-fashioned Portuguese red with a large splat of cowpat about it.

ROMANIA

Romanian Cellarmasters Red, Murfatlar
0 / MB / ▌   12/20

A blend of Cabernet Sauvignon and Feteasca Neagra from Murfatlar near the Black Sea. Coarse, rooty, old-fashioned stuff.

1985 Cabernet Sauvignon, Special Reserve, Dealul Mare
£££ / MB / ▌   14/20

Easily the best of Morrison's top ten reds. Cedary, leathery, mature Romanian Cabernet with a sweet, minty core and some attractively complex, gamey characters. Straight from the Ceaucescu cellar in Bucharest, no doubt.

SOUTH AFRICA

1992 Fair Cape Cinsault, KWV
£ / MB / ▌   13/20

Light, browning, rubbery red for fans of old-fashioned Cape styles.

SPAIN

1987 Carreras Dry Red, Valencia, Egli
0 / MB / ▌   10/20

A wine which had a headcold when it performed for us. Tart, plonkissimo red.

1993 Rioja, Bodegas Navajas
£ / MB / ▌   12/20

We felt that the barrel had been brought to this light, mushroomy, splintery red rather than the other way round.

1991 Jaume Serra Tempranillo, Penedes
£ / MB / ▌   13/20

A splintery, savoury Catalan red showing a bit of age and rustic vanilla oak flavours.

£3-5

AUSTRALIA

Woomera Vale Red
££ / MB / ▌   14/20

A good, basic Aussie red with pleasant juicy, minty fruit. On the rustic side, but still good value.

1991 McWilliams Hanwood Estate Cabernet Sauvignon
£ / MB / ▌   14/20

Mature Australian style, whose leathery, blackberry-like flavours reminded us more of Shiraz than Cabernet Sauvignon. Dry, peppery stuff for the barbecue-minded.

1992 Wyndham Bin 444 Cabernet Sauvignon
0 / FB / ▌   12/20

Tannic, extracted, overoaked warm climate red with soupy sweetness. At just under £5, you can do a lot better than this from Australia.

1992 Lindemans Bin 50 Shiraz
££ / FB / ▌   15/20

Cheaper than the Wyndham Estate and several times more enjoyable. This has the Lindemans stamp of soft, sweetly supple, blackberry fruit cocooned in spicy American oak.

CHILE

1992 Santa Carolina Cabernet Sauvignon
£££ / MB / ▌   16/20

One of the best Chilean reds on the market, especially at under £4, showing elegant blackcurrant leaf and spearmint characters. It has good acidity to keep it fresh, with firm tannins on the aftertaste.

FRANCE

Chais Cuxac Cabernet Sauvignon, Vin de Pays d'Oc
££ / MB / ▌   15/20
Sweet, ripe, chocolatey Cabernet Sauvignon with a bit of maturity under its neck-label. Craftily oaked stuff from the Cuxac co-operative.

Côtes du Rhône Villages, Epitalon
£££ / MB / ▌   15/20
From a well-known Burgundian merchant (we were given the info off the record, and we're respecting our sources), this is a rich, soft, aromatic blend of mainly Grenache and Syrah. Better value than most Beaujolais.

1990 Château de Lastours, Cuvée Arnaud de Berre, Corbières
£ / FB / ▌   14/20
Not quite up to the superb Simone Descamps from this unusual southern French estate, which houses a disabled community, but this is still a big ripe, warm-hearted red.

1992 Buzet Renaissance, Les Vignerons de Buzet
££ / MB / ▌   14/20
A good claret substitute from a reliable co-operative, which dominates the *appellation* of Côtes de Buzet. Gingery spice, firm tannins and smooth, grassy fruit.

ITALY

1990 Nebbiolo d'Alba, Ca' Bianca
£ / MB / ▌   13/20
Nebbiolo is the grape of Barolo, arguably Italy's finest red wine. It tends to austerity in its youth, but can soften with bottle age. This demandingly dry example needs food.

SPAIN

1993 Solana Cencibel
£££ / MB / ▌   16/20
The red counterpart to the brilliant Solana white. Also produced by Mitchelton Wines and Bodegas y Bebidas, this one is made

from Cencibel grown in Valdepeñas. An unoaked, vibrantly blackcurranty wine which is gradually settling into its stride.

1985 Navajas Reserva Rioja, Bodegas Navajas
££ / MB / 🍷   14/20

Soft, mature coconutty Rioja, which is beginning to dry out. Still, at under £5, this Reserva red is a good buy.

1990 Raimat Abadia
£££ / MB / 🍷   16/20

From the ultra-modern, New World influenced Raimat winery near Lerida in Catalonia, this is a complex blend of Cabernet Sauvignon and native Tempranillo. Full-flavoured with masses of spicy fruit and well-handled, smoky, coffee bean oak. A welcome return to form from this desert winery.

UNITED STATES

1992 Glen Ellen Merlot, Proprietor's Reserve
££ / MB / 🍷   14/20

A sweetish, gluggable California red with plummy fresh bite and lots of soft fruit.

1992 Sutter Home Zinfandel
£££ / MB / 🍷   15/20

Another good-value California red made from the near-indigenous Zinfandel grape. This is a light style of Zin with fresh, peppery, raspberry jelly characters.

£5–8

FRANCE

1990 Margaux, Peter Sichel
££ / FB / ▪━   16/20

Declassified from Château Palmer vines, Peter Sichel's part-owned, Third Growth property in Margaux, this lacks the elegance of the *appellation*'s top-notch wines, but it's still pretty good commune claret at a resonable price. The tannins need at least a couple of years to soften.

Rosé

Under £3

PORTUGAL

'M' Portuguese Rosé
£ / 3 / ▌   13/20
'M' doesn't stand for Mateus, in case you were wondering, or
marvellous, for that matter. Made by Borges & Irmão, it's a
pleasantly off-dry style with some Portuguese grip to it.

£3–5

UNITED STATES

Blossom Hill White Zinfandel
0 / 5 / ▌   11/20
A sickly, rose petal pink confection for fans of Dubonnet and
lemonade. The importers have been offering a free potted plant
with every bottle. Enough said.

Sparkling

£3–5

ITALY

Asti Spumante Gianni
££ / 5 / ▌   14/20
Frothy, sherbetty sweet fizz from Italy's latest DOCG, supposedly
the top rung of Italy's *appellation* ladder. It makes you wonder
what's on the bottom rung, but this is pleasantly quaffable stuff
with more freshness and acidity than many.

SPAIN

Cristalino Brut Cava, Jaume Serra
£ / 2 / ▮   14/20
Made from traditional Penedés grapes, this is a typically earthy, heavy cava with a hint of nuttiness.

£5–8

AUSTRALIA

Seaview Brut
££ / 2 / ▮   15/20
Back on form after a couple of indifferent years, this is fresh, toasty fizz with appealing tropical fruit ripeness.

Over £8

FRANCE

Nicole d'Aurigny Champagne, Réserve Brut, Union Auboise
£££ / 2 / ▮   17/20
Among the best inexpensive Champagnes on the market, this Pinot Noir-based fizz has none of the greenness often present in cheap bubbly from the region. Malty, soft and fruitily aromatic.

Paul Hérard Blanc de Noirs Champagne Brut
££ / 2 / ▮   15/20
A clean, fruity Pinot Boir dominated blend from the Aube district of southern Champagne. Light, pleasant, well-priced fizz.

Paul Hérard Champagne, Demi-Sec
££ / 4 / ▮   16/20
An unusual, off-dry Champagne, showing creamy, toasty flavours and nutty maturity. Fine if you've got a sweet tooth, but make sure you drink it well-chilled.

ODDBINS ****(*)

Head Office: 31-33 Weir Road, London, SW19 8UG

Telephone: 081 944 4400

Number of branches: 195

Credit cards accepted: Access, Visa, American Express, Switch

Hours of opening: Generally Monday to Saturday 10.00am to 9.00pm; Sunday 10.00am to 3.00pm and 7.00pm to 9.00pm

By-the-case sales: Yes

Glass loan: Yes (with deposit)

Home delivery: Free within locality of shop (minimum one case)

Clubs: The Catalyst magazine contains details of special offers and tastings and costs £5 for eight issues

Discounts: Ten per cent on mixed cases during Saturday tastings; five per cent on mixed cases at any time; seven bottles for the price of six on Champagne and sparkling wine at £5.99 and above

In-store tastings: Every Saturday, from 2.00pm to 5.00pm

Top ten best-selling wines: 1994 Lindemans Cawarra Colombard/ Chardonnay; 1993 Oddbins White Domaine de Jöy; 1993 Cockatoo Ridge; Seaview Brut; Glenloth Shiraz/Cabernet; Cuvée Napa Brut; Cuvée Napa Rosé; Perrier Jouët Champagne; 1992 Penfolds Bin 35 Cabernet/Shiraz; Veuve Clicquot Champagne

Range: GOOD: Burgundy, Australia, Bordeaux, Chile, California Beaujolais, Rhône, Bordeaux, Spain, New Zealand, Champagne and sparkling wines, Germany
AVERAGE: South of France, Alsace, Loire, Italy
POOR: South Africa, Eastern Europe, England

When lads' magazine *Loaded* ran an amusing article about Oddbins' annual consumer fair, it headlined the piece 'Into the

Valley of the Ponce'. The jibe was a bit below the waistline, given that Oddbins has done more than anyone in this country to make wine drinking fun and free of stuffed shirts. Ponces tend to buy their claret and Port from traditional City wine merchants. You couldn't imagine them taking to Oddbins, with its wacky Ralph Steadman-inspired image and cool, T-shirted shop staff.

Or could you? Oddbins made a well-publicised foray into the poncier end of the wine market this year when it snapped up £1m worth of smart 1992 Burgundies. The summer 1994 list was full of names like Carillon, Ramonet, Morey, Sauzet, Bonneau du Martray, Dujac and Gagnard Delagrange, complete with £20-plus price tags and tasting notes by American wine taster Robert Parker.

So has Oddbins wandered into the valley of the ponce? Over to senior buyer Steve 'style master' Daniel. 'Burgundy is good value at the moment when you look at the price of some of the best New World wines. We've been getting our customers to trade up through Australian wines like Leeuwin and Petaluma and I wanted some of the ultra-specialist share of the market. Burgundy is something we've never really touched.'

Daniel admits that it was a huge gamble. Oddbins offered 40 red and white Burgundies to its New World-inclined customers and sold them all within a month. It has also got its 'peg in the line for the 1993s', so watch out for more fine Burgundies early in 1995.

Burgundy may have occupied the front five pages of the summer list, but Oddbins' bread and buttered toast is still Australia. Statisticians may argue about who sells more Aussie wine – Tesco or Oddbins – but there's no denying that the latter shifts an awful lot of cases: 800,000 to be precise.

Talking to Steve Daniel and trading director John Ratcliffe, we got the impression that Oddbins was anxious to look beyond Australia. 'We're definitely expanding other areas,' says Ratcliffe. 'You have to be more selective now than when Australian wines first arrived here. It's still a key area for us, but short crops and heavy demand have made it more difficult to source good-value wines. Our policy has always been to buy where we've found the best value.'

Australia currently accounts for 40 per cent of Oddbins' sales – hence the pun 'Ozbins', sometimes used as a taunt by the chain's competitors. A case of too many eggs in the same picnic hamper? Perhaps. Oddbins is still the place to go if you want to get hold of top names such as Tim Knappstein, Cullens, Leeuwin, Coldstream Hills and Mount Langhi Ghiran, but these days Bottoms Up has a list which is just as good and Tesco is not far off.

What new areas has Oddbins targeted? Chile is the main one. Steve Daniel is excited by the intensity of flavour emerging from wineries such as Casablanca, Santa Carolina, Cono Sur and Carmen. In some cases, we feel the enthusiasm is warranted. Nevertheless, here too there is an element of duplication. The problem with Chile is that it doesn't produce a wide range of styles – Chardonnay, Cabernet Sauvignon and Sauvignon Blanc with a smattering of Pinot Noir, Merlot and Riesling about sums it up.

South Africa, largely ignored by Oddbins, might be a better long-term bet. So might the Languedoc-Roussillon, an area where Oddbins has been uncharacteristically slow out of the blocks. Given the quality of the stuff emerging from the Midi, 45 wines from the South of France looks a little thin when set against 186 from Australia.

Daniel has typically strong opinions on both counts. 'We were one of the first chains to sell wines from the South of France, but I only buy stuff I think is good enough. And Chile kicks shit out of South Africa at under £5. In terms of inherent potential, Chile has a lot more class.'

The other New World area Daniel rates highly is California, especially at over £5. Oddbins has come up with some innovative things from the West Coast and, crucially, it has persuaded producers to take a more realistic approach to pricing their wines. J. Lohr, Landmark, Wild Horse and Bonny Doon have all been introduced to the high street by Oddbins. So, this year, has L'Ecole 41, a brilliant new find up in Washington State.

There are, as always, two major attractions about Oddbins stores. The first is range – anywhere between 900 and 1,200 wines at a given moment – and the second is Oddbins' staff. Only Majestic and selected branches of Wine Rack and Bottoms Up can match Oddbins' managers for knowledge and enthusiasm.

Customers clearly appreciate this. At £5.47 a bottle (not including sparkling wines and Champagne), Oddbins has the highest average sale in the high street. Wine drinkers trust the recommendations they receive in an Oddbins store.

Oddbins has continued to expand in 1994 and has 'outperformed the market,' according to John Ratcliffe, even if it's getting 'really tough out there'. The number of shops is fast approaching 200 – up 22 on last year.

This creates a small problem of its own. Oddbins has always been quick on its feet, but with 200 stores to service, it needs to buy at least 100 cases of any given product. The way round this, Ratcliffe argues, is the Oddbins Fine Wine Stores. The first of these more specialised outlets was opened in November 1992 as a way of listing smaller parcels of wine and of 'attacking the ultra-specialist market'. There are four of them now – two in London, one in Glasgow and one in Edinburgh. Should keep the ponces happy.

Oddbins remains one of the most interesting and innovative places to buy wine in the world. It takes on a bewildering 600 new wines every year and has the managers to keep most of them moving through the shops. But, as Ratcliffe acknowledges, the competition is warming up. Bottoms Up in particular has a range which is every bit as good and the buyers to go on finding excellent new wines. Only two years ago, Oddbins seemed to have the high street to itself. These days, we're not so sure.

White

Under £3

FRANCE

1993 Domaine Lannemaison, Côtes de Gascogne
££ / 2 / 1   14/20
An unusual Gascon blend of Sauvignon Blanc, Ugni Blanc and Colombard, showing zingy, grassy, grapefruity characters and the added aromatic zip of the Sauvignon grape.

SPAIN

1993 Santara Dry White, Hugh Ryman
£££ / 2 / 1   15/20
From Conca de Barbera, a small *denominación* in Catalonia, this is a lemon-fresh blend of the native Macabeu and Parellada grapes. An excellent party white.

£3-5

AUSTRALIA

1994 Lindemans Cawarra Colombard/Chardonnay
££ / 3 / ▮ 14/20

Australian's answer to Vin de Pays des Côtes de Gascogne, this
top ten best seller is a soft, fresh, peachy white with a giveaway
off-dry finish.

CHILE

1994 Santa Carolina Sauvignon Blanc, Maipo Valley, Santa Rosa Vineyard
££ / 2 / ▮ 15/20

A grapefruit and ripe melon style of Sauvignon Blanc made by
consultant oenologist, Ignacio Recabarren. Good at under £4.

1994 Santa Carolina Sauvignon Blanc, Reserva
££ / 2 / ▮ 15/20

Using partial barrel-fermentation, Ignacio Recabarren has produced
a big, rich, tropical fruit Sauvignon Blanc with a hint of coconutty
oak and balancing zip.

1994 Casablanca Sauvignon Blanc, Lontue Valley
£££ / 2 / ▮ 17/20

**One of the best Sauvignon Blancs in Chile, which, at under £5,
is now selling at a realistic price. An intense apple and citrus
fruit-flavoured dry white with super concentration, heading
more towards New Zealand than the Loire Valley in style.**

1994 Carmen Chardonnay
££ / 2 / ▮ 14/20

A simple, but flavoursome, Chardonnay made by Alvaro Espinoza
in the Maipo Valley with full, rounded fruit in an appealing boiled-
sweets style and a light touch of oak.

1994 Santa Carolina Chardonnay, Lontue Valley
££ / 2 / ▮ 15/20

A nicely balanced, American oak-aged Chardonnay with focused,
refreshing fruit in the ascendant.

1994 Casablanca Chardonnay, Lontue Valley
£££ / 2 / ▌   16/20

Intense, pleasantly toasted Chardonnay, which has been through
partial barrel-fermentation for added texture and complexity.
Tropical fruit and grapefruit-like acidity in harmony.

FRANCE

1993 Oddbins White, Domaine de Jöy, Vin de Pays des Côtes de Gascogne
££ / 3 / ▌   14/20

A blend of Colombard, Ugni Blanc and the more interesting Gros
Manseng produced at the Gessler family domaine in Armagnac
country, a good grapefruit and boiled-sweets white with a touch
of sugar for popular appeal.

1993 Domaine St Hilaire Chardonnay, Vin de Pays d'Oc
££ / 2 / ▌   14/20

André Hardy pioneered premium grape varieties such as
Chardonnay and Cabernet Sauvignon at his 70-hectare estate near
Montpellier in the late 1950s and early 1960s, becoming one of
négociant Robert Skalli's star growers. These days he bottles and
sells his own production. This is a very ripe, buttery, unoaked
Chardonnay with good fruit concentration. Our only concern is
that it's a little short of acidity, so needs to be drunk a.s.a.p.

1993 Domaine de la Rénaudie, Sauvignon de Touraine
£££ / 2 / ▌   17/20

**A subtle, nettley Sauvignon Blanc with crisp, restrained
gooseberry flavours and a minerally edge more commonly
associated with Sancerre than more lowly Sauvignon de
Touraine. Made at an 18-hectare property in St Aignan-sur-
Cher from 20-year-old vines, it's incredible value at under
£5.**

1993 Gaillac Cave de Labastide de Lévis
££ / 2 / ▌   14/20

This unusual wine, made from the local Mauzac grape, was one of
Grapevine's wines of the year last year. While still pleasantly fresh
and distinctive, it didn't quite hit the high spot this year.

1993 Chardonnay, James Herrick, Vin de Pays d'Oc
££ / 1 / ▌   15/20

The second vintage from Englishman James Herrick's impressive
New World style vineyards near Narbonne. This is more elegant
and restrained than the 1992 with deftly handled oak and a lime-
like streak of acidity.

ITALY

1993 Pinot Grigio, Bidoli, Grave del Friuli
££ / 2 / ▌   14/20

A modern, cool-fermented white made by Arrigo Bidoli and French
winemaker Gaetane Carron during a productive vintage in Italy.

1993 Chardonnay del Salento, 'Le Trulle'
££ / 2 / ▌   15/20

A cleverly made southern Italian Chardonnay with plenty of fresh,
peachy fruit, grapefruity acidity and a touch of oak character from
flying Australian winemaker, Kym Milne.

1993 Albizzia Bianco di Toscana, Frescobaldi
££ / 2 / ▌   15/20

Apparently made predominantly from the Grechetto grape with a
dash of Ansonica and Chardonnay, this is a fresh, lemony dry white
of considerable character and finesse. More so than many a Tuscan
white, in fact.

PORTUGAL

1990 Esporão Reserva
0 / 2 / ▌   12/20

A Portuguese curiosity produced at the experimental, space-age
winery of Esporão in the Alentejo, which in 1990 was only just
starting to produce its own wines. The kindest thing we can say
about this American oak-aged oddball blend of Roupeiro, Diagalves,
Mantuedo and Perrum (if you've heard of three of them, you're
doing better than we are), is that the experiment didn't work.
Now that Australian winemaker David Baverstock is in charge, we
should see better things coming out of the lab.

SOUTH AFRICA

1992 Stellenzicht Noble Late Harvest Weisser Riesling, half-bottle
££££ / 7 / ➤   17/20
Stunning value for money at under £4 for a half-bottle, this is a raisiny, dessert wine with lots of crystallised citrus fruit freshness and zip. Made in limited quantities, so hurry, hurry, hurry.

1993 Danie de Wet Chardonnay sur lie, Robertson
££ / 2 / ▐   15/20
One of a large number of Chardonnays made in Robertson by white wine specialist, Danie de Wet. This is an unoaked style, relying on ageing on its yeast lees for flavour and freshness.

SPAIN

1993 Agramont Viura, Navarra
££ / 2 / ▐   14/20
A clean, modern, dry Navarra white with lashings of American oak, creating a Rioja lookalike.

1993 Sauvignon Blanc, Rueda, Hermanos Lurton
££ / 2 / ▐   15/20
Another cat's pee special from Jacques Lurton's Spanish operation. This is a grassy, grapefruity, easy-drinking in the New Zealand Sauvignon Blanc mould. Very upfront, and almost OTT.

1993 Solana White, Ribeiro
££££ / 2 / ▐   17/20
The offspring of a timely liaison between Australia's Mitchelton Wines and Spain's Bodegas y Bebidas. Winemakers Don Lewis and Francisco Diaz Ubero have used indigenous north-western Spanish grapes, Torrontes and Treixadura, to produce a brilliant, characterful white. A zesty, lemon and lime-like, modern white with some Australian fruit richness. Long may the partnership flourish.

£5–8

AUSTRALIA

1993 Balgownie Chardonnay
££ / 2 / 🍷   15/20
This is a barrel-fermented Chardonnay from vineyards in
Coonawarra and north-eastern Victoria. The cool climate origins
of the grapes add considerable elegance to the agreeable flavours
of vanilla fudge oak.

1993 Hill Smith Sauvignon Blanc
££ / 2 / 🍷   16/20
The Sauvignon Blanc in question was sourced from the Airstrip
Block, a vineyard in South Australia's idyllic, relatively cool Eden
Valley. The higher altitude gives the wine a green bean and
asparagus character, reminiscent of New Zealand's Montana
Sauvignon.

CHILE

1994 Casablanca Gewürztraminer, Santa Isabel Estate, Casablanca Valley
££ / 3 / 🍷   16/20
A fresh, aromatic Gewürztraminer, which takes its place alongside
Fairview in South Africa and Delatite in Australia's Victoria as one
of the best examples of the variety produced in the New World.
Orange zest and ginger spice make this a classic of its type.

1994 Casablanca Sauvignon Blanc, Santa Isabel Estate, Casablanca Valley
££ / 2 / 🍷   16/20
Made from a combination of grapes deliberately picked at different
levels of ripeness for a balance of rich fruit and fresh flavours. The
result is a successful grapefruit and melon style Sauvignon Blanc
with considerable intensity of flavour.

1994 Casablanca Chardonnay, Santa Isabel Estate, Casablanca Valley

££ / 2 / ⮕   16/20

Yet another well-honed Chilean white from superstar winemaker, Ignacio Recabarren. The buttery (malolactic) component has been toned down since the 1993 vintage to produce a balanced style with a hint of barley sugar sweetness, peachy fruit and deftly handled oak.

FRANCE

1993 Quincy, J M Sorbe

££ / 1 / ▋   15/20

Jean-Michel Sorbe is something of an exception in the small 100-hectare Loire *appellation* of Quincy as he's one of the few farmers in the village to concentrate exclusively on winemaking. This cool-fermented, bone-dry Sauvignon Blanc is attractively nettley with a charming touch of rusticity.

1993 Reuilly, Aujard/Mabillot

££ / 2 / ▋   15/20

Made by Bernard Aujard and Alain Mabillot, this is another dry Sauvignon Blanc from a tiny *appellation* in the eastern Loire. Fruitier and more rounded than the Quincy, it's full and fat, almost overripe in fact. Closer to a Graves than a Sancerre in style.

1993 Menetou-Salon, Morogues, Pellé, Cuvée Vanessa

££ / 2 / ⮕   16/20

We're not quite sure who Vanessa is, but we enjoyed this wine, which was named in her honour. A structured, aromatic Sauvignon, still on the tight side at the moment, this grassy dry white will develop well over the next year or two.

1993 Sancerre, La Croix au Garde, Pellé

££ / 1 / ⮕   16/20

Henri Pellé has been making Sancerre from his La Croix au Garde vineyard since 1982. The six-hectare site produces intense, concentrated wines with lots of backbone and bracingly fresh acidity.

1992 Bourgogne Aligoté, Jayer-Gilles
£££ / 2 / 🍾   16/20
Produced from 45-year-old vines, this remarkable Aligoté is a rich, leesy, old fashioned white Burgundy. Aligoté almost always loses out to Chardonnay in the Côte d'Or's popularity stakes, but this shows what can be done with ripe grapes and few low-yielding vines.

1992 St Véran, Roger Lasserat
££ / 2 / ➡   16/20
Roger Lasserat produces some of the oakiest wines in the southern Mâconnais, and this ultra-ripe, barrel-fermented example is no exception. His wines usually take time to come round, so tuck this one away for a year or two.

1992 Le Second de Floridène, Graves
££ / 2 / 🍾   17/20
As the name implies, this is the second label of Graves property, Clos Floridène, where academic and hands-on Bordeaux guru, Denis Dubourdieu, makes some of the most intense white wines in France. This is a clean, elegant, toasty Graves with a beautifully balanced, silky finish.

1992 Haut-Bertinerie Blanc, Côtes de Blaye
££ / 2 / 🍾   16/20
This is a Graves-style, barrel-fermented white Bordeaux with buttered asparagus-style Sauvignon Blanc in evidence, and pronounced smoky oak, which needs time to settle down.

ITALY

1993 Chardonnay del Salento, Vigneto di Caramia, Kym Milne
££ / 2 / 🍾   15/20
From the Caramia vineyard near Brindisi in southern Italy, this is a classy, barrel-fermented, New World-style Chardonnay made under Kym Milne's supervision by Warren Gibson. It's rich and well made, but lacks a little bit of local colour. Some might argue that's not a bad thing, but we rather like our Italian whites to taste Italian.

UNITED STATES

1992 J. Fritz Chardonnay
£ / 2 / ❧   14/20
This might sound like something produced in Germany, but it's
from the Russian River and Dry Creek Valleys in California's
Sonoma County. A big, rich, luscious wine with lots of alcohol
and peachy fruit, but a little lacking in finesse.

1992 L'Ecole 41 Semillon, Washington State
££ / 2 / ❧   16/20
Martin Clubb's excellent Washington State winery is housed in a
former school house – hence the name and a label which looks as
if it was designed by Ryan in fifth grade. The Yakima River region
produces some of the most exciting white wines in North America,
and this toasty, barrel-fermented white with its pungent yeast lees
character proves the point.

1992 Benziger Chardonnay
££ / 2 / ❧   15/20
Named after the family which founded the company, Benziger is the
up-market label of Sonoma County's unashamedly commercial Glen
Ellen winery. It's drier and more elegant than the tutti-fruity Glen
Ellen style, with nicely balanced vanilla oak flavours and fresh acidity.

1993 Kiona Late Harvest Gewürztraminer
£ / 7 / ❧   14/20
The Kiona winery and its wacky winemaker, Scott Williams,
specialise in sweet, late-harvest styles. From a 12-hectare vineyard
in Washington's Yakima Valley, this is a crystallised lychee-fruit
style with massive sweetness. We preferred the balance of the
admittedly more expensive ice wine (reviewed below).

Over £8

FRANCE

1992 Hautes Côtes de Beaune Blanc, Jayer-Gilles
£££ / 2 / ➥   17/20
It's extremely rare to find Pinot Blanc in top-class white
Burgundy, although maybe more seeps in than many

growers would like to admit. Astonishingly, this superbly crafted white is made entirely from old Pinot Blanc vines. Half of the wine is fermented in oak barrels, while the remainder goes into stainless steel to produce a balanced, textured style with richness from contact with its lees, and crisp acidity.

1992 Chassagne-Montrachet Maltroie Crets, Château de Maltroye
£ / 3 / 🕯   14/20
An off-the-winery-wall white Burgundy, whose super-ripe botrytis bouquet makes it smell more like a Sauternes than a Côte de Beaune white. It's coconutty and honeyed and tastes rather like a Sauternes, too. Catch out your nearest Master of Wine with this unusual buy.

1992 Chassagne-Montrachet, Morgeots Vignes Blanches, Château de Maltroye
££ / 2 / ➣   17/20
This is another ripe Chassagne-Montrachet, though this time there's no overt sweetness or botrytis in evidence. It's a powerful premier cru fermented in 100 per cent new oak, producing a concentrated, nutty style reminiscent of a top Chablis.

1991 Château l'Hospital, Graves
£ / 2 / 🕯   15/20
An assertively oaked, Graves-style white, whose vanilla hammer blow reminded us of an old-fashioned Rioja. Fine if you like the style.

1992 Clos Floridène, Graves
£££ / 2 / 🕯   18/20
A brilliant blend of mainly Semillon, with some Sauvignon Blanc and Muscadelle from star winemaker, Denis Dubourdieu. Concentration and class at a very good £12 price tag.

NEW ZEALAND

1993 Hunter's Sauvignon Blanc, Marlborough
£££ / 2 / ➣   17/20
This is the best New Zealand Sauvignon from the difficult 1993

vintage, confirming Hunter's standing as one of the New World's finest wineries. Fabulously aromatic with tropical flavours of passion fruit and melon, cut by elegant grapefruity acidity. Watch out, Cloudy Bay, there's a Hunter about.

UNITED STATES

1992 L'Ecole 41 Chardonnay
££ / 2 / ❱   16/20
Winemaker Martin Clubb's successful attempt at a Burgundian-style Chardonnay, which is barrel-fermented and aged for seven months on its yeast lees. The result is an immensely toasty, concentrated white with some toffee and fudge-like fruit, held together by fresh acidity.

1991 Franciscan Chardonnay, Cuvée Sauvage
0 / 2 / ❱   14/20
'Sauvage' refers to the ambient wild yeasts used to ferment this wine rather than the personal habits of winemaker Greg Upton. This can be one of California's best Chardonnays, but on the two occasions we've tasted it, the 1991 has seemed clumsy, old-fashioned and short of finesse.

1992 Landmark Two Williams Chardonnay
££ / 2 / ❱   16/20
A wine that sounds as if it's driven by Damon Hill, but is in fact a barrel-fermented Sonoma Valley white with plenty of rich, balanced, creamy, fudge-like flavours. In case you didn't know, Landmark is a tractor, not a racing car.

1992 Landmark Damaris Chardonnay
£££ / 2 / ▬   17/20
Modestly named after Damaris Deere W. Ethridge, the Nancy Reagan of Sonoma County, this is a very stylish, toasty, well-upholstered West Coast Chardonnay, with piercing fruit intensity and a hint of butterscotch oakiness. At this level of quality, California outperforms most Australian Chardonnay.

1993 Kiona Ice Wine, half-bottle
££ / 8 / ▬   16/20
Fruit basket aromas of melon and honey with some apple and

blackcurrant pie thrown in for good measure, this late-picked Chenin Blanc is the richest, most concentrated and best-balanced of Kiona's unusual sweet white wines. Not cheap at just under £10 a half, but worth a try.

Red

Under £3

ITALY

Puglian Red
£ / MB / 🍾   13/20
A spicy, fruity, sweetish blend of Negroamaro, Malvasia Nera and Sangiovese from Puglia's Salento peninsula made at a family-owned winery by Australian Kym Milne.

1993 Riva Sangiovese di Romagna
£££ / MB / 🍾   15/20
A fresh, savoury, unoaked barbecue red made in Emilia Romagna by French winemaker Gaetane Carron. Chocolate and cherry fruit with an Italian twist. Good value at under £3, and looks good on the dinner table too.

SPAIN

1993 Santara Red, Conca de Barbera
£ / MB / 🍾   13/20
A blend of Cabernet Sauvignon and Merlot from a small *denominación* in Catalonia made by Hugh 'The Guru' Ryman. Fine if you like the flavour of sawdust in your wine.

1993 Andelos, Palacia de la Vega, Navarra
£ / MB / 🍾   13/20
Soft, modern Navarra blend of Cabernet Sauvignon and the native Tempranillo and Garnacha with the emphasis firmly on fresh fruit flavours and not chippy oak. Pleasant, if basic.

Torrealdea Rioja
£££ / MB / ▊   14/20
From the enormous San Isidro co-operative in the Rioja Baja region,
which used to supply bulk wine to large private wineries such as
Marqués de Cáceres, this is a tradional blend of Rioja varieties
made in a highly modern, tank-fermented style. Once again
the emphasis is on fresh fruit, and here the result is more
successful.

£3-5

AUSTRALIA

1992 McWilliams Mount Pleasant Cabernet Sauvignon
£££ / MB / ▱   17/20
**McWilliams is one of the most underrated family wineries
in Australia, concentrating on substance rather than
publicity. Part of the reason is that until recently, its
reputation was based almost entirely on fortified wines. Now
it's adopted a more dynamic approach to table wine
production, we should start to see a few more stunners like
this. From irrigated vineyards in the New South Wales
district of Riverina, this is an intense, concentrated berry
fruit Cabernet Sauvignon with perfectly judged American
oak. Like most of McWilliams' wines, this one will age well
in bottle.**

1992 McWilliams Mount Pleasant Cabernet/Merlot
££ / MB / ▱   16/20
From the same area, this is a Cabernet Sauvignon dominated
Bordeaux blend with juicy, tobaccoey fruit and sweetly spicy
American oak. It's still young, but has the class and elegance to
age well.

Glenloth Shiraz/Cabernet, Private Bin 108
£ / MB / ▊   13/20
Soft, easy-drinking Kendal mint cake fruit flavours and a keen price
make this Penfolds blend the most popular Australian red at
Oddbins.

1992 Penfolds Bin 35 Shiraz/Cabernet, South Australia
££ / FB / ▐   15/20

A typically exuberant Penfolds blend with charred American oak and berry fruit. Let's hope they can keep the price under £5 during this period of pressure on grape prices in Australia.

CHILE

1993 Carmen Cabernet Sauvignon
££ / MB / ▐   14/20

Made by Alvaro Espinoza in Chile's Rapel Valley, this blend of Cabernet Sauvignon and a dash of Merlot is a well-priced introduction to what Chile has to offer. A young, herbaceous red with fresh acidity and a lick of oak.

1993 Carmen Cabernet Sauvignon Reserve
££ / MB / ►   15/20

Another wine from the pipette of Alvaro Espinoza, this time made from lower-yielding, older vines, and aged in French and American oak. Plenty of blackcurrant fruit concentration here and stylish balance, too.

1993 Carmen Merlot Reserve
£££ / MB / ►   16/20

Windsurfing winemaker Alvaro Espinoza fermented ten per cent of this chocolatey, concentrated Merlot in American oak barrels for smooth texture and harmonious oak integration. The result is a pretty impressive wine at under £5.

1991 Santa Carolina Cabernet Sauvignon Reserva
£££ / MB / ►   16/20

From the Santa Rosa del Peral vineyard in Chile's fertile Maipo Valley, a modern red made from Cabernet Sauvignon aged in French oak, Bordeaux-style, for 18 months. Yet another winner from the sure-footed Ignacio Recabarren.

1993 Cono Sur Pinot Noir
£££ / MB / ▐   15/20

From Cono Sur's Chimbarongo estate in the Rapel region, this is a raspberry and cherry lollipop style with distinct Pinot Noir character. A snip at under £4.50.

FRANCE

1992 Carignanissime de Centeilles, Minervois
££ / FB / ❚   15/20

John Lennon lookalike Daniel Domergue is one of the Languedoc's most uncompromising traditionalists, making wines from native varieties. This one comes entirely from a 100-year old plot of Carignan vines, although Domergue isn't allowed to advertise the fact on the label, owing to the silly rule that forbids the mention of a single grape variety on an *appellation* wine. His ingenious solution is to make a pun out of the name of this tarry, raspberry fruity red.

1993 Côtes de Ventoux Le Rouret, le Radical
£££ / FB / ❚   15/20

Another southern French red using much-denigrated Carignan to remarkable effect. The key to this fruity, supple, deeply coloured wine is once again the age of the vines.

1992 Domaine Croix Belle, Vin de Pays de Côtes de Thongue
££ / MB / ❚   15/20

A well-made, modern, juicy red from the Languedoc with what we thought tasted like a significant proportion of Cabernet Sauvignon.

1991 Château de Jau Côtes du Roussillon Villages
££ / MB / ❚   15/20

With its art gallery and set-menu restaurant, Château de Jau is one of the most appealing estates to visit in the Roussillon region. The quality of the wine has improved steadily over the last five years, so much so that, as well as providing Oddbins with its house red, it turns out concentrated, garrigue-scented numbers like this.

1993 Domaine Villerambert Julien, Minervois Cuvée Opera
£££ / FB / �corkscrew   16/20

Made by Marcel Julien, who looks as though he could be Gary Lineker's brother, this is a ripe, spicy, robust Minervois with plenty of the aromatic character of the Syrah grape.

ITALY

1993 Primitivo del Salento, Centele
£ / MB / ❚   13/20
Primitivo is said by pointy-headed ampelographers (that's grape scientists to you and us), to be the same grape as the Zinfandel of California. Tasting this Kym Milne southern Italian red, you can see the similarities between Zin and the jammy fruit and dry, rustic tannins on show here.

PORTUGAL

1990 Villa Regia, Douro
££ / MB / ❚   14/20

Made by Portuguese giant, Sogrape, this is a modern, tobaccoey, strawberry-soft Douro red with a touch of added sweetness.

1989 Quinta de Camarate, Fonseca
££ / MB / ❚   15/20
An oak-aged blend of Castelão Frances, Espadeiro and Cabernet Sauvignon made by California-trained winemaker Domingos Soares Franco. An elegant, minty red with sweet fruit concentration and deftly handled oak.

SPAIN

1991 Tempranillo Crianza, Bodegas Berberana, Rioja
£££ / MB / ❚   15/20
One of several vintages of Crianza Rioja on the market from the excellent-value Berberana stable. We marginally prefer the 1992 at Safeway over the 1990 and 1991. Still, at £3.99, this is a delicious, modern Rioja with toffee-like, supple fruit and finely handled oak-ageing.

1993 Garnacha, Veganueva, Navarra
££ / MB / ❚   14/20
Soft, juicy, unoaked Garnacha from go-ahead winery, Bodegas y Bebidas, made using the carbonic maceration technique to plane down the rustic edges.

1990 Agramont, Navarra
££ / MB / ⊷   15/20
A modern Rioja-style blend of native Tempranillo and Cabernet
Sauvignon, producing a smooth, ripe, pleasantly oaked red from a
go-ahead co-operative in Navarra.

1993 Solana Cencibel
£££ / MB / ▮   16/20
The red counterpart to the brilliant Solana white. Also produced
by Mitchelton Wines and Bodegas y Bebidas, this one is made
from Cencibel grown in Valdepeñas. An unoaked, vibrantly
blackcurranty wine which is gradually settling into its stride.

1988 Rioja Crianza Campillo
£££ / MB / ▮   17/20
**An outstanding bargain from Bodegas Campillo, one of the
youngest and best wineries in the Rioja region. The
peculiarity here is that Campillo uses only Tempranillo
grapes in its red wines, instead of the more usual blend of
varieties. The result is a gamey, mature Rioja with sumptuous
oak integration adding spicy complexity. As good as many
a Gran Reserva, but at a fraction of the price.**

UNITED STATES

Havenscourt Barbera
££ / MB / ▮   14/20
Havenscourt is a brand name developed by Oddbins in a joint
venture with winemaker Jason Korman at the Faux Winery in
Sonoma. Barbera is a commonly planted grape variety in Piedmont,
and, more surprisingly, in California's Central Valley. Now that
Italian grape varieties are becoming hot in the Napa and Sonoma
Valleys, growers have started to plant Barbera there too. This is
more approachable than the Piedmontese style with soft, sweetish,
plummy fruit.

Havenscourt Zinfandel
££ / MB / ▮   15/20
The bad news is that this is a wine with so much alcohol that it
almost makes it into the fortified wine bracket. The good news is
that there's no extra duty involved. A strapping American-oak aged

Zin with a dollop of Cabernet, presumably to get the alcohol below 15 per cent.

Havenscourt Cabernet Sauvignon
££ / MB / ▌   15/20
Another rich Havenscourt non-vintage red with herbaceous but concentrated blackberry fruit and a home-run of smoky American oak, finishing on the dry side. Like most of the Havenscourt reds, this is a one-glass wine. But what a glass.

£5–8

AUSTRALIA

1991 Jamieson's Run Cabernet Sauvignon, Coonawarra
£ / MB / ▌   15/20
An oaky, tarry Australian Cabernet which is tightly wound at the moment, needing time to soften and lose some of its tannins.

1991 Mount Langhi Ghiran Shiraz
£ / MB / ▌   14/20
From cool climate vineyards in the hills of southern Victoria, Mount Langhi Ghiran normally produces one of Australia's more elegant, minty Shiraz styles. This one is light, short and disappointingly lacking in fruit.

1991 Brown Brothers Cabernet Sauvignon
££ / MB / ▌   16/20
After some dullish years in the late 1980s, Brown Brothers in Victoria is once again producing some exciting, good-value red and white wines. This is a minty, elegantly oaked Cabernet from north-eastern Victoria with fresh fruit concentration and good depth of flavour.

1992 Leasingham Shiraz, Clare Valley, South Australia
££ / FB / ➥   16/20
Based in South Australia's Clare Valley, Leasingham makes approachable, fleshy reds, which appeal unashamedly to the senses. This is typical of the style, with luscious coconut and macaroon oak and spearminty freshness supporting sweet, blackberry Shiraz fruit.

1992 Wynn's Shiraz, Coonawarra

£££ / FB / ▮   16/20

This is Australia's answer to Crozes-Hermitage, produced in a juicy, fruit-packed style with distinctive peppery undertones, from temperate vineyards in the Coonawarra region of South Australia.

CHILE

1990 Santa Carolina Cabernet Sauvignon Gran Reserva

££ / FB / ▬   16/20

A big, chewy, tannic Chilean Cabernet Sauvignon, unusually fermented in South American beech casks, followed by two and a half years' ageing in American oak barrels. There's good fruit concentration, but it still needs time to slip past the wood.

1993 Cono Sur Pinot Noir Reserve

£££ / MB / ▮   17/20

Made by American winemaker Ed Flaherty at the Concha y Toro-owned Cono Sur Chimbarongo estate winery in the Rapel region, this second release is the best Pinot Noir we've come across so far from South America. It even rivals the likes of Saintsbury and Acacia in California, except on price, where, remarkably, it's under £6. A rich, chocolatey, nicely oaked Pinot Noir with voluptuous loganberry and raspberry fruit flavours.

1992 Cono Sur Cabernet Sauvignon Reserve

£££ / MB / ▮   17/20

Another outstanding red from Ed Flaherty at Cono Sur, only this time we're in Bordeaux rather than Burgundy country. Unusually for Chile, the fruit is soft, supple and ripe and the oak is beautifully integrated. Let's hope Cono Sur keeps the price below £6 for the 1993.

FRANCE

1992 Domaine de Triennes, 'Les Aureliens'

£££ / MB / ▮   16/20

Domaine de Triennes was bought five years ago by Burgundians Jacques Seysses and Aubert De Vilaine as an investment in the up-and-coming vineyards of southern France, situated in open country between Aix-en-Provence and the Mediterranean. This blend of Cabernet Sauvignon and Syrah is inspired by Eloi Durrbach of Domaine de Trévallon at Les Baux de Provence. Like a turbo-charged Cabernet Sauvignon, this is an oak-aged southern red with lots of spicy, brambly fruit and fine-grained tannins.

1991 Château Villerambert Julien, Cuvée Trianon, Minervois
£££ / FB / ↢   16/20
A blend of Syrah, Grenache, Mourvèdre and Carignan made at Marcel Julien's first-rate property in the Minervois, this vanilla and coffee bean style, smokily concentrated red has more than enough guts and fruit flavour to cope with the splinters. But it needs time.

1993 Beaujolais Villages, Domaine de St Ennemond
££ / MB / ↥   15/20
At last a real Beaujolais! From a family-owned domaine in the north of the Beaujolais region, this shows all the supple, juicy, come-hither charm of Gamay at its best, with classic red fruits character and freshly balancing acidity.

1993 Régnié, Domaine des Braves, Franck Cinquin
£££ / MB / ↢   16/20
Régnié has been generally disappointing since its elevation to the ranks of the Beaujolais crus in 1989, but this example, made by a former Tour de France cyclist, proves that the village has potential after all. It's a vibrant, rich, structured Gamay, which needs a year or more's age to get into top gear.

1993 Morgon, Domaine des Souchons
£££ / MN / ↢   16/20
Some producers in the Beaujolais cru of Morgon age their red wines in oak, but Serge Condemine has plumped for early bottling here in order to capture maximum aroma and cherry, plum and blackberry fruit. All the same, it's got the structure and backbone we expect from a good Morgon.

1989 Château de France, Pessac-Léognan
££ / MB / ↥   16/20
Lush, modern claret from the northern end of the Graves region, with plenty of caramel and vanilla oak, but solid, blackcurrant fruit flavours. Just getting into its stride.

ITALY

1988 Barbaresco, Castello di Neive
££ / FB / �   15/20
An aromatic, demandingly dry, but classically Italian red with the
mature, old-fashioned grip of the Nebbiolo grape. Not for
beginners, but Italophiles will find no trouble mopping up the
tannins.

1990 Chianti Rufina Riserva, Castello di Nipozzano, Frescobaldi
££ / MB / �   16/20
Serious Sangiovese-based red from a single estate in the high
altitude Rufina district of Chianti. The stylish oak gives the wine
an international façade, while the underlying fruit is classically
Tuscan. Give it time.

SPAIN

1991 Palacio de la Vega Cabernet Sauvignon Crianza, Navarra
££ / MB / ➊   16/20
A first Cabernet Sauvignon release from a Navarra winery, which
has only been making wine for four years. So well done Oddbins
for getting in early on this attractive, berry-fresh, Rioja-style red
with its spicy American oak character and good flavour intensity.

1992 Palacio de la Vega Merlot, Navarra
££ / MB / �   16/20
In contrast to the Cabernet Sauvignon, the Merlot was aged in
French oak, giving it a more restrained character, which will
develop nicely in time. A fruity, spicy Spanish red with one eye
on the future.

1985 Glorioso, Gran Reserva
££ / MB / �   16/20
Blended by French winemaker Michel Rolland, this Gran Reserva
Rioja was produced entirely from the patrician Tempranillo grape.
It was aged in American oak barrels for two and a half years and
spent a further three in bottle. At its peak now, but still showing
plenty of life. A modern-style Gran Reserva.

UNITED STATES

1993 The Catalyst III
£££ / FB / ▌   16/20
Named after a bar down the road from poet manqué Randall
Grahm's California winery, this is a hugely fruity, full-bodied,
peppery blend of 90 per cent Grenache and 10 per cent Barbera.
Soft, voluptuous drinking at just under £6.

1991 Fetzer Eagle Point Petite Sirah/Syrah
££ / FB / ▶   15/20
A chewy, deeply-coloured red from organic, lifestyle enhancement
specialists, Fetzer, showing masses of sweet fruit and charry
American oak. We're not sure it'll soften, but it's almost certainly
biodegradable.

Over £8

AUSTRALIA

1990 Yarra Yering Underhill Shiraz
£££ / MB / ▌   18/20
**The eccentric, tweedy Dr Bailey Carrodus was one of the
great, modern pioneers of cool climate viticulture in
Victoria's Yarra Valley north of Melbourne. This superb,
elegant Shiraz is like a cross between Australia's best and
the great Syrahs of the northern Rhône Valley. Matured in
French oak and unfiltered before bottling to retain every
ounce of flavour, it's a fresh, blackberry and eucalyptus-
style Shiraz with silky tannins and great finesse. About as
good as Shiraz gets.**

1991 Wynn's St Michael Hermitage
££ / MB / ▶   16/20
We assume that by the time this gets past the censors at the Wine
Standards Board, it will have lost the word Hermitage on the label
in favour of Shiraz. This is a contrasting style to the Yarra Yering,
with lots of soft, supple ripe fruit and coconutty American oak
flavours.

FRANCE

1991 Givry, Grand Berger, Domaine Tatraux Juillet
££ / MB / ⌐   15/20
From a small, family-owned estate in the Côte Chalonnaise
appellation of Givry, this is good honest Pinot Noir at just under
£8.50 with some dark chocolate and wild strawberry flavours.

1992 Hautes Côtes de Beaune, Jayer-Gilles
£££ / MB / ⌐   17/20
**Toasty, tobaccoey Pinot Noir with some deliciously savoury,
almost animal richness and fleshy, oaky concentration. A
hedonist's delight.**

1992 Hautes Côtes de Nuits, Jayer-Gilles
£££ / MB / ⌐   17/20
**As above, but with a touch more spicy, strawberry fruit and
firmer tannins.**

1990 Volnay Premier Cru Clos Audignac, Pousse d'Or
£ / MB / ⌐   16/20
At nearly £24, this is twice the price of the Jayer-Gilles reds, and
we're not convinced it offers twice the character, even if it is a
very good red Burgundy with composty, leafy fruit in the traditional
mould, give or take a veneer of vanilla oak.

1992 Chassagne-Montrachet, Carillon
££ / MB / ⌐   16/20
Carillon is better known as a white wine producer in Puligny-
Montrachet. But this comes from a hectare of vines which the
family owns in neighbouring Chassagne-Montrachet. This is
the best of the Carillon red Burgundies available at Oddbins.
It's an elegant, finely crafted Pinot Noir with good fruit
concentration.

1991 Château l'Hospital, Graves
££ / MB / ⌐   16/20
Considerably better than the same property's white wine, this is a
smoky Graves with lots of spicy new oak and concentrated,
blackberry fruit. Quite a mouthful at £8.99 a bottle.

1990 Bertineau St Vincent, Michel Rolland, Lalande de Pomerol
££ / MB / ➥   17/20
Last year we said this soft, plummy Merlot-based Bordeaux with its pronounced oak character should develop into something interesting, and it has. More aromatic and fleshier than it was a year ago, but it still has some way to go.

1990 Château Lilian Ladouys, St Estèphe
££ / MB / ➥   16/20
This is a recently created cru bourgeois, which used to sell its wines to the local co-operative. The co-op was getting a good deal if this characterful, oaky, modern claret is anything to judge by. The tannins are still tightly reined in, but the fruit quality suggests a good long life ahead.

1991 Châteauneuf-du-Pape, Château de Beaucastel
£££ / FB / ➥   17/20
A skunky, gamey, animal-like Provençal red from one of France's greatest estates. This is more forward than some Beaucastels, which usually need at least ten years to come round, but it's still a massive, savoury, farmyardy red with layer upon layer of complex flavours. Some say it's the sheep that graze in the vineyards that give it its distinctive character, others claim unorthodox winemaking techniques, while the owner, François Perrin, says the answer lies in the soil.

ITALY

1991 Lanaione Merlot, Frescobaldi
££ / FB / ➥   16/20
Very young, very tannic, very oaky and very Tuscan. Come back in five years' time.

1988 Castelgiocondo Brunello di Montalcino, Frescobaldi
£££ / FB / ➥   17/20
A rare sighting of a Brunello di Montalcino in a high street offie. Brunello is one of Italy's most highly prized, and often highly priced, reds. So it's good to see an example as good as

this selling at under £10. Unlike many a Tuscan superstar, it's an intensely fruity, savoury Sangiovese with class and balance. As recently recommended in *Loaded* magazine's wine column.

NEW ZEALAND

1992 Waimarama Estate Hawkes Bay Cabernet/Merlot
£££ / MB / ➡-   17/20
One of the few southern hemisphere reds to have achieved the concentration and elegance of a First Growth claret, this is New Zealand's answer to Mouton-Rothschild. Masses of supple fruit and toasty oak with a fresh acidity that promises good things for the future. The best red we've tasted from New Zealand in this vintage. Yours for only £11.

UNITED STATES

1992 L'Ecole 41 Merlot
££ / MB / ▮   16/20
More tales from the schoolhouse in Washington State. While Ryan in fifth grade's been doodling, winemaker Martin Clubb's been mixing Merlot with small amounts of Cabernet Sauvignon and Cabernet Franc to produce a soft, Pomerol-style Bordeaux blend with lashings of oak and chocolatey fruit. A Clubb-class red.

1991 Le Cigare Volant, Bonny Doon
0 / MB / ▮   14/20
Cigare Volant is the wine that made Randall Grahm's name as California's first Rhône Ranger. It's a blend of Syrah and Cinsault made in the style of a Châteauneuf-du-Pape. Perhaps as a result of popular demand, the wine isn't as good as it once was. At nearly £11, we'd rather drink the real thing.

1989 Flora Springs Trilogy
0 / MB / ▮   15/20
Trilogy is one of the horribly named Meritage wines. The term Meritage was issued for Bordeaux-style blends because the rules prevent producers from using the names of more than two grape varieties on any wine label. Flora Springs normally makes better Chardonnay than Cabernet. There's nothing wrong with this wine, but it's just a bit too serious and pricey for its own health.

Sparkling

£5–8

AUSTRALIA

Seaview Brut
££ / 2 / ▌   15/20
Back on form after a couple of indifferent years, this is fresh, toasty fizz with appealing tropical fruit ripeness.

Over £8

AUSTRALIA

1991 Green Point
£££ / 2 / ▌   17/20
This successful Yarra Valley winery has produced a brilliant successor to the 1990, which was one of *Grapevine*'s wines of the year in 1994. The Pinot Noir content has been increased, and Pinot Meunier has been added to the blend for the first time. Otherwise, this follows on nicely from the previous vintage showing considerable toasty complexity and finesse. Parent company Champagne house Moët et Chandon must be happy to see Dr Tony Jordan maintaining Green Point's high reputation.

FRANCE

Beaumont de Crayères, Cuvée Prestige
££ / 2 / ▌   15/20
From an Epernay-based co-operative, this is a fruity, young, Pinot dominated fizz with attractive aromas and mouth-filling mousse.

1986 Pol Roger Blanc de Chardonnay
£ / 2 / ▌   16/20
Nice wine, shame about the £30 price tag.

Perrier-Jouët NV Champagne
0 / 2 / 🍷   13/20

A disappointing, uninspired effort from a Grande Marque Champagne house. Simple, sweetish fizz of little finesse.

Veuve Clicquot Yellow Label Champagne NV Brut
£££ / 2 / 🍷   17/20

Veuve Clicquot is consistently among the best Grande Marque Champagnes, a fact reflected in its appearance among Oddbins' top ten best-selling wines. And at £20, it's easily the highest priced top ten performer in the country. Yellow Label is a rich, full-bodied blend of 56 per cent Pinot Noir, 28 per cent Chardonnay and 16 per cent Pinot Meunier. It's young, and although full-bodied, shows considerable finesse.

UNITED STATES

Mumm Cuvée Napa
££ / 2 / 🍷   15/20

After a couple of dodgy years and several advertising campaigns, Mumm Cuvée Napa appears to be back on the rails. The fruit quality is very good, but our reservation is that the wine is being released so young that it tastes somewhat tart and austere. Tuck it away for a few months and this one should reward your patience.

Cuvée Napa Rosé
££ / 3 / 🍷   15/20

We usually prefer the Cuvée Napa Rosé to the Cuvée Napa Brut, but on this occasion it was a case of honours even. Fresh and elegant with some strawberry sweetness, but a little rasping on the finish.

Fortified

£5–8

FRANCE

Muscat de Rivesaltes, Château de Jau
£ / 6 / 1   14/20

Mysteriously listed among southern French rosés in the Oddbins summer 1994 wine list, this is in fact a fortified, sweet Muscat from the Roussillon region. Not even Oddbins would claim it's perfect. Shame it couldn't find a better Muscat de Rivesaltes than this coarse, cloying example. Could someone pass the buyers the address of the Cazes brothers, please.

SAFEWAY ***(*)

Head Office: Safeway Stores Plc, Safeway House, 6 Millington Road, Hayes, Middlesex, UB3 4AY

Telephone: 081 848 8744

Number of branches: 371

Credit cards accepted: Visa, Access, Delta, Switch

Hours of opening: Monday to Saturday 8.00am to 8.00pm; Sunday 10am to 4.00pm

By-the-case sales: A five per cent discount is given on any purchase of 12 bottles or more of wines costing at least £2.99 a bottle. This discount applies even when a wine is on promotion

Glass loan: Free in selected stores

Home delivery: No

Clubs: No

Discounts: May Wine Fair, selection of price promotions every week including Multisaves and Linksaves. Case discounts described above.

In-store tastings: Occasionally

Top ten best-selling wines: Safeway Liebfraumilch; Safeway Hock; Safeway Lambrusco Bianco; Safeway Semillon, New South Wales; Lionel Derens Brut Champagne; Safeway Frascati Superiore Secco; Safeway Côtes du Rhône; Safeway Corbières; Safeway Romanian Pinot Noir, Dealul Mare; Safeway Cabernet Sauvignon, Svischtov

Range: GOOD: Eastern Europe, England, regional France, organic wines, Italy, Spain

AVERAGE: Bordeaux, Portugal, Chile, Australia, New Zealand, South Africa

POOR: California, Germany, Burgundy

'Rubbish,' said Master of Wine Liz Robertson in response to *Grapevine*'s suggestion that quality control was not all it might be in parts of Eastern Europe. 'Hungary and Bulgaria are just as reliable as Spain, France or Italy. You just have to go to the trouble of finding the right contacts in Eastern Europe.'

Safeway's Eastern European range, particularly its Hungarian selection, is the best in the country. Two years ago in tradition-bound Bulgaria, it pioneered the Young Vatted style, where wines were bottled while they still had some fruit rather than left to moulder in old wooden barrels. And it's followed that up with some good things too from Hungary, Romania and the Czech Republic.

Robertson says that innovation has brought handsome rewards. 'We stuck our necks out and we're very enthusiastic, so we tend to get first pick.' In Hungary it helps to have three trouble-shooters roaming the countryside – Nick Butler and his Eastern European partners, A'Kos Kamocsay and Agi Dezsenyi. 'We've expanded our range in Hungary,' she adds, 'because that's where we can do what we like. Bulgaria is a bit more institutionalised, but we work with very good wineries there in Russe, Sliven and Svischtov, so we're very happy.'

Happy, or 'chuffed to bits', would seem to describe the general atmosphere at Safeway, a friendly wine department with a trio of buyers working alongside Robertson. All three continue to source interesting new wines: Sarah Kynoch in the South of France, Clive McLaughlin in what he calls 'the war zones' of Africa and the Middle East and Piarina Hennessey in Spain.

Apart from Eastern Europe, Safeway is best known for its organic wines. There are more than a dozen, joined this year by two decent vegetarian wines. The organic list is much more than a gimmick, insists Robertson, although she concedes that it doesn't exactly zoom off the shelves. 'I'm committed to organic wines personally and I think the world of wine is starting to use fewer chemicals in the vineyard and cellar.'

To its credit, Safeway sponsors the annual Organic Fair at Ryton Gardens in the Midlands. And while it continues to offer wines from the likes of James Millton in New Zealand, Tenuta San Vito in Italy and Château Caraguilhes in France, we're not complaining.

English wines are another specialism. Until Bottoms Up's recent enthusiasm for this small, neglected corner of the market, Safeway was the only major retailer to show any real interest in our beleaguered national industry. There are 14 wines on the list at the time of writing, most of which sell well in stores close to the vineyard. As Robertson comments, 'We don't expect to sell a £6 wine from Hampshire in a supermarket in Hereford.'

If all these organic and English wines make the Safeway list sound excessively quirky, they shouldn't do. There are plenty of good mainstream things from the New and Old Worlds among the 400-strong range, too, with around 150 new wines bought this year alone. Italy and Spain, which we highlighted as weak areas last year, have both been given a shot in the arm. South Africa and Australia will benefit from expanded coverage later in the year, although in the autumn of 1994 the new wines hadn't arrived.

The focus of these additions are the May Wine Fair and a New World mini-fair held to celebrate the new vintage in the southern hemisphere. Safeway is concerned that in the past it hasn't made the most of its wine selection. 'I think we buy well wherever we go,' says Robertson, 'but now we're going to spend a bit more time selling the wines.'

The idea in 1995 is to have six major promotions – as well as the two wine fairs, there will be big pushes in January (bin ends), June (organic wines), September (around *Wine* magazine's International Challenge) and Christmas.

Robertson is keen to make the wine departments livelier places, with lots of posters and point-of-sale material. 'The fight is on at the moment for value and perception of value in the retail sector.'

Safeway itself is still committed to expansion, with 24 new branches opened in 1994. Not all of the stores have the complete wine range. Indeed, the full line-up makes it into only 35 or so supermarkets. The 'must stock' range numbers 200 wines, but you may have to order the more quirky things if your local Safeway isn't one of the larger sites.

In common with several of its competitors, Safeway is in the process of removing fine-wine racks from its branches. 'It's a graveyard,' says Robertson. 'If you lay a wine down that's selling perfectly well, it just dies.' The good thing about removing the racks, she adds, is that it will give Safeway more shelf space, which means more wines for the consumer to choose from.

So what does it all add up to? On the plus side, Safeway certainly has one of the more unusual supermarket wine ranges. It has done splendid, pioneering work in Eastern Europe. And we've seen some good new listings from Spain, Italy and Portugal, as well as a couple of very good southern French reds too.

But there are still areas which need improving. What concerns us most is a lack of excitement in several important areas. South Africa, Chile and California are good examples, as is Bordeaux, where *négociant* wines have apparently been bought in preference to more interesting crus bourgeois and petits châteaux. Burgundy is, similarly, a bit of yawn. It might offend the green and English wine lobbies to say so, but perhaps Safeway should spend a little more time on up-and-coming regions and a little less on curiosities.

White

Under £3

GERMANY

Safeway Hock, Deutscher Tafelwein
££ / 5 / 1   13/20
Grapey, sweet and fresh with pleasant, soft Müller-Thurgau fruit.

1992 Safeway Liebfraumilch
0 / 6 / 1   11/20
Sweet, tart and confected with far less personality than the Hock, but selling at the same price.

HUNGARY

1993 River Duna Sauvignon Blanc, Szekszard, Nick Butler
£££ / 3 / 1   15/20
One of the best Sauvignon Blancs we've tasted from Eastern Europe. Made by Nick Butler and sidekick, A'Kos Kamocsay, it's a wine where the aromatics don't quite deliver, but there's some good, gooseberry fruit on the palate.

ITALY

1993 'Le Montferrine' Moscato d'Asti
££ / 6 / 🍷   14/20
Softer and more appealing than many an Asti Spumante, this is a
sweet, frothy orange peel and sherbetty white with exuberant,
peachy fruit and only five per cent alcohol.

Safeway Lambrusco Bianco
£ / 5 / 🍷   12/20
Decent, appley, sweet and fizzy with less soupy sugariness than
some of its ilk.

MOLDOVA

1993 Hincesti Feteasca
££ / 3 / 🍷   14/20
One of the more successful collaborations between flying
winemaker Hugh Ryman and Australian giant Penfolds. Made from
the native Feteasca grape, this is like rich, grapefruity Sauvignon
Blanc with a rustic edge.

SOUTH AFRICA

1994 Roodezandt Colombard, Robertson
£ / 3 / 🍷   12/20
A neutral, peardroppy, cool-fermented white with a touch of
sweetness and sharpish acidity.

£3–5

AUSTRALIA

1993 Safeway Semillon/Chardonnay, South-East Australia
£ / 3 / 🍷   14/20
Light for Australia, this bespoke Penfolds' blend is a pleasant, toned
down, tropical fruit quaffer. A little pricey perhaps.

1993 Hunter Valley Chardonnay, Rosemount Estates, New South Wales
££ / 3 / 🍷   15/20
Rosemount specialises in rich, ultra-toasty, fudge and tropical fruit

Chardonnays, which have plenty of instant appeal, but can pall after the first glass. This one has more elegance than some, with spicy cinnamon flavours balanced by fresh acidity. Two glasses should do the trick.

ENGLAND

1993 Safeway Stanlake, Thames Valley Vineyards, Berkshire
££ / 2 / 🌓   15/20
A portmanteau blend of nine different grape varieties made by resident Australian winemaker, John Worontschak. It's a well-made and unusual English wine with cassis and tinned pea aromas that transported us to New Zealand's North Island. A fresh, zesty, quince-like white.

FRANCE

1993 La Coume de Peyre, Vin de Pays des Côtes de Gascogne
£ / 3 / 🌓   13/20
A basic, sweetish toffee apple white from Gascony's Plaimont co-operative. Is this style starting to replace Muscadet as yesterday's popular French white?

1993 Vegetarian White Wine, Domaine du Rey, Vin de Pays des Côtes de Gascogne
££ / 2 / 🌓   14/20
The only vegetarian white we know of in a national supermarket. On this context, vegetarian means that no animal products have been used during the processing of the wine (in case you didn't know, some of the wines you drink are clarified with animal blood or fish bladders). This is a blend of Colombard and Ugni Blanc and has more weight and zip than most Gascon whites we've tasted. This should put wings on your sandals.

1993 Château de Plantier, Entre-Deux-Mers
£££ / 2 / 🌓   15/20
A blend of Sauvignon Blanc and Semillon made using something that's known in the business as skin contact. This technique sounds more exciting than it is. It's a way of leaving grape juice in contact with its skins to extract flavour before fermentation. The technique has worked well here on this smooth, well-balanced Bordeaux

white with its grassy aroma and zippy, lemony flavours.

1992 Safeway Blanc de Bordeaux, Aged in Oak, Prodiffu
££ / 2 / ▌   15/20

From the Prodiffu operation, this is one of the better inexpensive oaked Bordeaux around. Most taste coarse and sawdusty, but this is stylish, fresh and grapefruity with restrained oak flavour.

1993 'Les Portailles' Vin de Pays d'Oc, Val d'Orbieu
££ / 2 / ▌   14/20

This is a 'versatile dry white wine', according to the rather baffling label. We're not sure what else you'd use it for, but we suggest drinking this clean, peachy, unoaked white with its pleasant fermentation lees-derived richness for inexpensive enjoyment.

1993 Domaine de Rivoyre Chardonnay, Vin de Pays d'Oc, Hugh Ryman
£££ / 2 / ▌   17/20

The 1992 Ryman Chardonnay was one of our wines of the year, and this elegant southern white with its tropical fruit and nicely judged oak intensity maintains the tradition.

GERMANY

1993 St Ursula/Hugh Ryman Rivaner/Scheurebe, Pfalz
££ / 2 / ▌   14/20

Another Hugh Ryman white, made in hitherto virgin territory for flying winemakers. It's a dry, aromatic, grapefruity blend of Rivaner (a synonym for Müller-Thurgau) and Scheurebe made at the giant St Ursula winery in Bingen.

1993 St Ursula/Hugh Ryman Riesling, Pfalz
££ / 2 / ▌   14/20

More austere than the Rivaner/Scheurebe blend, but this is still a pleasantly perfumed German white with attractive lime-like Riesling character.

HUNGARY

1993 Matra Mountains Chardonnay, Nagyrede
££ / 2 / 1   14/20
Made by Kym Milne and Brian Bicknell, this is a lemon, grapefruit
and toasty oak style Chardonnay with a crisp aftertaste. It shows
how superior Hungary is to its Eastern European competitors at
producing affordable, and drinkable, whites.

1993 River Duna Pinot Gris, Szekszard, Nick Butler
£££ / 2 / 1   15/20
So does this smoky, ripe, full-bodied Pinot Gris, which has unusual
richness, flavour and concentration for a wine at this price. It
reminded us of a cross between an Alsace Gewürztraminer and a
Hungarian Furmint.

1993 Nagyrede Sauvignon Reserve, Kym Milne and Brian Bicknell
££ / 2 / 1   14/20
According to Lancastrian wine supremo Liz Robertson, this wine
has lost a little bit of aroma in translation, but we still enjoyed its
fresh elderflower zing. Heading towards New Zealand in style,
which isn't surprising, given that it was made by Kym Milne,
formerly of Auckland's Villa Maria, and Brian Bicknell.

ITALY

1993 Safeway Chardonnay del Triveneto, GIV
0 / 2 / 1   12/20
One of the few disappointing wines we've had this year from the
Gruppo Italiano Vini, Italy's biggest wine company. Perhaps
Safeway should have employed Sainsbury's contract winemaker
Geoff Merrill to show them how it's done.

1993 Safeway Frascati Superiore Secco
££ / 2 / 1   14/20
We're not surprised that this moreish, dry Frascati is in Safeway's
top ten, even at £3.75. It's a characterful, almondy Roman white
with refreshing acidity.

1993 I Frari, Bianco di Custoza, Santi
£££ / 2 / ▌   15/20
In its chunky designer bottle, this is another very good Italian white.
It's a ripe, fruity, concentrated Bianco di Custoza with flavours of
pear and apricot and a refreshing lemony twist.

1993 Chardonnay del Salento, 'Le Trulle'
££ / 2 / ▌   15/20
A cleverly made southern Italian Chardonnay with plenty of fresh,
peachy fruit, grapefruity acidity and a touch of oak character from
flying Australian winemaker, Kym Milne.

1993 Pinot Grigio, Bidoli, Grave del Friuli
££ / 2 / ▌   14/20
A modern, cool-fermented white made by Arrigo Bidoli and French
winemaker Gaetane Carron during a productive vintage in Italy.

MOLDOVA

1993 Hincesti Premium Chardonnay, Hugh Ryman
0 / 3 / ▌   11/20
We weren't quite sure what a picture of the Kremlin was doing
on the label of this Moldovan Chardonnay. We weren't too sure
about the wine either, with its peculiar sweet and sour balance
and green, tart acidity. If Russia still sent people to Siberia, Hugh
Ryman would be in trouble.

SOUTH AFRICA

1994 Sauvignon Blanc, Vredendal
£ / 2 / ▌   13/20
A decent, pleasantly fruity, warm climate Sauvignon Blanc from
the Western Cape with a rather flat finish.

1994 Van Loveren Colombard/Chardonnay, Robertson
£ / 3 / ▌   13/20
A blend of 75 per cent Colombard and 25 per cent barrel-fermented
Chardonnay from Wynand Retief's Robertson estate, this is fresh
and well-made, but appears to have suffered from high yields in
the vineyard. Rather dilute.

1993 Danie de Wet Chardonnay Sur Lie, Robertson
££ / 2 / ▌   15/20

One of a large number of Chardonnays made in Robertson by white wine specialist, Danie de Wet. This is an unoaked style relying on ageing on its yeast lees for flavour and freshness.

SPAIN

Safeway Castilla de Sierra Rioja
£ / 2 / ▌   13/20

A blend of Viura and Malvasia with a strident yellow label that does it few favours, this is a light, lemony, modern white Rioja, which could do with a bit more flavour.

£5–8

AUSTRALIA

1989 Arrowfield Reserve Semillon, Hunter Valley
££ / 2 / ▌   15/20

A toasty Hunter Valley Semillon which gets much of its character and flavour from ageing in American oak rather than in bottle. It's a big, rich, luscious style with some barley sugar sweetness and plenty of fruit.

1993 Evans & Tate Two Vineyards Chardonnay, Western Australia
££ / 2 / ▬   15/20

So-called because the Chardonnay is blended from two separate vineyards; this is a full-bodied, oaky, Western Australian white, in which the two parts haven't quite yet come together. With a bit more time, they may do so.

AUSTRIA

1991 Seewinkler Impressionen Ausbruch, Neusiedlersee, half-bottle
£££ / 8 / ▬   17/20

Ausbruch is an Austrian speciality, somewhere between a sweet Beerenauslese and even richer Trockenbeerenauslese in style, and relying on shrivelled grapes for much of its character. Rich, peachy, honeycomb and raisin flavours with enough zip and acidity to stop it from cloying. Delicious stuff, but only to be found in Safeway's top 30 stores.

ENGLAND

1992 Thames Valley Vineyards Fumé
££ / 2 / 1   16/20
A daring, barrel-fermented English white made by Australian winemaker John Worontschak. It takes a bit of pluck to sell an English table wine at nearly £8 a bottle but, believe it or not, this toasty, elegant, almost Graves-style white blend is worth the money. Apart from the giveaway acidity, it could almost be French.

SPAIN

1991 Viñas del Vero Chardonnay, Barrel-Fermented, Somontano
££ / 2 / 1   15/20
Ripe, deeply coloured, butterscotch fudge and toast-like Chardonnay from a small Spanish *denominación* in Aragón's province of Huesca in northern Spain. A good attempt at a white Burgundy style. Again, though, only in limited distribution.

Red

Under £3

BULGARIA

1993 Safeway Young Vatted Merlot, Russe
££ / MB / 1   14/20
This is the second vintage of Safeway's mould-breaking Bulgarian red, with the emphasis on youthful fruit flavours rather than the more traditional oak-aged character. This is a deeply coloured, chocolatey red with a stalky undertone. Drink this in preference to the more austere Young Vatted Cabernet Sauvignon.

1991 Safeway Cabernet Sauvignon, Svischtov
0 / MB / 🍷   12/20
The palm trees label may hint at a Caribbean connection, but we
found this dry, raisiny Bulgarian red was closer to Romanian plonk
in style. Inexplicably, this features in the Safeway top ten. Could
it be something to do with the price?

FRANCE

Safeway Corbières
0 / FB / 🍷   11/20
This is what sometimes happens when you force the price of
Corbières under £3. You get a coarse, acid, old-fashioned, rooty
red.

1993 Safeway Côtes du Rhône
£ / MB / 🍷   13/20
Soft, soupy red from the Vaucluse department with a twist of
pepper and a rasp of rustic tannin. Drinkable at the price.

1993 Safeway Côtes du Ventoux, Mark Robertson
£ / MB / 🍷   13/20
Juicy, robust Provençal red made using the carbonic maceration
technique by flying winemaker Mark Robertson. There's a hint of
raisin and cinnamon, but not an inordinate amount of finesse
here.

HUNGARY

1993 Safeway Hungarian Country Wine, Kiskoros
££ / LB / 🍷   13/20
A light, fruity, peppery local Hungarian red made entirely from
the Kekfrankos grape in the carbonic maceration style by Agi
Dezsenyi, one of Hungary's few women winemakers.

1993 Safeway Hungarian Merlot, Szolo-Bor, Villány
£££ / MB / 🍷   16/20
Apparently Safeway pays good money to the designers of the truly
ghastly Jane Austen meets Brides of Dracula label adorning this
red. It's a soft, finely-textured Merlot with blackberry fruit and a
hint of pepper, which deserves better. Just as it's doing with its

whites, Hungary appears to be outpacing its neighbours on the red side too with wines like this.

ITALY

Safeway Sicilian Red
££ / MB / ▮   13/20
A dry, savoury, Mediterranean red from Vinicola Calatrasi.

1993 Tenuta Generale Cialdini, Lambrusco Secco
££ / MB / ▮   14/20
Unlike most of the Lambruscos on sale in Britain, this wine is red and dry rather than white and sweet. Frothy, cherried red with good fresh acidity and lots of character.

1993 Country Cellars Puglian Red, Vino da Tavola
£ / MB / ▮   13/20
A spicy, fruity, sweetish blend of Negroamaro, Malvasia Nera and Sangiovese from Puglia's Salento peninsula made at a family-owned winery by Australian Kym Milne.

PORTUGAL

1993 Safeway Ribatejo
££ / FB / ▮   13/20
Young vatted Ribatejo with chunky, plummy fruit flavours and a touch of mint and sweetness made by Portuguese oenologist João Ramos.

ROMANIA

1989 Safeway Romanian Pinot Noir, Dealul Mare, Nicolae Dumitru
££ / MB / ▮   14/20
Nicolae Dumitru, who's been making the wines at Dealul Mare for 40-odd years, seems to produce most of the Romanian wines we see in this country. Like many a Dumitru red, this one has a certain old-fashioned charm typified by the ox-drawn grape-cart on the label. A soft, sweetly rustic red which actually manages to taste of Pinot Noir – more than you can say for most sub-£5 red Burgundies. A top ten best seller at Safeway.

£3–5

AUSTRALIA

1992 De Bortoli Shiraz/Cabernet, New South Wales
££ / MB / ▌   14/20

A full, spicy Australian red blend from white wine specialists, De Bortoli, with upfront, berry fruit flavours and firm, warm climate tannins.

1992 Wildflower Ridge Shiraz, Western Australia
£££ / FB / ▬▸   16/20

One of a number of highly enjoyable wines we've had this year from the Houghton winery in Western Australia's Swan Valley. An interesting blend of mainly Shiraz with a touch of Malbec, aged for 15 months in oak. It's packed with vanilla oak, mint and sweet blackberry fruit, and nicely balanced by refreshing acidity.

BULGARIA

1987 Cabernet Sauvignon Reserve, Sliven
0 / MB / ▌   11/20

Even in Bulgaria, they don't make wines like this tannic, charmless red any more. And thank goodness for that.

1990 Vinenka Merlot/Gamza Reserve, Suhindol
0 / MB / ▌   12/20

Like an Eastern European Don Darias, this charry, rustic red is said to be aged in small American oak barrels. Arise, Don Vladimar.

FRANCE

1993 Château La Fôret, Bordeaux
£ / MB / ▌   13/20

More like a *négociant* wine than a Bordeaux château, this is a young, grassy claret with a dry finish.

1992 Vegetarian Red Wine, Oak-Aged Claret, Bordeaux Supérieur
££ / MB / ▌   14/20

Like its Vegetarian white counterpart, this is an interesting innovation at Safeway. It's a chunky, characterful claret with sweet oak and a chewy, texture for added roughage. Warning: not for vegans because the wine was clarified with egg whites.

1992 Médoc, Oak-aged
££ / MB / 🍷 14/20

A chunky, coconut oak-style claret from the *négociant* Ginestet, which appears to fill a pipeline to Britain's luncheon claret drinkers. Well made, if a little chewy.

1992 St Emilion, Gabriel Corcol
£ / MB / 🍷 14/20

Better than the rather fruitless 1990, this is another Ginestet claret, only this time we've crossed the Dordogne River to St Emilion and Merlot country. A soft, chocolatey red with a dry finish.

Safeway Côtes du Roussillon Villages
£ / MB / 🍷 13/20

A light, Beaujoloid quaffer from Les Vignerons Catalans, one of the largest producers in the Roussillon region. Pleasantly spicy, if unexciting.

1992 Château de Belesta, Côtes du Roussillon Villages
£££ / MB / 🍷 16/20

Surprisingly perhaps, this comes from the same producer. It's an equal blend of Syrah, Grenache and Carignan with intensely peppery aromas, vibrant young fruit and an elegance rarely found on cheap Roussillon reds. More like a Crozes-Hermitage or St Joseph than a Roussillon.

1992 Domaine Grange du Pin, Coteaux de Languedoc
££ / MB / 🍷 15/20

For a carbonic maceration red, this has a fair whack of robust southern fruit and tannin. We detected the animal presence of the Syrah grape and some of the herb and spice of the Mediterranean garrigue.

1991 Abbaye de Tholomies, Minervois
£ / MB / 🍷 13/20

A tannic, dry blend of Grenache and Syrah, showing slightly more charm than it did last year, but we still found it rather too firm and chewy for our liking.

1993 Fortant de France Cabernet Sauvignon, Vin de Pays d'Oc
£ / MB / 🍷   13/20

From a company which has pioneered international grape varieties in the Languedoc, this is a young, rather raw Cabernet with liquoricey, dry flavours.

HUNGARY

1993 Private Reserve Cabernet Sauvignon, Villány
££ / FB / 🍷   14/20

Aged in Hungarian oak, this is a juicy, modern Cabernet made by flying winemaker Nick Butler in a style which combines fruit sweetness with robust tannins.

1993 Great Plain Kekfrankos, Kiskunfelegyhaza
££ / MB / 🍷   14/20

Another Hungarian red which isn't short of gutsy tannins. Made from one of Eastern Europe's most interesting native grapes, this is a peppery, fresh Kekfrankos which reminded us of a Tuscan red. Needs food, but not necessarily goulash.

ITALY

1993 Safeway Chianti
£ / MB / 🍷   13/20

Decent, basic Chianti with dry tannins and some soupy sweetness.

Merlot/Cabernet Sauvignon, Vino da Tavola delle Tre Venezie
££ / MB / 🍷   15/20

A non-vintage, Veneto red from the GIV group, attempting to undercut the supertuscans with a well-priced, cool climate Bordeaux-style blend, showing good supple, blackcurrant fruit and nicely balanced tannins.

1992 Safeway Chianti Classico, Rocca della Macie
££ / MB / 🍷   15/20

Made by the reliable firm of Rocca della Macie, a winery owned by an Italian film producer, this is a good aromatic Sangiovese-based red with plenty of savoury, Tuscan character and an attractive almondy bite.

1990 Salice Salentino Riserva, Apulia
£££ / FB / 🍷 16/20

A rich, chocolatey southern Italian blend with aromatic angostura and thyme spiciness and mature, leathery Mediterranean fruit. Robust stuff, not to be undertaken without a corkscrew and mallet in hand.

1993 Tenuta San Vito, Chianti Putto (Organic)
£ / MB / 🍷 14/20

One of a baker's dozen of organic wines on Safeway's list, this is a youthful, but fairly barnyardy, Chianti with cherried fruitiness and fresh acidity.

PORTUGAL

1992 Quinta do Vale da Raposa, Douro
££ / FB / 👄 15/20

A red Douro Valley blend of the Port grapes, Tinto Roriz, Touriga Nacional and Touriga Francesa, this is a fruit-steered, modern red with the tannin you'd expect from such a warm region, but a fair amount of finesse and strawberry and plum fruit to match.

1990 Duque de Viseu, Dão
££ / FB / 👄 16/20

An even more obscure blend of Portuguese red grapes. This time the suspects are Touriga Nacional, Jaen, Alfrocheiro Preto and Tinta Pinheira. With grapes like these, we hope Portugal doesn't go down the international varietal route. And there isn't much chance while it's producing fine, modern reds, with a sheen of new oak, like this one. The acceptable modern face of Dão.

1990 Tinto da Anfora, Alentejo, J.P. Vinhos
£ / FB / 🍷 14/20

Australian Peter Bright may have moved on to international, jet-setting consultancy, but one of the wines he helped to create lives on. It's an old-fashioned contrast to the Duque de Viseu, with its game and eucalyptus aromas, soft strawberry fruit and dry aftertaste. Time to drink up.

SOUTH AFRICA

Kleindal Pinotage, Vinimark, Robertson
££ / FB / ❶   14/20

Pinotage is South Africa's main claim to an indigenous wine style. This is a sweet, ripe, alcoholic Cape red reflecting its warm climate origins in the Robertson region and showing masses of soft, baked-banana and raspberry fruitness. If this sounds off-putting, it shouldn't do.

SPAIN

1993 Young Vatted Tempranillo, La Mancha
££ / MB / ❶   14/20

Inspired by the success of the young vatted styles produced in Bulgaria, Sainsbury's did the same thing in Rioja, another region which has traditionally preferred to soften its wines with lengthy spells in old oak. The result is a vibrant, crunchy, strawberryish red with refreshing acidity.

Safeway Castilla de Sierra, Rioja Crianza
££ / MB / ❶   14/20

This is a more solid, four-square, old-fashioned Rioja, showing the oak flavours for which the region is famous. At the cheaper end, we generally prefer the unoaked wines.

1992 Tempranillo Oak-Aged, Rioja Berberana
£££ / MB / ❶   16/20

A wine which combines the best of traditional and modern-style Rioja. It's got the savoury, oak sweetness of the former and the intense, all-Tempranillo fruit of the latter. This adds up to a soft, attractively balanced red with lots of strawberry fruit and vanilla complexity.

£5–8

AUSTRALIA

1992 Hardy's Barossa Valley Shiraz
££ / FB / ☛   15/20

A substantial Barossa mouthful, which gets you by the short and curlies with its massively oaked, blackberry fruitiness and thick, robust flavours. Put it under the stairs or chain it to the wall.

1992 Hardy's Barossa Valley Cabernet Sauvignon
£££ / MB / ⌐-   16/20
From the same producer and the same region, this is even better: a Cabernet Sauvignon which has softened and settled down faster than its Shiraz stablemate. There's still plenty of robust, sweet fruit and coffee-bean oak, but there's a bit of elegance too. Don't tell the boys in Nuriootpa.

1989 Wynns Cabernet/Shiraz, Coonawarra
£££ / FB / ⌐-   16/20
A Coonawarra blend which is just beginning to show its class. A red wine made by Wynns' Peter Douglas with elegance and refreshing zip wrapped in voluptuously ripe blackcurrant and blackberry fruit flavours.

FRANCE

1990 Margaux, Barton & Guestier
£ / MB / ⌐   15/20
This claret from one of the Médoc's four top communes has the stylish bouquet you'd expect from a Margaux with some of the class of the vintage, although the oak is rather obtrusive at the moment.

1989 St Julien, Barton & Guestier
££ / MB / ⌐-   16/20
Also still a little on the oaky side, the St Julien nevertheless sneaks in front of the Margaux for its concentrated richness, voluptuously velvety texture and an intensity of fruit and balance which suggest a longer life ahead.

1988 Château Laroche Viella, Madiran
£ / FB / ⌐   15/20
This Madiran from the Plaimont co-operative looks like an expensive claret. Even though it's made from Tannat, Pinenc and Cabernet Sauvignon, it tastes rather like one too. Last year we felt that there was too much flashy new oak for the wine to cope with. Twelve months later, we think we've been

vindicated, as the wine's beginning to dry out.

1991 La Cuvée Mythique, Vin de Pays d'Oc
£££ / FB / ━   16/20

A blend of five southern French varieties from the go-ahead Val
d'Orbieu co-operative, this remarkable wine, with its smart ochre
label, looks more expensive than it is, even though it's crept just
over £5 since last year. Mourvèdre, Syrah, Carignan, Grenache
and Cabernet Sauvignon combine to produce one of southern
France's finest reds. Oaky, herby and packed with spicy flavours
of mint, angostura bitters and leather.

ITALY

1990 'Salvanza' Sangiovese di Toscana, Barrique-Aged, Vino da Tavola, Piccini
££ / FB / ━   15/20

Chewy, tannic, but well-made supertuscan red made entirely from
the Sangiovese grape. As the style demands, there's a lot of new
oak on show, but in this case the cherry, almondy fruit copes
well.

1988 Barolo, Terre del Barolo
££ / FB / ━   15/20

At just over £6.50, this Barolo from the local co-operative is pretty
good value for money. It's not one of the great Piedmontese reds,
but if it were, you'd be paying through the nose rather than sniffing
through it. A rich, dry, savoury Nebbiolo with a core of sweet
fruit and firm tannins.

PORTUGAL

1991 Quinta de Pancas, Vinho Regional Estremadura, Alenquer
£££ / FB / ━   16/20

A highly modern and highly appealing blend of 80 per cent
Cabernet Sauvignon with 20 per cent of the native Periquita. With
a veneer of silky, vanilla oak, this is a ripe, beautifully made red
with concentrated flavours of cassis and mulberry fruit. One of
Portugal's most exciting reds.

SOUTH AFRICA

1992 Kanonkop Kadette

££ / FB / ►   15/20

From Pinotage specialist, Beyers Truter, this is a well-priced blend of South Africa's indigenous grape with an almost equal proportion of the international Cabernet Sauvignon. Deeply coloured and oaky, it's a rich, fruity red with the concentration to age. We wouldn't say the two grapes are made for each other, but they do seem to have more than a little in common. Is this the first supercape red?

SPAIN

1987 Señorio de Nava, Ribera del Duero

£££ / FB / ►   16/20

Spain's most famous red wine, Vega Sicilia, comes from the Ribera del Duero region north of Madrid. This aged Tinto Fino (Tempranillo) has something of the same character, with lots of colour, sweet vanilla oak and seriously chunky blackberry fruit. Now into its stride and, apparently, getting younger.

Sparkling

£5–8

AUSTRALIA

Safeway Australian Brut, Seppelt

££ / 3 / ▌   14/20

Frothy, ripe Australian fizz with some tropical fruit sweetness and fresh acidity. Good at the price.

ENGLAND

Heritage Brut

££ / 2 / ▌   16/20

Made by English-based Australian, John Worontschak, this is one of the few drinkable sparkling wines made in England. Elegant and dry with Champagne-like toastiness and bottle-age. Surprise your Glyndebourne friends with this one.

Over £8

FRANCE

Lionel Derens Brut Champagne
0 / 3 / ◗   12/20
A coarse, sweetened-up, cider apple-like Champagne, which must sell on its £9 price rather than its quality. Otherwise we can't see why it's in Safeway's top ten best sellers.

Champagne Albert Etienne NV Brut
££ / 2 / ◗   15/20
An enjoyable, if young, basic Champagne, with pleasantly fruity Pinot character and a crisp aftertaste.

Champagne Albert Etienne Brut Rosé
£££ / 1 / ◗   17/20
With its attractive onion-skin colour, this is an elegantly dry rosé Champagne with delicate red fruit flavours and considerable finesse. When Champagne comes up with this sort of quality at around £13, it's hard to beat.

1988 Albert Etienne Brut Vintage
££ / 2 / ➛   15/20
A rich, young, vintage Champagne, with lots of fruit and flavour, but still rather tight on the finish.

Fortified

£3–5

SPAIN

Lustau Old Dry Oloroso, half-bottle
£££ / 1 / ▌   17/20
Oloroso Sherry doesn't get much better than this dry, tangy
example. Bronze-tawny in colour, it has a complex bouquet
of grilled almonds, orange peel and burnt toffee. If you
stopped drinking Sherry – or never started for that matter –
this should turn you on to one of the world's great fortified
wine regions.

£5–8

PORTUGAL

Safeway Vintage Character Port
££ / FB / ▌   16/20
From the Portuguese-owned house of Calem, this is a rich, strong,
fruit-cakey Port with sweet, intense fruit and good balance. For
once with an inexpensive Port, the fortifying spirit doesn't hit
you like a flamethrower.

Over £8

SPAIN

The Cream of Cream, Pedro Ximenez, Argueso
£££ / 9 / ▌   16/20
Not, as its name suggests, a deluxe version of Harvey's Bristol Cream.
Instead, this is one of the sweetest wines we've ever tasted. A black,
treacly, prune and raisin-like Sherry made from super-concentrated
Pedro Ximenez grapes, affectionately known as PX. One of the few
wines that actually works with chocolate and ice cream.

SAINSBURY'S ****(*)

Head Office: Stamford House, Stamford Street, London, SE1 9LL

Telephone: 071 921 6000

Number of branches: 360

Credit cards accepted: Visa, Access, Switch, American Express

Hours of opening: Branch specific. Regular late night opening

By-the-case-sales: Not in stores, but case offers made through Sainsbury's magazine

Glass loan: No

Home delivery: Through Sainsbury's magazine only

Clubs: No

Discounts: Multibuy offers, special offers, special purchases

In-store tastings: Yes, on an ad hoc basis

Top ten best-selling wines: Sainsbury's Muscadet de Sèvre-et-Maine; Sainsbury's Niersteiner Gutes Domtal; Sainsbury's Hock; Sainsbury's Liebfraumilch; Sainsbury's Lambrusco Bianco; Sainsbury's Claret; Sainsbury's Vin Rouge de France; Sainsbury's Valencia Oak Aged; Sainsbury's Bulgarian Country Red; 1988 Bulgarian Reserve Cabernet Sauvignon Lovico Suhindol Region

Range: GOOD: Bordeaux, Burgundy, Loire, Rhône, Australia, Languedoc-Roussillon, Germany, Eastern Europe, Italy, Portugal
AVERAGE: Beaujolais, Champagne and sparkling wine, Spain, New Zealand, South Africa
POOR: Alsace, California

Senior manager Simon Blower might have moved across to garden gnome and power drill land at Sainsbury's Homebase, but the wine department he helped to revitalise continues to be one of the most dynamic in the country. With no fewer than six different buyers and a support team than would keep the Paris–Dakar race on the road, Sainsbury's is obviously determined to keep its nose ahead of competitors Tesco, Asda and Waitrose.

Blower's was not the only departure in 1994. The wine department also lost Jon Woodriffe, one of the best young buyers in the country, to Thresher. On the plus side, Master of Wine Claire Gordon-Brown returned from absence, Gerard Barnes arrived from Cellar 5, and the buyers continued to list new wines at a palate-boggling rate.

At 450 wines, Sainsbury's range is not the largest supermarket line-up, but on current form it's the best. Three years ago, dullness and conservative buying had set in, but these days you're never short of interesting bottles at Sainsbury's.

Highlights of 1994 have included joint venture and flying winemaker projects with Australians Geoff Merrill, Peter Bright and Kym Milne, more listings from southern France and Australia, and some generally well-judged forays into the traditional heartland of Bordeaux and Burgundy.

This adds up to more than 120 new wines and nearly as many delistings. In some cases, it was a question of dead wood colliding with the departmental buzz-saw – we were particularly glad to see the demise of Sainsbury's Borba – but the turnover is largely down to buying 'new and exciting wines', according to senior buyer Mark Kermode. 'The crucial thing is to keep our momentum going.'

Sainsbury's has developed much closer relationships with its suppliers in the last couple of years. 'We used to buy wines off the peg,' says Kermode, 'but now we're looking much further ahead.' This involves developing partnerships between winemakers and various wineries, something which has been particularly successful in the case of Geoff Merrill and the Gruppo Italiano Vini.

The number of flying winemaker wines at Sainsbury's – currently hovering around the 40 mark – has resulted in a certain amount of criticism. Isn't this all a bit formulaic? Kermode disagrees. 'We do have certain wines that are sold specifically as flying winemaker wines, but we don't think the flying winemaker route is the only route. Our major drive is to improve the quality of our own-label wines and to work with local grape varieties wherever possible. Consumers don't really notice names like Geoff Merrill, Kym Milne or Peter Bright on the label. They're just interested in the stuff in the bottle.'

Fair enough. The excellent Peter Bright Torrontes was delisted this year because of poor sales, but this hasn't put Sainsbury's off the weird and wacky. The new Merrill wines include a Teroldego and a Grechetto – hardly grape varieties with mass appeal – and the Kym Milne Chapel Hill Irsai Oliver is almost certainly a new one on most consumers.

French, German and Italian wines still dominate sales, but Sainsbury's is keen to have as wide a range of countries as possible represented on its shelves. According to Kermode, research shows that 'experimentalists are more interested in country of origin than they are in grape varieties like Cabernet Sauvignon and Chardonnay'. Hence the appearance of bottles from Argentina, Uruguay, Moldova and the Czech Republic. 'Even if people aren't sure where the countries are,' he adds, 'they like to try their wines.' Let's hope no one's after interesting things from California.

But unusual wines are never going to be big sellers. One of the most impressive things about Sainsbury's is that its basic lines – the Hocks, clarets, Niersteiners and the vins de tables – are well-chosen in the main.

These delights notwithstanding, the big growth areas at Sainsbury's are Australia, South Africa, Spain and Eastern Europe. Germany, Italy, and France, on the other hand, have slipped. Alsace, table wines and the Rhône Valley have been the losers in France, while Lambrusco has taken a nose dive in Italy. Kermode feels that the 'underlying trend' is strong in both countries, however. There's certainly plenty of good stuff from GIV in Italy and the Languedoc-Roussillon in the South of France.

Not all of these wines have made it across the Channel to Sainsbury's slightly half-hearted attempt to join the Calais market. Sainsbury's Vins, Bières et Spiritueux (reviewed on page 518–19) lists some of the more interesting fare, but so far it has concentrated on big volume wines. We'd like to see a more daring approach to cross-Channel shopping.

Back on the British shop floor, Sainsbury's has nearly finished phasing out its Vintage Selection racks, in favour of 'wooden display boxes'; the finer wines are now known as Selected Vintage, believe it or not. The chain has also put a lot of work into point-of-sale material and a new cream and green look to make the department stand out from the rest of the store. Own-label branding has also been toned down to a blue strip on the bottom of the label.

In-store advisers, the last supermarket trend, have benefited from all-day training courses and are given tapes to listen to at home. They also receive a weekly bulletin with details of new lines and any supply problems.

Home delivery has not been developed as keenly as it has at Waitrose, but Sainsbury's does offer a monthly case, selected by the *Guardian*'s wine correspondent, through its magazine. 'We did a trial for home delivery two years ago,' says Kermode, 'and it didn't really take off. But people are beginning to trade up and Wine Direct reflects that.'

Trading up there may be, but, like its competitors, Sainsbury's has felt it necessary to offer regular £1.99 deals in 1994 to keep the customers satisfied. Nevertheless, Kermode says that price fighting is not as important as it was a year ago. 'The battle used to be all about price, but now it's changing. Quality, value and range are what people want now.' If he's right, Sainsbury's is in a position to provide all three.

NB Wines marked with an asterisk (*) are also available at Sainsbury's Vins, Bières et Spiritueux in Calais (see page 518-19).

White

Under £3

BULGARIA

Sainsbury's Bulgarian Chardonnay, Lyaskovets, Kym Milne
££ / 2 /   15/20
At last! A Bulgarian Chardonnay that actually tastes of the grape variety from which it was made. Clean, fruity, lemony stuff with some welcome weight. May this be the first of many.

CZECH REPUBLIC

1993 Sainsbury's Moravian Grüner Veltliner, Czech Republic, Nick Butler
££ / 3 /   14/20
Showing the peppery, green bean aromatics of one of Central

Europe's most distinctive grape varieties. The fruit is on the lean side and relies on cosmetic sweetness for balance.

FRANCE

*Sainsbury's Muscadet de Sèvre-et-Maine, Vignerons de Noëlle
£ / 2 / ◗   13/20
Pleasant, reliable Muscadet at under £3, with good fresh fruit.

Sainsbury's Bordeaux Sauvignon Blanc
££ / 2 / ◗   14/20
It's encouraging to come across affordable white Bordeaux as fresh and zesty as this. Thirst-quenching, grapefruity Sauvignon Blanc, which was left in contact with its skins for extra aroma.

GERMANY

Sainsbury's Niersteiner Gutes Domtal
££ / 4 / ◗   14/20
It's worth trading up a little bit from the likes of Hock and Liebfraumilch to get your hands on a bottle of this commendably fresh, grapey white. A little drier than most commercial German quaffers – and no bad thing.

*Sainsbury's Hock
£ / 5 / ◗   13/20
Sweeter than the Niersteiner, but still drinkable. Clean, floral stuff showing a touch of Müller-Thurgau grapefruit.

*Sainsbury's Liebfraumilch
£ / 6 / ◗   12/20
Sugary aromas and sugary flavours.

HUNGARY

*Sainsbury's Hungarian Country White, Balaton Boglar, Kym Milne
£ / 2 / ◗   13/20
A 50/50 blend of Müller-Thurgau and Királyleányka grapes, made in an appealingly floral style by airborne Australian Kym Milne.

Sainsbury's Hungarian Pinot Gris, Minosegi Bor, Nagyrede Region, Kym Milne

0 / 3 / ▋   11/20

Fat, confected white made from undistinguished raw material. A sow's purse, if ever we tasted one.

1993 Chapel Hill Irsai Oliver, Balaton Boglar, Kym Milne

££ / 2 / ▋   14/20

Nothing to do with the distinguished Australian winery of the same name, Chapel Hill is a clever brand name for Kym Milne's Hungarian wines. A light, fresh halfway house between Alsace Gewürztraminer and an Eastern European Muscat, showing typical lychee flavours and fragrance.

1993 Chapel Hill Sauvignon Blanc, Balaton Boglar, Kym Milne

££ / 2 / ▋   14/20

A winemaker who used to make some of the best whites in New Zealand ought to be good at Sauvignon Blanc. He is.

1993 Chapel Hill Oaked Chardonnay, Balaton Boglar, Kym Milne

££ / 3 / ▋   15/20

Sweeter than the other Chapel Hill whites, but still showing plenty of fresh, peachy fruit and a touch of New World smoky oak.

ITALY

*Sainsbury's Lambrusco Bianco

£ / 6 / ▋   13/20

Beery, frothy, sweet Italian white with a lime-like twist. A shandy-lover's dream.

*Sainsbury's Sicilian White, Settesoli

££ / 2 / ▋   14/20

An equal blend of Catarratto and Trebbiano, this is a well-made, Mediterranean white with soft, nutty, pine needle characters from the Settesoli co-operative.

PORTUGAL

*Sainsbury's Do Campo Branco, VR Terras do Sado, Peter Bright

£££ / 2 / 🍾   15/20

Made from 90 per cent Fernão Pires and 10 per cent Rabo de Ovelha grapes, this is a characterful, lemony white made by adopted Australian Peter Bright. About as good as inexpensive Portuguese whites get.

SPAIN

*Sainsbury's Vino de la Tierra Blanco, Extremadura, Peter Bright

0 / 3 / 🍾   12/20

Sweetish, baked white from western Spain. Not one of Peter's brightest.

£3–5

AUSTRALIA

1993 Peter Lehmann Semillon, McLaren Vale, South Australia

££ / 2 / 🍾   15/20

From one of the Barossa Valley's most engaging figures, this is a classic Semillon, showing waxy, ripe, lemony flavours and toasty aromas.

*1993 Mount Hurtle Sauvignon Blanc, McLaren Vale, Geoff Merrill

££ / 2 / 🍾   15/20

Mount Hurtle is Geoff Merrill's home base, or should that be eyrie? It's unusual to come across a Sauvignon Blanc in the warm McLaren Vale, especially one as good as this tinned pea and tropical fruit number.

1993 Lily Farm Vineyard Muscat, Grant Burge, Barossa Valley, South Australia

££ / 3 / 🍾   15/20

Zesty, lemon peel white with perceptible sweetness and lots of flavour, reminiscent of the popular Portuguese João Pires Muscat.

CHILE

*1993 Sainsbury's Chilean Sauvignon Blanc, Maipo Valley
0 / 2 / ▮   12/20
Overclean, overcropped and over here. Did someone forget to add the Sauvignon Blanc?

ENGLAND

Trinity, Wootton, Somerset
££ / 2 / ▮   14/20
A West of England blend of three grape varieties from three different counties. Müller-Thurgau, Schönburger and Bacchus in the first instance, Somerset, Devon and Dorset in the second. A pleasant clove and sweet pea fragrance makes this an appealing hedgerow white. At under £4, one of the best-value English wines on the market.

FRANCE

1993 Château les Bouhets, Bordeaux Blanc Sec
££ / 2 / ▮   15/20
Produced by a young winemaker Christophe Olivier, this is a balanced, refreshingly grapefruity white Bordeaux with good concentrated fruit and weight for the price.

1993 Château L'Ortolan, Entre-Deux-Mers, Hugh Ryman
££ / 2 / ▮   15/20
From you-know-Hugh, this is more of a New World style than the Château Les Bouhets made entirely from the Semillon grape. A crisp, fruity, new wave Entre-Deux-Mers.

1993 Séléction Peter Sichel, Bordeaux, Oak-Aged White
0 / 2 / ▮   11/20
A ham-fisted attempt to produce a modern style, with bungled oak-fermentation and bitter fruit. Back to the drawing board.

1993 Sancerre, Les Celliers de Cérès
££ / 1 / 🗲   14/20

From the improving co-operative in Sancerre, a good value eastern Loire dry white with the crisp, grassy fragrance of the Sauvignon Blanc grape. On the light side for Sancerre, but you don't find that many under £5.

1993 Chardonnay, James Herrick, Vin de Pays d'Oc
££ / 1 / 🗲   15/20

The second vintage from Englishman James Herrick's impressive New World style vineyards near Narbonne. This is more elegant and restrained than the 1992, with deftly handled oak and a lime-like streak of acidity.

1993 Chardonnay Vin de Pays d'Oc, Hugh Ryman
£££ / 2 / 🗲   17/20

The 1992 Ryman Chardonnay was one of our wines of the year in 1994, and this elegant southern white with its tropical fruit and nicely judged oak intensity maintains the tradition.

*Sainsbury's White Burgundy, Antonin Rodet
££ / 2 / 🗲   15/20

A new Sainsbury's own-label blend from Côte Chalonnaise merchant Antonin Rodet. And a very successful one too, with spicy fruit intensity and a light touch of oak.

HUNGARY

1993 Chapel Hill Chardonnay, Balaton Boglar, Barrique-Fermented, Kym Milne
££ / 2 / 🗲   15/20

Among the most flavoursome white wines to have emerged from the former Eastern bloc. A well-crafted, oak-fermented Chardonnay with good underlying citrus fruitiness.

ITALY

*Sainsbury's Orvieto Classico, Geoff Merrill
££ / 2 / 🗲   15/20

Proof that Australian winemakers don't only make Australian styles of wine, this is a characterfully herby, classic blend of five local grapes.

Sainsbury's Grechetto dell'Umbria, Geoff Merrill
££ / 2 / ▋   15/20

Another successful joint venture between Geoff Merrill and Italian wine giant, Gruppo Italiano Vini. Tannic bite, refreshing spritz and some richness of fruit make this a stylish Grechetto.

*1993 Sainsbury's Frascati Secco Superiore, Geoff Merrill
£££ / 1 / ▋   16/20

A distinctive blend of Malvasia del Lazio and Malvasia di Candia with 50 per cent Trebbiano for ballast. This weighty, rich, Roman white with its spicy stem ginger character almost restores your faith in Frascati.

1993 Bianco di Custoza, GIV, Geoff Merrill
£££ / 2 / ▋   16/20

Geoff Merrill has taken up where master blender Angela Muir left off last year to produce a superfresh, zippy, pear and ripe peach white from the shores of Lake Garda.

*Sainsbury's Chardonnay delle Tre Venezie, Geoff Merrill
££ / 2 / ▋   15/20

The most Australian of the wines Geoff Merrill made during his Italian *dolce far niente*. Buttery, sweet fruit and savoury oak make this a pleasure to drink. Come back next year, Geoff.

PORTUGAL

1993 Bright Brothers, Trincadeira das Pratas, Ribatejo
££ / 2 / ▋   14/20

The Costa del Sol label may be horrendous, but the wine is a revelation for Portugal. Made from the native Trincadeira grape, this is a full, fat dry white kept fresh by good acidity.

1993 Bright Brothers, Chardonnay, Ribatejo
££ / 2 / ▋   15/20

At João Pires, Peter Bright was the first man in Portugal to make world-class Chardonnay. His experience with the grape shines through in this nutty, rich white with its appealing Portuguese tang.

SOUTH AFRICA

1993 Vergelegen Chardonnay, Coastal Region
££ / 2 / ⟩   15/20
Like a spaceship built into the mountainside, Anglo-American
owned Vergelegen is one of South Africa's showpiece wineries.
This is the second release from an estate with enormous potential
and massive financial backing. Winemaker Martin Meinert has come
up with an elegantly oaked, citrus fruit Chardonnay, hinting at
spectacular things to come.

*1993 Danie de Wet Grey Label Chardonnay, Robertson
£££ / 2 / ⟩   17/20
**The bear-like Danie de Wet was one of our star winemakers
last year, and he's done it again in 1995. Trained at
Geisenheim in Germany, he has become South Africa's
leading Chardonnay specialist, making subtle, understated
wines of freshness, elegance and, above all, excellent value
for money. Partially barrel-fermented, this is a citrus and
vanilla-scented stunner with beautiful balance and intensity
of flavour.**

SPAIN

*1993 Sauvignon Blanc, Rueda, Hermanos Lurton
££ / 2 / ⟩   15/20
Another cat's pee special from Jacques Lurton's Spanish operation.
This is grassy, grapefruity, easy-drinking in the New Zealand
Sauvignon Blanc mould. Very upfront, and almost OTT.

1993 Sainsbury's Navarra, Viura/Chardonnay, Barrel-fermented
£ / 2 / ⟩   13/20
A bit of a disappointment after the high promise of last year's
release. The strong oak character of the 1992 is again in evidence,
but this time the fruit appears to have done a runner.

£5-8

AUSTRALIA

1993 Richmond Grove Cowra Verdelho
£££ / 3 / ❧   16/20
Surfing Australia's exciting new wave, an unusual Australian white
from the Cowra district of New South Wales with tropical
sweetness and a touch of smoky oak balanced by fresh acidity.

1993 The Rothbury Estate Cowra Vineyard Chardonnay, New South Wales
££ / 2 / ❧   15/20
Further evidence of a welcome lightness of touch at one of the
Hunter Valley's most esteemed wineries. Restrained melon fruit
and spicy oak with plenty of acidity and zip.

1993 Yarra Ridge Chardonnay, South-East Australia
££ / 2 / ❧   16/20
A French style Chardonnay showing barrel-fermentation and
buttery malolactic characters. The wine's cool climate origins are
apparent in its refreshing and restrained fruitiness.

CHILE

1992 Casablanca Valley Chardonnay, Santa Isabel Estate
££ / 2 / ❧   16/20
Proof that Ignacio Recabarren is now established as the best white
winemaker in Chile. A cool climate, barrel-fermented number,
showing richness and intensity on the palate, and a faintly
Sauvignon Blanc-like aroma.

FRANCE

1992 Château Carsin, Bordeaux Blanc
£££ / 2 / ☛   17/20
Mandy Jones is one of a small but growing band of
Australian woman winemakers, who's worked in Portugal,
Chile and Australia as well as Bordeaux. At Château Carsin,
she specialises in white wines, experimenting with
combinations of oaks, yeasts and grape varieties. The 1992

is the best Carsin to date, blending 20 per cent Sauvignon Blanc and 80 per cent Semillon in an elegant, toasty Graves-style white with a touch of Australian-style tropical fruit. Bordeaux could do with a few more Mandies. The equally excellent 1993 should be available in most stores by Christmas 1994.

1992 Menetou-Salon, Domaine Henri Pellé
£££ / 2 / ❶   17/20
Henri Pellé, the Mayor of Morogues just to the west of Sancerre, consistently produces Menetou-Salon to match the quality of nearby Sancerre. We said last year that this highly aromatic, almost New Zealand-style Sauvignon Blanc, is made for early drinking. But we've revised our opinion. Cracking stuff.

1993 Domaine de Grandchamp Sauvignon Blanc, Bergerac Sec
£££ / 2 / ❶   16/20
Château de la Jaubertie by another name. This was made by Charles Martin, maintaining this estate's high reputation for excellent Sauvignon Blanc. A crisp, assertive, ripe gooseberry white, combining the best features of the Loire Valley and New Zealand. The estate has recently been bought from father Nick by son Hugh Ryman in partnership with Esme Johnstone of Château de Sours. Watch out for fireworks.

*1992 Sainsbury's Chablis, Cuvée Pargues, Brocard
££ / 2 / ❶   15/20
An unusual Chablis which is eccentrically traditional in style. Old oak, sweetness and milk chocolate don't sound much like Chablis, but this is a fat but enjoyable white Burgundy in its own right.

1993 Sainsbury's Oak-Aged Chablis, Madeleine Mathieu, William Fèvre
0 / 2 / ❶   13/20
William Fèvre is the outspoken leader of the Chablis modernisers, using plenty of new oak to ram home his wooden stake. On his best wines, the oak is well-integrated, but here, it sticks out like a thumb with a large splinter in it. Call for Androcles, please.

1989 Château Bastor Lamontagne, Sauternes, 37.5cl
££ / 6 / ❶   16/20
1989 was a historically early vintage for Sauternes, producing
lusciously rich, honeyed wines. This is an intense, pleasantly oaked,
sweet white with surprising restraint and elegance for a 1989.

1990 Château de Sainte Hélène, Sauternes, 37.5cl
££ / 6 / ❶   16/20
The second wine of Château de Malle is richly barley sugared with
a refreshing citrus twist and a hint of marmalade.

NEW ZEALAND

1993 Villa Maria Private Bin, Sauvignon Blanc, Marlborough
££ / 2 / ❶   15/20
Slightly drier than the benchmark Montana Sauvignon Blanc, this
has an elderflower crispness typical of Marlborough in a cool
vintage. Good stuff.

1993 Jackson Estate Sauvignon Blanc, Marlborough
£££ / 2 / ❶   17/20
**Intensely aromatic passion fruit and melon cocktail from
one of the top names in New Zealand's South Island. Zesty,
but with surprising ripeness for the vintage, this is
Marlborough with knobs on.**

SOUTH AFRICA

1992 Boschendal Estate Chardonnay, Paarl
£ / 2 / ❶   14/20
Heavy bottle, heavy wine.

Over £8

AUSTRALIA

1989 Leeuwin Estate Chardonnay, Margaret River, Western Australia
£££ / 2 / ⊷ 18/20
The outstanding Chardonnay producer in Australia and possibly the entire southern hemisphere, Leeuwin is Margaret River's premier tourist attraction with its jazz concerts on the lawn and big noise promotions. The hype is more than justified here in this ultra-rich, Meursault-style Chardonnay with massive flavours of vanilla and butterscotch fudge balanced by crisp, finely-tuned acidity. In limited distribution.

FRANCE

1992 Puligny-Montrachet, Domaine Gérard Chavy
££ / 2 / ⊷ 16/20
Oaky, tightly focused Côte de Beaune village white Burgundy from one of Puligny's leading growers. A wine with good fruit concentration and a minerally, toasty character, which should age well over the next five years.

Red

Under £3

BULGARIA

*Sainsbury's Bulgarian Country Red, Cabernet Sauvignon and Cinsault, Russe
££ / MB / ❶ 14/20
Surprisingly demanding, given its position in Sainsbury's top ten. A dry, fruity expression of Cabernet Sauvignon with tobacco and green pepper character and a tannic edge.

1988 Bulgarian Reserve Cabernet Sauvignon, Lovico Suhindol Region
£ / MB / 🍷   13/20
Chewy, charry American oak and extracted blackcurrant fruit. Good value in a litre bottle, less so at 75cl.

1993 Sainsbury's Bulgarian Merlot, Oak-Aged, Liubimetz Region
££ / MB / 🍷   14/20
This wine follows in the footsteps of the Safeway-inspired Young Vatted Merlot with the emphasis on youthful, blackberry fruit and a sprig of mint for good measure. There's some oak here, but it's not obtrusive.

1993 Sainsbury's Bulgarian Cabernet Sauvignon, Oak-Aged, Russe
£££ / MB / 🍷   15/20
The American oak character is more marked here, but there's more than enough juicy young fruit to compensate.

1990 Bulgarian Reserve Gamza, Lovico Suhindol Region
££ / MB / 🍷   14/20
A fragrant, peppery indigenous red made from the Gamza grape, not a million miles from a Côtes du Rhône. A dry finish cries out for food.

*1989 Bulgarian Reserve Merlot, Lovico Suhindol Region
0 / FB / 🍷   12/20
Charmless and overoaked, this was our least favourite of Sainsbury's Bulgarian reds.

FRANCE

*Sainsbury's Claret
£ / LB / 🍷   13/20
Sainsbury's was in the process of changing suppliers for its basic claret from Castel Frères to Ginestet when we tasted our way through the range. This soft, grassy blend of the 1992 and 1993 vintages is decent enough at under £3, so it will be interesting to see what JS has got up its sleeves.

1993 Touraine Gamay
££ / LB / ❧   14/20
A fresh, fruity, pseudo-Beaujolais from Albert Besombes in the
Loire Valley. Light, easy slurping.

Sainsbury's Vin de Pays d'Oc Rouge, Hugh Ryman
££ / MB / ❧   14/20
Hugh Ryman has used Merlot and Cabernet Sauvignon to add a
touch of class to the Languedoc's rustic Grenache and Carignan.
The result is a solid, fruity glugger at a very attractive price.

ITALY

*Sainsbury's Sicilian Red
£££ / MB / ❧   14/20
A Mediterranean blend of 80 per cent Nerello Mascalese and 20
per cent Calabrese (both of whom, because of injuries, played for
Italy in the World Cup final) from Settesoli. A rosemary-scented,
plummy pasta basher.

MOLDOVA

*Moldova Pinot Noir, Cricova
££ / MB / ❧   14/20
There's been Pinot Noir in Moldova ever since the Czars brought
French grape varieties to the region in the last century. It's taken
them a while to get things right, but this is a bargain with lots of
raspberry fruit and that elusive Pinot Noir character. We hope this
wine stays consistent over the next year, since reliability is not
Eastern Europe's strongest suit.

*Moldova Codru, Cabernet Sauvignon/Merlot, Cricova
££ / MB / ❧   14/20
A chocolatey, traditional Bordeaux-style blend from the cavernous
underground cellars at Cricova. Another good-value red from up-
and-coming Moldova, provided, that is, it stays consistent.

PORTUGAL

*Sainsbury's Do Campo Tinto
££ / MB / ▌   15/20
Fresh, plummy, juicy Portuguese bacalhão-basher made by Peter
Bright from the undemanding Periquita grape. A chunky wine with
refreshing acidity.

SPAIN

*Sainsbury's Valencia Oak-Aged, Egli
££ / MB / ▌   14/20
From one of the best wineries in the Valencia region, this is a warm,
raisiny Spanish red with some sweet, juicy vanilla oak character.

£3-5

AUSTRALIA

1990 Arrowfield Pinot Noir, New South Wales
0 / MB / ▛   11/20
New South Wales is considered too warm to produce good Pinot
Noir, but that doesn't stop people trying. This leafy, shagged out
example illustrates the point. We'd rather drink root beer.

1992 Mount Hurtle Grenache/Shiraz, Geoff Merrill
££ / MB / ▌   14/20
Supple, juicy, forward blend with some attractive, leathery spice
and minty, dry fruit. A good, undemanding party red.

1992 Rosemount Estate Shiraz, South-East Australia
£££ / MB / ▌   16/20
Rosemount Estate made its name with its Chardonnays, but its
Shiraz can be equally good, if not better. This is a dense, but supple,
highly aromatic red with masses of peppery, spicy fruit. Blended
from vineyards in South Australia as well as Rosemount's native
New South Wales, it's a great introduction to the joys of a grape
which does brilliantly Down Under.

1992 Bright Brothers Shiraz, McLaren Vale
£ / FB / ▌   14/20
Old-fashioned, uncompromising, warm region Shiraz from an
Australian winemaker who produces better things in Portugal.

BULGARIA

1987 Bulgarian Stambolovo Special Reserve Merlot, Haskovo Region

££ / MB / ⌘   15/20

Showing more richness and concentration of flavour than most Bulgarian reds, this is a sweet tobaccoey Merlot with well-judged American oak spice. The special selection warrants the extra pound.

CHILE

1993 Sainsbury's Chilean Merlot, San Fernando

£ / MB / ⌘   14/20

Lightish, blackcurrant pastille style Chilean red from the ultra-modern Canepa winery.

FRANCE

Sainsbury's Vin Rouge de France, 1.5 Litre

££ / MB / ⌘   14/20

Wines in 1.5 litre plastic bottles are rarely the stuff of rapture, but this peppery, full-blooded southern blend is an excellent party red for drinking on its own or with food.

*Sainsbury's Red Graves Selection, Louis Vialard

££ / LB / ⌘   14/20

A light and fruity 50/50 blend of Merlot and Cabernet Sauvignon. A good introduction to the Graves with none of the rasping tannins you often find on inexpensive claret.

1991 Château de Clos Delord, Bordeaux Rouge

££ / MB / ⌘   15/20

This petit château red tastes more like a light, Loire red with its leafy, capsicum characters and fresh nip of acidity. Attractive stuff at a reasonable price.

1991 Château Segonzac, Cuvée Barrique, Premières Côtes de Blaye

££ / MB / ⌘   15/20

A firm, oaky, modern red situated across the Garonne from the

Graves. Marked by vanilla and youthful tannins, this claret could do with a year or two in bottle to show it at its best.

1990 Séléction Peter Sichel Oak-Aged Red
£ / FB / 🍷   13/20
A touch, chewy, prematurely aged number from *négociant* Peter Sichel. A bit pricey for what is a pretty basic Bordeaux red.

*1989 Château du Peyrat, Premières Côtes de Bordeaux
£££ / MB / 🍷   16/20
Exactly the sort of stuff that Bordeaux needs to produce to compete with the New World under £5. A blend of 50 per cent Merlot, 35 per cent Cabernet Sauvignon and 15 per cent Cabernet Franc from an ancient property owned by Paul and Henri Lambert. The ripeness of the vintage and some well-handled oak make this a pleasure to drink.

1993 Sainsbury's Gamay, Vin de Pays des Coteaux des Baronnies, Les Ramerottes, Jean-Claude Boisset
££ / MB / 🍷   14/20
A farmyardy aroma put us off a bit initially, but the underlying quality of the Gamay grape was so sweet and juicy that we forgave it.

1990 Sainsbury's Corbières, Domaine du Révérend
££ / MB / 🍷   14/20
This is a blend of mainly Carignan, Grenache and Syrah from Peter Sichel's property at Cucugnan in the shadow of the Cathar stronghold of Quéribus. A light, modern style of Corbières with savoury fruit and well-judged oak.

1990 Sainsbury's Corbières, Château La Voulte-Gasparets
£££ / FB / 🍷   17/20
Consistently among the best producers in the Languedoc-Roussillon, this estate makes wines to blow your socks and shoes off. Super concentration and masses of spicy, garrigue-scented fruit with a chunkiness that promises further development.

1990 Côtes du Rhône Villages, St Gervais, Laurent Charles Brotte
0 / MB / 🍷   12/20
A raisiny, alcoholic Grenache from a modest *négociant*, barely

worthy of the Villages suffix. Better Côtes du Rhônes abound, especially from 1990.

ITALY

Sainsbury's Teroldego Rotaliano, Geoff Merrill
££ / MB / ▌   14/20

A densely coloured northern Italian red made in a juicy, aromatic style by Australian Geoff Merrill in partnership with GIV. If you find the tannins in Italian reds a little demanding, try this crunchy red for a bit of relief.

1990 Chianti Classico, Briante
0 / MB / ▌   12/20

Dry, unappealing, rustic Chianti from the Grevepesa co-operative showing the downside of the Sangiovese grape. 1990 was an excellent vintage in Tuscany, so what happened here?

1982 Chianti Rufina Riserva, Fattoria di Galiga
££ / MB / ▌   14/20

It's unusual to find Chianti with 12 years' bottle-age under £5. This has good bitter-cherry concentration and the fresh acidity which is the hallmark of the Rufina zone, but we found the aftertaste on the rustic side.

1991 Sainsbury's Copertino Riserva
£££ / MB / ▌   16/20

From the Cantina Sociale of Copertino, this is the sort of mid-priced wine Italy needs more of. It shows rich, spicy, cherry, plum and tobacco fruit with plenty of life and character.

NEW ZEALAND

1992 Montana Cabernet Sauvignon, Marlborough
££ / MB / ▌   15/20

Like the same producer's admirable Sauvignon Blanc, this is tremendous value for money at under a fiver. 1992 was the first of two abnormally cool years in New Zealand, and, as a result, the wine is a little leaner than the excellent 1991.

PORTUGAL

1993 Bright Brothers Cabernet Sauvignon, Early Release, Ribatejo

£ / FB / ❶   13/20

Tannic, sturdy stuff from the South of Portugal. For an early release, this is a rather chewy wine. Fun it isn't.

1992 Sainsbury's Douro Tinto

0 / FB / ❶   12/20

There is a surprisingly large volume of red wine produced in the Port country of the Douro Valley. Some of it, especially Barca Velha, is outstanding. Much of it isn't. This is typically dour.

1990 Bairrada Terra Franca, Sogrape

££ / FB / ❶   14/20

A tobaccoey, aromatic Portuguese red made from the native Baga grape by Sogrape, one of the country's most enlightened producers. Needs food to mop up the tannins.

SOUTH AFRICA

Sainsbury's South African Pinotage, Coastal Region

££ / MB / ❶   14/20

A decent South African red made from the indigenous Pinotage crossing, showing characteristic flavours of raspberry and baked banana.

SPAIN

*Sainsbury's Rioja, Bodegas Olarra

££ / LB / ❶   15/20

Modern, light, fruity, carbonic maceration style Rioja. The sort of thing which may upset traditionalists, but which is easy on the palate and pocket.

*1989 Sainsbury's Rioja Crianza, Bodegas Olarra

££ / MB / ❶   15/20

Closer to what you'd expect to find in a bottle of Rioja. Appealing, sweet oak combined with soft raspberry fruit and some grip.

URUGUAY

1988 Castel Pujol Tannat, Canelones
££££ / FB / 🍷   17/20

A real find and one of the few wines, possibly the only wine,
available in the UK from Uruguay. To be honest, we didn't
even know wine was produced in Uruguay before we tasted
this astonishing red. The sturdy Tannat grape of south-
western France has been transformed here into a soft,
flavoursome, massively fruity red with balance and class.
Limited availability.

£5–8

ARGENTINA

1992 Bright Brothers Malbec, Las Palmas
££ / FB / 👄   15/20

There's an awful lot of Malbec in Argentina. This rich, concentrated
example is typical of the grape, which reaches its apogee in the
wines of Cahors. Strapping Argie red. Gotcha!

1985 Cavas de Weinert, Mendoza
££ / MB / 🍷   16/20

A curiosity to serve blind to dinner party fogeys and Masters of
Wine. An old-fashioned but well-made Bordeaux-style blend of
chocolatey complexity. There aren't many better reds than this in
Argentina. At its peak now.

AUSTRALIA

1992 Penfolds Koonunga Hill Shiraz/Cabernet, South Australia
£ / FB / 🍷   14/20

Like many an Australian wine, this has edged up in price over the
last year. Consistently reliable, it's true to the Penfolds formula of
lashings of American oak and juicy, spicy fruit. We'd like to see it
back under £5, though.

1992 Bailey's Shiraz, Glenrowan, Victoria
0 / FB / 🍷   12/20

From a hot area which specialises in fortified wines, this is an overextracted headbanger red for Iron Maiden aficionados. Stick to stickies, please, Bailey's.

1988 McWilliams Mount Pleasant Philip Shiraz, Hunter River Valley
£££ / MB / ▮   17/20
Hunter Valley Shiraz at its classic, old-fashioned best. It has all the leathery, gamey characteristics of the region's Shiraz, hence the unlovely expression 'sweaty saddle' to describe it, and a sumptuously smooth finish. A great wine from an underrated producer.

1991 Tim Knappstein Cabernet/Merlot, Clare Valley
£££ / MB / ▮   16/20
From Bruce Chatwin lookalike Tim Knappstein, this is an intense, mintily aromatic, Bordeaux-style blend, showing the elegance and balance that are typical of his brilliantly crafted wines.

*1992 St Hallett Cabernet Sauvignon/Franc/Merlot, Barossa Valley
££ / MB / ▮   15/20
For wine lovers who can't get their hands on St Hallett's legendary Old Block Shiraz, this is a sweetly fruity Barossa-meets-Bordeaux blend.

*1990 Penfolds Coonawarra Cabernet Sauvignon
££ / FB / ▬   16/20
Masses of colour, concentrated fruit and sweet sawdusty American oak give this the stamp of Penfolds, but there's some balancing Coonawarra elegance too. Poor persons' Bin 707.

FRANCE

1989 Château Lalande d'Auvion, Médoc
£££ / MB / ▮   17/20
Unusually for the Médoc, this is a Merlot-dominated claret from the windy, wide open spaces of Blaignan north of Bordeaux. A fleshy, slightly farmyardy red with soft tannins and the true character of the Médoc.

1990 Château Tour Prignac, Médoc, Cru Bourgeois
££ / FB / ↜   15/20
Another classic claret from the northern end of the Médoc, this
time from a property just east of the town of Lesparre. More tannic
and structured than the Lalande d'Auvion, but with plenty of
characterful, lead-pencil shavings fruit.

1990 Château Rozier, St Emilion, Grand Cru
££ / MB / ꟷ   16/20
From a family-owned property in the village of St Laurent des
Combes to the east of St Emilion, this is a ripe, seductive, Merlot-
dominated Right Bank claret. Available in Sainsbury's 50 top stores
only.

1990 Château Fournas Bernadotte, Haut-Médoc, Cru Bourgeois
££ / MB / ꟷ   15/20
From a cru bourgeois property situated on the northern side of
the world-famous village of Pauillac, this is a firm, traditional claret
with no new oak-ageing in evidence. As a result, the fruit occupies
centre stage.

1990 Vacquéyras, Paul Jaboulet-Isnard
0 / FB / ꟷ   12/20
Perhaps Gérard Jaboulet is trying to disown this dull, overpriced,
cooked southern Rhône red. Jaboulet-Isnard is not a terribly well
disguised synonym for Jaboulet Aîné.

1990 Gigondas, Tour de Queyron, Les Caves St Pierre
£ / FB / ꟷ   15/20
A heady, chocolatey, Grenache-based mouthfiller, long on alcohol,
but rather short on subtlety. Pricey at around £7.50 a go.

ITALY

1988 Barolo, Giordano
£ / FB / ꟷ   14/20
An old-style Barolo, getting on in years. It's going to be a photo
finish between the tannin and the fruit, but our money is on the
tannin.

1988 Valpolicella Classico Amarone, Sartori
££ / FB / ➘   15/20

Amarone is Valpolicella's claim to greatness, if that's not a contradiction in terms. This isn't one of the greats, but it's sweet, rich, super-ripe and savoury with a knee-bending punch of alcohol. Not for faint hearts.

NEW ZEALAND

1991 Corbans Private Bin Cabernet/Merlot, Marlborough
£££ / MB / ➘   17/20

Alan McCorkindale is one of the best red winemakers in New Zealand, producing a string of elegant Cabernets and Merlots and a good Pinot Noir from the company's Marlborough outpost. He's done as much as anyone to prove that New Zealand can make world-class red wines at relatively affordable prices. This supple, complex red reminds us of a slightly herbaceous Pomerol.

PORTUGAL

*1990 Quinta da Bacalhõa, Cabernet Sauvignon
£ / MB / ➧   15/20

This trail-blazing Portuguese Cabernet Sauvignon has built a following over the years, partly based on value for money. This isn't as good as the 1989, but it nicely combines ripe New World style blackcurrant and vanilla fruit with a hint of Portuguese rusticity.

Over £8

AUSTRALIA

1988 Wynn's John Riddoch Cabernet Sauvignon, Coonawarra, Penfolds
£££ / MB / ➘   17/20

The flagship wine from Wynn's historic Coonawarra estate has come down temptingly in price over the last year to below £10. A densely textured red with lots of sweet, tobaccoey fruit, combining power and finesse. You can

drink it now, but it will repay keeping for a good five years. In Sainsbury's top 30 stores.

1990 Limestone Ridge Vineyard Shiraz/Cabernet, Coonawarra
££ / MB / ➥ 16/20
Another top-notch Coonawarra red from the Lindemans branch of the Penfolds group. Lindemans has a justified reputation for more elegant styles than the blockbuster reds of Penfolds. This youthful, classic blend is rich in oak and blackcurrant fruit and will age well. In Sainsbury's top 30 stores.

***1991 Devil's Lair Cabernet Sauvignon, Margaret River, Western Australia**
£££ / MB / ➥ 17/20
Available in Calais as well as in Sainsbury's top 20 stores, this is one to frighten the life out of Bordeaux. From Margaret River in Western Australia, which rivals Coonawarra for the title of Australia's leading red wine region, this is a supple, intensely fruity Cabernet Sauvignon with wonderful, chocolatey flavours.

1990 Penfolds Cabernet Sauvignon Bin 707
£££ / FB / ➥ 17/20
If Penfolds' Grange is Australia's answer to the red wines of Hermitage, then this is its riposte to First Growth Pauillac. A blend of Cabernet Sauvignon from selected vineyards in South Australia, this is a tannic, concentrated monster designed for ageing. Come back in the next millennium. Available in six stores only.

FRANCE

1990 Château Poujeaux, Moulis-en-Médoc
££ / MB / ➥ 16/20
Château Poujeaux is among the leading crus bourgeois in Bordeaux, and price increases in recent vintages have reflected its growing status. This rich, modern, well-balanced claret often takes a while to come round owing to the high proportion of Petit Verdot in the blend. Needs a minimum of five years.

1990 Château Chasse-Spleen
££ / FB / ⚑ 17/20

This superb claret will serve as a memorial to Bernadette Villars, who tragically died while walking in the Pyrenees. With the 1986 and 1989, this is the best Chasse-Spleen of the last decade. Well-structured with fine-grained tannins and toasty, vanilla oak, the wine has the backbone to age gracefully.

1991 Nuits-St-Georges, Paul Dugenais
£ / MB / ⚑ 14/20

Paul Dugenais is one of the bewildering number of aliases for the ubiquitous Labouré-Roi, a *négociant* making better whites than reds on the whole. This would make a good, basic house red Burgundy with its fresh, cherry-strawberry Pinot Noir fruitiness, but we expect more from a village wine.

*1990 Château de Rully Rouge
££ / MB / ⏴ 16/20

Until merchant company Antonin Rodet bought the Côte de Beaune estates of Jacques Prieur, Château de Rully was its top property. Performing above its Côte Chalonnaise *appellation*, this is a seductive, savoury, concentrated red Burgundy at just over £8.

1989 Savigny-lès-Beaune, Jean-Marc Pavelot
££ / MB / ⏴ 16/20

Limited, unfortunately, to six stores, but well worth hunting down. Jean-Marc Pavelot's wines are consistently among the finest in Savigny, showing the fresh charm and succulence typical of the village. A wine which is hugely enjoyable now, but with the potential for ageing.

*1990 Châteauneuf-du-Pape, Domaine André Brunel
£££ / FB / ⏴ 17/20

Even better than the much praised 1989, this is a strong, heady, aromatic red with masses of Grenache fruit sweetness and herby concentration. Excellent stuff from a great vintage, which will benefit from further ageing.

PORTUGAL

1989 Quinta da Bacalhôa, Cabernet Sauvignon, Magnum
££ / MB / ▮   16/20
Sainsbury's has done much to promote Peter Bright's cedary
combination of Bordeaux varieties, Cabernet Sauvignon and
Merlot, to the extent that it currently stocks two different vintages
of Portugal's answer to Bordeaux. This is the more enjoyable of
the pair, with better balance and richness than the 1990. The
magnum seems to bring out the best in the wine.

Rosé

Under £3

FRANCE

Sainsbury's Blush Wine, Vin de Table Français
0 / 4 / ▮   11/20
A 100 per cent Grenache rosé from the Sète-based Fortant de
France operation. Given Fortant de France's American-style
marketing, it's no surprise to find them producing a French
wine modelled on the blush wine craze in California. Mawkish
rather than moreish.

HUNGARY

**Sainsbury's Hungarian Cabernet Sauvignon Rosé,
Szoloskert, Nagyrede Region**
££ / 3 / ▮   13/20
Softish, strawberry jam style Hungarian rosé from the ubiquitous
Kym Milne. A cool, green pepper edge adds extra interest.

£3–5

FRANCE

1993 Domaine de la Tuilerie, Merlot Rosé, Vin de Pays d'Oc, Hugh Ryman

££ / 3 / ♪   14/20

Hugh Ryman has come up with an attractively off-dry style of rosé showing good ripe fruit and a herbaceous, fresh note.

1993 Domaine des Blancs, Sainsbury's Côtes du Lubéron Rosé

££ / 1 / ♪   14/20

Weird name for a rosé. A dry, early-picked, cherryish, day-glo style, which will go well with food.

Sparkling

£3–5

SPAIN

*Sainsbury's Cava, Mont Marçal

££ / 2 / ♪   15/20

One of the more appealing supermarket cavas around. Instead of the usual earthiness, this has clean citrus fruit flavours and a degree of finesse.

£5–8

FRANCE

Sainsbury's Sparkling Chardonnay, Tradition Brut, Charles de Fère

££ / 2 / ♪   15/20

Proof that France can produce good Champagne substitutes at an affordable price. Delicately toasty, creamy fizz for under £6.

SOUTH AFRICA

Madeba Brut, Robertson
££ / 2 / 🍾   15/20
The first commercial release from futuristic millionaire and ex-
Natal coalminer Graham Beck's playground in the Cape. Warm
Robertson is not the first place you'd think of setting up a sparkling
wine operation, but Graham Beck's faith in the region is bearing
quality fruit and elegant bubbles.

Over £8

AUSTRALIA

1991 Green Point
£££ / 2 / 🍾   17/20
This successful Yarra Valley winery has produced a brilliant
successor to the 1990, which was one of *Grapevine*'s wines
of the year in 1994. The Pinot Noir content has been
increased, and Pinot Meunier has been added to the blend
for the first time. Otherwise, this follows on nicely from
the previous vintage, showing considerable toasty
complexity and finesse. Parent company Champagne house
Moët et Chandon must be happy to see Dr Tony Jordan
maintaining Green Point's high standards.

FRANCE

*Sainsbury's Extra Dry Champagne, NV
£ / 2 / 🍾   14/20
From Duval-Leroy, this is a forward, Chardonnay-based Champagne
showing the gawkiness of youth. We didn't enjoy this quite as
much as last year's excellent offering, but with the volumes that
Sainsbury's get through, batches are bound to vary.

Sainsbury's Blanc de Noirs Champagne, NV
£££ / 2 / 🍾   17/20
A fine blend of 80 per cent Pinot Noir and 20 per cent Pinot
Meunier from patrician merchant, Bruno Paillard. A malty,
Ovaltine-like fizz with style and finesse.

*1989 Sainsbury's Vintage Champagne, Blanc de Blancs

££ / 2 / ▌ 15/20

At around £14, this is a comparatively inexpensive vintage Champagne with delicately mouth-filling fruit and good structure. If you want a Champagne to drink with food, you could do worse than this.

*Sainsbury's Rosé Champagne Brut, NV, Beaumet

££ / 1 / ▌ 15/20

From the house of Beaumet, this is a fruity but markedly dry style of rosé Champagne with pleasant strawberry fruit.

Fortified

£3–5

SPAIN

Sainsbury's Pale Dry Manzanilla, Bodegas Del Ducado, Dry Sherry, half-bottle

£ / 2 / ▌ 13/20

This Manzanilla has the typical, savoury aromas of Sherry's flor yeast, but the wine is a little heavy and coarse.

Sainsbury's Pale Dry Amontillado, Croft

£ / 3 / ▌ 13/20

Amber-coloured, sweetish, commercial Amontillado rather lacking in finesse.

Sainsbury's Oloroso Old Dry Sherry, Croft, half-bottle

££ / 1 / ▌ 15/20

The most distinguished and characterful of Sainsbury's dry Sherry range, this has nutty, burnt caramel aromas and a refreshingly dry tang. Granny wouldn't like it.

Sainsbury's Palo Cortado Medium Dry Sherry, Emilio Lustau, half-bottle

££ / 3 / ▐   16/20

Halfway between a dry Amontillado and a tawny Port in aroma, this is a beautifully balanced, mature Sherry with notes of coffee, caramel and almonds, and a distinctive orange peel twist for added complexity.

Over £8

PORTUGAL

Sainsbury's 10 Year Old Tawny Port, Quinta do Noval

££ / 5 / ►   15/20

An aromatic, sweet, slightly spirity tawny with good raisin and red fruits character.

1978 Fonseca Guimaraens, Vintage Port

££ / FB / ►   16/20

Guimaraens is the name Fonseca gives to its wines in years in which their top wine, Fonseca Vintage Port, is not released. This is not quite in the same league as the densely peppery 1976, but it's still immensely enjoyable stuff. Smooth, chocolate and raisin rich and full of life.

SOMERFIELD ***
(INCLUDING GATEWAY)

Head Office: Somerfield House, Hawkfield Business Park, Whitchurch Lane, Bristol, BS14 0TJ

Telephone: 0272 359359

Number of branches: 650, of which 137 are Somerfield Stores, 47 SoLo and 26 Food Giant

Credit cards accepted: All

Hours of opening: Varies from store to store, but generally Monday to Saturday 8.30am to 6.30pm and Sunday 10.00am to 4.00pm

By-the-case sales: No

Glass loan: No

Home delivery: No

Clubs: No

Discounts: No, but regular promotions

In-store tastings: Monthly, day-long tastings in top 100 stores

Top ten best-selling wines: Liebfraumilch; Lambrusco Bianco; Hock; Valencia Medium Sweet; Bulgarian Cabernet Sauvignon; Valencia Red; Bulgarian Country Red; Valencia Sweet; Muscadet; Valencia Dry

Range: GOOD: French country wines, Italian red, Australia
AVERAGE: Bordeaux, Burgundy, Rhône, Portugal, Italian white, South Africa, South America, England, Champagne and sparkling wines, New Zealand
POOR: Germany, Spain, Eastern Europe, United States

You may not have noticed, but Gateway has changed names in the last year from the snappy Gateway Foodmarkets to the even snappier Somerfield Stores. Gateways are being converted faster than you can say 'major modernisation programme' and, at the time of writing, Somerfields are on their way to making up a quarter of the chain's 631 licensed stores.

If the name switch weren't confusing enough on its own, Somerfield also trades under the Food Giant, SoLo (sic) and David Greig banners. So how is the poor, befuddled consumer coping with all this? Pretty well, according to wine-buying controller, Angela Mount. 'Most of our customers think the Somerfields are completely new shops. We've retained our regulars but we've also managed to attract a lot of new people.'

The Somerfield concept was first mooted four years ago – neatly coinciding with Angela Mount's own arrival in Bristol – as a response to Gateway's rather dowdy image. The idea, says Mount, was 'to be the leading high street supermarket, not develop a chain of superstores. It was difficult to inject new life and excitement into the Gateway name, which has a slightly older, downmarket feel.' Wine sales are up in all the Somerfield outlets, according to Mount, already rewarding the chain's £200 million investment.

The Somerfield stores may look a lot better than your average Gateway, but Mount has no intention of abandoning her value-for-money crusade. She launched something called Price Check in May 1993 and has developed the idea over the last year. 'Every month we have three or four wines at outrageous prices. When we put a £1.99 Vin de Pays d'Oc on the shelves, we sold 30,000 cases in two weeks.' Rioja, white Burgundy and a southern French Merlot have all been similarly attractive.

The other good thing is that, in the new stores, more space has been allocated to wine. This means that the full range is available in 40 stores, and 90 per cent of it is available in a further 60 stores. These days, good wines are no longer restricted to the lucky few.

Mount is one of the most dynamic supermarket wine buyers, sourcing good deals and creating interest where previously there was none. Gateway (as it was then) barely had a wine range in 1990. Her hard work has resulted in large volume increases and a growing reputation as a canny negotiator.

The promotions are a good way of 'getting people to try new wines without taking a financial risk'. Somerfield's excellent white Burgundy, for example, was on offer in 1994 at £3.49 and sold 10,000 cases. The price has gone back up to £4.99, but the wine continues to sell well. 'An outrageous price created a new customer base,' adds Mount.

All this is fine and dandy, but the promoted wines are not always as special as they might be. The hit rate seems to be an Ancient Mariner-style one in three, with albatrosses given shelf space alongside the good stuff. Still, at £1.99 it's worth taking a punt on a Price Check wine.

The Somerfield range has not increased in the last 12 months and still floats around the 350-wine mark. There have been 40 new listings and a corresponding number of delistings, but far fewer changes than in previous years. There are two reasons for this: first, Angela Mount is happier with the range; and second, the focus has been on new labels, own-brand wines and in-store promotions.

The New World is still under-represented at Somerfield and Mount intends to increase her range of South African, Californian and Chilean wines. Flying winemaker wines are another possibility for the coming months. And Eastern Europe still needs attention. Otherwise, it's more of the same.

As it stands, the range has several high points, especially in Italy, southern France and Burgundy, a well-chosen middle and some pretty nasty stuff at the bottom. Mount says that 'given that we have a smaller range than many of our competitors, I can't afford to hide any wines. I have to be proud of all of them.'

We're not so sure. She has done a good job in the £3-4 range, but there are some truly awful wines among the cheapies. Indeed, what worried us most was that several of the poorest wines at Somerfield are top ten best sellers. By definition, these are the wines that customers buy in considerable volume, so they really ought to be more enjoyable. Otherwise, how do you persuade them to come back for more?

White

Under £3

GERMANY

Hock Deutscher Tafelwein
0 / 4 /]   10/20
A sweet, bland confection, marginally superior to sugar water.

Liebfraumilch, Rheinhessen
0 / 5 /]   11/20
Hello? Is there anyone or anything there?

Somerfield Baden Dry, ZBW
££ / 2 /]   14/20
No sign of Gothic script or labyrinthine labelling here. This is a
French-style German white, albeit made mainly from Müller-
Thurgau, with a floral bouquet and pear and grapefruit characters.

HUNGARY

1992 Gyöngyös Muscat, Hugh Ryman
0 / 3 /]   6/20
Customers who enjoy this sort of thing need a brain scan. We
poured this down the sink and had to call in the plumber to replace
the pipes.

ITALY

Lambrusco Bianco dell'Emilia, Vino Frizzante
0 / 5 /]   10/20
Tired and fruitless. The sort of stuff that could give Lambrusco a
bad name.

1993 Lazio Bianco, Pallavicini
££ / 2 /]   14/20
Gazza may be recuperating from a broken leg, but the wine he
inspired lives on. Rather like England's mercurial star, this baked
off-dry Frascati tastealike has lost some of its zip since last year.

MOLDOVA

1993 Hincesti Moldovan Chardonnay, Hugh Ryman
0 / 3 / ⬤   12/20

Hugh Ryman makes wine, not to mention beer, in so many places these days, that he runs the risk of spreading his undoubted talents a little thin. Perhaps that's what's happened with this cosmetic, sweet and sour number.

SOUTH AFRICA

1993 Simonsvlei South African Chenin Blanc
££ / 3 / ⬤   14/20

Drinkable, commendably cheap, cool-fermented Cape white with boiled sweets to the fore. A bit dilute.

SPAIN

Valencia Dry White Spanish Wine
0 / 3 / ⬤   8/20

The most interesting thing about this coarse, tired, old-style white is the Flamenco guitarist on the label.

Valencia Medium White Spanish Wine
0 / 4 / ⬤   12/20

Sugary, baked white from Spain's eastern seaboard. Considerably better than the dry version, but still two picadors short of a bullfight.

Valencia Sweet White Spanish Wine
0 / 6 / ⬤   11/20

Cloying liquid sugar in a glass. Weight watchers and wine drinkers beware.

£3–5

AUSTRALIA

1993 Penfolds Bin 21 Semillon/Chardonnay, South-East Australia
££ / 2 / ⬤   15/20

In common with many commercial Australian whites, the 1993 is more restrained than the 1992 vintage. Fresh melon and peachy fruit with a dab of smoky oak and herbal Semillon character. Perfect party and house white.

1993 Berri Unwooded Chardonnay
££ / 3 / ▐   14/20
Unwooded Chardonnays are a welcome new development for Australia in general and for this South Australian co-operative in particular. Mango fruit exoticism and a fresh citrus streak make this an appealing drink.

1993 Hardy's Nottage Hill Chardonnay
£ / 3 / ▐   13/20
Rather obvious, sweet white from Down Under. Half a glass would be more than enough.

CHILE

1993 Somerfield Chilean Sauvignon Blanc, Canepa
0 / 2 / ▐   12/20
Clumsy, alcoholic Chilean white with negligible Sauvignon Blanc character. A winery as well equipped as Canepa should be able to do better than this.

FRANCE

1992 Oak-Aged Bordeaux Blanc, Eschenauer
£ / 2 / ▐   13/20
The words 'oak-aged' definitely sell this wine, according to buyer, Angela Mount. Who are we to argue with the bottom line, but we found the wine clumsily oaked and a bit long in the molars.

1993 Chardonnay Vin de Pays d'Oc, Domaine de la Tuilerie, Hugh Ryman
££ / 2 / ▐   15/20
This is the sort of wine Hugh Ryman does best, perhaps because he's more closely involved than in Moldova or Hungary. A restrained New World style Chardonnay with pineapple and lime fruit flavours and a bit of toast and buttery richness.

1993 Chardonnay, James Herrick, Vin de Pays d'Oc
££ / 1 / ▌   15/20
The second vintage from Englishman James Herrick's impressive
New World style vineyards near Narbonne. This is more elegant
and restrained than the 1992 with deftly handled oak and a lime-
like streak of acidity.

1992 Mâcon Blanc Villages, G. Désiré
£ / 2 / ▌   13/20
Fudge-like, overoaked, basic white Burgundy from the merchant
house of Labouré-Roi.

1992 Somerfield White Burgundy, G. Désiré
£££ / 2 / ▌   16/20
Considerably more enjoyable stuff for an extra 50 pence.
Beautifully balanced Chardonnay with far more complexity than
you'd expect at this price and level of quality.

HUNGARY

1993 Gyöngyös Hungarian Chardonnay, Hugh Ryman
0 / 2 / ▌   12/20
Sweet, flat and lacking in freshness, a wine which has its ups and
downs owing to rather primitive cellar technology. When it's good,
it's very good, but when it's bad . . .

ITALY

1993 Somerfield Chardonnay del Piemonte
££ / 2 / ▌   15/20
A crisp, fresh northern Italian Chardonnay from the Araldica co-
operative for people who don't like oak. Bottled with a bit of carbon
dioxide for extra zip and life.

NEW ZEALAND

1993 Nobilo White Cloud, Gisborne
£ / 3 / ▌   14/20
Along with Montana and Cloudy Bay, this consistent blend of
Müller-Thurgau and Sauvignon Blanc is one of New Zealand's most
successful exports. A massively commercial, fruity, off-dry white

with a pleasant edge of greenness to slice through the sugar.

PORTUGAL

Somerfield Bairrada Branco, Caves Aliança
££ / 2 / 🌡   14/20
Bet you've never knowingly tasted Bical, Maria Gomes and Sercial
grapes in the same wine before. Nor had we until we encountered
this modern, lime-like dry white.

£5–8

FRANCE

1993 Sancerre, Domaine Brock
0 / 1 / 🌡   13/20
A light, somewhat tart Sancerre made from the Sauvignon Blanc
grape. As one of the few wines over £6 at Somerfield, it really
ought to be more exciting.

Red

Under £3

BULGARIA

Bulgarian Country Wine, Sliven, Merlot and Pinot Noir
£ / MB / 🌡   13/20
A young, unusual combination of classic Bordeaux and Burgundy
grapes. Light, soft red with plenty of fruit.

1989 Bulgarian Cabernet Sauvignon, Svischtov Region
£ / MB / 🌡   13/20
Mature, old-style Cabernet Sauvignon with a gamey, tinned tomato
character and softish tannins.

FRANCE

Somerfield Côtes du Roussillon, Jeanjean
££ / MB / 🥂

An appealing, juicy southern French blend of Syrah, Mourvèdre, Carignan and Cinsault from a company which specialises in Languedoc *appellations*.

Somerfield Claret, Eschenauer
££ / MB / 🥂   14/20

Soft, grassy, well-made claret with appealing fruit sweetness and grip. One of the better cheap Bordeaux reds on the market.

ITALY

1993 Lazio Rosso, Casale San Giglio
£££ / MB / 🥂   15/20

A real find, especially at this price. A stylish blend of Merlot and Sangiovese with plenty of richness and soft, but fresh fruit. A southern Italian red to appeal to Francophile palates.

PORTUGAL

Leziria Red, Almeirim
£££ / MB / 🥂   15/20

A value-for-money red that never lets you down. The tannins are softer than last year's more robust version, but there's still plenty of peppery Portuguese character on offer.

SPAIN

Valencia Full Red Spanish Wine
0 / MB / 🥂   9/20

Souped-up, sweetish, coarse red. As subtle as Carmen's lipstick.

£3–5

AUSTRALIA

1992 Penfolds Bin 35 Shiraz/Cabernet, South Australia
££ / FB / ▌   15/20

True to the successful Penfolds' formula, this is a rich, full-bodied, blackberry fruity, modern red with oak in abundance.

Somerfield Australian Cabernet Sauvignon, Penfolds
£ / FB / ▌   14/20

Minty, robust and more rustic than the Bin 35.

1992 Nottage Hill Cabernet Sauvignon
0 / FB / ▌   13/20

Coarse, obvious minty red with hefty tannins from the sprawling BRL-Hardy operation.

CHILE

1993 Somerfield Chilean Cabernet Sauvignon, Viña Segu Olle
£££ / MB / ▌   16/20

Segu Olle is part of the Villa Montes operation, responsible for some of Chile's best red wines. This is a supple, well-made claret substitute with no oak, but plenty of chocolate and blackcurrant fruit.

FRANCE

1992 Domaine des Salaises, Saumur Rouge, Rémy Pannier
£ / MB / ▌   14/20

Light, aromatic, herbaceous Cabernet Franc, which has replaced the more pricey Chinon on the Somerfield list. Strawberry softness gives way to a slightly tart finish.

1993 St Tropez, Côtes de Provence, Les Caves de Provence
££ / MB / ▌   14/20

One for the posing pouch, although the skittle bottle could do you permanent damage if you're not careful. Good soft, juicy Syrah-based stuff.

1992 Mâcon Rouge, G. Désiré
0 / LB / ⌘   11/20
Light, tart and overcropped Gamay. Completely pointless.

1990 Somerfield Red Burgundy, Cave de Buxy
£ / MB / ⌘   13/20
Basic strawberryish red Burgundy with a bit of oak. Getting on a
bit, so drink up.

1993 Somerfield Syrah, Vin de Pays d'Oc, Jeanjean
££ / FB / ⌘   15/20
Deep-hued Languedoc red with lots of chunky, sweet fruit and
tannic bite.

1990 Somerfield Oak-Aged Claret, Eschenauer
££ / MB / ⌘   15/20
Well-integrated oak and sweet ripe Merlot-based fruit make this
claret a pleasure to drink at under a fiver.

1991 Vacquéyras, Arnoux et Fils
££ / FB / ⌘   15/20
Rich, raisiny, rustic Grenache-dominated red (that's enough
alliteration, Ed), with a spicy, chocolatey finish.

ITALY

1989 Copertino, Cantina Sociale
££ / MB / ⌘   15/20
Baked southern Italian red with a core of sweet and savoury fruit
at a good price.

1991 Chianti Classico, Montecchio
££ / MB / ⌘   15/20
Made by star oenologist and natty dresser, Franco Bernabei, this is
a fresh, characterful Tuscan red in which the sharp edges of the
Sangiovese grape have been stylishly toned down and the fruit
enhanced.

PORTUGAL

1993 Terras d'el Rei, Co-operativa da Reguengos
££ / FB / ▌   15/20

Vibrant, robust, Portuguese quaffer from the southern Alentejo region. It's good to see this quality-minded co-operative doing well in Britain.

SPAIN

1992 Berberana Tempranillo, Rioja
£££ / MB / ▌   16/20

Lashings of coconutty American oak blend succulently with Spain's best red grape variety to produce a sumptuous, savoury Rioja in a modern mould.

Sparkling

£3–5

FRANCE

Chardonnay Brut, Varichon et Clerc, Cuvée Privée
£ / 3 / ▌   14/20

Packaged in royal blue and gold, this is an innocuous, light, appley fizz, which would make a good Buck's Fizz base.

Fortified

£3–5

Somerfield Moscatel de Valencia, J. Gandia
0 / 8 / ▌   11/20

Hardly a wine. You'd be better off pouring the contents away and replacing with aftershave.

SPAR **(*)

Head Office: Spar Landmark Ltd, 32-40 Headstone Drive, Harrow, Middlesex, HA3 5QT

Telephone: 081 863 5511

Number of branches: 2,200 stores of which 1,700 are licensed

Credit cards accepted: At individual retailer's discretion

Hours of opening: Varies. Average of 91 hours a week per store

By the case sales: At individual retailer's discretion

Glass loan: Yes, in some branches

Home delivery: No

Clubs: Not for consumers, but 458 retailers belong to the Spar Wine Club

Discounts: At individual retailer's discretion

In-store tastings: Yes

Top ten best-selling wines: Liebfraumilch; Lambrusco; Valencia Red; Bulgarian Country Wine; Hock; French Country Wine; Cabernet de l'Aude; Claret; Jacob's Creek White; Don Darias

Range: GOOD: Regional France, Italy, Bordeaux, white Burgundy
       AVERAGE: Germany, South Africa, Spain, Eastern Europe, Australia, South Africa
       POOR: Sparkling wines, California

We all know what happens to acorns. They turn into large trees, albeit oaks rather than the firs which Spar uses as its logo. From the dozen or so wines which Master of Wine Philippa Carr inherited six years ago, the Spar range has grown to an impressive, oak-like 150, 30 of them added in the past year alone.

Quantity doesn't necessarily imply quality, but the hit rate is impressive in Britain's largest independent chain of convenience stores. With branches dotted throughout the country and a strong base in the Midlands and the North, an increased range is good news for British wine drinkers.

Once an afterthought, wine now represents a substantial proportion of Spar's total sales and has increased by 18 per cent in the last year. Most of Spar's 1,700-odd licensed stores stock the basic range of 60 or so wines. Beyond that, they are free to pick and choose, which means that some of the best wines don't filter down into the less enthusiastic stores.

This is where the Spar Wine Club comes in – an initiative which Carr and sidekick Liz Aked have developed further in 1994.

'We thought we'd have to bully people to take a bigger wine range,' says Carr, 'but we've found that you just have to enthuse them and provide access to information.' As a result, the club has expanded its membership from 250 to over 400 in the last year.

Apart from organising tastings, visits to vineyards and information packs, the Spar Wine Club has this year targeted New World wines to help establish Spar as a wine-friendly convenience store, not just a place to buy Spar Crumpets, Spar Low Fat Dairy Spread and Spar Choc 'O' Dot biscuits.

The increased knowledge at store manager level is paying off. The average Spar 'till ring', as it's known in the trade, is £2.30, so getting customers to spend £4 on a bottle of wine is no mean feat. 'We try to keep things under a fiver,' adds Carr, 'because we have to be realistic. People aren't going to walk into their local store and spend £8 on a bottle of wine they don't know.'

The focus remains on inexpensive drinking from Italy, Germany, France and Spain because, as Carr says, 'we simply have many more products from those countries'. But the horizons of Spar's customers are expanding. According to Carr, 'New World wines have been an instant success', with Jacob's Creek, red and white, the best-selling New World wines in Spar stores. Significantly, both are over £4.

The new Table Mountain Pinot Noir from South Africa has been a 'hot seller' and, with new quality wines from Australia's Orlando and Lindemans, an extremely fruity Chilean Cabernet/Merlot and a good robust South African red, Spar's customers are being given a glimpse of the southern hemisphere wines previously confined to more up-market emporia.

Eastern Europe has come into sharper focus, too, as Bulgaria reasserts itself with better reds and Hungary starts to establish a following, thanks in part to flying winemakers such as Nick Butler and Kym Milne producing clean, fruity wines to a formula. Even the Czech Republic gets a look in at Spar with a velvety (put it down to the Velvet Revolution) Moravian Hills red. Carr and Aked have continued to champion the South of France, most notably with excellent-value wines from Domaines Virginie and the giant Val d'Orbieu co-operative.

Spar means thrift in Dutch as well as fir tree, hence the Spar logo (the business was founded in Holland in 1932). The founders and their heirs must be happy with the expanding, but good-value wine range on offer in their British outlets. We said last year that there aren't many chains with a better picked range under £5, and we haven't changed our minds. Long may the acorns grow.

White

Under £3

FRANCE

Vin de Pays du Gers, Le Mounerot
0 / 3 / ▍   12/20
Sweetish, green apple white from Gascony. The Plaimont co-operative usually comes up with better things than this.

Spar Vin de Pays des Côtes Catalanes
££ / 2 / ▍   15/20
A blend of the Mediterranean grape varieties, Macabeu, Grenache and Muscat from the go-ahead Rivesaltes co-operative. Fragrant, fresh dry white with a bit of southern weight.

GERMANY

Spar Rosenlieb 5% volume
£ / 6 / ▍   12/20
Rose petal and beeswax aromas characterise this sweet, fizzy Liebfraumilch from the St Ursula stable.

HUNGARY

Spar Danube White
0 / 3 / ▊   12/20
Szurkebarat and Rajnai Rizling are the grapes here, as if you hadn't
guessed. A dullish, sweet white with a bit of spice.

ITALY

Spar Soave
£ / 3 / ▊   13/20
Clean neutral Soave (just for a change) with a soft finish.

PORTUGAL

Spar Portuguese Table Wine
££ / 2 / ▊   14/20
From the Benfica co-operative, presumably near Lisbon, this
peachy Muscat-style white was made by Paolo Nigra, an acolyte
of pioneering Australian winemaker, Peter Bright. Eusebio probably
drinks this one.

£3-5

AUSTRALIA

1993 Lindemans Cawarra, Colombard/Chardonnay
££ / 3 / ▊   15/20
Low in alcohol for an Australian white at ten per cent, but not
short of mouth-filling, ripe tropical fruit and oak flavours.

1993 Hardy's Nottage Hill Chardonnay
£ / 3 / ▊   13/20
Rather obvious, sweet white from Down Under. Half a glass would
be more than enough.

1992 Orlando RF Chardonnay
££ / 3 / ▊   15/20
The best vintage of RF we've had yet, with more restrained oak
handling and fresh melon and citrus fruit flavours.

1993 Jacob's Creek Riesling
£££ / 2 / ◖   16/20

No longer sold in a Germanic flute bottle, but this is still a textbook Aussie Riesling with fresh, zesty, lime-like fruit and a refreshingly dry streak of acidity holding the wine nicely in balance.

CHILE

1993 Andes Peaks Sauvignon Blanc, Santa Emiliana
0 / 3 / ◖   12/20

Basic undistinguished Chilean white with very little in the way of Sauvignon Blanc character. Peaked a little early.

FRANCE

Spar Viognier, Cuxac
££ / 2 / ◖   16/20

One of the best of the new wave of Languedoc Viogniers made by Serge Dubois at the Cuxac co-operative. Fruity, complex apricot and orange peel flavours with none of the sickliness sometimes associated with cheap Viognier.

1992 Chablis, La Chablisienne
£ / 2 / ◖   15/20

Not the greatest 1992 Chablis from the top-notch La Chablisienne co-operative. Fatness and opulence have replaced the elegance we have found in other blends from the same vintage.

1992 Côtes de Saint-Mont, Tuilerie du Bosc
££ / 2 / ◖   14/20

An oak-aged blend of Gros Manseng, Corbu and Arrufiac, the three white musketeers of Gascony. A touch of angelica spice and fruit marked by green acidity.

Chasan, Oaked Vin de Pays d'Oc
££ / 2 / ◖   15/20

A Languedoc curiosity made by Australian John Weeks at Domaines Virginie near Béziers. This Chardonnay/Listan crossing has produced a crisp, lightly oaked white.

GERMANY

1992 Piesporter Goldtröpfchen Riesling QbA, Grans-Fassian
££ / 3 / ▌   15/20

A powerfully floral bouquet and plenty of sweet and sour grapefruity intensity from one of the Mosel's better producers.

1992 Niersteiner Spiegelberg Kabinett
£ / 3 / ▌   13/20

Light, grapey Müller-Thurgau, one step up from Liebfraumilch.

HUNGARY

Dunavar Prestige Chardonnay
££ / 2 / ▌   15/20

Made at Antinori's new winery in Hungary, this is a stylishly packaged, unoaked Chardonnay that would cost twice as much if it were produced in Italy, or Burgundy for that matter.

PORTUGAL

Spar Vinho Verde, Alamo
£ / 3 / ▌   13/20

Davy Crockett wouldn't have given up his racoon-fur hat for this neutral, off-dry blend of Encruzado and Trajaduro. Not one of Sogrape's greatest hits.

1992 Duque de Viseu, Dão, Sogrape
££ / 2 / ▌   15/20

This is more like it. Another Portuguese white based on the Encruzado grape, but this time greater ripeness and fermentation in new Portuguese oak have given the wine a lot more texture and character.

Red

Under £3

BULGARIA

Spar Russe, Cabernet/Cinsault
££ / MB / 🍷   14/20
Fruity, savoury Bulgarian blend with plenty of charred, coconut
oak character.

CZECH REPUBLIC

Moravia Hills Czech Red Wine
£££ / MB / 🍷   15/20
Produced near the Austrian border from Vavrinecke and Frankovka
grapes by flying winemaker Nick Butler, this is a pepper and plum
style red with some cool climate elegance.

FRANCE

Spar Vin de Pays des Côtes Catalanes
£ / MB / 🍷   13/20
Clean, light, aromatic Roussillon red which falls short on the finish.

HUNGARY

Spar Danube Red
££ / MB / 🍷   15/20
A KKK special, but nothing to do with pointed white hoods and
flaming crosses. The KKK in question are Kekfrankos and Kadarka
from Kiskoros, and very enjoyable they are too. A soft, juicy red
with beetroot and pepper undertones.

ITALY

Spar Merlot del Veneto
£ / LB / 🍷   13/20
From Boscaini, which also supplies Spar's Soave and Valpolicella,
this is a herbaceous, light quaffer with notable acidity.

£3-5

AUSTRALIA

1992 Nottage Hill Cabernet Sauvignon
0 / FB / 🍾   13/20
Coarse, obvious minty red with hefty tannins from the sprawling BRL-Hardy operation.

1991 Orlando RF Cabernet Sauvignon
£££ / MB / 🍾   16/20
An elegant toffee, liquorice and blackcurrant style Cabernet with pleasing intensity and depth of fruit flavour.

1992 Lindemans Bin 45 Cabernet Sauvignon
££ / MB / 🍾   15/20
Smoky, brambly, classic Lindemans elegance without quite the class of the Orlando RF.

CHILE

1992 Andes Peaks Cabernet/Merlot, Santa Emiliana
£ / MB / 🍾   14/20
Cooked blackcurrants and fresh acidity make this a drinkable, if unexciting, New World red. Hardly gets past base camp.

FRANCE

1993 Spar Merlot Vin de Pays d'Oc
££ / MB / 🍾   14/20
Bottled in Bordeaux by the merchant Dulong, this Languedoc red is not a million miles away from a pleasantly ripe claret.

Spar Coteaux du Languedoc
££ / FB / 🍾   14/20
A sweet, peppery blend of Grenache and Carignan made using the carbonic maceration technique by the giant Val d'Orbieu conglomerate.

1993 Château Bories Azeau, Corbières
£££ / FB / 🍷   16/20
A spicy, Syrah-based Languedoc red with masses of colour and sweet, ripe cherry fruit. Excellent value from Val d'Orbieu.

1992 Syrah Vin de Pays d'Oc, Domaine Montariol
££ / MB / 🍷   14/20
From Domaines Virginie, this is a soft, Beaujolais-style southern French red. Enjoyable enough, but short on local colour.

Domaine de Moulin Faugères, Domaines Virginie
££ / FB / 🍷   15/20
A chewier Virginie winter warmer with more backbone and some pronounced oak character.

Spar Claret
£ / MB / 🍷   13/20
From Bordeaux merchant, Dulong, this is a light, grassy claret suffering from the dilution of the 1993 vintage.

ITALY

1993 Montepulciano d'Abruzzo, Tollo
£££ / FB / 🍷   16/20
A hugely enjoyable, unoaked, modern Italian rosso from the Abruzzi on the Adriatic coast. Fragrant, soft and full of damson fruit.

SOUTH AFRICA

1993 Table Mountain Pinot Noir
££ / FB / 🍷   15/20
Fruity, cherryish Pinot Noir with a hint of South African earthiness. Still, at just over £3, you wouldn't find anything as good from Burgundy.

1992 Oak Village Vintage Reserve
£ / FB / 🍷   13/20
Faintly minty, dry South African blend with chunky fruit and bitter tannins.

SPAIN

1989 Palacio de León
££ / MB / 🍷   14/20
A Tempranillo-based red from a co-operative in León with plenty
of coconutty, Bounty Bar style oak. A thinking person's Don Darias.

1989 Domino de Espinal, Yecla
££ / MB / 🍷   14/20
Savoury, faintly rustic Rioja-style red from Yecla, a little known
denominación in Spain's south-eastern corner.

£5–8

PORTUGAL

Vinho do Monte, Alentejo, Sogrape
£££ / FB / 🍷   16/20
A classically Portuguese blend of the southern Moreto, João
Santarem and Alfrocheiro grapes from one of the Iberian
Peninsula's most dynamic producers. Chunky, aromatic, minty stuff
with plenty of oak barrel treatment.

SPAIN

1987 Señorio de Nava, Ribera del Duero
£££ / FB / ➡   16/20
Spain's most famous red wine, Vega Sicilia, comes from the Ribera
del Duero region north of Madrid. This aged Tinto Fino
(Tempranillo) has something of the same character, with lots of
colour, sweet vanilla oak and seriously chunky blackberry fruit.
Now into its stride.

Rosé

Under £3

FRANCE

Spar Rosé de Syrah, Vin de Pays d'Oc
££ / 2 / ▌   14/20
A dry, almost steely, southern French rosé cool-fermented to
produce a strawberryish wine with a note of bubblegum. Another
success from the Cave de Cuxac.

£3-5

PORTUGAL

Spar Portuguese Rosé, Alamo
£ / 3 / ▌   13/20
A Mateus Rosé substitute for those sentimental, sepia-tinted moments.

Sparkling

£3–5

AUSTRALIA

Great Western Brut
££ / 3 / ▌   14/20
Sherbetty, tangy off-dry Aussie fizz from the deservedly popular
Seppelt offshoot of the Penfolds group.

FRANCE

Spar Roi de Paris, Vin Mousseux Brut
0 / 3 / ▌   12/20
Which king of Paris gave his name to this rather undistinguished
fizz? Off with his head.

SPAIN

Cava, Codorniu
££ / 2 / 🍷   15/20
Toasty, modern cava from the reliable Codorniu giant in Catalonia.
A third of the wine is made from Chardonnay grapes and the
balance from a trio of lesser local varieties.

£5-8

AUSTRALIA

Orlando, Carrington Brut Rosé
££ / 3 / 🍷   15/20
Strawberry fresh and fruity, pale pink fizz from Australia's Orlando
group, with enough sweetness to keep granny happy.

Over £8

FRANCE

Spar Champagne, Marquis de Prével
0 / 3 / 🍷   13/20
Perhaps the Marquis de Prével is somehow related to the Roi de
Paris. If so, put him in a tumbril too.

Fortified

Under £3

FRANCE

Muscat St Jean de Minervois, half-bottle
£ / 7 / 🍷   13/20
Sweet, alcoholic, floral, fortified white with lots of honey and
brandy snap fruit. A touch spirity. Good barbecue fuel.

TESCO ***(*)

Head Office: Old Tesco House, Delamere Road, Cheshunt, Herts, EN8 9SL

Telephone: 0992 632222

Number of branches: 497 (of which 50 have the full range) including 57 William Lows

Credit cards accepted: Access, Visa, Switch

Hours of opening: Monday to Friday 9am to 8pm; Saturday 9am to 6pm; Sunday 12am to 4pm

By-the-case sales: On specific promotions and through the Tesco wine club

Glass loan: Currently being tested in certain metropolitan stores

Home delivery: Through new wine club, Wine Select

Clubs: Wine Select. Contact Freephone 0800 403403

Discounts: No

In-store tastings: Yes, in selected stores. Permanent tasting area in top branches

Top ten best-selling wines: Tesco Hock; Tesco Liebfraumilch; Tesco Lambrusco Bianco; Tesco Claret; Tesco Vin de Pays de l'Hérault; Bulgarian Cabernet Sauvignon; Tesco Australian Red; Tesco Australian White; Tesco Escoubes, Vin de Pays des Côtes de Gascogne; Tesco Côtes du Rhône Villages

Range: GOOD: Australia, Champagne, South Africa, South America, New Zealand, regional France, Italy
AVERAGE: Bordeaux, Spain, Rhône, United States, Fortified
POOR: Eastern Europe, Alsace, Burgundy

Tesco is a supermarket chain that's going places. Literally so, in fact. After buying the northern French Catteau stores, it's now poised to hoover up to-ing and fro-ing Channel tunnel traffic with a massive off-licence in the so-called Cité de l'Europe at the French entrance to the tunnel. The giant 22,000 square foot store, devoted solely to drink, is set to open in 1995. It will be bigger than the biggest Tesco store, dwarfing poor Sainsbury's half-hearted little effort at the Mammouth hypermarket in Calais.

'Putting a toe into local markets is part of Tesco's policy of expansion,' says Stephen Clarke, Tesco's wine trading manager. 'We hope it's bringing in much-needed investment and technology.' Clarke thinks Sainsbury's underestimated its shoppers in Calais, believing they would be content to buy wines at prices where the saving is no more than the difference in duty. Tesco is aiming for a more aggressive sales pitch. The range will be 'huge' and there will 'generally be a price differential of more than just the duty'.

Not content with rolling back southern frontiers, Tesco has breached the Scottish border too with its takeover of the Dundee-based supermarket chain, William Low. After a big bucks battle with arch-rival Sainsbury's, Tesco was pushed up from its original bid of £154m to £247.4m. Until the takeover, only 16 of Tesco's 440 stores were in Scotland. Tesco now plans to turn the 57-strong William Low chain into Tesco Scotland.

Low was already being severely squeezed by the encroaching discounters on the one hand, and the likes of Safeway and Asda on the other. This is presumably why it could originally accept an offer nearly £100 million less than the final figure.

The takeover did not come as great news to the staff at Low's head office, which is being disbanded, but the move may well prove popular with Scottish shoppers, not just because they see Sainsbury's as the Sassenach enemy (Tesco's MD, Sir Ian MacLaurin is, after all, a Scot, even if he does take a bloated £1m salary), but because Tesco's development plans will favour the many Low stores outside Scotland's main conurbations.

Tesco's move across the Channel was in large part an attempt to recoup some of the estimated £40m lost on beers, wine and spirits to cross-Channel shopping. In the wine market as a whole, however, the chain remains just a nose behind Sainsbury's. Despite the drain of its customers' forays across the Channel, Tesco claims it increased turnover on wine by 12 per cent last year, although Stephen Clarke concedes that in order to do so, a lot of price cutting was needed.

The wine department, which shed its only Master of Wine during the year, continues to spend a great deal of time and energy travelling widely – 'more than any of our competitors', says Clarke – looking for interesting new things as a way of maintaining Tesco's hard-won reputation for having one of the best, if not *the* best, New World wine ranges. As Stephen Clarke says, 'We've always tried to be the most innovative of the supermarket groups, and you can't buy wines sitting behind a desk in Cheshunt.' Smaller stores now have a better representation of New World wines than in the past.

South Africa has been the biggest growth area over the past year, thanks in part to the country's move into the modern, post-apartheid winemaking era. With 23 South African wines on the list, Tesco has more than any other supermarket, and the line-up includes a clutch of excellent wines from the Swartland co-operative and Danie de Wet, the Chardonnay king of Robertson.

Tesco's claim to be the market leader in Australian wines (with 18 per cent of sales) is backed by a list of no fewer than 67 Aussie wines. The list is about much more than well-known brands and cheap own-labels. Among Tesco's more exciting Oz wines are several higher priced estate wines from Tarrawarra, Delatite and Mitchelton in Victoria, St Halletts, Chapel Hill, Tim Adams and Pewsey Vale in South Australia, and Western Australia's Cape Mentelle. As Australian wine becomes more expensive owing to the current grape shortage, it is encouraging to see a supermarket favouring quality and diversity.

Tesco continues to work with flying winemakers, mainly Jacques Lurton and Kym Milne, and has signed up John Worontschak, the Aussie behind the current success of English wines, to make Tesco's first two own-label Brazilian wines, a Cabernet/Merlot and a Chardonnay/Semillon called Aurora.

In the increasingly difficult classic wine regions of Europe, the area that impressed us most this year was Tesco's range of £3 to £5 Italian wines. The buying team has come up with some characterful Italian whites and a handful of even better reds, such as the Rosso del Salento, the Casale del Giglio Shiraz, the Villa Pigna Rosso Piceno and a much-improved Chianti range. In France, the Les Domaines range continues to provide good-value substitutes from the South of France for the pricier classics.

We pointed out last year that for an innovative supermarket, it was surprising to see Tesco lagging behind in Eastern Europe, where it was undoubtedly less enterprising than Safeway and Sainsbury's. This is still true, although Tesco does claim to be the biggest retailer of Hungarian wines. According to Stephen Clarke, 'It is still very difficult to ensure continuity of supply, because they've gone from a command economy to a free market so fast that they're missing a generation of middle managers. The sample you get is often great, the first lorryload not quite so good, the second less good, and the third undrinkable.'

Another innovation has been the introduction of in-store wine advisers at the large Tescos in Amersham, Sandhurst and New Malden. The idea has been so successful that the number will be increased to 50 over the coming months. 'They're there to provide basic, confidence-building knowledge for people,' says Clarke. Tesco is also developing a wine guide as part of something called 'touch-screen purchasing', presumably for the stores where there are no in-store advisers.

All in all, then, this has been an exciting year for Tesco, with further expansion planned for the next 12 months. The direct-mail wine club, reported to be in the offing last year was finally launched at the beginning of October 1994. Otherwise, the range continues to be one of the largest and most interesting in the high street.

One small moan is that wine label design could be improved. This doesn't mean Tesco should go the Asda route of weird and colourful fantasy labels. But the package, in many cases, could definitely do with some brightening up. Mind you, there are so many other things going on at Tesco that improved packaging may have to wait.

White

Under £3

AUSTRALIA

Tesco Australian White, Rhine Riesling, South-East Australia
£ / 3 / 🌢   13/20
An off-dry Aussie Rhine Riesling from the giant Penfolds corporation. Pleasantly floral, but not up to the previous vintage.

CHILE

Tesco Chilean White
£ / 2 / ▌   13/20
A cool-fermented, modern blend of 95 per cent Sauvignon Blanc
and 5 per cent Semillon from the Canepa winery near Santiago.
Zesty citrus fruit with a faintly bitter finish.

FRANCE

Tesco Escoubes, Vin de Pays des Côtes de Gascogne, Yves Grassa
0 / 2 / ▌   12/20
A wine which has crept below the £3 mark in the last year, and has
found its way into Tesco's top ten as a result. We liked this confected,
under-ripe vin de pays about as much as we did last year.

GERMANY

Tesco Hock, Deutscher Tafelwein
££ / 5 / ▌   14/20
Pleasant, clean grapefruity Müller-Thurgau-based white with some
fresh acidity. Better value than most cheap German whites.

Tesco Liebfraumilch, Nahe
£ / 5 / ▌   13/20
Fresh acceptable stuff, if a wee bit lacking in concentration. Wee's
the word.

ITALY

1993 Tesco Bianco del Salento
££ / 2 / ▌   14/20
An unusual marriage of 75 per cent Verdeca, 17 per cent
Chardonnay and 8 per cent Sauvignon Blanc made by travelling
Australian, Kym Milne. Peachy, soft white with a lime-like streak.

Tesco Lambrusco Bianco, Vino Frizzante Naturale
0 / 6 / ▌   11/20
A sweet confection in a screwtop bottle, apparently with natural
bubbles.

SOUTH AFRICA

Tesco South African White
££ / 3 / █   14/20
An enjoyable, off-dry blend of three parts Chenin Blanc to one
part Muscat of Alexandria. The perfume of the latter grape certainly
hits you between the eyes. A good introduction to South African
whites – wines, that is.

£3–5

AUSTRALIA

Tesco Australian Colombard/Chardonnay, Kingston Estate
£ / 2 / █   13/20
Made by Greek winemaker Sarantos Moularadellis in the Australian
Riverland, this is a ripe, if dilute Aussie quaffer.

Tesco Australian Chardonnay, South-East Australia
££ / 3 / █   15/20
From the same producer, this is a considerably more convincing
wine. Forget the naff, surfer label and enjoy soft, tropical fruit
flavours of pineapple and melon.

1993 Pewsey Vale Rhine Riesling
£££ / 2 / █   16/20
From a vineyard which was established in the mid-nineteenth
century, this shows the crisp, cool climate intensity of Rhine
Riesling from South Australia's elevated Adelaide Hills. Intensely
tangy stuff with loads of lime fruit flavour.

1992 Old Triangle Semillon/Chardonnay
£ / 3 / █   14/20
Like Pewsey Vale, this comes from a small vineyard belonging to
the Hill-Smiths of Yalumba. An oaky blend trying to be more elegant
than it is.

FRANCE

Tesco Graves, Yvon Mau
0 / 2 / 🍷   12/20
This partially oak-aged Bordeaux blend of Sauvignon Blanc and
Semillon sounds more interesting on paper than it proves to be in
the bottle. So let's leave it there, shall we.

1993 Tesco Domaine Saubagnère, Vin de Pays des Côtes de Gascogne, Yves Grassa
£ / 2 / 🍷   13/20
At nearly £4, this is not cheap for a Gascon white. It's better than
the basic Escoubes, also from Yves Grassa, but still has an off-
putting green apple tartness. Has Yves Grassa lost his magic touch?

1993 Domaine Lapiarre, Côtes de Duras
££ / 2 / 🍷   15/20
A wine which was rescued from the clutches of the local co-
operative by innovative English wine importer, Andrew Gordon.
An aromatic Sauvignon Blanc, from south-western France with a
good stab at New Zealand-like tropical, grapefruity flavours.

1993 Tesco White Burgundy, Cave de Viré
£ / 2 / 🍷   14/20
A new supplier for Tesco's house white Burgundy. A pleasant,
slightly spicy, unoaked Chardonnay from the reliable Viré co-
operative.

1992 Gaston Dorléans Vouvray Demi-Sec
££ / 4 / 🍷   15/20
The Bourillon-Dorléans family make some of the best wines in
Vouvray. This smoky, medium dry Chenin Blanc pulls off a deft
balancing act between sweetness and the grape variety's high
natural acidity.

1993 Marsanne, Domaine de Montaubéron, Vin de Pays des Côtes de Thongue
££ / 2 / 🍷   15/20
In 1969 proprietor Paul de Saret de Bertier was one of the first in
the Languedoc to plant the Rhône Valley's Marsanne grape just a
few kilometres from the Mediterranean. The old vines have given

depth and concentration to this creamy, aniseedy dry white.

1992 Domaine Saint James Viognier
£ / 2 / 🍾   14/20
A strident, apricot jam style white from the Corbières region with
an almost overpowering bouquet and barrel-fermentation
characters. A fattish, idiosyncratic wine.

1992 Tesco Les Domaines de la Source, Muscat, Vin de Pays de l'Hérault
££ / 2 / 🍾   15/20
An elegant, grapey dry Muscat from Delta Domaines' unusual,
volcanic soils between Béziers and the Mediterranean.

1993 Les Domaines de St Pierre, Chardonnay, Vin de Pays d'Oc
££ / 2 / 🍾   15/20
A modern, fresh, unoaked Chardonnay from the Languedoc, closer
to the restrained French style than the New World.

GERMANY

1992 Bereich Johannisberg Riesling, QbA, Krayer
£ / 3 / 🍾   13/20
A sweetish Rheingau Riesling showing the neutral flavours you'd
expect from comparatively high yields of 88 hectolitres per hectare.

ITALY

Tesco Bianco del Piemonte
£ / 2 / 🍾   13/20
An appley, typically sharp Cortese from the Monferrato region of
Piemonte. A bit of a yawn.

Tesco Bianco del Lazio, Fontana Candida
££ / 2 / 🍾   14/20
This southern Italian blend of Trebbiano, Malvasia and Chardonnay
comes from Frascati wine merchants Fontana Candida. A citrusy
white with a bitter lemon twist. Ideal for post penalty shoot out
nerves. If he weren't a Buddhist, Roberto Baggio would be drinking
this by the containerload.

1993 Tesco Verdicchio Classico
££ / 2 / ▋   15/20

A classically nutty Verdicchio with plenty of concentration and character made by Garofoli. It shows what cool-fermentation can add to this native grape variety when it's done well.

1992 Tesco Villa Cerro Soave Recioto, 50cl
£ / 5 / ━   14/20

A sweet, barrel-aged white from the Veneto region made from sugar-rich dried grapes in the traditional way. A pleasant ripe pear and honey style, which lacks the intensity of the best Reciotos.

1993 Chardonnay del Salento, Le Trulle
££ / 2 / ▋   15/20

A cleverly made southern Italian Chardonnay with plenty of fresh, peachy fruit, grapefruity acidity and a touch of oak character from flying Australian winemaker, Kym Milne.

NEW ZEALAND

Tesco New Zealand Dry White
£ / 3 / ▋   13/20

Specially blended for Tesco by Villa Maria's retiring, white-haired ventriloquist, George Fistonich, this is a fragrant, commercial blend of New Zealand's most widely planted grape variety, Müller-Thurgau, with a dash of Gewürztraminer for character.

1992 Tesco New Zealand Sauvignon Blanc, Riverlea Wines, Gisborne
££ / 2 / ▋   14/20

A green bean and tropical fruit Sauvignon Blanc from Cooks, with asparagus shoots thrown in for good measure. Good value at under £4.

Tesco New Zealand Chardonnay, Cooper's Creek, Gisborne
££ / 2 / ▋   15/20

Made by pony-tailed winemaker Kim Crawford, from grapes grown at Matawhero near Gisborne, this is a caramel fudge and toasty oak Chardonnay cut by zippy, cool climate acidity.

SOUTH AFRICA

1994 Tesco Robertson Chardonnay
££££ / 2 / 🖢   ··   **16/20**
A wine which shows Chardonnay specialist Danie de Wet on top
form. Using one-third barrel-fermentation for some buttery
richness, this is a refreshing, citrusy white with a balance typical
of de Wet's superb Chardonnays.

1993 Tesco Swartland Sauvignon Blanc
££ / 2 / 🖢   **15/20**
Produced at the first-rate Swartland co-operative by Johan de Villiers
and the delightfully named Christo Kock, this is a grassy,
gooseberry-scented white in the assertive New Zealand mould.

Tesco Robertson Chardonnay/Colombard
££ / 2 / 🖢   **14/20**
A crisp, dry, citrus-fruity blend of Chardonnay and Colombard
grapes made at the high-tech Madeba estate by itinerant Aussie
winemaker John Worontschak, better known for his myriad English
wines.

1994 Oak Village Sauvignon Blanc, Stellenbosch
£ / 3 / 🖢   **13/20**
Commercial, fruity Cape Sauvignon Blanc with a prickle of carbon
dioxide. Not one of South Africa's greatest Sauvignon Blancs.

SPAIN

1992 Galician Albariño
££ / 2 / 🖢   **15/20**
Believe it or not, £4.99 is cheap for an Albariño, the most coveted
white grape variety in Spanish restaurants. A rich, aromatic, honey
and grapefruit-like dry white reminiscent of Alsace at its best.

£5–8

AUSTRALIA

1993 St Halletts Semillon/Sauvignon
£ / 2 / ▌   15/20
From a Barossa Valley winery better known for its Old Block Shiraz
and Cabernet/Merlot reds, this is an opulent, lemony, unoaked
blend with lots of grassy character. Ought to be £2 cheaper.

1992 Tesco McLaren Vale Chardonnay, Ryecroft
££ / 2 / ▌   16/20
McLaren Vale, with its Mediterranean climate, is one of the best
vineyard areas in South Australia. This ripe, richly oaked
Chardonnay is just the sort of wine to conquer British palates.

1992 Delatite Dead Man's Hill Gewürztraminer
££ / 3 / ▌   15/20
Fresh, zesty, cool climate Gewürztraminer, an unusual variety in
Australia, from winemaker Rosalind Ritchie, with lime and spice
fruit sweetness and a crispness rarely found in Alsace examples of
the grape.

FRANCE

1991 Domaine de la Jalousie, Cuvée Bois, Vin de Pays des Côtes de Gascogne, Yves Grassa
£ / 2 / ▌   14/20
Further evidence that Yves Grassa's mantle has slipped in recent
vintages. This overpriced, clumsily oaked Gascon white is not a
patch on the 1990.

1993 Tesco Sancerre, Alphonse Mellot
££ / 1 / ▌   15/20
The iconoclastic Alphonse Mellot has been associated with Tesco
for five years now, selecting elegant, finely balanced Sancerres
with fresh acidity. This doesn't live up to his estate wines, but it's
still pretty good.

Château Liot, Sauternes, half-bottle

££ / 7 / ▌ 16/20

A dessert wine curiosity from Bordeaux, bottled specially for Tesco by Château Liot in the commune of Barsac. The peculiarity lies in the fact that this is a blend of two vintages, 1991 and 1992. Otherwise, it's an elegant, Semillon-dominated Sauternes with classic wax, honey and lemon-curd characters, polished by flavours of new oak and peachy botrytis.

GERMANY

1991 Grans-Fassian Riesling Trocken

££ / 1 / ► 16/20

Winemaker Gerhard Grans produces sculpted, demanding Mosel Rieslings with pure, if austere, green apple fruit flavours. Some may find this ultra-dry white a little too lean, but we loved it. Its petrol and lime-like character should evolve nicely.

Over £8

AUSTRALIA

1993 Tim Adams Semillon, Clare Valley

££ / 2 / ▌ 16/20

A ripe, creamy, toasty, barrel-fermented Semillon from one of the best producers in the comparatively cool Clare Valley. Herbal freshness, lots of fruit concentration and a crisp, dry finish. A wine that will age – if you let it.

FRANCE

1990 Château Magneau, Graves

£ / 2 / ► 15/20

From a vineyard tucked away in a pine forest, this is a rich, massively toasty, barrel-fermented white Graves with plenty of Semillon padding to absorb the shock of the barrel staves.

Red

Under £3

AUSTRALIA

Tesco Australian Red, Shiraz/Cabernet Sauvignon, South Australia
£££ / MB / 🍷   14/20
A classic Aussie blend from the Penfolds group. This is a minty, somewhat chewy red relying on fruit rather than oak for effect.

BULGARIA

Tesco Bulgarian Cabernet Sauvignon
0 / MB / 🍷   11/20
Raisiny, stewed and rustic, a Bulgarian Cabernet from the old school.

CHILE

Tesco Chilean Red
£ / MB / 🍷   13/20
A modern, blackcurrant pastille style blend of Cabernet Sauvignon and Malbec made by the go-ahead Canepa operation.

FRANCE

Dorgan, Vin de Pays de l'Aude, Mont Tauch
0 / MB / 🍷   12/20
Produced by the normally excellent Mont Tauch co-operative from Carignan grapes grown around the Corbières village of Tuchan, this is sturdy southern plonk, which could have done with a term or two at charm school.

1993 Grand Carat, Vin de Pays du Comté Tolosan
0 / LB / 🍷   10/20
A 2- rather than 24-carat red.

Tesco Vin de Pays des Côtes de Perignan
££ / MB / ▌   14/20
A fresh, lively, spicy southern quaffer with some tannic grip at a
very affordable price.

Tesco Claret, Yvon Mau
£ / MB / ▌   13/20
A herbaceous young claret with pleasant light fruit but a slightly
tart, astringent finish.

Tesco Vin de Pays de l'Hérault
££ / MB / ▌   14/20
The star of Tesco's top ten best-sellers, this is a juicy, gluggable,
spicy southern French red with cherry fruit and soft-textured
carbonic maceration character.

ITALY

Tesco Rosso del Salento
£££ / MB / ▌   15/20
A brilliant-value southern Italian blend of Negroamaro, Malvasia
Nera and Sangiovese. A sweet, baked Mediterranean red with warm,
spicy flavours.

SOUTH AFRICA

Tesco South African Red
£££ / FB / ▌   15/20
Made from a highly unusual combination of mainly Cinsault, Tinta
Barroca and Shiraz, this is a smooth, minty red with soft tannins
and a distinctively animal South African bite. Rather like the
Springbok prop forward, Hennie Le Roux.

£3–5

AUSTRALIA

Tesco Australian Shiraz
£ / FB / ▌   14/20
Produced by someone or something known as The Vales, this is a

sweet, leathery old-fashioned Shiraz with a tough finish.

BULGARIA

1988 Tesco Bulgarian Cabernet Sauvignon Reserve, Suhindol
££ / MB / **❚**   14/20

A comparatively modern Bulgarian Cabernet Sauvignon from the much-vaunted (by the Bulgarians) Suhindol region. Loads of charred, toasty American oak and sweet berry fruit.

CHILE

Tesco Chilean Cabernet Sauvignon, Mondragon, Maipo Valley
££ / MB / **❚**   15/20

Considerably better than Tesco's basic Chilean red, this is a wine with more fruit sweetness and grip. Thoroughly enjoyable stuff.

FRANCE

1992 Tesco Vintage Claret, Yvon Mau
££ / MB / **❚**   14/20

Aged in new oak, this Merlot-dominated claret has plenty of soft, fruitcake sweetness and good balance for a young red produced in one of Bordeaux' lesser recent vintages.

Tesco St Emilion
£ / MB / **❚**   14/20

Aromatic, soft, lead-pencil Right Bank Merlot with a slightly astringent aftertaste.

Tesco Graves
0 / MB / **❚**   13/20

A rather rustic Left Bank claret from Pierre Coste, one of Bordeaux's winemaking gurus, better known for his white wines than his reds.

1989 Tesco Les Domaines, Buzet, Domaine de la Croix
££ / MB / **❚**   15/20

A Bordeaux-style blend from a reliable *appellation* in south-western France dominated by the Buzet co-operative. At under £4, this supple red is a good claret substitute.

1990 Domaine Beaulieu, Saint Sauveur, Côtes du Marmandais
£££ / MB / ▌   16/20
A blend of Merlot, Cabernet Franc and Cabernet Sauvignon, this Bordeaux-style wine comes from a small region in south-western France, just east of the Entre-Deux-Mers. A rich, soft red which has markedly improved over the past year. One to frighten complacent Bordeaux châteaux owners.

1989 Domaine de Lanestousse, Madiran
£££ / FB / ▌   17/20
From the most southerly domaine in Madiran in the foothills of the Pyrenees, this is a chocolatey, gamey Cabernet Franc dominated red with a lovely core of sweet and savoury fruit. At 45 per cent, the traditional Tannat grape component is lower than in most Madiran. Could that be why the wine tastes so good?

Tesco Beaujolais
£ / MB / ▌   13/20
Acceptable, if unexciting, basic Gamay from the Bully co-operative in the Bas Beaujolais. Both are better-known for Beaujolais Nouveau.

1993 Tesco Côtes du Rhône Villages
£ / MB / ▌   13/20
A faintly peppery, Grenache-based red, which would be fine for a Côtes du Rhône rather than a supposedly superior Côtes du Rhône Villages.

1991 La Vieille Ferme, Côtes du Rhône
££ / MB / ▌   15/20
This one is a Côtes du Rhône – confusingly, perhaps, given that it's £1 more expensive that Tesco's Côtes du Rhône Villages. The fact that this wine was made by François Perrin of Châteauneuf-du-Pape's Château de Beaucastel may have something to do with the price differential. It's certainly in a different class, with rich, chocolatey fruit and plenty of oomph.

1992 Domaine de Prebayon, Côtes du Rhône Villages
£ / MB / ◗ 14/20

From Gabriel Meffre, one of the southern Rhône's better *négociants*, this is a modern, carbonic maceration style quaffer with enjoyable sweet fruit.

1991 Tesco Les Domaines des Baumelles, Côtes du Lubéron
££ / MB / ◗ 15/20

The grapes from this Rhône Valley domaine are vinified by well-known winemaker Jean-Louis Ribeyrolle at Château Val Joanis. It's a perfumed, Grenache-based spicy red with commendable concentration given that half of the Rhône Valley was under water during the 1992 vintage.

1992 Domaine Maurel Fonsalade, Oak-Aged, St Chinian
££ / FB / ▬ 15/20

Produced on the heavier clay soils of St Chinian in the Languedoc, this is a chunky, almost rustic style with masses of colour, tannin, oak and concentrated sweet fruit. Give it time.

1993 Tesco Domaine de la Source, Syrah
£ / LB / ◗ 13/20

A light, raspberry fresh Languedoc Syrah made in an easy-drinking wine bar mould. Wallpaper wine for couch potatoes.

ITALY

Tesco Rosso del Piemonte
£ / MB / ◗ 13/20

Basic, sweetish, north-west Italian red. Piemonte's answer to *négociant* Bourgogne Rouge.

Tesco Rosso del Lazio
££ / MB / ◗ 15/20

A Roman blend of Merlot and Sangiovese made in an attractively soft, cherry fruity style. Brilliant value at just over £3.

1993 Casale del Giglio Shiraz, Vino da Tavola del Lazio
££ / MB / ◗ 15/20

This old-style Roman co-operative has been transformed in private hands, producing a series of experimental wines from Merlot,

Cabernet Sauvignon, Syrah and Petit Verdot. A delightfully fresh, berry fruit style with no oak to get in the way of the exuberance.

1989 Villa Pigna Rosso Piceno
£££ / MB / ▌   16/20
From the Italian Marche region on the Adriatic, this is like a rustic Chianti, blending Sangiovese and local Montepulciano grapes aged in old oak for three years. The wine has turned into a meaty, bitter-chocolate style bargain.

1992 Tesco Chianti Classico
£££ / MB / ▭   16/20
A surprisingly good follow-on to the excellent 1990 from the Grevepesa co-operative. This is an approachable, almost sumptuous Chianti, just the sort of thing to turn French wine lovers on to the delights of Tuscany.

1993 Primitivo del Salento, Le Trulle
£ / MB / ▌   13/20
Primitivo is said by pointy-headed ampelographers (that's grape scientists to you and us), to be the same grape as the Zinfandel of California. Tasting this Kym Milne southern Italian red, you can see the similarities between Zin and the jammy fruit and dry, rustic tannins on show here.

MEXICO

1990 Tesco Mexican Cabernet Sauvignon, LA Cetto
££ / FB / ▭   15/20
Not quite as good as the astonishingly concentrated 1988 and 1989 Cabernet Sauvignons, but this massively fruity, oaky red from Mexico's Baja California peninsula is still great value at under £4.

NEW ZEALAND

1990 Tesco New Zealand Cabernet Sauvignon, Auckland, Cooper's Creek
£ / MB / ▌   14/20
This weedy blend of Cabernet Sauvignon and 15 per cent Merlot from vineyards near Auckland on North Island is beginning to show its age, so drink up.

1991 Tesco New Zealand Cabernet Sauvignon/Merlot, Riverlea Wines, Gisborne

££ / MB / ❜   15/20

From the Corbans stable, this is a Gisborne blend with typical elegantly grassy fruit and well-judged oak. One of the cheaper New Zealand reds on the British market.

PORTUGAL

1991 JP Barrel Selection

0 / FB / ❨   11/20

JP stands for João Pires rather than Just Passable. Made from the Periquita grape in the Terras do Sado region of southern Portugal, this dried-out, jammy red is on the way to a premature grave.

SOUTH AFRICA

Tesco Stellenbosch Merlot

£ / FB / ❜   13/20

A grassy, slightly cooked South African Merlot from two separate producers, the Heldeberg co-operative and Overgaauw estate. Closer to a Cabernet Franc than a Merlot in style.

1992 Oak Village Vintage Reserve, Vinfruco

££ / MB / ❜   15/20

An oaky Cape blend of Shiraz, Merlot, Cabernet Sauvignon and Cinsault made using the combined efforts of two co-operatives and the Overgaauw estate. With its rustic, strawberry sweetness and firm tannins, it reminded us of an Hautes-Côtes red Burgundy.

SPAIN

1987 Tesco Rioja Reserva, Viña Mara, Berberana

££ / MB / ❜   14/20

A mature Tempranillo-based Rioja, showing plenty of coconut and vanilla oak and supple fruitiness. Drink up.

UNITED STATES

Tesco Californian Zinfandel
£ / MB / ▐   14/20
From Zinfandel specialists Stratford, this is a light, tobacco-pouch style of Zinfandel, leavened with a dash of Cabernet Sauvignon. Slightly marred by residual sugar, presumably catering for the sweet-toothed American palate.

£5–8

AUSTRALIA

1992 McLaren Vale Merlot, Ryecroft
£ / FB / ►   14/20
Thick, sweet, obvious Australian red with lots of oak and rather hard tannins. Fair enough, but one-dimensional.

1991 Delatite Devils River Cabernet/Merlot
££ / MB / ►   16/20
From the cool climate vineyards in the foothills of the Victorian Alps, this is an Australian red with a difference. Fresh, elegant and distinctly minty, with a fine balance between herbaceous berry fruit and unobtrusive oak.

1992 Tesco Yarra Glen Pinot Noir
££ / MB / ▐   16/20
The second wine of Pinot Noir specialists Tarrawarra, this comes from Victoria's Yarra Valley, recognised in Australia as the variety's second home. Fruit sweetness and a touch of oak spiciness make this a good-value alternative to red Burgundy.

FRANCE

1990 Château de Goelane, Bordeaux Supérieur
££ / MB / ▐   15/20
Traditional, mature but tannic claret with Cabernet Sauvignon in the ascendant. Will benefit from robust food.

1990 Clos de Chenôves, Bourgogne Rouge, Cave de Buxy
£ / MB / ▐   13/20
An oak-aged red from one of Burgundy's better co-operatives in
the Côte Chalonnaise. Unfortunately, this dry, slightly green Pinot
Noir is not one of their best efforts.

1992 Domaine de Conroy, Brouilly, St Charles
£ / MB / ▐   14/20
From the largest of Beaujolais' ten crus, this is a sweet, well-made
Gamay from eccentric barrel broker Jean de St Charles' estate.

1991 Châteauneuf-du-Pape, Les Arnevels, J. Quiot
£ / FB / ➖   14/20
A traditional, Grenache-dominated Châteauneuf from Jérôme
Quiot's extensive 86-hectare vineyard. Quiot is currently President
of the Institut National des Appellations d'Origine, so perhaps he
spends rather too much time away from home. Heady but distinctly
bitter stuff.

ITALY

1991 Villa Pigna, Cabernesco
£ / MB / ➖   14/20
A supertuscan red made entirely from Cabernet Sauvignon, with
the obligatory heavy duty designer bottle and plenty of oak flavour.
Good, if a little overworked, and not particularly Italian.

1990 Tesco Chianti Classico Riserva
£ / MB / ➖   14/20
Dry and serious Chianti from the Grevepesa co-operative. A little
too austere for its own good, but showing some concentrated
underlying fruit.

1986 Villa Cerro Valpolicella Amarone
0 / FB / ▐   13/20
A composty, raisiny blend of traditional Valpolicella varieties,
starting to fall apart at the seams. Chewy, hefty stuff. Not the best
example of Amarone on the market.

SOUTH AFRICA

1992 Kanonkop Pinotage
£££ / FB / ⮕   17/20
At just under £7, you can experience South Africa's best
Pinotage, produced in a traditional style by winemaker
Beyers Truter. Deeply coloured, concentrated, strapping
stuff with lots of ripe tannin, sawdusty, vanilla oak and sweet
raspberry and plum fruitiness.

Over £8

FRANCE

Château Michelet, Bordeaux, 2 Litres
££ / MB / ▌   14/20
Soft, juicy, full-flavoured claret in a box. Just the thing for
Conservative Association dinners, jumble sales and garden parties.

1987 Château St Georges, St Georges St Emilion
££ / MB / ▌   16/20
1987 was more successful on the Merlot-dominated Right Bank of
the Dordogne in Bordeaux than in the Médoc. This supple, minty,
mature claret from a St Emilion satellite *appellation* proves the
point. Cry God for claret, England and Michael Portillo!

SPAIN

1982 Campillo Gran Reserva Rioja
£££ / MB / ▌   17/20
Campillo is one of the few estates in Rioja to make its wines
solely from the Tempranillo grape. This is a modern style,
which uses American and French oak combined with
prolonged bottle-ageing to achieve its effect. And the effect
is stunning in this savoury, mature red, which still has
plenty of life left in it.

Rosé

Under £3

FRANCE

Domaine de la Done, Rosé de Syrah, J.P. & M. Dardé
££ / 2 / ⌐   13/20
Clean, dry, delicately strawberry-flavoured Syrah rosé from a 70-
hectare estate in the Languedoc. With that many hectares to choose
from, it ought to have a bit more oomph.

Sparkling

£5-8

AUSTRALIA

Tesco Australian Sparkling Wine
£ / 2 / ⌐   14/20
Commercial, sherbetty, big-bubbled sparkler from Seppelt's Great
Western winery in Victoria.

FRANCE

1989 Tesco Crémant de Bourgogne, Cave de Viré
£ / 2 / ⌐   14/20
Appley, toasty fizz from the Cave de Viré in southern Burgundy.
Starting to show its age.

**Crémant de Loire Rosé, Cave des Vignerons de Saumur,
Cuvée de la Chevalerie**
££ / 2 / ⌐   16/20
An intriguingly grassy pink fizz dominated by the Cabernet Franc
grape. Dry, elegant, characterful stuff, as used by the Saumur
Cavalry for sabre practice.

Over £8

FRANCE

Tesco Premier Cru Brut Champagne
££ / 2 / ▮   15/20
A young Champagne with the accent on fresh lemony fruit rather than nutty bottle-development characters. A good house fizz at just under £12.

Tesco Blanc de Noirs Champagne
£££ / 2 / ▮   17/20
A brilliant-value own-label Champagne with Pinot Noir character in abundance. Beautifully balanced, refreshingly clean strawberry fruit with the faintest of pink tinges and bottle-aged character.

Champagne Herbert-Beaufort, Carte d'Or Brut Grand Cru
££ / 2 / ▮   17/20
A grand cru grower's Champagne from family-owned vineyards in and around the aptly named village of Bouzy, showing lots of rugged individuality. It's a big, honest mouthful of Champagne, made mainly from Pinot Noir grapes.

1982 Tesco Vintage Champagne, Premier Cru
£ / 2 / ▮   15/20
Well-developed vintage Champagne from a good year, which has preserved good lively, lemony fruit and fresh acidity to balance the mature bouquet and biscuity character.

Fortified

Under £3

SPAIN

Tesco Superior Manzanilla, 37.5cl, Sanchez Romate
£££ / 1 / ⬛   16/20
Superior, for once, says it all. This is a salty, fresh, tangy, dry Sherry sold in a practical half-bottle. Chill, close your eyes, and imagine you're on holiday in Andalucia.

Tesco Superior Oloroso Seco, 37.5cl, Sanchez Romate
££ / 1 / ⬛   14/20
Despite what Orson Welles used to imply on television, the best Olorosos are dry. This toasty, amber coloured example is good, if a little short on flavour.

£3–5

SPAIN

Tesco Superior Palo Cortado, 37.5cl, Sanchez Romate
£££ / 1 / ⬛   16/20
Palo Cortado is a halfway house between Amontillado and Oloroso. This is an intensely dry, complex wine, showing beguiling flavours of toffee, almond and butterscotch. If Sanchez Romate can't sell the wine, they could always repackage it as an ice-cream.

£5–8

AUSTRALIA

Tesco Australian Aged Tawny Liqueur Wine
££ / FB / ⬛   15/20
Moderately fiery Australian blend of Shiraz, Grenache, Cabernet Sauvignon and Semillon grapes from vineyards in McLaren Vale and the Hunter Valley. It's a very sweet, raisiny Tawny lookalike with little of the spirity hardness you often find in Port.

PORTUGAL

Tesco 1987 Late Bottled Vintage, Smith Woodhouse
£ / FB / ▌   13/20
An aggressive, deeply coloured, surprisingly well-preserved LBV
with masses of sweet, plummy fruit, headbanging alcohol and
chewy tannins.

Over £8

PORTUGAL

Tesco 10 Year Old Tawny Port, Smith Woodhouse
0 / FB / ▌   12/20
Spirity, hard, sweet and unbalanced. Even another ten years are
unlikely to bring this one round.

THE THRESHER GROUP

THRESHER *(*)**
WINE RACK **
BOTTOMS UP **(*)**

Head Office: The Thresher Group, Sefton House, 42 Church Road, Welwyn Garden City, Herts, AL8 6PJ

Telephone: 0707 328244

Number of branches: 117 Wine Rack; 70 Bottoms Up; 1,410 Thresher (divided into 841 Thresher Wine Shops, 467 Drinks Stores from Thresher, 100 Food and Drinks Stores and two Home Runs)

Credit cards accepted: Access, Visa, American Express, Switch

Hours of opening: Monday to Saturday 9am to 10.30pm; Sunday 12pm to 3pm and 7pm to 10pm. Food and Drinks Stores the same except open from 8am

By-the-case sales: Yes. Bottoms Up offers a price guarantee: buy any wine cheaper by the case within seven days of purchase, and it will refund the difference and add a free bottle of the same wine

Glass loan: Yes

Home delivery: Free locally. Free nationally where possible

Clubs: Cellar Key and Exclusively Alsace (Wine Rack); Imbibers at Bottoms Up; Wine with Food Club at Thresher Wine Shop

Discounts: On cases of Table Wine (including sparkling wine) under £120: ten per cent at Bottoms Up, five per cent at Wine Rack and Thresher Wine Shops. On cases of table wine (including sparkling wine) over £120: ten per cent at Bottoms Up, Wine Rack and Thresher Wine Shops. On mixed cases of Champagne: 15 per cent (ten per cent off six if under £120) at Bottoms Up and seven for the price of six at Wine Rack. Generally there are special discounts for club members

In-store tastings: Every Friday and Saturday at Bottoms Up and Wine Rack; occasionally at Thresher Wine Shops

Top ten best-selling wines:

Thresher Wine Shops: Liebfraumilch Gustav Prince; Lambrusco Own-Label; Tollana Dry White; 1993 Vin de Pays d'Oc Chardonnay; Tollana Red; Figaro, Vin de Pays d'Oc; Jacob's Creek Red; Tollana Medium Dry; Hock Gustav Prince; Mâcon-Villages, J.P. Bartier

Range: GOOD: Champagne and sparkling wines, regional France, Alsace, Rhône, Italy, Spain, Australia, New Zealand
AVERAGE: Bordeaux, Burgundy, Beaujolais, Loire, Portugal, Eastern Europe, South Africa, Chile
POOR: Germany, California

Bottoms Up: Jacob's Creek White; Jacob's Creek Red; Tollana Dry White; Mâcon-Villages, J.P. Bartier; Figaro, Vin de Pays d'Oc; Penfolds Bin 35; Domaine de Tariquet; Frascati; Gyöngyös Estate Chardonnay; Muscadet, J.P. Bartier

Range: GOOD: Champagne and sparkling wines, regional France (especially Languedoc-Roussillon), Alsace, Rhône, Bordeaux, Burgundy, Italy, Spain, Portugal, Australia, New Zealand, England, fortified wines
AVERAGE: Beaujolais, Loire, Eastern Europe, South Africa, Chile
POOR: Germany, California

Wine Rack: Figaro, Vin de Pays d'Oc; Domaine de Tariquet; Tollana Dry White; Mâcon-Villages, J.P. Bartier; Jacob's Creek White; Jacob's Creek Red; Gyöngyös Estate Chardonnay; Albor Tinto; Penfolds Bin 35; Penfolds Koonunga Hill Chardonnay

Range: GOOD: Alsace, Champagne and sparkling wines, England, regional France (especially Languedoc-Roussillon), Rhône, Bordeaux, Burgundy, Italy, Spain, Portugal, Australia, New Zealand, fortified wines
AVERAGE: Beaujolais, Loire, Eastern Europe, South Africa, Chile
POOR: Germany, California

If you haven't yet got to grips with the complicated workings of the Thresher Group, don't worry, we're still trying to work it out ourselves. The Thresher Group comprises Britain's biggest off-licence chain, which is divided into a number of different types of store. At the base of the pyramid, there are 1,410 Thresher stores, of which

841 are Thresher Wine Shops and 467 Drinks Stores from Thresher, plus 100 Food and Drinks Stores and two new, experimental Home Runs. Higher up the pyramid, there are 117 Wine Racks, and at the top, 70 Bottoms Up stores. Still with us, we hope.

For the rest, the differences are mainly to do with wine range and the services the shops offer. Broadly speaking, Thresher Wine Shops and the smaller Drinks Stores are high street off-licences; Thresher's answer, if you like, to Victoria Wine. Thresher Wine Shops are more wine orientated, with a range of up to 500 wines in their bigger stores, compared to the stronger 'beer and fag' presence in Thresher Drinks Stores. Although less glamorous or high profile than Wine Rack or Bottoms Up, the combined horsepower of the 1,308 nationwide Thresher Wine Shops and Drinks Stores is what actually drives the whole caboodle.

If the high street shops keep the business ticking over, then Wine Rack and Bottoms Up are the catwalk supermodels. Wine Rack, which has grown from five stores in 1989 to 117 is, in a sense, Thresher's answer to Oddbins, albeit with a distinctly traditional, even formal, atmosphere. Whereas Oddbins' baskets spill carelessly onto the floor in untidy heaps, at Wine Rack they're as neat and tidy (sometimes a little too stiff and forbidding in fact), as the managers themselves. Wine Racks cover England and Wales.

If Wine Rack is Thresher's Oddbins, then Bottoms Up is its Majestic Wine Warehouses. And it's Bottoms Up which is currently the Thresher Group's favoured son. Like Majestic, Bottoms Up stores are the largest in size and carry the full Thresher range of 700 wines (compared to Wine Rack's average of 500), including all the higher priced, top quality stuff. Currently, they stretch from Bristol in the south-west to Newcastle in the north-east. With its bigger storage area, Bottoms Up can sell more wines by the dozen, and that's what it's been doing this year, with more than 40 per cent of its sales currently by the case.

Range and size apart, Bottoms Up encourages a more relaxed approach to wine buying. Bought as part of the old Peter Dominic empire at the end of 1990, it took until the end of 1993 to muck out all the old Bottoms Up stables. Now, at last, it's starting to function as it should. Compared to the 12 per cent growth rate of the overall operation last year, Bottoms Up grew by 20 per cent. So much so that Thresher appears to see Bottoms Up as the way forward. Indeed, the Thresher Group's retail flourish is provided by Bottoms Up's wine list, a come-hither tabloid paper with cameos of winemakers and evocative black and white photos.

So much for the form. How about the content? Well, we're pleased to report good news on this front too. The wine buying team has expanded to four, taking on Jon Woodriffe, previously one of Sainsbury's most dynamic young buyers. 'Our aim over the past year,' says wine buyer Kim Tidy, 'has been to fill the gaps where the range was weaker, such as South America, South Africa and the South of France. We've expanded our range of unoaked wine styles and grape varieties, with, for instance, more wines based on Riesling, Semillon and Müller-Thurgau. We've come up with some different things from Eastern Europe and, in France, we've tried to bring in more Burgundies under £10 and expand the Rhône.'

Agreeing that 'possibly our enthusiasm got the better of us on occasions', Kim Tidy has returned his scattergun to its holster, toning down the over-enthusiasm for expensive New Zealand Sauvignon Blancs and Alsace whites. Generally, the range looks more exciting and better focused than a year ago. The Burgundy and Rhône sections have expanded with some excellent estate wines. The regional French range is second to none, with its emphasis on local colour and the individuality and diversity of some of the best estates and co-operatives, particularly in the Languedoc-Roussillon.

In the New World, Australia and New Zealand are still important, and the team continues to come up with not just safe, easy-to-buy brands, but interesting, good-value wines. With estates such as Villiera, De Wetshof and Kanonkop, there are signs that Thresher is moving beyond the KWV to some more interesting wines in South Africa. Chile is better too, although there is still some way to go. One of the most improved areas is Spain, where buyer Julian Twaites has managed to unearth a handful of exciting modern whites alongside some super reds.

Eastern Europe, particularly Hungary, has been plundered to good effect, although there still seems to be an excess of old-fashioned Bulgarian stuff around. We also question whether the new range of 30 English wines, which includes some good things from Australian winemaker, John Worontschak, couldn't do with a bit of canopy management. We were distinctly underwhelmed, too, by the so-called Regional Classics range. This seems to consist of taking the lowest common denominator wine in any particular region and slapping a Regional Classics label on it to make it look more interesting.

One of Thresher's major achievements, given its vast and often unwieldy bulk, has been in taking customers by the hand and getting them to enjoy and appreciate the excitement and diversity of good-quality wines. As buyer Jo Standen says, 'We are very efficient and very good at selling wines over £5 a bottle. The supermarkets may be successful at pushing through large volumes of wine at £1.99, but instead of attracting new customers to wine, I'm not convinced it doesn't encourage existing customers to trade down.'

What Thresher is trying to achieve is not easy when the whole thrust of the market is downwards. With its better-balanced range and increasing confidence, we hope it continues to take the high road.

NB Wines are listed at all three stores unless otherwise indicated.

White

Under £3

BULGARIA

Slaviantzi Muscat and Ugni, Regional Classics
££ / 3 / 🌓   13/20
Sweetish, aromatic Bulgarian blend of grapey fruit with a cloying finish. Like most of Thresher's so-called Regional Classics, this is lowest common denominator stuff.

FRANCE

1993 Terret, Les Acacias, Vin de Pays des Côtes de Thau
£ / 2 / 🌓   13/20
A clean, cool-fermented, peardroppy curiosity from the shores of the Bassin de Thau made from the unusual Terret grape. Wines from this area were traditionally used as a base for Vermouth, but are starting to emerge as styles in their own right.

1993 Muscat, Vin de Pays des Collines de la Moure, Hugh Ryman, half-bottle
£££ / 6 / 🌓   16/20
An elegant, sweetly aromatic grape-and-melon flavoured curiosity

made by Englishman Hugh Ryman from cool climate vineyards in the Languedoc hills.

GERMANY

Hock Deutscher Tafelwein, St Amandus Weinkellerei
0 / 5 / ░   11/20
Dull, cardboardy German blend from unidentifiable grapes.

1993 Liebfraumilch, Regional Classics
£ / 5 / ░   12/20
Marginally fresher than the Hock, with some grapey fruit and a bit of spritz.

HUNGARY

1993 Irsai Oliver, Magyar Vineyards
££ / 3 / ░   14/20
An Eastern Europe answer to Alsace's Gewürztraminer, showing similar spicy characteristics, fresh acidity and an appealing off-dry fruitiness.

1993 Hungarian Muscat
£££ / 2 / ░   14/20
Fresh, zesty, grapefruity aperitif material with a pungent aroma and a crisp, lime-like finish.

ITALY

Lambrusco dell'Emilia Bianco, Vinicola Sant'Ilario
£ / 5 / ░   12/20
Hoppy, rustic, sweetish Italian fizzy white with a coarse aftertaste.

MOLDOVA

1993 Moldova Rkatsiteli, Hugh Ryman
£££ / 3 / ░   14/20
Tropical guava fruit with a touch of Sauvignon Blanc like cattiness from flying winemaker Hugh Ryman. Great value at under £3, and a good example of one of Moldova's more interesting native grape varieties. We just wish we could pronounce it.

SPAIN

1993 Santara Dry White, Hugh Ryman
£££ / 2 / ▌   15/20

From Conca de Barbera, a small *denominación* in Catalonia, this
is a lemon-fresh blend of the native Macabeu and Parellada grapes.
An excellent party white.

£3-5

ARGENTINA

1993 Etchart Torrontes
££ / 2 / ▌   15/20

Torrontes is one of the most interesting South American aromatic
grape varieties, and this example from top producer Etchart shows
the grape at its zesty, floral best. Refreshing, clean and well-
balanced, like a cross between fragrant Muscat and spicy
Gewürztraminer.

AUSTRALIA

1993 Penfolds Bin 202 Rhine Riesling
££ / 3 / ▌   14/20

A fairly recent addition to the Penfolds range, reflecting the consumer's
growing interest in Australian Riesling. Unashamedly commercial,
with sweet lime and orange peel fruitiness and crisp acidity.

1993 Tollana Dry White
£ / 2 / ▌   13/20

A clean, fresh fruit salad of grape varieties from Australia's sauna-
hot, irrigated Riverland region. It must be popular because
Thresher, Bottoms Up and Wine Rack all have it in their top ten
best-selling wines.

1993 Bridgewater Mill Riesling, Clare Valley
££ / 3 / ▌   15/20

Bridgewater Mill is the second label of Brian Croser's Petaluma,
one of Australia's highest profile wineries. Sweeter than the much
acclaimed Petaluma Riesling, this is soft and tropically fruity with
plenty of up-front flavour.

1993 Katnook Estate Riddoch Coonawarra Riesling
£££ / 2 / 】   16/20
An intensely aromatic, cool climate Riesling from Katnook Estate
in the Coonawarra region of South Australia. This has focused lime
and passion fruit characters with a crisp, zingy finish.

1993 Red Cliffs Estate Colombard Chardonnay
£££ / 2 / 】 (BU/WR only)   15/20
The sort of stuff which flies out of the off-licence door. At under
£4, this pleasantly fruity Aussie blend is particularly well-balanced
and elegant.

1993 Red Cliffs Estate Chardonnay
£££ / 2 / 】 (BU only)   15/20
The oak is on the prominent side here, giving the wine a toasty
overlay, but the underlying fruit is so fresh and peachy that it's
not overdone.

CHILE

1993 Las Colinas Semillon/Sauvignon, Santa Rosa Vineyard
£ / 3 / 】   13/20
An unoaked, off-dry Chilean blend from the Maipo Valley. At nearly
£4, it's the sort of thing that South Africa tends to do better.

1994 Villa Montes Sauvignon Blanc, Cuvée Ryman
££ / 2 / 】   14/20
All the whites Hugh Ryman and Aurelio Montes make together in
Chile taste of Sauvignon Blanc for some reason. So why not have
the real thing, a soft, aromatic, modern Sauvignon with good fruit
flavour and fresh acidity?

ENGLAND

Trinity, Wootton, Somerset
££ / 2 / 】   14/20
A West of England blend of three grape varieties from three different
counties. Müller-Thurgau, Schönburger and Bacchus in the first
instance, Somerset, Devon and Dorset in the second. A pleasant clove
and sweet pea fragrance makes this an appealing hedgerow white.
At under £4, one of the best-value English wines on the market.

FRANCE

1993 Muscadet de Sèvre-et-Maine, Regional Classics
0 / 2 / 🍶   11/20

Fat, old-fashioned Muscadet, which, surprisingly for a 1993, has seen better days. If this is a regional classic, then we're Beavis and Butthead.

1993 Domaine du Tariquet, Vin de Pays des Côtes de Gascogne
££ / 2 / 🍶   14/20

Made from Gascon Yves Grassa's own vineyards, this is a fresh, tangy grapefruity Ugni Blanc white, which makes the top ten at Wine Rack and Bottoms Up.

1993 Le Cordon, Vin de Pays d'Oc
££ / 2 / 🍶   14/20

A big, ripe, New World style southern French white made from Roussanne, Grenache Blanc and Chardonnay from vineyards in the Gard by Gabriel Meffre's young winemaker, Thierry Boudinaud.

1993 Domaine des Salices, J. & F. Lurton, Vin de Pays d'Oc
££ / 2 / 🍶   15/20

A soft, green bean and asparagus-like Sauvignon Blanc, made by flying winemaker Jacques Lurton in the New Zealand style.

1993 Chardonnay Vin de Pays d'Oc
££ / 2 / 🍶   14/20

Unoaked, butter and citrus-fruit Chardonnay from the cool, southern French region of Limoux.

1993 Mâcon-Villages, Regional Classics, J.P. Bartier
£ / 2 / 🍶   13/20

A basic, unoaked, village Chardonnay from Burgundy's southern end with faint butteriness and sharp acidity.

1993 La Chapelle de Cray Tour, Sauvignon Blanc
£££ / 2 / 🍶   16/20

A nettley, intensely aromatic, dry Sauvignon de Touraine, with the length and richness of many a Sancerre at twice the price.

1993 White Burgundy, Chardonnay, Cave de Viré
££ / 2 / 🍾   14/20

Viré is one of the more quality-conscious co-operatives in the Mâconnais region, turning out large volumes of honest, fruity Chardonnay, of which this is a textbook example.

HUNGARY

1993 Disznoko Tokaji Furmint
££ / 2 / 🍾   15/20

The first release from an interesting new venture headed up by Jean-Michel Cazes, the dynamic showman of the Médoc. Insurance company AXA, which already owns vineyards in Portugal as well as France, has invested in the ancient, but dilapidated Hungarian region of Tokay, famous for its legendary sweet wines. This is a dry style made from the local Furmint grape, showing honeyed, ginger spice and good balancing acidity. Presumably the grapes are in safe hands.

1993 Gyöngyös Chardonnay
0 / 3 / 🍾   12/20

Souped-up, spritzy, boiled-sweets style white with tart acidity from Hugh Ryman's Hungarian outpost.

ITALY

1993 Frascati Superiore, Vino Secco
££ / 2 / 🍾   14/20

Spritzy, nutty dry Roman white from the giant Verona-based GIV organisation. Fresh and well balanced with an appealing bitter twist.

1993 Pinot Grigio, Fiordaliso
£££ / 2 / 🍾   15/20

Fine, fresh, well-made Italian dry white with peachy fruit and an attractively nutty aftertaste.

NEW ZEALAND

1993 Kapua Springs Dry White, Villa Maria
££ / 3 / 〗   14/20

Better than the medium-dry version, this is still a sweetish, floral
Kiwi white made from Müller-Thurgau, New Zealand's most widely
planted grape variety.

SOUTH AFRICA

1994 Boland Colombard
££ / 3 / 〗   14/20

Light, early-picked Cape white with aromatic tropical banana and
guava fruit and fresh acidity.

1994 Winelands Chenin Blanc
£££ / 3 / 〗   15/20

A thoroughly enjoyable, grapey Chenin Blanc with crisp, appley
fruit and clean, lively acidity.

1994 Winelands Muscat d'Alexandrie
£££ / 3 / 〗   15/20

Rich, ginger spice-like Muscat with good balance. Demure, Lady
Penelope lookalike wine buyer Jo Standen seems to have found
her feet in the Cape. Perhaps Parker's been showing her around.

SPAIN

Señorio de los Llanos, Valdepeñas
£££ / 2 / 〗   16/20

Amazing to discover that you can extract this much flavour from
Airen, one of the world's most widely planted grape varieties.
Normally it's yawn-inducingly neutral, but this is characterful and
richly peachy with the added complexity of a year's oak-ageing.

1993 Colegiata, Toro
££ / 2 / 〗   15/20

We've been disappointed this year by the red wines from Toro, a
rugged region close to the Spanish border with Portugal. But this
lemon-fresh, rounded Malvasia restored some of our faith in its
potential.

1993 Agramont Blanco, Navarra

££ / 2 / 🌢 (BU only)   15/20

A good follow-up to last year's innovative blend of the native Viura with international superstar Chardonnay. Unusually for Spain, this citrusy white is fermented in small oak barrels, giving it an attractively toasty, vanilla fudge-like character.

1993 Señorio de Elda Moscatel, Alicante

££ / 4 / 🌢   15/20

An off-dry, aperitif-style white from Spain's eastern coast opposite the Balearic Islands. Despite the up-front sweetness, there's plenty of grapey fruitiness and good balance. Buyer Julian Twaites has come up with a commendable selection of unusual Spanish whites.

£5–8

AUSTRALIA

1993 Chapel Hill Riesling, Eden Valley

£££ / 2 / 🌢 (BU only)   17/20

Made by Pam Dunsford, one of a growing band of women winemakers in Australia, this superb, cool climate Eden Valley Riesling has nothing to do with the Hungarian wine of the same name. Highly aromatic, fresh and zesty – definitely one of Australia's most delicate Rieslings.

1993 Rosemount Unoaked Semillon, Hunter Valley

££ / 2 / �'   15/20

It's unusual to find the word Unoaked on the label of a white wine, especially at Rosemount, which pioneered barrel-fermented styles of Chardonnay in Australia. It's part of a welcome general trend towards lighter, food-friendly wines from Down Under. This is textbook Semillon, with pure herby flavours and concentrated fruit. A little austere now, but should improve with age.

CHILE

1993 Santa Carolina Special Reserve Sauvignon Blanc

££ / 2 / 🌢   16/20

A super wine from cellar wizard, Ignacio Recabarren. This is a ripe, rich, buttered asparagus style Sauvignon Blanc with grapefruity crispness for balance. Chile finally seems to be getting good depth of flavour into its white wines.

1993 Santa Carolina Cinco Estrellas Chardonnay, Gran Reserva
£ / 2 / 1 (BU/WR only) 15/20
Another ripe Santa Carolina white, with peach and pineapple fruit, citrusy acidity and classy oak. The only disappointment is the £7.50 price tag.

ENGLAND

1992 Thames Valley Vineyards Fumé
££ / 2 / 1 16/20
A daring, barrel-fermented English white made by Australian winemaker John Worontschak. It takes a bit of pluck to sell an English table wine at nearly £8 a bottle, but, believe it or not, this toasty, elegant, almost Graves-style white blend is worth the money. Apart from the giveaway acidity, it could almost be French.

FRANCE

1991 Edelzwicker, Rolly Gassmann
££ / 2 / 1 16/20
Although it sounds like something Julie Andrews might have sung, Edelzwicker is the name the Alsace region gives to its basic blended whites. In the hands of a family domaine like Rolly Gassmann, lowly Edelzwicker is transformed into a smoky, spicy dry white of considerable character.

1992 Zind-Humbrecht Gewürztraminer, Turckheim
£ / 3 / 1 15/20
Darling of wine competition judges, Olivier Humbrecht makes a large variety of opulent Alsace whites with conspicuous fruit sweetness. This hefty, spicy, rose petal Gewürztraminer with its exotic lychee character is typical of the Zind-Humbrecht style.

1993 Château de la Jaubertie, Sauvignon Blanc, Bergerac Sec
£££ / 2 / 1 16/20
This was made by Charles Martin, maintaining this estate's high

reputation for excellent Sauvignon Blanc. A crisp, assertive, ripe gooseberry white, combining the best features of the Loire Valley and New Zealand. The estate has recently been bought from father Nick by son Hugh Ryman in partnership with Esme Johnstone of Château de Sours. Watch out for fireworks.

1993 Sancerre, La Cresle de Laporte, Laporte
£££ / 1 / �데-   17/20
Elegant, smoky Sancerre made by Henri Bourgeois of Domaine Laporte, with a jazzy label. Bourgeois took over the property in 1987, since when quality has distinctly improved. A stylish, concentrated classic.

1993 Pouilly-Fumé, Les Duchesses
££ / 1 / ➝-   16/20
Tight, flinty, nettley Loire Sauvignon Blanc that needs a good year for its flavours to unfurl.

1992 Petit Chablis, Goulley
££ / 2 / ▮   16/20
Petit Chablis is such a discredited *appellation* – the petit usually refers to quality rather than the extent of the vineyards – that it's encouraging to come across a rich, fruity, modern example such as this with classic Chablis character and excellent buttery richness.

1991 Chablis Vieilles Vignes, La Chablisienne
££ / 2 / ➝- (BU only)   16/20
Structured, concentrated, intensely flavoured Chardonnay from old vines belonging to the excellent La Chablisienne co-operative. This one should run and run.

1992 St Véran, Domaine des Deux Roches, Les Terres Noires
££ / 2 / ➝-   16/20
A super, partially oak-aged Chardonnay from one of the best domaines in southern Burgundy. This is a beautifully crafted, ripe, rich white with the zesty acidity and freshness typical of this producer.

1993 Côtes du Rhône Viognier, Séléction Marc Français
££ / 2 / ▮ (BU only)   15/20
Soft, peachy, stone fruit style Viognier with aromas of honeysuckle

and grapefruit. Good value for Viognier, whose low vineyard yields make it an expensive luxury to produce.

ITALY

1992 Arneis, Castello di Neive
£££ / 1 / ⚑   17/20
Arneis is a local Piedmontese white grape sometimes known as Barolo Bianco. It was on the verge of disappearing – like many an Italian native grape – but has made something of a resurgence. The price of this fragrant, angelica spicy, unoaked wine has come down in the last couple of years to the point where it's at last become excellent value.

1993 Lugana, Ca' dei Frati
££ / 2 / ⚑   16/20
Intensely fresh, fruity and tangy with excellent weight, this Lake Garda dry white is one of the few Italian whites to wring some character out of the Trebbiano grape.

NEW ZEALAND

1993 Villa Maria Private Bin, Sauvignon Blanc, Marlborough
££ / 2 / ⚑   15/20
Slightly drier than the benchmark Montana Sauvignon Blanc, this has an elderflower crispness typical of Marlborough in a cool vintage. Good stuff.

1993 Vidal Sauvignon Blanc, Hawkes Bay
£ / 2 / ⚑   15/20
A rather vulgar, sweetish tropical fruit and tinned peas Sauvignon Blanc from Hawkes Bay in New Zealand's North Island. Hawkes Bay generally makes better Cabernet Sauvignon than Sauvignon, as is evident here.

SOUTH AFRICA

1993 De Wetshof Rhine Riesling, Robertson
££ / 1 / ⚑   15/20
Danie de Wet is the Chardonnay king of South Africa, but he also makes a few other odds and sods at his modern, Robertson winery

in the eastern Cape. This dry white has good aromatic Riesling character, but falls away on the finish. Don't we all.

1993 De Wetshof Chardonnay d'Honneur
£££ / 2 / ➡   17/20
Danie de Wet on more familiar territory, producing a rich, barrel-fermented Chardonnay with masses of fruit flavour, some buttery malolactic characters and good underlying finesse. One of an impressive range of world-class Chardonnays. Let's hope he keeps his prices tethered to reality.

1994 Villiera Sauvignon Blanc
££ / 2 / 🍾   16/20
A gooseberryish, lemony dry white made by Jeff Grier at Villiera in Paarl, which is not far from the assertive New Zealand style of Sauvignon Blanc. Well, what's a few thousand miles between Sauvignons? One of South Africa's best.

UNITED STATES

1992 Newtonian Chardonnay, Napa Valley
££ / 2 / 🍾   16/20
Newtonian is the second label of Newton Vineyards, one of the top names in the Napa Valley. Experienced winemaker John Kongsgaard has produced a stylish, balanced Chardonnay with creamy fruit, a spicy touch of cinnamon oak and great depth.

Over £8

AUSTRALIA

1993 Samuels Bay Riesling, South-East Australia, Adam Wynn
£ / 2 / 🍾   15/20
A joint venture between Thresher and roly-poly, wisecracking Australian winemaker Adam Wynn. We didn't find the £9 price tag very funny on this perfumed, well-crafted Riesling, but perhaps Adam's bank manager is having the last laugh.

FRANCE

1989 Blanck Riesling Grand Cru Schlossberg, Vieilles Vignes
£££ / 2 / �   17/20
Delicate, intensely flavoured, slatey Alsace Riesling from an
over-extended grand cru which too often disappoints. Not
here, though. Buyer Kim Tidy's enthusiasm for Alsace wines
is vindicated by Rieslings like this.

1991 Zind-Humbrecht Tokay Pinot Gris, Vieilles Vignes
££ / 3 / � (WR only)   17/20
Super-ripe, late-picked Pinot Gris showing masses of smoky,
honeyed fruit and the benign influence of the botrytis
mould. A powerful, heady mouthful with opulent fruit
richness. A little pricey at £14 a caber toss.

1987 Chablis Premier Cru, Côte de Lechet
££ / 2 / ➊   16/20
A mature, surprisingly concentrated premier cru white from a
problematic vintage, showing how well top Chablis can age. It
has the lean acidity of the vintage and appealing, almost creamy
flavours.

1992 Rully Les Saint Jacques, Laborbe-Juillot
££ / 2 / �   16/20
The village of Rully generally makes the best white Burgundies in
the Côte Chalonnaise. This grower's Chardonnay is a full-flavoured
delight, with restrained nutty oak character, buttery fatness and
excellent balance.

NEW ZEALAND

1993 Hunter's Sauvignon Blanc, Marlborough
£££ / 2 / � (BU/WR only)   17/20
This is the best New Zealand Sauvignon from the difficult
1993 vintage, confirming Hunter's standing as one of the
New World's finest wineries. Fabulously aromatic with
tropical flavours of passion fruit and melon, cut by elegant
grapefruity acidity. Watch out, Cloudy Bay, there's a Hunter
about.

1992 Hunter's Oak-Aged Sauvignon Blanc
££ / 2 / ➤ (BU only)   16/20
One of the best fumé styles of Sauvignon Blanc produced in New
Zealand. But the unoaked Hunter's Sauvignon is so brilliantly
focused and intense that the Graves-style oak makes this wine a
little less distinctive. Try it with food.

1991 Hunter's Marlborough Chardonnay
£££ / 2 / ➤ (BU/WR)   17/20
**Another winner from Jane Hunter, OBE. The richness and
concentration of this toasty Chardonnay are balanced by
intense, grapefruity acidity. It's a fresh, mouthwatering
white, every bit as good as her outstanding Sauvignon Blanc.**

Red

Under £3

BULGARIA

1993 Bulgarian Vintage Première Merlot, Iambol Region
£££ / MB / ▐   15/20
Soft, young, plummy Bulgarian Merlot in the young vatted mould
pioneered by Safeway. Low on tannin, high on fruit.

FRANCE

1993 Côtes du Ventoux, La Mission
£ / MB / ▐   13/20
A rather rustic, chewy southern French blend made at the UCVC
co-operative in the South of France by Kiwi Mark Robertson.

HUNGARY

Butler's Blend Hungarian Country Wine, Kekfrankos Merlot, Villany Region 39
££ / MB / ▐   14/20
Fresh, peppery, savoury sweet red made by eponymous flying
winemaker, Nick Butler. Hungary's answer to basic Côtes du Rhône.

1993 Hungarian Cabernet Sauvignon Villány Hills
££ / MB / ▋   14/20
A fresh, elegant, blackcurranty Cabernet Sauvignon with appealing
fruit sweetness.

ITALY

1993 Merlot Grave del Friuli
££ / MB / ▋   14/20
A young, plum and tobacco young red from the cool hills of north-
eastern Italy.

ROMANIA

Romanian Cellars Country Wine, Pinot Noir/Merlot, Dealul Mare
£ / MB / ▋   12/20
As with last year's Feteasca Neagra and Cabernet Sauvignon blend,
this jammy Romanian red is a little shy about its birth year. We're
still offering a weekend in Bucharest to anyone who can enlighten
us. Third prize . . .

SLOVAKIA

St Laurent Slovakian Red
£££ / MB / ▋   15/20
From the region of Nitra near Bratislava, this is a smoky Pinot
Noir-like red with cherry and strawberry fruit and a touch of tannin.

SPAIN

San Valero Cariñena
££ / MB / ▋   14/20
Good basic Spanish plonk in a frosted bottle, showing fresh, juicy
fruit and a little less obvious oak than the Don Darias clones.

1993 Santara Red, Conca de Barbera
£ / MB / ▋   13/20
A blend of Cabernet Sauvignon and Merlot from a small
denominación in Catalonia made by Hugh 'The Guru' Ryman.
Fine if you like the flavour of sawdust in your wine.

Don Domingo
0 / MB / 🍾   11/20
Talking of Don Darias clones, this is a coarsely oaked, tart, would-be Rioja with few redeeming features. Look out for Don Darren, son of Don Domingo, at a store near you.

£3–5

ARGENTINA

1991 Etchart Cabernet Sauvignon, Cafayate
£££ / MB / 🍾   16/20
One of the best-value Argentinian wines on the market, showing good fruit concentration and fine-grained tannins. An elegant, cool climate red that ought finally to lay the ghost of the Falklands to rest. Perhaps they should send a case to Baroness Thatcher.

AUSTRALIA

Tollana Red
££ / MB / 🍾   14/20
A well-priced introduction to the robust charms of Australian red wines. A ripe, fruity Ribena-style blend from the Penfolds group.

1991 Tollana Black Label Cabernet Sauvignon
££ / MB / 🍾   14/20
An oakier, more robust Aussie quaffer, with similarly overt blackcurrant fruit and a pronounced vanilla oak aftertaste.

1991 Red Cliffs Coonawarra Cabernet Sauvignon
£££ / MB / 🍾   16/20
A contrast in style for readers who prefer more elegant Australian reds. This supple, well-balanced Cabernet Sauvignon from the premium quality district of Coonawarra is excellent value at under £5.

1992 Penfolds Bin 35 Shiraz/Cabernet
££ / FB / 🍾   15/20
True to the successful Penfolds formula, this is a rich, full-bodied, blackberry fruity, modern red with oak in abundance.

CHILE

1993 Las Colinas Merlot/Cabernet
£ / MB / ⁑   14/20
A typical, basic Chilean red with flavours of mint and blackcurrant
and some chewy, stalky tannins for good measure.

FRANCE

1993 Figaro, Vin de Pays de l'Hérault, Cave Co-operative de Villeveyrac
£ / MB / ⁑   13/20
Take traditional southern French grapes, vinify them by the modern
carbonic maceration technique and you almost end up with a silk
purse. Damson fruitiness, high acidity and a rustic dry finish.

1993 Domaine les Colombies, Corbières
£££ / FB / ⁑   15/20
Spicy, vibrantly fruity Languedoc red with chunky, winter-warming
flavours and tannins. Another great-value southern French wine.
Buy this in preference to the cheaper Corbières Regional Classic.

1993 Le Cordon, Vin de Pays d'Oc
££ / MB / ⁑   14/20
Made by Thierry Boudinaud at Gabriel Meffre's winery in the Gard,
this is a soft cherry and strawberry style southern blend of Syrah,
Merlot and Cabernet Sauvignon. Perfect for TV dinners.

1992 Domaine Ste Eulalie, Minervois
££ / FB / ⮞   15/20
A robust, but finely balanced, fruit-dominated southern French
red with chocolate, spice and chunky blackberry flavours and
powerful Syrah character.

1993 Beaujolais, Pierre Yves, Regional Classics
0 / MB / ⁑   11/20
Soft, soupy, bog-standard Gamay. Does anyone actually enjoy
drinking this stuff? At £3.99, it's out of its depth.

Claret, Sichel, Regional Classics
0 / MB / 🍾   **13/20**
Light on fruit with a hard, rustic finish, this wine reflects the generally poor quality of recent Bordeaux vintages.

Côtes du Rhône, Regional Classics NV
£ / MB / 🍾   **13/20**
From a co-operative in the Gard region of southern France, this is a soft, raisiny, Grenache-based quaffer with a rough edge.

1992 Coteaux du Tricastin, Domaine de Montine
££ / MB / 🍾   **15/20**
If you like southern French reds with elegance as well as tannin, you'll go a bundle on this Syrah-based red from the cool hills of the Provençal hinterland. Good value at under £4.

HUNGARY

1993 Hungarian Cabernet Franc Private Reserve, Villány Region
££ / MB / 🍾   **15/20**
It's unusual to come across Cabernet Franc, a variety more closely associated with the Loire, in Eastern Europe. But this is a real treat, showing typically grassy aromas and soft, spicy fruit.

ITALY

1993 Primitivo del Salento, 'Le Trulle'
££ / MB / 🍾   **14/20**
Made from a grape that sounds like someone who works for the Cosa Nostra, this is a sweet and savoury, American oak and strawberry fruit, southern Italian red from the Kym Milne corporation.

1993 Valpolicella, Regional Classics
£ / LB / 🍾   **13/20**
A light, fresh, northern Italian red, which, like many a Valpolicella, lacks a bit of concentration. Hardly a regional classic.

1990 Merlot/Cabernet Sauvignon Fiordaliso, Vino da Tavola
££ / MB / ▌ (Th only)   15/20

Juicy, cool climate Merlot from northern Italy in an expensive-looking bottle. An elegant Bordeaux-style blend, which would happily grace your dinner table.

1993 Chianti, Regional Classics, L. Cecchi
££ / MB / ▌   14/20

One of the better regional classics in the Thresher range, this Tuscan red has some distinctive Sangiovese character and a robust, dry finish. The sort of thing that used to come in those just-one-Cornetto wicker flasks.

1990 Chianti Rufina Riserva, Villa di Vetrice
££ / MB / ▌   15/20

Made by the Grati family in the Rufina hills east of Florence, this is an attractively savoury, rustic Chianti from an excellent vintage for Tuscany. Good characterful stuff.

1991 Parrina
£££ / MB / ▌   16/20

Parrina is one of a number of Tuscan wines made by designer-oenologist, Franco Bernabei, who consults for many of the top Chianti estates. This red from a tiny *denominazione* in southern Tuscany is a characterful follow-up to the 1990, one of *Grapevine*'s wines of the year in 1994. Once again, it has distinctive aromas of lavender and thyme and lots of Mediterranean fruit character. We hear that instead of walking on water, Franco Bernabei walks on pine needles.

1990 Salice Salentino Riserva, Taurino
£££ / FB / ▌   16/20

A rich, chocolatey southern Italian blend with aromatic angostura and thyme spiciness and mature, leathery Mediterranean fruit. Robust stuff, not to be undertaken without a corkscrew and mallet in hand.

SOUTH AFRICA

1994 Boland Dry Red, Paarl
£££ / MB / ♦   15/20
Juicy, bubblegummy Pinotage-based Cape red with plenty of soft, strawberryish carbonic maceration fruit and firm tannic bite.

1994 Winelands Cinsault Tinta Barocca, Stellenbosch
£££ / MB / ♦   15/20
Equally good value at under £4, this is a liquorice and plum style Cape blend of the Port grape, Tinta Barocca, and the Mediterranean's Cinsault.

SPAIN

1990 Agramont, Navarra
££ / MB / ♦   15/20
A modern Rioja-style blend of native Tempranillo and Cabernet Sauvignon, producing a smooth, ripe, pleasantly oaked red from a go-ahead co-operative in Navarra.

1989 Chivite Reserva, Navarra
£££ / MB / ♦   15/20
A savoury, super-value red from the large, family-owned winery, Chivite. It's an intensely flavoured, slightly gamey blend of Tempranillo and Garnacha aged in French and American oak for 18 months, which is just getting into its stride. Hard to beat at under £4.50.

1990 Berberana Tempranillo Rioja
£££ / MB / ♦   15/20
Young, savoury Rioja made entirely from the top-notch Tempranillo grape by a company which consistently produces value-for-money reds. Exceptionally well-balanced with the oak nicely in harmony with the fruit.

1993 Valdemar Rioja Tinto
£££ / MB / ♦   16/20
Another all-Tempranillo Rioja, this time without oak, but plenty of juicy pepper and plum fruit. Traditionalists may find the absence of oak disconcerting, but it shouldn't take them long to come round.

£5-8

AUSTRALIA

1990 Riddoch Coonawarra Cabernet Shiraz
££ / FB / ᴗ-   15/20
A minty, concentrated Coonawarra blend with overtones of
tobacco and spicy American oak. Come back in three years.

1991 Riddoch Limited Release Shiraz
£££ / FB / ᴗ-   17/20
**Rich, classic Coonawarra Shiraz with tarry but elegant,
blackberry fruit flavours and fresh acidity. Another one for
the long haul.**

1992 St Hallett Barossa Shiraz
£££ / FB / ᴗ-   17/20
**A hulking Barossa Valley monster with lashings of malty,
chocolatey Shiraz fruit and full-blown, ripe tannins. A
substantial chip off the Old Block.**

CHILE

1990 Santa Carolina Special Reserve Cabernet Sauvignon, Los Toros Vineyard, Maipo Valley
££ / MB / ᴗ-   15/20
A juicy, full-flavoured Maipo Valley Cabernet made by Ignacio
Recabarren in the modern style. Soft, minty fruit and firm tannins.

1990 Caliterra Reserve Cabernet Sauvignon, Maipo Valley
££ / FB / ᴗ-   16/20
Straddling the New World and France, this is like a cross between
an Australian Cabernet Sauvignon and a claret with intense, smooth-
textured blackcurrant fruit and well-handled oak.

FRANCE

1990 Domaine du Vieux Relais, Costières de Nîmes
££ / FB / ❶   15/20
From vineyards close to the Languedoc-Provence frontier, this is a
strapping, fresh southern French red with lots of chocolatey,

savoury fruit. Like Côtes du Rhône on steroids.

1992 Domaine de l'Hortus, Coteaux du Languedoc, Pic St Loup

£££ / FB / ➤   16/20

Founded as late as 1980, Jean Orliac's Domaine de l'Hortus has rapidly become one of the most exciting properties in the Languedoc. Until 1989, Orliac sold most of his production to the local co-operative. Now he's making his own wine, the potential has been realised. His rosés are good, but his reds are even better. This blend of Syrah, Mourvèdre and Grenache is an intensely aromatic, tightly structured red packed with flavours of blackberry and black olive. Delicious stuff.

1993 Domaine Gauby, Cuvée des Rocailles, Côtes du Roussillon

££ / FB / ➤   16/20

Deeply-coloured red from rugby-playing winemaker Gérard Gauby. Like the man who made it, it's a muscular, warm-hearted Roussillon blend with far less oak than some of Gauby's other wines. A winemaker who's fast emerging as one of the stars of southern France.

1993 Fleurie, Duboeuf

££ / MB / ➤   15/20

On the serious side for a Fleurie, which tends to be among the more elegant of Beaujolais' ten crus, but there's some good Gamay fruit concentration, and the wine will get better as it softens.

1991 Moulin-à-Vent, Tour de Bief, Duboeuf

£££ / MB / ➤   17/20

King of the Beaujolais Georges Duboeuf reserves new oak treatment for his best estate wines. Moulin-à-Vent usually makes the most structured wines in the region, and this oaky, chocolatey red proves the point. As it ages, it's started to take on the gamey character of a good red Burgundy.

1990 Château Coucheroy, Graves

££ / MB / ▌   15/20

A fresh, light elegant Graves red with attractive vanilla oak flavours. Given the excellence of the 1990 vintage, it could do with a bit more concentration.

1990 Château de Francs, Côtes de Francs
££ / MB / ⤙ 16/20

The Côtes de Francs is a tiny Right Bank *appellation* of Bordeaux producing wines in the style of St Emilion. This up-and-coming property is run by Dominique Hébrard, whose family owns the famous Château Cheval Blanc, and Hubert de Bouard of Château l'Angélus. Given the pedigree of the men behind it, it's not surprising that they've come up with a grassy, focused claret with a sweet core of fruit and layers of vanilla oak. One for the cellar.

1992 Château Grand Prebois, Côtes du Rhône
££ / FB / ⤙ 15/20

A heady, chunky Provençal red heading in the direction of Châteauneuf-du-Pape with good spicy, concentrated fruit and robust tannins. Expensive for a Côtes du Rhône, but worth the money.

1990 Rasteau, La Ramillade, Château du Trignon, Côtes du Rhône Villages
£££ / FB / ⤙ 17/20

Spicy, savoury, massively concentrated Rhône blend from one of the best of the Côtes du Rhône villages. A super wine which combines soft, fleshy fruit and firm backbone and seems to linger for ever on the palate.

1992 Coudoulet de Beaucastel, Côtes du Rhône
££ / FB / ⤙ 16/20

This is the second label of the prestigious Châteauneuf-du-Pape property, Château de Beaucastel. It's more forward than the first wine, but there's still a strong resemblance. Solid tannins, softened by sweet, juicy fruit and freshened by acidity.

ITALY

1993 Dolcetto, Pian Romualdo, Mascarello
££ / FB / ⤙ (BU/WR only) 16/20

As well as making one of the best traditional Barolos, Mauro Mascarello produces dark, concentrated Dolcetto in a juicy, rich chocolate and damson-skin style. Most Dolcetto is made to be drunk young, like Beaujolais, but this one should age nicely for a good couple of years.

1990 Cappello di Prete, Vino da Tavola del Salento, Candido
£££ / FB / ❒ (BU only)   17/20
A mature, southern blend from Italy's Mediterranean heel,
full of savoury raisin and tobacco fruitiness and delightfully
fresh acidity. At just over £5, this is one of the best-value
Italian reds on the market.

PORTUGAL

1989 Cartuxa, Evora
£££ / FB / ⬤   17/20
A structured, old-fashioned blend of Periquita, Moreto,
Aragones and Trincadeira from the flatlands of southern
Portugal's Alentejo region. With its tarry, peppery fruit and
raisiny sweetness, this is the Iberian Peninsula's answer to
first-rate Cahors.

SPAIN

1989 Conde de Valdemar Rioja Reserva
£££ / MB / ⬤   17/20
A sweetly oaked Rioja made entirely from the Tempranillo
grape by modern winery, Martinez Bujanda. The integration
between wild strawberry fruit and vanilla-flavoured oak is
close to perfection. Yet another triumph for Rioja.

1987 Baron de Ley Rioja Reserva
££ / MB / ❒   16/20
This is an unusual blend (for Rioja) of 90 per cent Tempranillo
and 10 per cent Cabernet Sauvignon, aged, equally unusually, in
French rather than American oak. This wine has taken a while to
emerge from its shell, but it's turned into an elegant, seductively
textured stunner.

1989 Viña Amezola Crianza
££ / MB / ⬤   16/20
A good contrast in style to the Baron de Ley, this Crianza Rioja has
the sweet, coconutty hallmark of traditional Rioja rounded out
with mature, gamey flavours.

Over £8

AUSTRALIA

1991 David Wynn Patriarch Shiraz
££ / MB / ▬   16/20

David Wynn, the man who pioneered Coonawarra reds, is the father of barrel-chested winemaker, Adam Wynn. This is intended as a tribute to the white-haired patriarch of the Wynn family, and very good it is too. A rich, minty South Australia style with the cool climate elegance and natural acidity which comes from hillside vineyards. Needs time to fulfil its potential.

FRANCE

1992 Givry Clos Marceaux Premier Cru, Laborde-Juillot
££ / MB / ▬   16/20

A modern-style red Burgundy from the village which makes many of the best Pinot Noirs in the Côte Chalonnaise, with well-balanced flavours of new oak and raspberry-like fruit.

1992 Chorey-lès-Beaune, Tollot Beaut et Fils
££ / MB / ▬   16/20

Tollot Beaut make some of the most approachable Pinot Noirs in Burgundy, and this is a typical example. A wine with fresh, plump fruit and pronounced smoky oak from one of the less well-known villages on the Côte d'Or.

1990 Gérard Julien, Côtes de Nuits Villages
££ / MB / ▬   16/20

Another oaky red Burgundy, this time with a more rustic edge to it, but plenty of full-flavoured plum and chocolate character.

1989 Château Ramage la Batisse, Cru Bourgeois, Haut-Médoc
££ / FB / ▬   16/20

A *Grapevine* favourite. Lots of classy new oak on show, but more than enough concentrated, savoury fruit to compensate for the splinters. Just goes to show that oak barrels don't have to be clumsily handled.

1991 Châteauneuf-du-Pape, Château de Beaucastel
£££ / FB / ⊷ (BU/WR only)   17/20
A skunky, gamey, animal-like Provençal red from one of
France's greatest estates. This is more forward than some
Beaucastels, which usually need at least ten years to come
round, but it's still a massive, savoury, farmyardy red with
layer upon layer of complex flavours. Some say it's the sheep
that graze in the vineyards that give it its distinctive
character, others claim unorthodox winemaking
techniques, while the owner, François Perrin, says the
answer lies in the soil.

1992 Châteauneuf-du-Pape, Domaine Font de Michelle
££ / FB / ⊷   16/20
Affectionately known as the Gonad Brothers, Jean and Michel
Gonnet consistently produce one of the best Châteauneufs
around. At the opposite end of the spectrum to Beaucastel, this
is a raisiny, peppery, warm-throated red with masses of alcohol
and ripe tannin.

1992 Collioure, Domaine de la Rectorie, La Coume Pascole
££ / FB / ⊷   16/20
A tarry, rich blend of Syrah and Grenache from the hills behind
the pretty Mediterranean port of Collioure near the Spanish border.
Savoury and oaky with a gamey, pleasantly rustic touch. A top-
notch Roussillon red.

SOUTH AFRICA

1991 Kanonkop Pinotage
£££ / FB / ⊷ (BU only)   17/20
Big, rich, blackberry fruit and coconutty American oak make
this one of South Africa's few world-class red wines.
Winemaker Beyers Truter produces this cult wine, using old-
fashioned, open fermenters and ancient bush vines provide
the raw material.

Rosé

£3–5

FRANCE

1993 Château de la Jaubertie Rosé
£££ / 3 / ▌   16/20
A *Grapevine* wine of the year last year, Château de la Jaubertie's
rosé is consistently one of this Bergerac property's best wines.
The 1993 is a little paler than the day-glo stunner from the previous
vintage, but still packed with assertively grassy, strawberryish
flavours and balanced by refreshing acidity.

SOUTH AFRICA

Winelands Cinsault Rosé, Stellenbosch
££ / 3 / ▌   16/20
Light, aromatic bubblegum and strawberry-style Cape rosé with a
touch of residual sweetness.

£5–8

NEW ZEALAND

1993 Vidal Merlot Hawkes Bay Rosé
£££ / 2 / ▌   17/20
1993 was a dilute red wine vintage in New Zealand, so several
producers made rosé as well. This juicy, grassy, capsicum-
scented pink from Hawkes Bay winery Vidal is the best Kiwi
rosé we've come across. Could this be the start of something
interesting?

Sparkling

Over £8

FRANCE

Jean de Praisac Brut NV Champagne, F. Bonnet
£££ / 2 / 🍾   16/20
Very impressive for a house Champagne, this is a toasty blend
with a surprising degree of complexity for a wine at just over a
tenner. Showing more maturity than you'd expect from a non-
vintage Champagne.

Drappier Carte d'Or Brut NV Champagne
£££ / 3 / 🍾   17/20
**Almost entirely made from Pinot Noir, this young, but well-
balanced Champagne shows the classically creamy, red-fruit
character of the Aube district. Intensely fruity and stylish
with considerable elegance and length.**

Perrier-Jouët NV Champagne
0 / 2 / 🍾   13/20
A disappointing, uninspired effort from a Grande Marque
Champagne house. Simple, sweetish fizz of little finesse.

Fortified

£5–8

FRANCE

**1993 Banyuls, Domaine de la Rectorie, Cuvée Parcé Frères,
half-bottle**
£ / FB / 🍾   15/20
Aromatic, sweet blackberry fruit and a nip of tannin make this
young southern French fortified red from the Roussillon coastline
an interesting change from spirity Port. Should improve with age,
but we'd like to see it retail at under £5 for a half-bottle.

SPAIN

Manzanilla Pasada, Lustau, half-bottle
££ / 2 / ▌   16/20
From top Jerez-based Sherry *négociant*, Emilio Lustau, this is a
savoury Manzanilla Pasada with salty yeast character, softened by
extra ageing. The result is a rounded complex Sherry of great
individuality, heading towards an Amontillado.

Oloroso Viejo de Jerez, Lustau, half-bottle
£££ / 1 / ▌   17/20
Oloroso Sherry doesn't get much better than this dry, tangy
example. Bronze-tawny in colour, it has a complex bouquet
of grilled almonds, orange peel and burnt toffee. If you
stopped drinking Sherry – or never started for that matter –
this should turn you on to one of the world's great fortified
wine regions.

Don Zoilo Very Old Oloroso
££ / 2 / ▌   16/20
Brown-gold in colour, this Sherry has lots of caramel oak character
and a pruney, austere, dry finish. The sort of Sherry that needs to
be drunk with olives and salted almonds.

Don Zoilo Very Old Cream
£££ / 6 / ▌   17/20
Nut-brown in colour, this has a sweet *crème brûlée* bouquet
and powerful raisiny fruit with hints of caramel and coffee.
A brazenly rich, dessert Sherry.

Over £8

PORTUGAL

1976 Fonseca Guimaraens
££ / FB / ➤   16/20
Fonseca Guimaraens is the name Fonseca gives to its wines in
years which are not declared for its vintage Port. It must have
been a close decision here, because this dense, peppery animal
has the concentration and power of a vintage Port.

1983 Fonseca
£££ / FB / ➪   17/20
Fonseca is owned by an English company in Portugal –
Taylor, Fladgate & Yeatman. This is the antithesis of the
Graham style with a powerful bite of dry tannin and richly
concentrated, spicy fruit.

Cossart and Gordon Five-Year-Old Malmsey
££ / 5 / ➪   16/20
Madeira can sometimes resemble an Amontillado Sherry. This
excellent wine certainly has some of the burnt-toffee and savoury
elements of a top Sherry, but is distinguished by a raisiny, hot
climate richness.

1952 Rutherford and Miles Verdelho
£ / 3 / ➪ (WR/BU only)   18/20
You just have to put the £69 price tag out of your mind here
and hope one of your friends or relations is feeling
generous. It's pretty amazing stuff with a highly aromatic,
minced pie spice and toffee bouquet, richness of fruit and
refreshing tangy acidity.

UNWINS **

Head Office: Birchwood House, Victoria Road, Dartford, Kent, DA1 5AJ

Telephone: 0322 272711

Number of branches: 296

Credit cards accepted: Access, Delta, Switch, Visa, Master Card, American Express, Diners Club, Transax

Hours of opening: Monday to Saturday 9.00am to 10.00pm; Sunday 12pm to 3.00pm and 7.00pm to 10.00pm

By-the-case sales: Yes

Glass loan: Free

Home delivery: Most branches deliver free

Clubs: No

Discounts: Ten per cent on table and sparkling wines (may be mixed); five per cent on special offers; 12.5 per cent on orders over £150

In-store tastings: Yes

Other facilities: Monthly accounts; mail order; gift vouchers

Top ten best-selling wines: La Mancha Red; La Mancha White; Frascati; French Country Red (Vin de Pays du Gard); Mauregard White Bordeaux; French Country White (Vin de Pays de l'Hérault); Hock; Lambrusco Bianco; Fitou; Duchatel

Range: GOOD: Red Bordeaux, Port

AVERAGE: Sparkling wines, Champagne, Australia, Sherry, Spain, Italy, Germany, white Bordeaux, white Burgundy, Loire, Rhône

POOR: Red Burgundy, United States, Eastern Europe, England, regional France, New Zealand, South Africa, Chile

Last year Unwins celebrated 150 years as an independent retailer. Actually, perhaps 'celebrate' is overstating it. Were there fireworks? Was there singing and dancing in the streets of the Home Counties? Did anyone hear a Champagne cork pop? We didn't. In fact, it was all rather quiet on the south-eastern front as Unwins slouched quietly towards the twenty-first century like a camel train crossing the Kalahari. Perhaps there wasn't that much to celebrate after all.

At the very least, we'd like to report that it's a case of business as usual. When we said last year that Unwins had moved out of Central London into the commuter belt and beyond, where life was quieter and a little less competitive, we added that even here the battle for custom was intensifying. What we hadn't realised was how much cross-Channel shopping might affect Unwins, whose 296 stores are concentrated in leafy suburbia and sleepy coastal towns such as Shoreham and Peacehaven.

It's difficult to be precise about the effects, but of all the high street chains, it seems that Unwins has been the worst hit. So much so that the rumours started to fly. Would Unwins be taken over by the ambitious Greenalls Cellars group? Would it merge with another chain? Would it put up the shutters once and for all?

As it happens, it did none of these things. Unwins just soldiered on. It may not be the high street's most dynamic operation, but with most of its properties owned freehold, it suffers from little of the pressure affecting chains with high rents to pay.

Being at one remove from the realities of life in the high street has not necessarily worked to Unwins' advantage. The image remains that of the traditional wine merchant with a list of mature claret and vintage Port and an emphasis on the service offered by its long-standing staff.

These two positive points notwithstanding, Unwins relies too much on brand names, both in Europe and the expanding New World. There's Torres in Spain, Mateus in Portugal, the KWV in South Africa, Penfolds in Australia, Gallo in California, Montana in New Zealand. Anyone still awake? There's nothing inherently wrong with brands in themselves (Montana and Penfolds are reliable and good). It's just that they tend to be safe but staid. And crucially, they don't encourage the sense of adventure the new wine drinker increasingly craves.

We aren't suggesting that Unwins managers suddenly ditch their traditional clientele, dye their hair blonde and stick rings through their nostrils. But the reality of high street trading is that to survive, you have to move with the times and encourage customers to follow you. We've seen it happen at Oddbins, and latterly at Victoria Wine, Thresher and Fuller's. But we're still waiting for Unwins to make a move.

To be fair, Unwins has not entirely sat on its hands over the past year. It's taken on a bright new marketing executive, Jim Wilson. And, responding to increasingly aggressive pricing from competitors, it put out a La Mancha red and white at £1.99. The two wines have stormed to numbers one and two in their hit parade, displacing Liebfraumilch and Lambrusco Bianco. Anything which does that can't be all bad.

Italy and Australia have seen some interesting new additions to the list, too. There are even some excellent higher priced wines on offer, such as the recherché delights of Frescobaldi's 1990 Chianti Riserva Castello di Nipozzano, Sardinia's 1990 Terre Brune from Santadi and the 1989 Orlando St Hugo Coonawarra Cabernet Sauvignon.

We don't see these wines flying off the shelves at Unwins, though. To be honest, stock is about as likely to fly off an Unwins shelf as the geese over our mantelpiece are to take wing for Greenland. As things stand, too much of Unwins' range is overpriced and uncompetitive.

We said last year that if Unwins was going to survive to see its 160th birthday, it needed to address weaker areas of the range such as Australia, New Zealand, Eastern Europe, South Africa and the Languedoc-Roussillon. A start has been made on Australia, but not much more than that. We'd like to see changes move from first into top gear over the next 12 months. Happy 151st birthday!

White

Under £3

ITALY

1993 Tocai del Veneto Bartolomeo, Vino da Tavola del Veneto
£ / 2 / 1   13/20
A decent, basic Italian white with characteristically neutral fruit quality and a hint of green olive.

SPAIN

La Mancha
£ / 2 / 🍾   12/20
Introduced to combat the flood of supermarket £1.99 specials,
this is a baked, slightly tart central Spanish white bottled in the
Loire to keep the price down.

£3–5

AUSTRALIA

Penfolds Stockman's Bridge
££ / 3 / 🍾   14/20
Stockman's Bridge presumably connects Jacob's Creek to Oxford
Landing. This is an early-picked, unusually light Australian white with
pleasant Rhine Riesling style fruit and a touch of residual sweetness.

1993 Lindemans Semillon/Chardonnay Bin 77, South-East Australia
££ / 3 / 🍾   15/20
A well-made, ripe melon and tropical fruit-like white with a kiss of
oak character and good, zesty acidity for balance. Enjoyable stuff
at under a fiver.

1989 Wakefield White Clare Crouchen/Chardonnay, Clare Valley
£££ / 2 / 🍾   16/20
A fruit salad of tropical flavours from South Australia's Clare Valley,
combining elements of mango and orange in an old-fashioned,
idiosyncratic style. It's not often you find Crouchen and
Chardonnay blended together.

CHILE

1993 Canepa Sauvignon Blanc, Sagrada Familia
££ / 2 / 🍾   15/20
One of the better Sauvignon Blancs produced at the ultra-modern
Canepa winery near Santiago. This is an elderflower and orange
zest-like white with crisp acidity and more concentration than many
Chilean whites.

FRANCE

1992 Pinot Blanc Woelfelin
£ / 2 / ▪   14/20

A pleasantly smoky, peachy Alsace white with soft fruit sweetness.
A little dilute perhaps.

1992 Château Ducla, Entre-Deux-Mers
£ / 2 / ▪   13/20

This wannabe modern blend of Semillon and Sauvignon Blanc has
lost the freshness and zing it had a year ago.

GERMANY

1990 Louis Philippe Riesling, Louis Guntrum
£ / 3 / ▪   15/20

One of a growing number of German wines appearing on British
shelves in Burgundian, as opposed to flute-shaped bottles. This
Rheinhessen Riesling has some pleasant lime and kerosene-like
fruit, but it ought to be £1 cheaper.

HUNGARY

1993 Gyöngyös Hungarian Chardonnay, Hugh Ryman
0 / 2 / ▪   12/20

Sweet, flat and lacking in freshness, a wine which has its ups and
downs owing to rather primitive cellar technology. When it's good,
it's very good, but when it's bad . . .

1993 Gyöngyös Estate Sauvignon Blanc
££ / 2 / ▪   14/20

This is the best Sauvignon Blanc we've encountered from the
pioneering Gyöngyös Estate. Made in a mini-New Zealand style,
it's a zesty, aromatic dry white with citrus fruit sweetness and
acidity. A caveat: we have noticed inconsistency between
Gyöngyös bottlings.

ITALY

1993 Bianco di Custoza La Cenge, Associati Soave
£££ / 2 / ▮   15/20
Yeasty, nutty, limey white, which reminded us of Robinson's Barley
Water. Perhaps we've been watching too many old Wimbledon
clips. Good, characterful stuff from the Soave co-operative.

1993 Breganze Bartolomeo
££ / 1 / ▮   14/20
Good toasty, nutty Tocai from the Veneto region of northern Italy,
with a characteristic bitter twist and a dry aftertaste.

1993 Frascati Superiore Tullio San Marco
££ / 2 / ▮   14/20
Nice wine, shame about the packaging. Decant before drinking
this fresh, perfumed, lime and pine resin-like Roman dry white.

SOUTH AFRICA

1993 Pearl Springs Sauvignon Blanc, Breede River Valley
£ / 3 / ▮   13/20
A sweetened-up, cool-fermented Cape white with flavours of
peardrop and green bean.

1993 Cape Cellars Chardonnay, Coastal Region
£ / 3 / ▮   13/20
Fat, buttery, unoaked Cape Chardonnay with a confected aftertaste,
from the KWV giant.

SPAIN

1992 El Coto Rioja Bodegas El Coto
£ / 2 / ▮   13/20
A strange white Rioja, which can't seem to decide whether it's in
the modern or traditionalist camp. A coconut and grapefruit
segment cocktail with underlying heaviness. Perhaps it's just a bit
long in the tooth.

UNITED STATES

Blossom Hill, California
0 / 3 / ▐   10/20

We'd rather drink a wine cooler than this sweetened-up concoction. Blossom Hill should be moved to Boot Hill.

£5–8

AUSTRALIA

1993 Penfolds Bin 21 Semillon/Chardonnay, South Australia
£ / 2 / ▐   15/20

In common with many commercial Australian whites, the 1993 is more restrained than the 1992 vintage. Fresh melon and peachy fruit with a dab of smoky oak and herbal Semillon character. Perfect party and house white. Should be under £5.

1992 Orlando RF Chardonnay
££ / 3 / ▐   15/20

The best vintage of RF we've had yet, with more restrained oak handling and fresh melon and citrus fruit flavours.

AUSTRIA

1991 Eiswein Neusiedlersee, Burgenland, half-bottle
££ / 8 / ➥   16/20

From vineyards in Burgenland close to Austria's border with Hungary, this Eiswein was made from frozen grapes picked in late autumn at sub-zero temperatures. It's an unctuously sweet, honey and raisin style dessert wine with soft, peachy fruit and a frostbite of acidity. They'll probably preserve Kurt Waldheim in this one.

FRANCE

1993 Sancerre Les Roches, Vacheron
££ / 1 / ➥   16/20

A lively, citrus and gooseberry-scented Sancerre from one of the leading producers in the eastern Loire's most famous *appellation*. Still young and taut, but with enough minerally intensity to stay the distance.

GERMANY

1989 Oppenheimer Herrenberg Scheurebe Spätlese, Louis Guntrum
£ / 4 / ❶   15/20

Scheurebe is looked down upon in Germany, perhaps for its embarrassingly catty aromas, but at its best the grape makes smoky, grapefruity white of great intensity. This is on the restrained side for Scheurebe, which may not be a bad thing.

NEW ZEALAND

1993 Montana Sauvignon Blanc
£££ / 2 / ❶   16/20

A wine that never lets you down. Montana's hugely successful Sauvignon Blanc has been selling at under a fiver for as long as we can remember, so it's hardly surprising to see it among the top ten best-selling wines in the UK. Textbook elderflower and asparagus style with lively acidity and rounded, tropical fruit.

Over £8

FRANCE

1976 Vouvray Cave des Viticulteurs du Vouvray
££ / 4 / ❶   15/20

A year ago, we commented that it was a pleasure to see a high street chain taking a risk on a very mature and unusual, off-dry Vouvray. The fact that this is still around would suggest that it's not as popular as it deserves to be.

Red

Under £3

ITALY

1992 Merlot del Veneto, Bartolomeo
£ / LB / 🌓   13/20
Easy-drinking north Italian rosso with light, bitter-cherry fruit.
Pleasant trattoria fare.

SPAIN

La Mancha
££ / LB / 🌓   13/20
The red counterpart to the white £1.99 La Mancha, made in a soft,
fruity, carbonic maceration style.

£3–5

AUSTRALIA

Penfolds Stockman's Bridge
£ / MB / 🌓   13/20
A simple, blackcurrant and mint-flavoured Aussie red with a slightly
coarse, rustic finish. You'd be better off paying an extra £1 for the
Penfolds Bin 2 or Bin 35.

1992 Penfolds Bin 35 Shiraz/Cabernet, South Australia
££ / FB / 🌓   15/20
A typically exuberant Penfolds blend with charred American oak
and berry fruit. Let's hope they can keep the price under £5 during
this period of pressure on grape prices in Australia.

1992 Lindemans Bin 50 Shiraz, South-East Australia
££ / MB / 🌓   15/20
An easy-drinking introduction to the pleasures of Australian Shiraz,
with aromatic white pepper, spicy American oak and sweetly
supple, blackberry fruitiness.

1992 Lindemans Bin 45 Cabernet Sauvignon
££ / MB / 🍷   15/20

Smoky, brambly, classic Lindemans elegance without the class of the Bin 50. So many bins, so little wine to put in them.

CHILE

1993 Canepa Cabernet Sauvignon, Sagrada Familia
£ / MB / 🍷   13/20

Not up to the Sauvignon Blanc sourced by Unwins from the Santiago-based Canepa operation. It's on the medicinal side with a stalky, unripe aftertaste.

FRANCE

1990 Château Mingot, Côtes de Castillon
££ / MB / 🍷   15/20

An almost Rioja-style Bordeaux from the eastern hills of Castillon, where the English were defeated in the Hundred Years War. Soft Merlot fruit, vanilla oak and fresh acidity make this an attractive claret.

1991 Château Ducla, Yvon Mau
£ / MB / 🍷   14/20

Solid, green pepper fruit and unyielding, four-square tannins from the large Bordeaux *négociant*, Yvon Mau.

1992 Buzet Renaissance, Les Vignerons de Buzet
££ / MB / 🍷   14/20

A good claret substitute from a reliable co-operative which dominates the *appellation* of Côtes de Buzet. Gingery spice, firm tannins and smooth, grassy fruit.

ITALY

1992 Breganze Bartolomeo, Rosso Breganze
££ / LB / 🍷   14/20

A fresh, food-friendly, savoury Italian red from the Veneto region with more middle palate weight than you often find in a spag bol red.

1993 Valpolicella Classico, Rocca Sveva, Associati Soave
££ / MB / ♦   14/20

Charming, carbonic maceration style Valpolicella with flavours of bubblegum and raspberry, and a not unpleasant touch of residual sweetness.

1992 Barbera del Piemonte, Giordano
££ / MB / ♦   15/20

A wine in an appealing, dinner party worthy package, showing the soft, savoury characters of the Barbera grape with fresh, but not rasping, acidity.

1992 Chianti, Villa Selva
££ / MB / ♦   15/20

An old-style, Sangiovese-based Tuscan red with pleasant plumskin characters and robust tannins. Good to know Italy can still produce honest wines like this at under £4.

1993 Montepulciano d'Abruzzo, Miglianico
££ / MB / ♦   15/20

Almost fizzing with vibrant damson fruit and purple colour, this is a wine with backbone as well as forward, come-and-get-me appeal.

PORTUGAL

1992 Borba Adega
££ / MB / ♦   14/20

We draw the line at giving this region as curt a dismissal as we did last year. Not because we've been showered with offers of free trips (chance would be a fine thing), but because we enjoyed the wine a bit more. A Portuguese Beaujolais with a bit of indigenous spice.

SOUTH AFRICA

1992 Cape Cellars Cabernet Sauvignon, Breede River Valley
0 / FB / ♦   11/20

A tough, earthy, tannic old boot of a Cape red. Wake up boys, we've entered a new era now.

UNITED STATES

Zinfandel, Cartlidge & Brown, Central Coast
££ / MB / ▸   15/20

If you've never tasted Zinfandel, California's near-native grape, this peppery, aromatic example is a good one to cut your teeth on. Avoid the same winery's clumsy Chardonnay.

£5–8

AUSTRALIA

1993 Rosemount Cabernet Sauvignon, South Australia
£ / MB / ▸   14/20

One-dimensional blackcurrant fruit juice, oak and tannin do not a wine make, especially at nearly £7.

FRANCE

1990 Vieux Château Negrit, Montagne St Emilion
£ / MB / ▸   14/20

Full, ripe, deeply coloured St Emilion satellite red with a bitter, overextracted finish. It may soften in time, but don't (Right) Bank on it.

1989 Château Charmail, Haut-Médoc
£ / MB / ▸   14/20

Aromas of coffee bean oak sweetness give way to a rasp of green tannins – surprising given the vintage.

1992 Fleurie Domaine Meziat, Pierre Dumont
£ / MB / ▸   13/20

Soft, soupy, prematurely ageing Gamay from a normally reliable *négociant*. One of a number of poor value Beaujolais crus we've tasted this year.

1991 Fitou Château de Ségure, Les Producteurs de Mont Tauch
£££ / FB / ▸   16/20

Château de Ségure is the flagship estate of the Mont Tauch co-operative, which nestles in the Corbières hills within sight of the

Pyrenees. After the successful 1989, they didn't make a wine in 1990, moving on instead to the excellent 1991 vintage. This is a wine with aromatic sandalwood spice and flavours of angostura bitters and chunky, sweet fruit. Super stuff.

PORTUGAL

1984 Garrafeira Reserva Particular, Antonio Bernadino
£££ / FB / 🍷   16/20
The top Portuguese reds age surprisingly well. This wine from Antonio Bernadino is a rich, alcoholic, concentrated marvel, which has matured with considerable grace, and is still showing remarkable freshness and Portuguese character.

SPAIN

1989 Gran Sangredetoro Reserva Penedès, Miguel Torres
0 / FB / 🍷   11/20
A dry, old-fashioned blend of Garnacha and Cariñena grapes aged in a wooden container somewhere in the Penedès. You can do better almost anywhere at £6 a bottle.

1984 Castillo Fuentemajor Rioja Gran Reserva, Bodegas AGE
££ / MB / 🍷   16/20
Good value Gran Reserva from giant producer AGE, with well-preserved vanilla oak and savoury, leafy fruit sweetness. At its peak.

UNITED STATES

1993 Elysium Black Muscat
0 / 6 / 🍷   12/20
A sweet California confection, showing aromas of rose-hip syrup and talcum powder. Overmarketed, overpriced, and too often to be found over here. Apparently, some people like it.

1990 Columbia Crest Merlot, Columbia Valley, Washington State
££ / MB / 👈   16/20
Washington State's surprisingly cool vineyards on the eastern side of the Cascade Mountains are not yet regarded as an alternative to

California. But with a few more wines like this chocolatey, black-cherry red, with its fine balance of oak and fruit, it shouldn't be long.

Over £8

AUSTRALIA

1989 Orlando St Hugo Cabernet Sauvignon, Coonawarra
££ / FB / ↝   16/20
After Jacaranda Ridge, this is Orlando's top-of-the-range Cabernet Sauvignon. There's plenty of vanilla oakiness on show in this restrained, European-style Coonawarra red, but there's enough underlying fruit to cope.

1990 Penfolds Cabernet Sauvignon Bin 707, South Australia
£££ / FB / ↝   17/20
If Penfolds' Grange is Australia's answer to the red wines of Hermitage, then this is its riposte to First Growth Pauillac. A blend of Cabernet Sauvignon from selected vineyards in South Australia, this is a tannic concentrated monster designed for ageing. Come back in the next millennium.

FRANCE

1991 Domaine de la Salle, Beaune Premier Cru, Les Champs Pimont, Bichot
0 / MB / ↑   13/20
An attempt at a modern red Burgundy, where the Pinot Noir is so smothered in new oak that we've sent for the Missing Grape Varieties Bureau to locate the elusive fruit.

1990 Châteauneuf-du-Pape, Château des Fines Roches, Barrot
£ / FB / ↝   15/20
A hefty, aromatic Châteauneuf with leathery, cedary spice and a dry stewed-fruit aftertaste.

ITALY

1990 Chianti Rufina Riserva, Castello di Nipozzano, Frescobaldi

££ / MB / ➡   16/20

Serious Sangiovese-based red from a single estate in the high altitude Rufina district of Chianti. The stylish oak gives the wine an international façade, while the underlying fruit is classically Tuscan. Give it time.

1990 Terre Brune, Santadi

££ / FB / ➡   16/20

Made by Antinori winemaker Giacomo Tachis in Sardinia, this rich, supple, toffeed, modern red has a nice veneer of vanilla oak and lots of dry, leafy complexity. A little on the expensive side at nearly £14.

Sparkling

£5–8

AUSTRALIA

Angas Brut Rosé

£ / 3 / ▌   14/20

Easy-drinking strawberry-cup fizz, which has lost its value-for-money edge in the last three years.

1990 Seaview Pinot Noir/Chardonnay Brut

££ / 2 / ▌   16/20

A toasty, bottle-aged bouquet and classic fudge-like blend of the Champagne grapes Pinot Noir and Chardonnay, make this an interesting contrast in style. Even at a pound more, this is very good value.

FRANCE

Crémant d'Alsace, Mayerling Brut

£ / 2 / ▌   14/20

Made entirely from the Pinot Blanc grape, this is a frothy, basic fizz with flavours of apple and pear. At least £1 overpriced.

Over £8

AUSTRALIA

1991 Green Point
£££ / 2 / ⟩   17/20
This successful Yarra Valley winery has produced a brilliant
successor to the 1990, which was one of *Grapevine*'s wines
of the year in 1994. The Pinot Noir content has been
increased, and Pinot Meunier has been added to the blend
for the first time. Otherwise, this follows on nicely from
the previous vintage, showing considerable toasty
complexity and finesse. Parent company Champagne house
Moët et Chandon must be happy to see Dr Tony Jordan
maintaining Green Point's high reputation.

UNITED STATES

Mumm Cuvée Napa
££ / 2 / ⟩   15/20
After a couple of dodgy years and several advertising campaigns,
Mumm Cuvée Napa appears to be back on the rails. The fruit quality
is very good, but our reservation is that the wine is being released
so young that it tastes somewhat tart and austere. Tuck it away for
a few months and this one should reward your patience.

Fortified

£5–8

PORTUGAL

1988 Smith Woodhouse LBV
££ / FB / ➼   15/20
A sweet, fiery Late Bottled Vintage Port with good, rich fruit and
tobaccoey, spicy bite.

VICTORIA WINE ***(*)

Head Office: Victoria Wine Company Ltd, Brook House, Chertsey Road, Woking, Surrey, GU21 5BE

Telephone: 0483 715066

Number of branches: 1,531 including 40 Victoria Wine Cellars and 178 Haddows in Scotland

Credit cards accepted: Access, Visa, Amex

Hours of opening: Variable. Majority of stores open from 10am to 10pm Monday to Friday/Saturday

By the case sales: Yes

Glass loan: Free with large orders

Home delivery: On a local basis by arrangement

Clubs: No

Discounts: Five per cent off mixed cases; seven for six on non-promoted Champagnes

In-store tastings: On an occasional basis by arrangement

Top ten best-selling wines: Liebfraumilch; Sansovino Lambrusco Bianco; Casa Barco Spanish Red; Bulgarian Merlot/Pinot Noir, Sliven; Merlot del Veneto; Chianti Piccini; Vin de Pays de l'Hérault Dry White; Leziria Red; Fitou, Mme C. Parmentier; Hardy's Stamp Series Shiraz/Cabernet

Range: GOOD: Germany, Eastern Europe, Portugal, Champagne and sparkling wine, Australia, Rhône, Spain, New Zealand, Italy
AVERAGE: Portugal, red Burgundy, California, regional France, Bordeaux, Chile, South Africa
POOR: England, Loire, Alsace, Beaujolais

At a time of closures, mergers and general pessimism among the

British wine trade, Victoria Wine opened a new set of stores this year. Called Victoria Wine Cellars, the first ten were opened in June 1994 in a variety of London and commuter-belt sites. And they were so successful that, at the time of writing, the number has increased to 40, with more planned for the coming months.

Hang on a second, you're thinking, haven't we been here before? Didn't Victoria Wine launch something rather similar in the 1980s? Those of us with reasonably good memories recall Gare du Vin and South of the Bordeaux, Victoria Wine's previous attempts to 'do an Oddbins' by taking, respectively, the wacky and minimalist stripped pine routes. With names like those, who needs fickle customers?

Victoria Wine Cellars are genuinely different. In appearance, they are not unlike a branch of Wine Rack, with lots of dark wood, green paint and designer lighting. But the resemblance ends there. Cellars, as they are known in the vernacular at Victoria Wine, are less stuffy than many branches of Wine Rack and are aimed not at wine buffs, but at existing customers and what product group manager, Thomas Woolrych, calls 'professional experimenters'. In other words, people who like to shop around.

The stores opened with some genuinely amazing half-price offers on vintage Port – good news for colonels in places such as Cranleigh, Windsor, Henley and Harpenden – but the signs are that customers like the format of the new stores, with or without the come-in-and-try-us deals. More important, Cellars don't appear to have alienated the sort of shopper who wanders in for a packet of fags and a tin or four of Special Brew. Not something that could be said of South of the Bordeaux. 'We've gone for approachability,' says Woolrych. 'The previous ideas were experiments; this is building on Victoria Wine's existing strengths.'

Elsewhere in the business, the revamping of former Augustus Barnett sites was finally completed in 1994. The two ranges were harmonised and, by the end of August, the name Augustus Barnett had disappeared from British high streets. All that remains for posterity are 50 Augustus Barnett wines.

If you're prone to nostalgia, it was a sad moment. But no one could claim that Augustus Barnett was a dynamic retailing force in its final months. Things are more promising now it's in the hands of Victoria Wine and the street-wise, suntanned trading director Adrian Lane. Owners Allied-Lyons finally seem to have decided to put some investment behind Victoria Wine. As a result, the stores have consolidated their position in the high street in 1994.

Apart from a handful of very good wines, Augustus Barnett provided Victoria Wine with a series of larger shops. 'Augustus Barnett increased our number of shops by 50 per cent,' says Woolrych, 'but selling space went up by 75 per cent.' This means the larger stores can now stock more wines. A Cellars can have as many as 550 wines on the shelf, the bigger Victoria Wines 400.

Wine sales continue to increase at Victoria Wine, although much of the growth has come at the lower end of the market. Nevertheless, the Victoria Wine top ten is better than most, with a good Fitou, a decent Chianti and an Australian Shiraz/Cabernet adding lustre to the best sellers. Significantly, the Aussie red retails at £3.79. 'We're very successful at selling wine at under £3,' says Woolrych, 'but what we're trying to do now is raise the level of interest among our customers so that we sell more wine at £3.99 and £4.99.'

It's a laudable enough aim. Yet for the time being 80 per cent of Victoria Wine's sales are provided by 20 per cent of the range. No prizes for guessing which the big turnover wines are. Woolrych believes that advice and a pleasant wine-buying environment are the way to get people to spend more money. That and the elusive 'personal element'.

The wines are vital, too, of course, And this is why Adrian Lane has been so keen to expand the range. He's introduced a few old favourites from his Tesco days, but he's also sent his team of buyers out to find new things in South Africa, Italy, Australia and southern France. The five of them are even pictured in the new Victoria Wine list, perched over barrels in arty pools of studio lighting. Well, it's better than photographs of wine writers . . .

The aim at Victoria Wine is to provide a balanced but interesting line-up of wines. 'I don't see the point in being, say, the Uruguayan wine specialist,' adds Woolrych. 'If you sell to a narrow part of the market or to an elite, you're never going to make any money out of wine retailing.' This is another point of difference with Wine Rack, which in the past allowed enthusiasm to get the better of its buying policy in Alsace and Madeira.

The Victoria Wine range is better now than it has ever been, with some good things available from France and Eastern Europe and a growing number of New World wines from California, South Africa and Australia. The entire 550-strong range is available from all branches of Victoria Wine and Haddows, although you may have to order the posher wines if your local is not in a prime location.

This is the lingering problem with Victoria Wine. The best stores, especially the new Victoria Wine Cellars, are very good indeed but in the less salubrious parts of the country, the shops have a war-zone feel to them at times. Perhaps this says more about Britain than it does about Victoria Wine, but we'd still like to see better managers in all the stores, not just the lucky few.

All the same, this has been a positive year for Victoria Wine. It's brought some badly needed optimism to the high street and there are signs that it's developing into a major wine retailing force, set to follow Thresher's dynamic lead, and who knows, even given Thresher a run for its money. Let's hope so.

White

Under £3

BULGARIA

1993 Bear Ridge Bulgarian Dry White
£ / 3 / 1   13/20
From the Lyaskovets region of Bulgaria, this is an off-dry blend of Aligoté, Rkatsiteli, Dimiat and Muscat Ottonel. Rather a lot of grapes for what is a neutral, faintly cloying white.

CZECH REPUBLIC

1993 Moravia Hills Czech Dry White
£££ / 2 / 1   15/20
Another flying winemaker white, made this time by Australian Nick Butler in the comparatively virgin vineyard territory of the Czech Republic. Blending Olasz Rizling with a small amount of Grüner Veltliner, Butler has come up with some interesting tropical fruit and white pepper character. Excellent value. Let's hope they're selling this in the bars of Prague.

FRANCE

1993 Vin de Pays de Vaucluse Blanc, La Mission
0 / 2 / ❱   12/20
Kiwi Mark Robertson of the Matua Valley Estate has produced a
variable range of wines in his first flying winemaker vintage in the
South of France. This earthy southern blend of Ugni Blanc and
Bourboulenc is one of the duffers.

French Dry White, Vin de Pays de l'Hérault, Chais Comtal, 1 Litre
0 / 3 / ❱   11/20
Sweetish, unbalanced, southern French white sold by the litre. A
case of quantity triumphing over quality.

GERMANY

Liebfraumilch, Rheinhessen Winzer
£ / 4 / ❱   12/20
On the dry side for a Lieb, this is decent, clean, boiled-sweets stuff
with refreshing, grapefruity acidity.

HUNGARY

1993 Magyar Vineyards Hungarian White
0 / 3 / ❱   12/20
Coarse, oily, old-fashioned Hungarian blend from the Gyöngyös
Estate. Hungary and winemaker Adrian Wing can do better than
this.

1993 Chapel Hill Irsai Oliver
££ / 2 / ❱   14/20
Nothing to do with the distinguished Australian winery of the same
name, Chapel Hill is a clever brand name for Kym Milne's
Hungarian wines. A light, fresh halfway house between Alsace
Gewürztraminer and an Eastern European Muscat, showing typical
lychee flavours and fragrance.

ITALY

Sansovino Lambrusco Bianco
0 / 5 / ▋   11/20

Not as sweet as some Lambruscos on the market, otherwise this frothy baked-apple white is par for the Emilia Romagnan course. Unlike Asti Spumante, not yet a DOCG; more of a DOG, really. Woof, woof.

1993 Dry Muscat di Puglia, 'Le Trulle'
£ / 2 / ▋   13/20

A fresh, aromatic, lime-juice cordial white from the Corato region in the heel of southern Italy. Light, modern, fruity stuff. Are there any countries left untouched by flying winemakers?

SOUTH AFRICA

1994 Cape White
£ / 4 / ▋   13/20

A sticky, medium-dry Cape white made at the Simonsvlei co-operative from the ubiquitous Chenin Blanc grape. South Africa's answer to Liebfraumilch.

£3–5

AUSTRALIA

1993 Deakin Estate Colombard/Chardonnay
££ / 3 / ▋   14/20

An unoaked, new-wave blend of 70 per cent Colombard and 30 per cent Chardonnay from the State of Victoria. Pleasantly fruity in a melon and grapefruit mould.

1993 Deakin Estate Sauvignon Blanc
£ / 3 / ▋   13/20

Thinner than the other Deakin Estate whites with little in the way of Sauvignon Blanc character to commend it. You'd be better off in the Loire or New Zealand.

1993 Deakin Estate Chardonnay
££ / 2 / ❶   15/20
The best of the Deakin Estate whites, this is a fresh, modern, cool climate white with a light touch of smoky oak and an attractive passion fruit character.

1993 Penfolds Bin 21 Semillon/Chardonnay, South-East Australia
££ / 2 / ❶   15/20
In common with many commercial Australian whites, the 1993 is more restrained than the 1992 vintage. Fresh melon and peachy fruit with a dab of smoky oak and herbal Semillon character. Perfect party and house white.

1993 Hardy's RR, Medium Dry White
£ / 4 / ❶   14/20
RR stands not for rest and recreation, but for Rhine Riesling. We preferred the new vintage to last year's soupy performance. Still a touch cloying, but showing some nice lime peel fragrance and fresher acidity.

BULGARIA

1993 Bear Ridge Bulgarian Chardonnay
££ / 2 / ❶   14/20
According to winemaker Kym Milne, this wine was 'oak-handled', which we take to mean he's dangled a bag of oak chips in the vat. The technique, rather like putting hickory chips on a barbecue, is a legitimate way of adding some oak interest. That's what's happened here on this coconutty, dry white.

CHILE

1994 Caliterra Sauvignon Blanc
££ / 3 / ❶   15/20
More restrained in style than some of Caliterra's other wines, this is an unoaked, citrus fruit Sauvignon Blanc from Chile's leading exponent of the grape, Ignacio Recabarren.

FRANCE

1993 Domaine de L'Argentier, Terret, Vin de Pays des Côtes de Thau

££ / 2 / ▌   14/20

From the shores of the oyster-rich Bassin de Thau, this is an unusual dry white made from an undervalued grape variety. A fresh, full, citrusy style with a lively bite.

1993 La Serre Sauvignon Blanc

££ / 2 / ▌   15/20

Made by Englishman Hugh Ryman at the Foncalieu-owned Domaine de Corneille, this is a grassy, intensely aromatic white with lots of the classic gooseberry flavours of the Sauvignon Blanc grape.

1993 Angelico, Calvet, Yves Barry

£ / 2 / ▌   13/20

The Angelico in the title has nothing to do with fat monks, bad habits or sickly liqueurs. It refers instead to the Muscadelle grape, for which it is apparently a synonym. If this light, ascetic white is anything to go by, you can see why Muscadelle is rarely used on its own. One for silent contemplation.

1993 Muscat Sec, Domaine Montrabech, Vin de Pays d'Oc

££ / 2 / ▌   15/20

A spicy, fresh apéritif white made by Australian John Weeks at Domaines Virginie near Béziers. The Muscat used here is the superior Muscat à Petits Grains version, much of which goes into the region's best fortified wines.

1993 Muscat Cuvée Tradition, Turckheim, Alsace

£ / 2 / ▌   14/20

This is part of the Turckheim co-operative's basic range. It's on the light side for an Alsace white (not always a bad thing) with some delicate spice to it.

1993 Chardonnay, James Herrick, Vin de Pays d'Oc

££ / 1 / ▌   15/20

The second vintage from Englishman James Herrick's impressive New World style vineyards near Narbonne. This is more elegant and restrained than the 1992, with deftly handled oak and a lime-like streak of acidity.

HUNGARY

1993 Chapel Hill Oaked Hungarian Chardonnay
££ / 2 / ❚   15/20

Among the most flavoursome white wines to have emerged from the former Eastern Bloc. A well crafted, oak-chipped Chardonnay with good underlying citrus fruitiness.

ITALY

1993 Verdicchio Classico, Villa Pigna
£ / 2 / ❚   13/20

A soft, cool-fermented coastal Italian dry white made entirely from the Verdicchio grape. Fairly neutral with a hint of bitter almond.

1993 Lugana, Pasqua
£ / 2 / ❚   13/20

A fresh, appley white from northern Italy. The local Trebbiano di Lugana grape can produce more concentrated, characterful wines than this.

PORTUGAL

1991 Bairrada Reserva, Sogrape
£ / 2 / ❚   14/20

An oak-fermented hotch-potch of six indigenous grape varieties from Sogrape, the company which invented Mateus Rosé. With its curious aromas of linseed oil and baked bananas, it could do well in Caribbean restaurants.

1993 Chello, Dry Vinho Verde
£ / 1 / ❚   13/20

It's unusual to come across dry Vinho Verde in this country, although the Portuguese themselves drink little else. But this is almost too austere for its own good.

1993 Quinta de Azevedo Vinho Verde
£££ / 1 / ❱   16/20

This Lorero-based example is much more like it. With fresh apple and pear fruit, zesty acidity and a smidgeon of clove spice, it finishes nicely zippy and dry.

SOUTH AFRICA

1994 Simonsvlei Chenin Blanc
££ / 2 / ❱   14/20

Drier than the same co-operative's Cape White. Cool fermentation has produced a refreshing, peardrop and banana style white bearing little resemblance to the austerity of the Loire's Chenin Blanc.

1994 Goiya Kgeisje Sauvignon/Chardonnay, Vredendal Co-operative
£ / 2 / ❱   13/20

The great selling point of this northern Cape white is that it is the first wine to appear on UK shelves in any given vintage. In marketing terms, it's South Africa's answer to Beaujolais Nouveau. We enjoyed this fresh, green bean style white blend a little more in 1993.

1994 Cape View Chardonnay Sur Lie
££ / 2 / ❱   15/20

Lees-ageing has given this unwooded Stellenbosch Chardonnay a bit of extra concentration and personality. Good-value stuff from air miles specialist Kym Milne.

1994 Neetlingshof Gewürztraminer
££ / 3 / ❱   15/20

Soft, perfumed, lychee-like Gewürztraminer from Günter Brözel, one of the Cape's most experienced winemakers. Picked early for elegance, this is a respectable South African riposte to Alsace.

1992 Stellenzicht Noble Late Harvest Weisser Riesling, half bottle
£££ / 7 / ⬗   17/20

Stunning value for money at under £4 for a half-bottle, this is a raisiny, dessert wine with lots of crystallised citrus fruit freshness and zip. Made in limited quantities, so hurry, hurry, hurry.

UNITED STATES

1992 Corbett Canyon Chardonnay
££ / 2 / ▌   15/20

From cool vineyards in the coastal California region of Santa Barbara, this elegant, lively Chardonnay was partially fermented and aged in French oak barrels for added complexity. Not quite up to the stunning 1991, but still good value at under £5.

£5–8

AUSTRALIA

1993 Moondah Brook Verdelho
££ / 3 / ▌   15/20

Made from the Madeira grape, Verdelho, which has found a second home in Western Australia. The result is an attractive greengage and melon style alternative to Chardonnay. For those who can't face yet another glass of the Big C.

1993 Basedow Semillon
£ / 2 / ▌   13/20

A rich, overcharred, American oak-dominated Semillon from the Barossa Valley. Drink with barbecued Barramundi.

1993 Basedow Chardonnay
£ / 2 / ▌   14/20

More of the same. A somewhat brash, American oak, tropical fruit and cinnamon toast style of Chardonnay. A one-glass wine.

1993 Colonnade Chardonnay
£££ / 2 / ▌   16/20

This elegant Yarra Valley Chardonnay, made at sparkling wine specialist, Domaine Chandon, shows how good new-wave Australian whites can be. A restrained, subtly oaked wine with excellent length on the palate.

ENGLAND

1993 Penn Vineyards Dry
££ / 1 / ↭   15/20

A bone-dry, Home Counties blend of the aromatic Bacchus and Reichensteiner grapes. This has benefited from the hand of Australian John Worontschak, who has produced a steely, almost Sauvignon-like white with good ageing potential. At just over £5 it may look expensive, but it could take its place happily alongside French wines at a similar price without blushing.

ITALY

1993 Soave Classico Superiore, Anselmi
££ / 2 / ▮   16/20

A £7 price tag might look excessive for a Soave, but then this is no ordinary Veneto white. Made by one of the region's leading white wine producers, it's a rich, concentrated Soave made from old vines of Garganega and Trebbiano. To paraphrase a well-known Master of Wine, it screams Garganega.

1993 Chardonnay del Salento, Vigneto di Caramia
££ / 2 / ▮   15/20

Toasty New World style oak is the dominant feature of this southern Italian Chardonnay made by Kym Milne and Warren Gibson with a helping hand from Augusto Cantele. On the pricey side.

NEW ZEALAND

1993 Stoneleigh Sauvignon Blanc
£ / 2 / ▮   14/20

If you like green salads of asparagus, artichokes and green beans, this vegetal Marlborough Sauvignon Blanc is the one for you. We found it suffered from the cool 1993 vintage more than some of its competitors.

1993 Vidal Sauvignon Blanc
£ / 2 / 🗲   15/20

Hawkes Bay usually produces riper, if less assertive, styles of
Sauvignon Blanc. Not a bad thing in this case, since the tropical
fruit character compensates for high natural acidity and pungency
of flavour. Too expensive.

SOUTH AFRICA

1993 Cathedral Cellars Sauvignon Blanc
£ / 2 / 🗲   13/20

From a single estate in the western Cape, this is the giant KWV co-
operative's flagship brand. As such, it's a disappointment, showing
insufficient Sauvignon Blanc character to justify a £6 price tag.
Sauvignon Blanc still has some way to go in South Africa.

SPAIN

1992 Torres Gran Viña Sol, Chardonnay
0 / 2 / 🗲   13/20

This pioneering Penedès winery has gone off the boil in the last
few vintages. Gran Viña Sol, an oaked blend of mainly Chardonnay
and the native Parellada, used to be one of Spain's better whites.
Latterly, it's been overtaken by the competition.

Over £8

FRANCE

1993 Pouilly-Fuissé, Duvergey-Taboureau
£ / 2 / 🗲   14/20

From a small Meursault-based *négociant* business, whose managing
director plays in a country and western band in his spare time,
this is an aptly rustic white Burgundy with some oak, but not
enough fruit. Pricey at nearly £9.

1992 Chablis Premier Cru, Les Vaudevey, Bacheroy-Josselin
££ / 2 / ☛   16/20

A wine that grows on you. Nutty, concentrated and old-fashioned,
this is a premier cru Chablis with balance and character.

1993 Château de Vaudieu Blanc, Châteauneuf-du-Pape, Gabriel Meffre
£££ / 2 / 〗   17/20
Made at Gabriel Meffre's vineyard in Châteauneuf-du-Pape, best known for its powerful red wines, this is an interesting blend of Clairette, Grenache Blanc, Picardan and Roussanne. A broad-shouldered white with intense, aniseedy complexity and concentration.

1990 Riesling Grand Cru Schoenenbourg, Turckheim, Alsace
££ / 2 / ↞   16/20
From one of Alsace's bewildering number of grand cru sites, this is a pungently aromatic, toasty Riesling from the usually excellent Turckheim co-operative. A crisp, elegant white just getting into its stride.

1988 Château Filhot, Deuxième Cru Classé, Sauternes
£ / 7 / ↞   15/20
1988 was the first of a trio of great vintages in Sauternes. This honeyed, old-fashioned example has good botrytis character and concentration, but lacks something in the finesse department.

Red

Under £3

BULGARIA

Bulgarian Country Wine, Merlot/Pinot Noir, Sliven
£ / LB / 〗   12/20
An unusual combination of Bordeaux's Merlot and Burgundy's Pinot Noir, producing something that tastes like neither. Smells of instant coffee and tastes of stewed plums. A top ten best seller at Victoria Wine.

1993 Bear Ridge Bulgarian Gamza
£ / LB / 〗   13/20
Made by New World winemaker Steven Bennett (perhaps it's Kym Milne under a pseudonym), this is a basic, jammy, light

red with soft, carbonic maceration fruit. Good to come across
a Bulgarian red made from a native grape. Shame it's not a bit
more interesting.

1993 Debut Bulgarian Cabernet Sauvignon
££ / MB / ▌   14/20
Fresh, juicy Bulgarian quaffer from the Russe winery, made in a
style inspired by Safeway's successful Young Vatted Cabernet
Sauvignon, where the emphasis is on young fruit rather than barrel-
ageing character.

CZECH REPUBLIC
1993 Moravia Hills Dry Red
£££ / MB / ▌   15/20
Nick Butler and Mark Nairn can take the credit for this unusual
Czech blend of Vavrineke and Frankovka, a vibrant pepper and
cherry-like red with fresh acidity. Very palatable.

FRANCE
1993 La Mission, Vin de Pays de Vaucluse Red
0 / LB / ▌   11/20
A light, rustic attempt at a southern French Beaujolais. Mission,
sadly, unaccomplished.

HUNGARY
1993 Hungarian Country Red, Villány
£££ / MB / ▌   15/20
Another Beaujolais lookalike, this time from southern Hungary
made from Kekfrankos, Kekoporto, Cabernet Sauvignon and
Merlot. Soft, juicy and brilliant value.

1993 Hungarian Cabernet Sauvignon, Szekszard
££ / MB / ▌   14/20
Similar in style to the Country Red with a bit of wood ageing.
Blackcurrant essence and soft tannins for easy quaffing.

ITALY

1993 Merlot del Veneto Vino da Tavola, Cantina della Torre
££ / LB / ❲   13/20
Pale ruby, almost a rosé, with light, cherried flavours, and some
sweetness. Easy-drinking northern Italian red at a good price.

PORTUGAL

Leziria Red, Almeirim
£££ / MB / ❲   15/20
A value-for-money red that never lets you down. The tannins are
softer than last year's more robust version, but there's still plenty
of peppery Portuguese character on offer.

SPAIN

Casa Barco Spanish Red
0 / LB / ❳   10/20
Rooty, oak-chipped, confected Spanish Tinto Plonko. Almost
undrinkable.

1993 Puerta da la Villa, Cencibel, Valdepeñas
££ / MB / ❲   14/20
Deeply coloured, chunky, eastern Spanish red from the native
Cencibel grape with the accent on clean, modern fruit flavours.

1989 CVNE, Viña Real Rioja, half-bottle
££ / MB / ❲   16/20
CVNE is one of the leading producers in Rioja, and this atypical
blend of Tempranillo, Graciano and Mazuelo shows the region at
its best. An elegant, gamey style with seductive supple fruit and
subtle vanilla oak in a practical half-bottle.

£3–5

AUSTRALIA

1992 Deakin Estate Victoria Cabernet Sauvignon
££ / MB / ❲   15/20
A concentrated, but well balanced, Cabernet from cool climate

Victoria, showing fresh, spearmint and blackcurrant fruit and an elegant touch of oak.

1993 Hardy's Stamp Series Shiraz/Cabernet, South-East Australia
££ / FB / 🍷   15/20
A well-made, vanilla, mint and soft, berry fruit style red from the Hardy group. This has enough dry, tannic grip for winter drinking. Great to see a wine like this among Victoria Wine's top ten best sellers.

CHILE

1991 Caliterra Cabernet Sauvignon
££ / MB / 🍷   14/20
Ignacio Recabarren appears to have lightened up the winemaking at Caliterra to bring the wines closer to European styles. An almondy, sweetly fruity red with a nip of tannin and balancing acidity.

FRANCE

Fitou, Cuvée Mme Claude Parmentier
£££ / FB / 🍷   15/20
Heartening to see this characterful, southern red established in Victoria Wine's top ten best sellers. From Val d'Orbieu, it has plenty of spicy aroma and robust but quaffable, peppery fruit.

1993 Beaujolais, Philippe de Courcelettes
0 / LB / 🍷   11/20
Very light, dilute Beaujolais with negligible Gamay fruit character from the Cellier des Samsons umbrella co-operative. If Beaujolais can't do better than this at £4, it should pack up and move south. Or north.

1993 Minervois, Cave des Hauts Coteaux
£££ / MB / 🍷   15/20
With its Cézanne-style label and pepper and cinnamon aromas, this is an upfront, juicy red with masses of fruit. A wine that knocks spots off basic Beaujolais.

1993 Big Frank's Red
££ / MB / ⚑ 15/20

Aromatic, characterful southern French blend of Syrah, Grenache and Carignan with plenty of sweet, spicy fruit and well-handled French oak. This was made by humorous Polish-American painter, Frank Chludinski, who claims it does wonders for your virility. We wonder if the Advertising Standards Authority has noticed his back label.

ITALY

1993 Lambrusco Rosso Grasparossa di Castelvetro
££ / LB / ⚑ 14/20

Most Lambrusco drunk in this country is sweet, white alcoholic lemonade. This is drier than the white stuff and more enjoyable. A fizzy, cherry and raspberry cordial.

1993 Merlot/Sangiovese, Casal del Giglio, Vino da Tavola del Lazio
£ / LB / ⚑ 13/20

A Merlot-dominated blend from Gazza's adopted home. Dry, plummy and a bit stalky.

1993 Primitivo del Salento, 'Le Trulle'
££ / MB / ⚑ 14/20

Made from a grape that sounds like someone who works for the Cosa Nostra, this is a sweet and savoury American oak and strawberry fruit, southern Italian red from the Kym Milne corporation.

1991 Valpolicella Classico 'Il Maso', Zonin
0 / MB / ⚑ 11/20

Although this light Valpolicella hails from a single vineyard, it tastes no better than the basic Valpol – and that's not saying much. No wonder some of the best producers want to distance themselves from the Valpolicella name altogether.

1992 Chianti Piccini
££ / MB / ⚑ 14/20

This basic Chianti is one of Victoria Wine's top ten best sellers, so clearly their customers know a bargain when they taste one. Fresh, clean, cherryish fruit with a nip of tannin.

1991 Chianti Rufina Riserva, Fattoria di Galiga
££ / MB / 🢒   15/20
From Villa di Vetrice, a large family estate in the heart of the Rufina
district near Florence, this is a traditional, savoury Chianti with an
appealingly mature, sweet middle. A good price for a Chianti Riserva.

PORTUGAL

1991 Grão Vasco, Dão
££ / FB / 🢒   14/20
Grão Vasco is the Dão Estate of the go-ahead Sogrape operation.
The wines of this region are never the most immediately attractive
in Portugal, on account of their rustic edge, but this richly tarry,
dry red is appealing in its own way.

1989 Quinta da Camarate, Fonseca
££ / MB / 🢒   15/20
An oak-aged blend of Castelão Frances, Espadeiro and Cabernet
Sauvignon made by California-trained winemaker Domingos Soares
Franco. An elegant, minty red with sweet fruit concentration and
deftly handled oak.

SOUTH AFRICA

1994 Belvedere du Cap, Syrah
£ / MB / 🢒   14/20
A wine which sounds like a Cape contraceptive, and, after a bottle
or two, probably has the same effect. The brief for the Welmoed
co-operative was apparently to make a Crozes-Hermitage style.
The boys couldn't quite pull it off.

1992 Stellenzicht Cabernet/Malbec
£ / MB / 🢒   14/20
A light, modern upfront blend of 60 per cent Cabernet Sauvignon
and 40 per cent Malbec aged for eight months in new oak. Sweet,
gluggable fruit and soft tannin.

1994 Fairview Gamay Noir
££ / MB / 🌓   15/20
The sort of soft, abundantly fruity red that Beaujolais ought to be making. Winemaker Charles Back has used the carbonic maceration technique to produce a vibrant, cherry and raspberry-like red with a nip of tannin.

SPAIN

1991 Marqués de Monistrol Cabernet Sauvignon
£ / MB / 🌓   13/20
Marqués de Monistrol are better known for their much advertised cavas than their red table wines. This overoaked Penedès Cabernet Sauvignon shows you why.

1987 Campo Viejo Rioja Reserva
££ / MB / 🌓   15/20
Campo Viejo make some of the best-value, traditional Riojas. This is a good seven-year-old example with sweet, leafy, mature fruit flavours and Rioja's vanilla hallmark.

£5–8

AUSTRALIA

1992 Basedow Cabernet Sauvignon
0 / MB / 🌓   13/20
Oak-fermented, oak-aged and oak-flavoured. That's enough oak.

1992 Basedow Shiraz
£ / MB / 🌓   14/20
The blackberry fruit of the Shiraz grape seems to work better with American oak here than on the Basedow Cabernet Sauvignon. The hefty oak could still do with toning down.

1992 Riddoch Shiraz
££ / MB / 👈   15/20
Aged in a combination of French and American oak, this is an elegant Coonawarra Shiraz with a peppery, Rhône-like freshness and firm tannins.

1983 Brown Brothers Shiraz/Cabernet
££ / MB / 🏴   15/20
When this wine was made, Australian wines weren't even a gleam
in wine buyers' eyes. Brown Brothers were one of Australia's
pioneering exporters, so it's fitting that this mature, mint-toffee
red Victoria blend has turned up now, like an old timer at a party.

1992 Penfolds Koonunga Hill Shiraz/Cabernet, South Australia
£ / FB / 🏴   14/20
Like many an Australian wine, this has edged up in price over the
last year. Consistently reliable, it's true to the Penfolds' formula of
lashings of American oak and juicy, spicy fruit. We'd like to see it
back under £5, though.

1990 Penfolds Coonawarra Cabernet Sauvignon
££ / FB / ►   16/20
Masses of colour, concentrated fruit and sweet sawdusty American
oak give this the stamp of Penfolds, but there's some balancing
Coonawarra elegance too. A poor person's Bin 707.

FRANCE

1991 La Cuvée Mythique, Vin de Pays d'Oc
£££ / FB / ►   16/20
A blend of five southern French varieties from the go-ahead Val
d'Orbieu co-operative, this remarkable wine, with its smart ochre
label, looks more expensive than it is, even though it's crept over
£5 since last year. Mourvèdre, Syrah, Carignan, Grenache and
Cabernet Sauvignon combine to produce one of southern France's
finest reds. Oaky, herby and packed with spicy flavours of mint,
angostura bitters and leather.

1993 Côte de Brouilly, Philippe de Courcelettes
£ / MB / 🏴   14/20
Wines from the Côte de Brouilly, one of the smallest of Beaujolais'
ten crus, are normally noted for their finesse. This example from
the Cellier des Samsons is more like a straight Beaujolais, and, as
such, should be considerably cheaper.

1993 Morgon, Les Vignerons du Prieuré
££ / MB / ▌   15/20

Morgon is among the most ageworthy Beaujolais crus. This juicy, full-flavoured Gamay from the Cave des Producteurs in Juliénas is pleasant enough, but it's hardly one for the cellar.

1992 Alsace Pinot Noir, Cuvée Médaille d'Or, Pfaffenheim
££ / MB / ▌   15/20

A pale rosé-hued Pinot Noir from the Pfaffenheim co-operative. Pure, delicate fruit with a touch of oak and more character than you'd expect from the pallid colour.

1992 Hautes Côtes de Beaune, Denis Carré
£ / MB / ▌   14/20

Pleasant, if light, raspberryish Pinot Noir from the cool, upper hills of the Côtes de Beaune. The acidity is bracing, just like the air in the Hautes Côtes.

1992 Hautes Côtes de Nuits, Oak-Aged, Les Caves des Hautes Côtes
0 / MB / ▌   12/20

Clumsy, green oak and insufficient fruit make this red Burgundy a rather dour prospect.

ITALY

1990 Vigneti di Marano, Amarone, Boscaini
££ / FB / ▌   15/20

A hefty wine in a hefty bottle, this single vineyard, classic style of Valpolicella is sweet and rustic with loads of alcohol from raisined grapes and a bitter chocolate aftertaste. Not for wimps, quiche eaters or anorak wearers.

NEW ZEALAND

1992 Corbans Merlot
££ / MB / ▌   15/20

This wine has been so good in recent vintages that even tight-fisted wine-writing hacks have been seen investing in a case or two. The 1992 version is a slight disappointment, but still good in an oak, green pepper and blackcurrant cast.

PORTUGAL

1988 Garrafeira TE, Fonseca
£££ / MB / 🍷   16/20

One of the best-value reds in Portugal, made from a combination
of Cabernet Sauvignon and Castelão Frances grapes by talented
winemaker Domingos Soares Franco. The wine's Portuguese
origins are more in evidence than the classic cassis character of
Cabernet Sauvignon on this minty, savoury, nicely evolved red.
And no, we've no idea what TE stands for.

SOUTH AFRICA

1984 Neetlingshof Pinotage
£££ / MB / 🍷   16/20

Pinotage doesn't often age well, but this example made by veteran,
ex-Nederburg winemaker Günter Brözel has held up exceptionally
well. About as elegant as Pinotage gets, the fruit is sweet and mature
with elements of raspberry and wild strawberry, rather like an
ageing red Burgundy.

SPAIN

1992 Las Torres Merlot
£ / MB / 🍷   14/20

Miguel Torres made his name with a Spanish Cabernet Sauvignon,
which beat top classified Bordeaux in international blind tastings.
Now he's using Cabernet's Bordeaux stablemate, Merlot, in a more
commercial, fruity style. There's nothing wrong with the wine, it
just isn't worth £6.

1982 Campo Viejo Rioja, Gran Reserva
£££ / MB / 🍷   17/20

**Remarkable value for a 13-year-old Gran Reserva, this
gamey, old-style Rioja was aged for four years in American
oak barrels before bottling. It's smooth, sweet and supple
with fresh, balancing acidity to keep it in trim.**

Over £8

AUSTRALIA

1990 Katnook Merlot
£ / FB / ➡ 15/20

An oaky, firmly tannic Coonawarra Merlot, which needs plenty of time before it softens into an approachable mouthful.

1990 Katnook Cabernet Sauvignon
££ / FB / ➡ 16/20

Another Coonawarra red for the long haul, aged in French oak barrels for two years. It's serious stuff, but the length of flavour is an encouraging sign for future development.

1990 Penfolds Cabernet Sauvignon Bin 707, South Australia
£££ / FB / ➡ 17/20

If Penfolds' Grange is Australia's answer to the red wines of Hermitage, then this is its riposte to First Growth Pauillac. A blend of Cabernet Sauvignon from selected vineyards in South Australia, this is a tannic, concentrated monster designed for ageing. Come back in the next millennium.

FRANCE

1991 Cornas, Thierry Allemand
£££ / FB / ➡ 18/20

Powerful, aromatic Syrah from one of the best growers in the northern Rhône. £16 is a lot to pay for a red wine, but when it's as good as this smoky, hugely concentrated, spicy number, we reckon it's well worth it.

1989 Sancerre Rouge, Henry Natter
£ / LB / ▌ 14/20

From a small family estate in Sancerre run by the tweedy Henry Natter, this is a light, pungent Pinot Noir with a faintly earthy character. We prefer his whites.

1990 Château de Mercey, Mercurey Premier Cru
0 / MB / ♦ **13/20**
From *négociant* Duvergey-Taboureau, this is an oaky, rather pricey Côte Chalonnaise Pinot Noir, which fails to rise above its rustic origins.

1983 Domaine de Bigarnon
0 / MB / ♦ **12/20**
Domaine de Bigarnon is the third wine of Second Growth Château Léoville Lascases in St Julien. We can see the point of a second wine, but if the fruit isn't good enough to go into it, surely it should be sold off to the *négociants*. Tired and bitter, rather like the château's owner.

1988 Clos Fourtet, St Emilion Premier Grand Cru Classé
£££ / MB / ➡ 17/20
A fresh, structured Merlot with lots of coffee bean new oak, pencilly, soft fruit and a hint of the farmyard. Needs at least another five years to reach its peak.

NEW ZEALAND

1992 Vidal Cabernet/Merlot
£ / MB / ♦ **14/20**
A light, oaky, elegant would-be claret from a lean vintage in New Zealand. If New Zealand reds are going to gain a foothold in Britain, they've got to be more realistically priced.

Rosé

£3–5

FRANCE

1993 Syrah Rosé, Fortant de France
£ / 2 / ♦ **13/20**
Good, basic modern rosé made using the *saignée* method (literally, bleeding), where pink juice is run off from a red-wine vat at the start of fermentation. Pleasantly strawberryish stuff from Skalli in the Languedoc.

ITALY

1993 Puglian Rosé, 'Le Trulle'
££ / 2 / ⌐ 14/20
Australian winemaker Kym Milne has used the *saignée* technique here on the Puglian Negro Amaro grape variety to produce an attractively dry, redcurrant-like rosé.

SOUTH AFRICA

1994 Shiraz Blanc de Noirs, Van Loveren
££ / 3 / ⌐ 14/20
An unusual style for South Africa, made in the warm Robertson region by Wynand Retief from Shiraz grapes vinified like a white wine. Pale pink, almost a blush style, with soft strawberry fruit and saving acidity.

SPAIN

1993 Jacques and François Lurton Rosado, Tempranillo
££ / 2 / ⌐ 15/20
One of the fruitiest, dry rosés on the market, made at a Spanish co-operative by itinerant Frenchmen, Jacques and François Lurton. A wine with good red fruits concentration and crisp acidity.

Sparkling

£3–5

FRANCE

Marquis de la Tour Brut
£ / 4 / ⌐ 13/20
Sweetish, eggy Loire fizz, all right if you bombard it with fresh orange juice.

£5–8

ENGLAND

Heritage Brut
£££ / 2 / ♪   16/20
Made by English-based Australian, John Worontschak, this is one
of the few drinkable sparkling wines made in England. Elegant
and dry with Champagne-like toastiness and bottle-age. Surprise
your Glyndebourne friends with this one.

FRANCE

1992 Maison la Motte, Chardonnay
£ / 2 / ♪   14/20
Chardonnay with bubbles from James Herrick's vineyards near
Narbonne. A creditable first effort that could have done with a bit
more bottle-age before release. As it stands, it's on the short side.

Crémant de Bourgogne, Blanc de Noirs, Cave de Bailly
0 / 3 / ♪   13/20
Sweetened up, appley fizz with a coarse, bitter finish.

1992 Clairette de Die, Cuvée Cybèle
£ / 5 / ♪   13/20
In a fin de siècle, flower-print bottle, this is a sweet and rather
obvious grapey fizz from the Rhône Valley. Asti does this sort of
thing with a lighter touch.

SPAIN

1990 Torre del Gall Gran Reserva
££ / 2 / ♪   15/20
From Moët et Chandon's Spanish outpost, this is one of the best
cavas on the market. A rich mouthful of refreshingly zesty fruit
with none of the usual cava bitterness. Clean, well balanced and
elegant.

Over £8

AUSTRALIA

1991 Croser Sparkling Brut

££ / 2 / ▌   16/20

An idiosyncratic, sweet and savoury, smoky bacon blend of Pinot Noir and Chardonnay grown in cool climate vineyards near Adelaide. Winemaker Brian Croser has modestly named this wine after himself. But then so do the Champenois, and Croser is in partnership with Champagne Bollinger. Consistently among the best Australian sparkling wines.

1991 Green Point

£££ / 2 / ▌   17/20

This successful Yarra Valley winery has produced a brilliant successor to the 1990, which was one of *Grapevine*'s wines of the year in 1994. The Pinot Noir content has been increased, and Pinot Meunier has been added to the blend for the first time. Otherwise, this follows on nicely from the previous vintage, showing considerable toasty complexity and finesse. Parent company Champagne house Moët et Chandon must be happy to see Dr Tony Jordan maintaining Green Point's high standards.

FRANCE

Crémant d'Alsace, Cuvée Julien, Dopff au Moulin

££ / 2 / ▌   15/20

Full, pear and peach style Alsace fizz with a crisp acid bite and considerable elegance.

1986 Victoria Wine Vintage Champagne

£ / 2 / ▌   14/20

This is nothing like as good as the wine we remember with affection from last year. It has an eggy smell and the more acid fruit seems rather young. Perhaps our palates have changed.

Fortified

£5–8

ITALY

Pellegrino Superiore Secco Marsala
£££ / 2 / ⟩   17/20
A large part of the pleasure of this Sicilian fortified wine is
its astonishing amber-gold colour. The aroma and flavours
in the bottle live up to the advance billing: caramel fudge
and orange peel with attractively balanced fruit sweetness
and a dry, almondy finish. Who said Marsala was just for
cooking?

PORTUGAL

1989 Moscatel de Setúbal, Fonseca Successores
£ / 7 / ⟩   13/20
A young, fortified blend of Moscatel, Boal and Malvasia grapes
from the Setúbal peninsula south of Lisbon. An infusion of dates,
raisins and candied peel with a rather hard, spirity finish. Perhaps
these wines need longer to soften in the barrel.

Dow 10-Year-Old
£ / 7 / ⟩   13/20
Closer to ruby than tawny in colour, this is a young, sweet and
faintly spirity Aged Tawny Port, which is usually a good deal more
enjoyable.

SPAIN

La Ina, Pale Dry, Domecq
££ / 2 / ⟩   16/20
Domecq's Fino brand is regularly among the most enjoyable dry
Sherries on the market. As always with Fino Sherry, the watchword
is freshness. This is a slightly fuller, richer style than the equally
popular Tio Pepe from González Byass, but it still has the typical
savoury bite of a good Fino.

La Concha Medium Dry Amontillado, González Byass
££ / 4 / 🔳   15/20

A commercial, off-dry Amontillado from a producer better known for its premium dry Sherries. This is a good, mature, nutty style, most likely to be of interest to the sweet of tooth.

WAITROSE ****

Head Office: Doncastle Road, Southern Industrial Area, Bracknell, Berkshire, RG12 8YA

Telephone: 0344 424680

Number of branches: 108

Credit cards accepted: Switch, Visa, Delta

Hours of opening: Monday and Tuesday 8.30am to 6.00pm. Wednesday and Thursday 8.30am to 8.00pm. Friday 8.30am to 9.00pm. Saturday 8.30am to 6.00pm. Closed Sunday (except for a few branches)

By-the-case sales: Yes

Glass loan: Free against returnable deposit of £5

Home delivery: No, but carry to car at all Waitrose supermarkets. Mail order: some Waitrose wines available through Findlater Mackie Todd, acquired by the John Lewis Partnership in 1993. Tel: 081 543 0966

Clubs: No

Discounts: Wines of the month discount of 12 bottles for the price of 11 (without five per cent discount) or five per cent discount on a whole case of wine, including Champagne and fortified wines

In-store tastings: Occasional customer tastings

Any other facilities: Ice, gift packing and wine list produced ten times a year

Top ten best-selling wines: 1993 Domaine des Fontaines Merlot; Waitrose Good Ordinary Claret; 1988 Cabernet Sauvignon Russe; Don Hugo Red; 1993 Hardy's Southern Creek Shiraz/Cabernet; Castillo de Liria Dry; 1993 Waitrose Muscadet de Sèvre-et-Maine; 1993 Hardy's Southern Creek Semillon/Chardonnay; 1993 Mâcon-

Villages Chardonnay; Waitrose Liebfraumilch

Range: GOOD: Bordeaux, Burgundy, regional France, Australia, Champagne and sparkling wine, Eastern Europe
AVERAGE: Rhône, Italy, New Zealand, Germany, United States, South Africa, South America
POOR: Spain, Portugal, England

The John Lewis Partnership in-house journal is a surprising fund of information. It will tell you anything from whether men's underpants are up or down, to the movement of garden gnomes. And the weekly league tables inside this highly professional publication are so accurate and up-to-date that the Chancellor is said to be an avid reader. So is Julian Brind, the head of wines, spirits, beers and soft drinks at John Lewis' supermarket chain, Waitrose.

Every Friday morning, Brind flicks open his copy of *The Gazette* to see where he stands in the league table of percentage increases over the past week and the previous half-year. When *Grapevine* visited Waitrose in the early autumn, his department was standing second behind fruit, vegetables and horticulture, and showing more than a seven per cent increase over the same period in 1993. Soft drinks, beer and cider had no doubt been given a boost by the continuing warm weather, but since the beginning of 1994, wines too have done well.

One reason has been the success of the new mail order service. This time last year, Waitrose's parent, John Lewis, was just getting its mail order operation off the ground, allowing it to expand its catchment area beyond the local radium of its 108 stores to customers nationwide. Having bought wine merchant company Findlater Mackie Todd in February 1993, the plan was to bring Findlater and John Lewis account customers together and offer a range of wines which combined the old-fashioned virtues of Findlater's list with the more up-to-date range of the Waitrose wine department.

The result is a Findlater list with a choice of 400 wines, around half of which overlap with the Waitrose range. The new range has given Findlater's customers access for the first time to the excitement and adventure of the New World. According to Findlater's managing director, Jane Turner, 'A lot of the customers we inherited tended to be in the 50-plus age group. It's been nice to be able to introduce them to the New World. Many of them are surprised when they taste the wines to find they prefer the New World to Burgundy.'

Customers receive a glossy brochure, *Wine News*, which is sent out ten times a year and contains offers of six to eight different cases, from a mixed Wines of the Month dozen to cases based on a wine region or grape variety. With the average case price varying between £39 and £80, the scheme has 'snowballed since Christmas' says Turner. 'From the start we set a high standard of service. Customers get their wines within the week and we deliver free to customers who order two cases or spend more than £100. We get the feeling that the independent wine trade is nervous of our success.'

Another much expanded area over the past year has been Eastern Europe. Not hard perhaps, given that, as we pointed out last year, Waitrose shelves were devoid, Bulgaria apart, of Eastern European wines. The man responsible for the changes is Master of Wine David Gill, who brought the valuable experience of working for Bulgarian Vintners Company when he joined Waitrose last year. (Incidentally, Gill's appointment brought the number of Masters of Wine in the Waitrose wine buying team to five. If there are any unemployed MWs out there, you know where to send your CV.)

Since the beginning of the year, David Gill has busied himself providing Waitrose with a balanced range of Eastern European wines. According to Gill, 'Hungary is ahead of the game, Slovenia is very forward looking, while Romania has huge, but as yet unrealised, potential. I'm not yet convinced by the wines I've seen from Moldova.' He is a fan of indigenous Eastern European grape varieties, many of which, such as Harslevelu, Kekfrankos, Oremusz and Babiasca, can be as characterful as they are unpronounceable.

For this reason perhaps, he has been less reliant than some on Australian flying winemakers, tending to use the resources of local wineries to provide most of the range rather than bring in just another Chardonnay and Cabernet Sauvignon. He is aware that the tongue-twisting names of so many grape varieties can be off-putting. 'But I think we can get through to our customers with these styles through price, packaging and tastings.'

Gill is aware that there are problems of continuity with some of the wines, simply because many Eastern regions lack the necessary funding, equipment and know-how to apply consistent quality standards all the way from vineyard to bottle. 'You have to work with your supplier and make friends with the people you deal with,' he says. 'Waitrose has always been very good at that.' To date, Hungary has been the main area of expansion; there are also some good wines from Slovenia, Romania, Slovakia and a handful of new Bulgarians.

With most of the wines from Eastern Europe in the £2.99 to £4 price bracket, and an increasingly good-value selection from the Languedoc-Roussillon, the latest range is much better balanced. More wines in this critical price range also help Waitrose to avoid having to stock the shelves with endless cheap German wines or taking the down-market promotional route of putting on wines at £1.99 just to maintain sales. 'I don't believe you're giving good value at £1.99,' says Julian Brind, 'and I'm not convinced it brings new customers in.' The full range of just under 500 wines is now available in 51 stores and 80 per cent of it in all stores.

In the New World, the Australian range is as good as ever, but with the problem of demand starting to outstrip supply, Waitrose is continuing to expand in South Africa and looking hard at Chile. Italy 'remains a nightmare,' says Brind, 'because people still don't understand it.' Perhaps Waitrose don't understand it very well either, because their Italian section is one of the less exciting parts of the range and could do with a bit of fleshing out. So, for that matter, could Spain and Portugal.

It may have escaped your attention, but Waitrose has been introducing the EPOS scanning system over the past year. By 1995 all its branches, from Dorchester to Birmingham, will be converted to the new system. EPOS is all part of bringing Waitrose, one of Britain's most conservative supermarket chains, up to date. The same is true of the wine department, which for the first time has been allowed to do a bit of local advertising, an activity once frowned upon by the board. Last year, Brind was so surprised to win *Wine* magazine's Supermarket of the Year award, he nearly fell off his chair. This year, Waitrose is better prepared all round.

White

Under £3

BULGARIA

1993 Lyaskovets Aligoté
££ / 3 / ❗   13/20
This wine, according to Eastern European wine buyer David Gill,
'consistently came through in blind tastings by simply outclassing
trendier Bulgarian whites'. Cynics might say this isn't hard, but
this is a clean, weighty, pleasantly fruity dry white, which makes
it exceptional by modest Bulgarian standards.

FRANCE

1993 Waitrose Muscadet de Sèvre-et-Maine
0 / 1 / ❗   12/20
Tart, faintly grubby Muscadet which reminded us of an
overcropped Chenin Blanc.

GERMANY

Waitrose Liebfraumilch, Pfalz
£ / 5 / ❗   12/20
With its imperial eagle label, this is a sweet, basic Lieb with typically
floral Müller-Thurgau characters.

HUNGARY

1993 Chapel Hill Irsai Oliver, Balaton Boglar, Kym Milne
££ / 2 / ❗   14/20
Nothing to do with the distinguished Australian winery of the same
name, Chapel Hill is a clever brand name for Kym Milne's
Hungarian wines. A light, fresh halfway house between Alsace
Gewürztraminer and an Eastern European Muscat, showing typical
lychee flavours and fragrance.

SPAIN

Castillo de Liria Dry, Valencia
££ / 2 / 🍷   13/20
A clean, dry, lime-fresh Valencian white from the ubiquitous
Vicente Gandia. A decent, if rather light, top ten best seller at
Waitrose.

£3–5

ARGENTINA

1994 Santa Julia Torrontes Riojano, Mendoza
£££ / 2 / 🍷   15/20
We're slightly baffled by the mention of the word Riojano on this
wine's label, as we weren't aware there was any Torrontes planted
in Rioja. No matter – we enjoyed the restrained grapey, Muscat-
like fruit of this near-native Argentinian variety. An interesting
curiosity.

AUSTRALIA

1994 Houghton Wildflower Ridge Chenin Blanc, Western Australia
£££ / 2 / 🍷   17/20
From Hardy's Western Australian operation, this is a hugely
aromatic Chenin Blanc with masses of cassis, grapefruit and
tropical fruit flavours and a hint of smokiness from partial
oak-ageing. It's nice to see an interesting white from
Australia made from something other than Chardonnay and
Semillon.

1991 Wakefield Crouchen/Chardonnay Clare Valley, South Australia
£££ / 2 / 🍷   16/20
A 40/60 blend of Chardonnay and Crouchen, an unusual variety,
which has been grown in Australia's Clare Valley, where it's known
as Clare Riesling, since the 1850s. Wakefield specialises in this
style, which tastes almost like a mature, unoaked, herbal Semillon.
Fresh acidity gives the wine lift and staying power.

1993 Hardy's Southern Creek Semillon/Chardonnay, South East Australia
££ / 3 / ▌   14/20

Commercial, off-dry, inexpensive Australian white blend with ripe, tropical fruit flavour and a bit of oak character on the aftertaste. A top ten best seller.

1994 Nanya Estate Riesling/Gewürztraminer, South Australia
£ / 3 / ▌   13/20

Nothing to do with popular author C. S. Lewis or his wardrobe. Indeed, we thought the label looked suspiciously like a cannabis-leaf, so perhaps Ganja estate would be more appropriate. The wine is an aromatic blend of two-thirds Riesling, one-third Gewürztraminer, showing confected flavours of pineapple and melon and a hardish finish.

CHILE

1993 Montenuevo Chardonnay
££ / 2 / ▌   14/20

An unoaked Chardonnay from the modern Canepa winery near Santiago with lemon and pineapple chunks fruit and bracing acidity.

ENGLAND

1993 Chapel Down Epoch V, East Sussex
£ / 3 / ▌   13/20

Epoch V sounds rather pompous, when all you've got in the bottle are the comparatively humble Müller-Thurgau and Reichensteiner grapes with a little bit of oak-ageing. David Cowderoy is one of England's better winemakers, but this toasty, tongue-tingling white is not yet epoch-making.

FRANCE

1993 Chasan Domaine la Roque, Vin de Pays d'Oc
££ / 3 / ▌   13/20

A Chardonnay/Listan crossing from Domaines Virginie, a New World influenced operation based in Béziers. Australian winemaker John Weeks can do this sort of thing with his eyes closed. A pleasant peardroppy white quaffer.

1993 Vin de Pays d'Oc Sur Lie
££ / 2 / ⬩   14/20
Picked at night to retain freshness, this is another Australian-style
Languedoc white, in this case an all-comers blend of Chasan,
Sauvignon, Grenache Blanc, Ugni Blanc and Terret, kept on its
lees for three months. The result is a honeyed, soft modern dry
white with appealing freshness.

1993 Pinot Blanc d'Alsace, Blanck Frères
££ / 3 / ⬩   15/20
Waitrose is one of the few supermarkets with a following for Alsace
wines. Perhaps this has something to do with the fact that it buys
well in the region. This one from the family firm of Blanck is a
plump, ripe, smoky white, halfway between a Pinot Blanc and
more interesting Pinot Gris in style.

1993 Bourgogne Aligoté, Jean-Marc Brocard
££ / 1 / ⬩   14/20
A nettley, almost Sauvignon-like Aligoté from cool, northern
vineyards near Chablis. The acidity makes the wine a little austere.
Pass the cassis, Bishop.

1993 Touraine Sauvignon, Domaine Gibault
£££ / 2 / ⬩   15/20
Ripe and rich for a simple Sauvignon de Touraine, it outclasses its
appellation with ripe, gooseberryish flavours and textured,
honeyed fruit. A bargain at under £4.

1993 Château Haut-Rian, Bordeaux AC, Michel Dietrich
£££ / 2 / ⬩   15/20
Made by flying winemaker, Hugh Ryman (not a pseudonym for
O'Ryan), this is a soft, aromatic Bordeaux blend with the Semillon
grape in the ascendant. Excellent value too.

1993 Muscat Bondevilles, Vin de Pays de l'Hérault
£££ / 2 / ⬩   16/20
Produced from low-yielding vines, whose Muscat grapes used to
find their way into the fortified wines of Muscat de Frontignan,
this is a fresh, appealingly dry style, which could bring about a
change in the fortunes of a threatened *appellation*.

Muscat de Beaumes-de-Venise
£ / 8 / ⬧   13/20

Like Muscat de Frontignan, Muscat de Beaumes de Venise is a
fortified wine *appellation* in southern France. It just happens to
have done a better job of publicising its sweet, heady wines, some
of which are enjoyable in a boudoir sort of way. This gets as far as
reception, but doesn't quite make the chaise-longue.

1993 Mâcon-Villages Chardonnay
£ / 2 / ⬧   13/20

It's quite an achievement for a white Burgundy to make a
supermarket top ten. At under £4, this is a soft, unoaked, quaffing
Chardonnay with no great pretensions.

GERMANY

1993 Hochheimer Reichestal Riesling Kabinett
£ / 3 / ⬥—   14/20

Made by the winningly named Holger Schwab, this is a young,
almondy Rheingau Riesling, which needs time to develop a bit
more personality.

HUNGARY

1993 Szekszard Chardonnay
££ / 2 / ⬧   14/20

A rich, honey and clove scented, unoaked Chardonnay from
consultant Australian winemaker, Nick Butler. Hungary's white
wines are starting to draw away from the rest of the Eastern
European field.

1993 Lakeside Oak Chardonnay
££ / 2 / ⬧   15/20

A cleverly oaked Chardonnay made at the Balaton Boglar co-
operative by Australian flying winemaker, Kym Milne. It's a peachy,
fresh, New World style with carbon dioxide for added zip.

ITALY

1993 Orvieto Classico, Cardeto, Orvieto Co-operative
££ / 2 / ▊   14/20
From the largest producer of Orvieto Classico, this is a selection
of what the co-operative regards as its best wines, made from a
blend of the native Procanico, Verdello and Grechetto grapes. A
nutty Umbrian dry white with bracing acidity.

1993 Lugana, Villa Flora, Zenato
££ / 2 / ▊   15/20
From a family-owned property at the southern end of Lake Garda,
this is a single vineyard Lugana made entirely from the normally
undistinguished Trebbiano grape. A ripe, peachy number with a
spicy aftertaste and lime-peel zest.

1993 Cortese dell'Alto Monferrato, Ca' Bianca
£ / 1 / ▊   13/20
Austere, almost acerbic, bone-dry white made from the characterful
but demanding Cortese grape of Piedmont.

SLOVENIA

1993 Labor Chardonnay
££ / 2 / ▊   14/20
Wine buyer David Gill only popped over the Italian border into
Slovenia because Waitrose bottles its Vermouth in nearby Trieste.
But this lightly oaked, green-olive Chardonnay with its curious,
but not unpleasant, Ovaltine-like undertone, is an interesting find
in an imposing Italian bottle. Let's hear it for the village of Koper,
overlooking the Gulf of Trieste.

1993 Vipava Sauvignon
££ / 2 / ▊   14/20
From a winery between Ljubljana and the Italian border, this is a
decent stab at a Sauvignon de Touraine-style white. The bouquet
doesn't exactly scream Sauvignon Blanc, but there's some pleasant
boiled-sweets character on the palate.

SOUTH AFRICA

1993 Stellenzicht Chardonnay, Stellenbosch
£ / 2 / ▌   13/20
A straight-up, oaked Cape Chardonnay, where the splinters are
more in evidence than the fruit flavours.

£5–8

AUSTRALIA

1993 Brown Brothers King Valley Riesling, Victoria
££ / 2 / ▌   15/20
Dry, crisp, cool climate Riesling from some of Brown Brothers'
best vineyards in north-eastern Victoria's King Valley, showing
zesty flavours of lemon and lime. Good with oriental food.

1993 Arrowfield Show Reserve Chardonnay, New South Wales
£ / 3 / ▌   14/20
Big, broad-shouldered, old-style Australian Chardonnay from
vineyards in the Hunter Valley and Cowra. Fine if you like tropical
fruit and toasty, vanilla-fudge oak in superabundance, but hard to
force down more than a glass.

1992 Mitchelton Reserve Wood Matured Marsanne, Goulburn Valley, Victoria
£££ / 2 / ➽   17/20
**Mitchelton make two styles of Marsanne, oaked and
unoaked. As its label suggests, this is the barrel-aged one.
It's a big, rich, waxy mouthful of concentrated, full-flavoured
fruit, but exceptionally well-balanced too. Should improve
with age.**

1987 Lindemans Botrytis Semillon
££ / 8 / ▌   15/20
Now that the European Union and Australia's winemakers have
settled their differences over sweet wines, among other things,
we should see many more good-value stickies from Down Under.
This deep, golden, mature Semillon wine oozes honey and barley
sugar sweetness, but has lost the refreshing acidity it once had.

CHILE

1993 Valdivieso Chardonnay Barrel Fermented, Lontue Valley

£££ / 2 / 🍷   17/20

When we tasted this wine in the early autumn of 1994, it had just been drawn from a blending vat, so we couldn't be sure it would be quite as astounding once it arrived in bottle over here. Otherwise it was wine-of-the-year material, a superbly crafted, French-style Chardonnay with toasty, butterscotch oak and a fresh core of acidity, like a young Meursault premier cru. Brilliant value at just over £5.

FRANCE

1992 Château Carsin, Bordeaux Blanc

£££ / 2 / ↜   17/20

Mandy Jones is one of a small but growing band of Australian woman winemakers, who's worked in Portugal, Chile and Australia as well as Bordeaux. At Château Carsin, she specialises in white wines, experimenting with combinations of oaks, yeasts and grape varieties. The 1992, a blend of 80 per cent Semillon and 20 per cent Sauvignon Blanc, is a New World interpretation of Graves-style white with ultra-fresh, grapefruity flavours and deftly handled oak.

1993 Tokay Pinot Gris, Beblenheim

££ / 3 / 🍷   15/20

Although normally over a fiver, this full, ripe, almost off-dry Pinot Gris is on promotion at £4.99 for Christmas 1994. One to sip during the Queen's annual message to the nation.

1993 Waitrose Gewürztraminer, Beblenheim

££ / 3 / 🍷   15/20

Typically rich, full-frontal lychee and rose petal Gewürztraminer. This one is also on promotion at Christmas at £5.45. Not much subtlety perhaps, but there's plenty of concentrated spicy fruit.

1992 Pouilly-Vinzelles, Bouchard Père

0 / 2 / 🍷   12/20

To clamber onto the shelves at Waitrose, samples have to get past no fewer than five Masters of Wine. We're not sure how this lumpen, old-fashioned white Burgundy pulled it off. Homer must have nodded on this occasion.

1990 Château Tour Balot Premières Côtes de Bordeaux
0 / 6 / ▮　　　　　　　　　　　　　　　　　　　　　　　13/20
And this one.

1991 Château la Caussade, Ste Croix du Mont
££ / 7 / ▮　　　　　　　　　　　　　　　　　　　　　　15/20
This poor person's Sauternes is a blend of 75 per cent Semillon and 25 per cent Sauvignon Blanc with good, honey and peach-like concentration.

1990 Château Bastor-Lamontagne, Sauternes, half-bottle
££ / 7 / ▰▸　　　　　　　　　　　　　　　　　　　　　16/20
For more than twice the price of a Ste Croix du Mont, you get a wine with considerably more weight, colour and barley-sugared richness. Just short of the first division, it has oodles of brandy snap and apricot fruit and balancing acidity.

SOUTH AFRICA
1993 Backsberg Chardonnay, Paarl
£££ / 2 / ▮　　　　　　　　　　　　　　　　　　　　　16/20
Sydney and Michael Back pioneered South African Chardonnay in the early 1980s, and their experience with the variety is starting to pay off. This mainly barrel-fermented style is still a little tight at the moment, but has the elegance to age. Cinnamon oak and citrus fruit flavours make this one of the best Cape Chardonnays.

Over £8

FRANCE
1990 Château Roumieu-Lacoste, Sauternes
£££ / 8 / ▰▸　　　　　　　　　　　　　　　　　　　17/20
A blend of mainly Semillon with some Muscadelle, this is a **botrytis rich, partially barrel-fermented Sauternes with intense flavours of apricot and honey, lifted by elegant, fresh**

acidity. Good to see a supermarket selling a wine like this, even if it does cost nearly £14.

1992 Meursault de Ropiteau
££ / 2 / ➡   15/20

Closer to a village Puligny-Montrachet than a Meursault in flavour, this is a modern, toasty, citrus fruit and mineral style of Chardonnay, which was aged for 12 months in oak barrels.

Red

Under £3

BULGARIA

1993 Oriachovitza Barrel-Aged Merlot Vintage Première
£ / MB / ◗   13/20

From Stara Zagora in the Balkan hills, this is a baked, coarsely oaked Bulgarian red with a dry finish. Perhaps it should have spent a bit more time in barrel.

1988 Cabernet Sauvignon Russe
£ / MB / ◗   13/20

From the go-ahead Russe co-operative near the Danube, this is a sweet blackcurrant pastille red with more youthful tannins than you'd expect on a six-year-old wine. A top ten best seller at Waitrose.

FRANCE

1993 Masquerade Vin de Pays de l'Aude
££ / MB / ◗   14/20

A colourful carnival-style label heralds this interesting blend of Cabernet Sauvignon, Merlot, Malbec and Syrah from cool climate vineyards near Limoux. A good-value red at under £3 with oodles of soft, plummy, carbonic maceration fruit.

1993 Le Secret Vin de Pays de Vaucluse
0 / LB / ◗   11/20

This light, rustic attempt at a southern French Beaujolais is a secret that's not worth keeping.

1993 Domaine des Fontaines Merlot, Vin de Pays d'Oc
££ / MB / ▌   14/20

A soft, juicy, claret-like quaffer from the reliable Domaines Virginie stable near Béziers. If only claret could come up with the same sort of value.

1993 Merlot/Cabernet Sauvignon, Vin de Pays d'Oc
££ / MB / ▌   14/20

A ripe, green pepper and blackcurrant Bordeaux-style blend from the Pays d'Oc. We generally prefer the Languedoc's indigenous varieties, but it's hard to quarrel with wines like this, especially if you're a claret lover.

HUNGARY

1993 Nagyrede Kekfrankos
£ / MB / ▌   13/20

From Hungary's Matra Hills, this is a peppery, surprisingly mature Kekfrankos with the native grape's characteristic strawberry-cup fruitiness.

ROMANIA

1993 Simburesti Pinot Noir
££ / MB / ▌   14/20

Bottled by the West Country wine merchant and brewer, Eldridge Pope, this is a light, raspberry fruity red from southern Romania, with distinctive Pinot Noir character. It's the first truly modern Romanian red we've come across, and bodes well for the future.

SPAIN

Don Hugo Alto Ebro
£ / MB / ▌   13/20

This Don Darias clone has had a few of the oak chips extracted at Waitrose's request. As such, it's a definite improvement. Is it too much to hope that Uncle Don Darias and his extended family will follow Don Hugo's lead?

£3–5

AUSTRALIA

1993 Hardy's Southern Creek Shiraz/Cabernet, South East Australia
££ / MB / ⅃   15/20

The best wine in Waitrose top ten best sellers is a supple, attractively oaked Aussie blend with lots of vibrant blackcurrant fruit and soft, chocolatey tannins. An excellent introduction to Australian reds at just over £3.50.

1994 Nanya Estate Malbec/Ruby Cabernet, South Australia
£ / MB / ⅃   13/20

Back in ganja-land, this is a tarry, chunky blend of two unusual (for Australia) grape varieties from Angove's own vineyards in the Riverland. A bit of a doughnut wine.

CHILE

1993 Valdivieso Merlot Barrel Fermented, Lontue Valley
£££ / MB / ⅃   16/20

Like the Chardonnay from the same winery, this was in tank-sample form when we tasted it, so we hope it travels as well in bottle. A lush, stylishly oaked Chilean Merlot with backbone. Extraordinary value at under £5.

ENGLAND

1992 Chapel Down Epoch 1, East Sussex
£ / MB / ⅃   13/20

The red counterpart to David Cowderoy's Epoch V white. Decent red wines are even harder to make than whites, so he deserves credit for this one. It's made from a grape called GM 6494/5, a crossing of the Eastern European grapes, Saperavi and St Laurent. A curious oak-aged wine with dry, slightly herbaceous fruit and rasping acidity.

FRANCE

1993 Château de la Roche Gamay, Touraine Amboise AC
££ / MB / 🍷   14/20

A young, peppery Loire red with more substance and character than most Gamays from Touraine.

1993 Fleurie, Roland Dagneau, half-bottle
££ / MB / ☛   15/20

Roland Dagneau is another name for Georges Duboeuf, the so-called king of the Beaujolais. A young crimson red with a chocolatey richness that reminded us of good red Burgundy. It needs time, but should blossom into something interesting over the next three years.

1993 Red Burgundy Pinot Noir, Jean-Claude Boisset
££ / MB / 🍷   14/20

We said last year that we were looking forward to better things from the *négociant*, Jean-Claude Boisset, after the arrival of the dynamic new managing director, Bernard Repolt. Sure enough, this is a chunky, but pleasantly oaked house red Burgundy using Pinot Noir fruit from the Hautes Côtes de Beaune.

1991 Domaine de Pigeonnier Corbières
££ / MB / 🍷   15/20

From an estate near the Cistercian Abbé de Frontfroide, this is a spicy, aromatic, softly fruity Languedoc red made from a blend of Mourvèdre, Syrah, Grenache and Carignan, employing the carbonic maceration technique for texture.

1992 Cabernet Sauvignon, Vin de Pays d'Oc, Hugh Ryman
££ / MB / 🍷   15/20

Classic, supple, capsicum and blackcurrant Cabernet Sauvignon from 'Hugh the Guru', as his marketing set-up would have it. It would be nice to see a few more clarets offering this sort of value for money.

Waitrose Good Ordinary Claret, Bordeaux
£ / MB / 🍷   13/20

Ordinary's the word.

1992 Château St-Maurice Côtes du Rhône
££ / FB / ❳   14/20

Old vines of Syrah, Cinsault and Grenache have produced an old-fashioned, hefty, baked, raisiny Côtes du Rhône in the Châteauneuf-du-Pape mould.

1990 Château les Tonnelles de Fronsac
£ / FB / ⊷   14/20

You'd be surprised to discover that this Fronsac red from close to St-Emilion is made from 85 per cent Merlot vines. We certainly were, because Merlot is normally a bit more supple than this firm, highly extracted claret. It's mouth-puckering at the moment, but may soften in time.

HUNGARY

1993 Villány Cabernet Sauvignon
£££ / MB / ❳   15/20

An indication of the sort of value for money Hungary is starting to offer with its juicy, unoaked reds. This fresh, blackcurranty Nick Butler Cabernet Sauvignon is brilliant value at just over £3. And we suspect that it's the first of many such enjoyable wines to come.

ITALY

1992 Dolcetto Vino da Tavola del Piemonte, Gemma
£ / MB / ❳   13/20

A light, made-for-trattorias northern Italian red with firm tannin and damsony tartness.

1993 Waitrose Monica di Sardegna DOC
££ / MB / ❳   14/20

You only need one whiff of this raisiny, Sardinian rosso to spot its hot Mediterranean origins. Good stuff from the thyme, chocolate and black cherry, Marcella Hazan school of Italian wine and food.

1992 Waitrose Chianti
££ / MB / ❳   14/20

A decent rather than spectacular house Chianti with supple, savoury, dry fruit. But at just over £3, who's complaining?

SOUTH AFRICA

1994 Avontuur Cabernet/Merlot, Stellenbosch
££ / MB / 1   14/20
Lots of colour, supple texture and intensely minty flavours
produced in the modern idiom by winemaker Jean-Luc Sweerts in
Stellenbosch. Good value at under £4.

1991 Backsberg Cabernet Sauvignon, Paarl
£££ / MB / ⮞   17/20
The 160-hectare Backsberg estate is best known for its elegant
Chardonnays. But this excellent red, made from recently
planted South African clones of Cabernet Sauvignon, is equally
exciting in its own way. Halfway to a Coonawarra Cabernet
in style, it's an elegant tobacco, mint and blackcurrant-like
wine with balance and ageing potential.

SPAIN

1990 Cosme Palacio Rioja
£ / MB / ⮞   14/20
A pure Tempranillo Rioja from grapes grown in the Alavesa region
and matured, unusually, in French oak. There are so many good
value Riojas on the market at the moment that we found this tannic
example almost too much of a mouthful. Look again in a year or two.

£5–8

AUSTRALIA

1992 Goundrey Langton Cabernet/Merlot, Western Australia
££ / MB / 1   15/20
From cool vineyards in the wilds of Western Australia's Mount
Barker, this is another elegant Coonawarra-style red with ripe
blackcurrant fruit, soft chocolatey tannins and fresh acidity.

1991 Château Reynella Basket Pressed Shiraz McLaren Vale, South Australia
££ / FB / ⮞   15/20
This is a solid, Australian Shiraz with a minty character and lashings
of coconutty American oak. Named in homage to Rocky

O'Callaghan's original Basket Press Shiraz, it is a good wine, but we preferred the excellent 1992.

1990 Penfolds Bin 407, Cabernet Sauvignon
££ / FB / ⌐ 15/20

A blend of Coonawarra and Padthaway grapes, which has opened out and softened a teeny bit since we saw it last year. But it's still a densely coloured, tarry, tightly packed, oaky red.

1992 Leasingham Shiraz, Clare Valley, South Australia
££ / FB / ⌐ 16/20

Based in South Australia's Clare Valley, Leasingham makes approachable, fleshy reds which appeal unashamedly to the senses. This is typical of the style, with luscious coconut and macaroon oak and spearminty freshness supporting sweet, blackberry Shiraz fruit.

FRANCE

1990 Châteauneuf-du-Pape, Les Calcerniers, Delas Frères
££ / FB / ⌐ 16/20

Delas is one of the largest merchants in the northern Rhône, but in common with rivals Chapoutier and Jaboulet, makes a Châteauneuf from the southern Rhône too. This powerful, hefty, peppery red is only just getting into its stride.

1990 Baron Villeneuve de Château Cantemerle, Haut-Médoc
£ / MB / ⌐ 15/20

A seductive Graves-style red from Fifth Growth Château Cantemerle in the upper Médoc, with coffee and vanilla oak and supple, ripe fruit. You might expect a bit more oomph at the price.

1990 Château Maine-Bonnet, Graves
££ / MB / ⌐ 15/20

Traditional, chewy claret needing a year or so to soften into something more approachable. At the moment, it's on the rustic side.

1990 Château d'Arche, Haut-Médoc
££ / MB / ⌐ 16/20

Unusually for a Médoc, this is made entirely from Merlot and Cabernet Franc, with not a Cabernet Sauvignon grape in sight. Showing the quality of the 1990 vintage, it's a concentrated, stylish claret with a good future ahead of it.

ITALY

1989 Grifi, Avignonesi
££ / FB / ⮞   16/20
Once priced well over £10, this supertuscan blend of Cabernet
Sauvignon and Sangiovese has dropped its price over the past year
and is now back on Planet Earth. Elegant pine and cherry fruit
flavours and muscular vanilla oak make this an excellent buy.

SOUTH AFRICA

1991 Fairview Shiraz Reserve, Paarl
££ / FB / ⮞   15/20
A beefy, minty Cape Shiraz from cheese and wine producer Charles
Back. We hope the American oak flavours tone down over the
next year, because they're a bit strident at the moment.

UNITED STATES

1991 Fetzer Valley Oaks Cabernet Sauvignon, California
£ / FB / ⮞   15/20
Charry, chewy, concentrated red from a California winery whose
mission is to promote organic causes and lifestyle enhancement.
Come back in another three years.

Over £8

AUSTRALIA

1992 Coldstream Hills Cabernet/Merlot Yarra Valley, Victoria
£££ / MB / ⮞   17/20
**Prolific ex-corporate lawyer, wine writer, winemaker,
author and show judge James Halliday has made Pinot Noir
his Holy Grail in Victoria's cool Yarra Valley. So much so
that people sometimes overlook the potential for elegant
Cabernet Sauvignon and Merlot in the region. This is a
seductive, Right Bank Bordeaux-style blend with fine-
grained tannins, green pepper fruit, well-integrated oak**

and considerable length of flavour.

FRANCE

1990 Château Lascombes, Margaux
£££ / MB / ←   17/20
Under winemaker René Vannetelle, Second Growth Château Lascombes in Margaux has enjoyed an upturn in fortunes over the last decade. This excellent 1990 is structured to age in bottle, but has enough supple fruit and Margaux elegance to be enjoyed now. And at under £13, there's no need to feel guilty about indulging yourself.

1988 Carruades de Lafite Rothschild, Pauillac
££ / MB / ←   16/20
This is Château Lafite's answer to Château Latour's second wine Les Forts de Latour, and has replaced the latter on the Waitrose list. A tight, concentrated classy mini-Lafite, which still needs plenty of time to unfurl. One for your cellar.

UNITED STATES

1991 Robert Mondavi Pinot Noir, Napa Valley
££ / MB / ▌   15/20
Not quite as good as the previous vintage's spectacular success, but winemaker Tim Mondavi's Pinot Noir is still one of the best in California. Sweetly oaked, spicy, ripe Pinot for immediate drinking.

Sparkling

£5–8

AUSTRALIA

Yalumba Pinot Noir/Chardonnay
£££ / 2 / ▌   16/20
Although you might mistake it on the shelf for Bollinger RD, there's no mistaking the New World origins of this creamy, frothy, mouth-filling blend of 70 per cent Pinot Noir and 30 per cent Chardonnay.

FRANCE

Crémant de Bourgogne Rosé, Cave de Lugny
££ / 2 / ▮   15/20
An attractive copper pink blend of Chardonnay, Pinot Noir and
Gamay from a Burgundian co-operative which specialises in
sparkling wines. Soft, malty, easy-drinking stuff.

Clairette de Die Tradition
££ / 6 / ▮   14/20
Sherbetty, grapey sweet fizz from the Rhône Valley with the
marked, take-it-or-leave-it perfume of the Muscat grape. Asti for
adults.

Over £8

AUSTRALIA

1991 Green Point
£££ / 2 / ▮   17/20
This successful Yarra Valley winery has produced a brilliant
successor to the 1990, which was also one of *Grapevine*'s
wines of the year in 1994. The Pinot Noir content has been
increased, and Pinot Meunier has been added to the blend
for the first time. Otherwise, this follows on nicely from
the previous vintage, showing considerable toasty
complexity and finesse. Parent company Champagne house
Moët et Chandon must be happy to see Dr Tony Jordan
maintaining Green Point's high reputation.

FRANCE

Waitrose Brut NV, Blanc de Noirs
£££ / 2 / ▮   17/20
This was also one of *Grapevine*'s sparkling wines of the
year in 1994 and it, too, has done it again. Made entirely
from Pinot Noir grown in the Aube region of Champagne
near Les Riceys, it's a ripe, malty, forward fizz with charming
strawberry fruitiness. We defy you to dislike it.

1986 Waitrose Extra Dry Vintage
££ / 2 / ▌   16/20
A nutty, toasty, digestive biscuit style of Champagne with lots of
rich flavours from prolonged contact with its yeast lees. A good
value vintage blend of the three Champagne grapes: Chardonnay,
Pinot Noir and Pinot Meunier. Well priced at under £15.

UNITED STATES

Mumm Cuvée Napa
££ / 2 / ▌   15/20
After a couple of dodgy years and several advertising campaigns,
Mumm Cuvée Napa appears to be back on the rails. The fruit quality
is very good, but our reservation is that the wine is being released
so young that it tastes somewhat tart and austere. Tuck it away for
a few months and this one should reward your patience.

Fortified

£3–5

GREECE

Mavrodaphne of Patras
££ / FB / ▌   14/20
Mavrodaphne is a small *appellation* in the far south-eastern corner
of Cephalonia. It's a sweet, raisiny, Port-like red with a baked
Mediterranean character. At under £3.50, it's better value than
many a tawny Port, but don't expect too much in the way of
finesse.

THE *GRAPEVINE* GUIDE TO CROSS-CHANNEL SHOPPING

Setting the scene

It all began on 1 January 1993. After years of red tape, hesitation and foreboding, the Single European Market had finally arrived. The Eurosceptics may have seen the whole business as further evidence of creeping federalism, but most Brits welcomed the changes by popping the corks on bottles of foaming Champagne.

But what did it all mean in practical terms? Several questions hung in the New Year air. Had excise duty now been brought into line with the rest of Europe? Had customs allowances been abolished? What on earth were minimum indicative levels (or MILs)? And was it time to buy a transit van? Few people seemed to know the answers, waiting, like spotty teenagers at their first discotheque, for someone else to take the dance floor.

Almost two years on, the party has turned into an unprecedented cross-Channel knees-up. The Wine & Spirit Association in London estimates that overseas purchases account for more than ten per cent of the wine drunk in the UK and may be as high as 15 per cent. The Brewers Association, too, has warned that the tidal wave of duty-paid beer imports has reached the equivalent of one million pints a day.

The independent consultancy, London Economics, is a little more cautious, estimating that the ten per cent figure quoted by the W&SA is still five years away. But it does predict that Britain will soon follow the likes of Denmark, Canada and Ireland by cutting duty rates to halt the flow of cross-border booze.

The Single Market

'The whole point of excise duties is to stop people drinking too much and to raise revenue,' comments London Economics director Bill Robinson. 'Cross-border shopping frustrates these objectives. It enables people to drink more while paying less tax. If we had the correct revenue-maximising rates before the advent of cross-border shopping, we now have rates that are too high. Cutting them would probably raise revenue.'

This is a moot point. As the then paymaster general, Sir John Cope, told the *Off-Licence News* conference in April 1994, cross-border shopping, at an estimated £250 million per annum, represents a loss of less than five per cent of total alcohol duty of £5.1 billion.

This figure, despite the Single Market bonanza, actually increased in 1993 from £5.06 billion in 1992 and £4.85 billion in 1991. The Treasury, by all accounts, is not convinced that lower duty rates would produce a corresponding increase in sales (and therefore revenue). 'We are losing some money to cross-border activity,' said Sir John, 'and if we were to cut duty significantly, we would lose a lot more.'

As Hylton Bearman, head of British Customs' Excise Division, International Branch, puts it: 'You have to remember that not everyone drinks in Britain. There are social issues involved, because if you lose £6 billion in revenue, you have to make it up somewhere else. You have to take the total tax regime into account.'

1995 and all that

Whatever happens to British duty in the long term, cross-Channel buying has become a way of life. Fifty years after the Normandy landings, the opportunity for tax avoidance, not to mention tax evasion, has given rise to a sustained invasion of the Channel ports. So huge is the volume of traffic, in fact, that the French have been taken by surprise, especially in Calais, or Bootleg City, as it's been affectionately called. They've never seen so many gleeful day-trippers, tourists and bootleggers.

The British wine trade, partly because of prohibitive initial costs, but also from fear that duty on drink might be dropped, was initially cautious about setting up in France. But caution was thrown to the trade winds once they saw the phenomenal success of the early pioneers, EastEnders, Calais Wine & Beer, La Maison du Vin, The Grape Shop and The Wine Society.

Substantial losses caused by the cross-Channel shopping drain have encouraged the big boys to follow suit. First Sainsbury's set up a store within a store at the Mammouth hypermarket in Calais. Now Tesco, which has bought the northern French chain Catteau, plans to open its biggest off-licence yet in the new Cité de l'Europe at the French entrance to the Channel tunnel in 1995.

Cross-Channel Shopping – where to buy?

With British and French supermarkets, hypermarkets, wine merchants and cash-and-carry operations all slugging it out, the choice of wines, beers and spirits available to the cross-Channel shopper is bewildering. But, before you blunder into the first cross-Channel hypermarket and load your car to the gunwales with ten cases of vin de table, be warned. There are plenty of pirates who'll sell you Jolly Roger instead of Jolly Good Rouge. If possible, taste before you buy. If not, let *Grapevine* be your guide.

Most cross-Channel shoppers make for Calais. Eight million Brits visited the French Channel ports in 1993, and the majority took one of the many ferries to Calais. Boulogne, served by the Seacat, and Cherbourg, by a longer and more expensive crossing, are less popular destinations But that shouldn't put you off for a second. Both towns are considerably more attractive than Calais (the sort of place that makes you hanker longingly after Milton Keynes), and both contain at least one top-notch wine merchant.

Inevitably, buying wine in France is a hit-and-miss affair, with considerable variation in the quality and range of wines available. Stumble into the wrong retailer and you'll be faced with endlessly dull *négociant* blends. Go to one of the more quality-conscious outlets and you can take your pick of estate wines and growers' Champagnes. In the most enlightened retailers, such as The Grape Shop in Boulogne and La Maison du Vin in Cherbourg, you can even come across a smattering of wines from New World countries, too.

The French hypermarkets, on the other hand, have struggled to keep up with events. It is only in the last few months that the likes of Auchan and Mammouth have started to tailor their wine ranges to British palates. But it would be wrong to think that all the French retailers are totally fixated on price and *appellation contrôlée* wines. Shops like Perardel, Le Chais and Bar à Vins could well surprise you with their range and quality.

What's your limit?

And what are the rules governing cross-Channel buying? The first point to bear in mind is that provided you are buying wine for your own use (and that includes parties, weddings and other celebrations), there is no limit to the amount of booze you can bring into the country.

Customs can stop you at the roadside and ask whether the wine, or more likely beer, is really for your own consumption. They have even been known to gatecrash the odd wedding. If it isn't for your own use, you are breaking the law by carrying smuggled goods. The definition of bootleg booze (so-called, because the first smugglers used to hide drink inside their boots) is anything you plan to sell to someone else without paying duty.

To avoid bothering the vast majority of honest shoppers, Customs has created something called Minimum Indicative Levels. These, according to Hylton Bearman, are 'the point at which we start to ask if the goods are of a commercial nature'. The current limits are 90 litres of table wine (of which not more than 60 may be sparkling), 20 litres of fortified wine, 110 litres of beer and 10 litres of spirits. If you want to bring back more, the burden of proving it's for your own consumption is on you, guv.

In theory, the duty differential makes buying wine in France a very attractive proposition. The saving is equivalent (at the time of going to press) to £12.13 a dozen excluding VAT on table wine, £18.66 on fortified wines and £20.03 on Champagne and sparkling wines. That's roughly £1 a bottle on table wine, £1.55 on Port, Sherry, Madeira and fortified Muscats, and a whacking £1.67 on fizz.

Bon Voyage

All in all, this is a great time to buy wine in France, with better wines available in the Channel ports than ever before. Le Chais, Perardel, La Maison du Vin, Bar à Vins, The Wine Society and The Grape Shop are all excellent outlets. British wine merchants may not approve, but their protests should be taken with a pinch of *sel de mer* given that, in some cases, they themselves are spearheading the invasion and wine sales are still rising in the UK.

We'd still like to see a few more New World wines on sale in French-owned stores, but you can't expect miracles overnight. A lot of them have to cater for their Gallic clientèle as well as the hordes of day-trippers. And French consumers buy French wines.

The French are responding in their own way to the competition from British-owned chains. Some continue to sell rubbish, but a lot more have increased the quality of their ranges. We were pleasantly surprised by a handful of wines in French supermarkets, which we dismissed *en masse* in last year's guide. They are not yet a match for the likes of Sainsbury's or Tesco, but now that Britain's two wine retailing giants have set up on French soil, that day may not be too far away.

SUPERMARKET AND WINE SHOP ADDRESSES (BY PORT)

Boulogne
Auchan, Route Nationale 42, 62200 St Martin lès Boulogne (21 92 06 00)

Le Chais, Rue des Deux Ponts, 62200 Boulogne (21 31 65 42)

The Grape Shop, 85–87 Rue Victor Hugo, 62200 Boulogne (21 31 28 28 or 071 924 3638 in the UK); Gare Maritime, 62200 Boulogne (21 30 16 17)

Intermarché, 62360 Pont de Briques (21 83 28 28)

Prix Gros, Boulevard Diderot, 62200 Boulogne (21 30 43 67)

Les Vins de France, 11 Rue Nationale, 62200 Boulogne (21 30 51 00)

The Wine Society, Rue Fressin, 62140 Hesdin (21 81 61 70)

Calais
Bar à Vins, 52 Place d'Armes, 62100 Calais (21 34 68 22)

Calais Wine & Beer Company, Rue de Judée, Zone Marcel Doret, 62100 Calais (21 97 63 00 or 081 875 1900 in the UK)

Le Chais, 40 Rue Phalsbourg, 62100 Calais (21 97 88 56) and at 67 Boulevard Jacquard, 62100 (21 97 47 00)

Charlie's, 14 Rue de Cronstadt, 62100 Calais (21 97 96 49)

EastEnders, 110–112 Rue Mollien, 62100 Calais (21 34 53 33)

Intermarché, 56 Avenue Antoine de St-Exupéry, 62100 Calais (21 34 42 44)

Mammouth Centre, Route de Boulogne, 62100 Calais (21 34 04 44)

Perardel, Zone Industrielle Marcel Doret, 190 Rue Marcel Dassault, 62100 Calais (21 97 21 22)

Pidou, Zone Industrielle Marcel Doret, 190 Rue Marcel Dassault, 62100 Calais (21 96 78 10)

J. Sainsbury Bières Vins et Spiritueux, Mammouth Centre, Route de Boulogne, 62100 Calais (21 34 04 44)

Le Terroir, 29 Rue des Fontinettes, 62100 Calais (21 36 34 66)

Cherbourg
Auchan, Centre Commercial Cotentin, 50470 La Glacerie (33 44 43 44)
Continent, Quai de l'Entrepôt, 50104 Cherbourg (33 43 14 11)
La Maison du Vin, 71 Avenue Carnot, 50100 Cherbourg (33 43 39 79 or 0929 480352 in the UK)
Leclerc, 21 Rue des Claires, 50460 Querqueville

Dieppe
Intermarché, 76370 Rouxmesnil Bouteilles (35 82 57 75)
Leclerc, 76370 Etran-Martin Eglise (35 82 56 95)
LC Vins, 1 Grande Rue, 76200 Dieppe (35 84 32 41)
Mammouth, ZAC Val Druel, 76200 Dieppe (35 82 65 50)

Roscoff
Les Caves de Roscoff, Zone de Bloscon, Ateliers 7–9 29680 Roscoff (98 61 24 10 and 071 376 4639 in the UK)

USEFUL TELEPHONE NUMBERS:
Customs and Excise Single Market Unit: 071 620 1313
Hoverspeed: 21 46 14 14 (France); 0304 240101 (UK)
P&O Ferries: 21 46 10 10 (France); 081 575 8555 (UK)
Brittany Ferries: 98 29 28 28 (France); 0705 827701 (UK)
Stena Sealink: 21 46 80 00 (France); 0233 647047 (UK and European head office)
Sally Line Ferries: 28 21 13 42 (France); 071 409 2240 (UK)

AUCHAN **(*)

Address: Route Nationale 42 (direction St Omer), 62200 Saint Martin lès Boulogne, Boulogne

Telephone: 010 33 21 92 06 00

Hours of opening: Monday to Friday 8.30am to 10pm. Saturday 8am to 10pm

Manager: Yves Rouet

Payment methods: Access, Visa; French francs

Discounts: Promotions and annual Foire aux Vins in October with special discounts

English spoken: No

In-store tastings: No

There are 50 Auchan hypermarkets in five regions throughout France from Boulogne in the north to Perpignan down near the Spanish border. At the Boulogne Auchan, just outside town on the road to St Omer, the Brits tend to go for beer, spirits and wines around the 50 franc mark, while the French are more likely to plump for the mixed delights of Bordeaux classed growths.

Auchan, unlike many French hypermarket chains, has a central buying unit near Lille, although Monsieur Rouet, who is in charge of 14 northern French branches, can and does buy wines to embellish the core range. The average British customer, he says, has become more wine-orientated since 1 January 1993. Apart from stuffing five cartons of beer into their supermarket trolleys, British customers cram an average of 15 bottles of wine on top.

In common with arch-rival Mammouth, Auchan was rather slow to welcome the Single Market invasion. But with Sainsbury's and Tesco entering the running, Auchan, to cater for British palates, is planning to expand its range to include southern French varietals, Eastern European and New World wines.

During its Foire aux Vins in October, which concentrates on Bordeaux, customers can taste 15 to 20 different wines. Claret remains Auchan's strongest area, but there are other positive aspects too. Rouet has an open mind and of all the French supermarkets we visited Auchan was the most committed to wine.

White

Under 20FF

FRANCE

1992 Château Gireme, Entre-Deux-Mers, Yvon Mau
££ / 2 / ▌   14/20
Drinkable, grassy, modern white Bordeaux from the usually reliable Yvon Mau stable.

1993 Anjou, Les Caves de la Loire
£ / 3 / ▌   13/20
Slightly cloying, stewed-apple Chenin Blanc with lively acidity.

20–30FF

FRANCE

1992 Château Plessis-Brezot, Muscadet de Sèvre-et-Maine Sur Lie
£ / 3 / ▌   13/20
Soft, sweetish Muscadet. The sur lie character appears to have done a runner.

1993 Bourgogne Chante Fluté, Philippe d'Argenval
££ / 2 / ▌   14/20
Comparatively interesting for a hypermarket Bourgogne Blanc. There's a touch of oak and some pleasant, appley Chardonnay fruit complexity.

1992 Coteaux du Layon, Albert Besombes
£ / 4 / ▌   13/20
Light, rather coarse, sweet Chenin Blanc from a Loire *appellation*
that is capable of better things.

30–50FF

FRANCE

1992 Pouilly-Fumé, Les Champs de Gri, Albert Grebet
££ / 1 / ▌   15/20
Good value, nettley Sauvignon Blanc with crisp, citrus-like acidity
and a minerally note.

1992 Sancerre, Michel Vattan
£ / 2 / ▌   14/20
Closer to a Sauvignon de Touraine than a Sancerre.

1992 Mouton-Cadet, Bordeaux Blanc
0 / 2 / ▌   12/20
An undistinguished waxy blend of Sauvignon Blanc, Semillon and
Muscadelle from the Baron Philippe de Rothschild empire.
Hilariously overpriced for a Bordeaux Blanc.

1991 Alsace Gewürztraminer, Cave de Sigolsheim
£ / 2 / ▌   13/20
Ah! It's that unmistakeable tinned lychee aroma of slightly coarse
Gewürztraminer. A decent introduction to an aromatic and rather
obvious style.

1990 Château Haut Larrivat, Ste Crois du Mont
£ / 5 / ▌   14/20
Light, elegant sweetie that should be displaying a bit more weight
and richness from such a good vintage for the sweet wines of
Bordeaux.

Over 50FF

FRANCE

1991 Chablis, Communaux d'Aronce, Moillard
0 / 2 / ▌   13/20
A boiled-sweets, confected Chablis with ungainly acidity. Basic
Chablis should be better – and cheaper – than this.

Red

Under 20FF

FRANCE

1992 Bordeaux, Jean de Nuit
£ / MB / ▌   13/20
Baked rough-and-ready claret for around 10 francs a bottle. Yer
pays yer money . . .

1992 Versant Royal, Bordeaux Supérieur
££ / MB / ▌   15/20
An old Auchan standby, this is a well-made, Merlot-dominated,
juicy claret blend and, at less than 20 francs, very good value.

1993 Gaillac, Carte Noire
££ / MB / ▌   14/20
Light, fresh drinkable south-west French red in a good Beaujolais
mould. Good house wine material.

1993 Côtes du Ventoux, Vignerons de Canteperdrix
££ / MB / ▌   14/20
A young, fruity southern Rhône glugger, with good colour and a
grind of the pepper mill.

1993 Château de Bastet, Côtes du Rhône
££ / MB / 🍷   15/20

Fresher and more concentrated than the Côtes du Ventoux, this is a good-value winter warmer.

1991 Côtes du Rhône Villages, Cellier des Dauphins
££ / FB / 🍷   15/20

Aromatic carbonic maceration style Rhône red with robust, punchy fruit.

1991 Château Mesnard, Minervois
££ / MB / 🍷   15/20

Not a wine that you'd immediately place in the Languedoc. But this is another enjoyably gluggable, carbonic maceration red.

1992 Château Capendu, Grande Réserve, Corbières
££ / FB / 🍷   15/20

Considerably more weight and tannin than the Minervois. Cleverly used oak adds a bit of polish to the robust southern fruit.

1992 Château des Mazes, Coteaux du Languedoc
£££ / FB / 🍷   16/20

At less than the price of a café crème in most French bars, this chunky, spicy, characterful Mediterranean red is an incredible bargain.

20–30FF

FRANCE

1993 Mâcon Supérieur, Philippe d'Argenval
£ / MB / 🍷   14/20

Light, soft, strawberryish Gamay fruitiness at a decent price.

1992 Bergerac, Maison Peyrarede
0 / MB / 🍷   12/20

Browning at the rim and beginning to show its age already. The underlying fruit is sound enough, but may not last the course.

1990 Médoc, Pierre Chanau
££ / MB / ▰   14/20
Vanilla oak and fruitcake sweetness make this a soft, approachable, drink-me claret.

30–50FF

FRANCE

1993 Brouilly, Antonin Dubayeu
££ / MB / ▰   15/20
Vibrant, youthful Gamay fruit in a zippy, bubblegum and strawberry style. Textbook stuff.

1991 Mouton Cadet, Bordeaux
0 / MB / ▰   12/20
We find it hard to understand why anyone would part with nearly 50 francs for this overpriced, browning claret. A triumph of marketing over substance.

1990 St Emilion Grand Cru, Porte du Roy, Union des Producteurs
£££ / MB / ▰   16/20
For 11 francs less than the Mouton-Cadet, why not buy a claret with some character? The delicious, tobaccoey Merlot spice and sweetness makes this a bargain. Drinking nicely now, but will keep too.

1991 Gigondas, Domaine St François-Xavier
££ / FB / ▰   15/20
Meaty, full-bodied Syrah spice with the sort of robust tannins that need food for the wine really to sing.

1992 Châteauneuf-du-Pape, Château Saint-André
££ / FB / ▰   16/20
Fine, powerful Châteauneuf-du-Pape with smooth, flavoursome fruit and gingerbread spice. One to enjoy now or keep for next Christmas.

Rosé

Under 20FF

FRANCE

Listel Gris de Gris, Vin de Pays des Sables du Golfe du Lion
0 / 3 / ⅃   12/20
A popular if dull rosé produced on the sandy littoral of the French
Mediterranean. Fat and on the sweet side.

20–30FF

FRANCE

1993 Domaine Pont du Roi, Tavel, Les Caves Saint-Pierre
££ / 2 / ⅃   15/20
Day-glo pink rosé with the sort of liquorice and blackcurrant fruit
to make Listel Gris de Gris blush. This full-bodied, dry Rhône Valley
rosé can be drunk happily with food.

BAR À VINS ***

Address: 52 Place d'Armes, 62100 Calais

Telephone: 010 33 21 34 68 22

Hours of opening: 9am to 8pm except Wednesdays, Monday to Saturday

Manager: Luc Gille

Payment methods: Access, Visa; sterling and French francs

Discounts: Negotiable

English spoken: Yes

In-store tastings: Yes

Luc Gille's claim to be the only wine merchant in Calais is a mite exaggerated, but with little more than cash-and-carry warehouses and hypermarkets for competition, you can see what he means. Monsieur Gille is one of those passionate, though increasingly rare, souls who cares about his job.

Holding court behind the bar in the Place d'Armes, this former off-shore oceanographer affects a fierce exterior to ward off the evils of marauding lager louts, beer runners and what he calls 'just-looking day trippers'. This latter group tends to wander in off the streets of Calais asking for strong carrier bags for the wines they've just bought at Mammouth. Gille speaks English, but his response to this question is invariably in curt French.

In the ordered anarchy of this old curiosity shop of wine paraphernalia, Gille dispenses hospitality and wine in bulk in addition to a range of 250-odd fine wines, most of which he sources himself from French vineyards. If you speak a little French, it's worth going along just to mix with the locals at aperitif time. Bar à Vins is a café and wine bar as well as a retail outlet.

Gille's strengths include Muscadet, Vouvray, red and white Bordeaux, Champagne and an excellent Châteauneuf-du-Pape.

Unlike his competitors, he refuses to sell Piat d'Or and Mouton-Cadet. 'I'm a wine merchant,' he protests. He sure is.

White

20–30FF

FRANCE

1992 Domaine de Tarrit, Vin de Pays des Côtes de Gascogne
£ / 2 / 🍾   13/20
Fresh, light white with a touch of pineapple and grapefruit. Drink up.

1992 Domaine Barreau-la-Grave, Blayais
££ / 2 / 🍾   15/20
An idiosyncratic, organic Bordeaux white from Patrick Pouvreau, showing flavours of pepper and celery and an intriguingly waxy texture.

30–50FF

FRANCE

1993 Muscadet de Sèvre-et-Maine Sur Lie, Cuvée des Lions, Serge Saupin
£££ / 1 / 🍾   17/20
If only all Muscadet tasted like this fresh, concentrated example. Honey and ripe pears with a textbook sur lie bite.

1990 Mâcon-Villages, Claudius Rongier
£ / 2 / 🍾   14/20
An old style Mâcon with the emphasis on ripe, honeyed fruit, a bit of old oak and rusticity.

1992 Réserve du Domaine Tokay Pinot Gris, Gérard Metz
££ / 2 / 🍾   16/20
Plenty of alcohol here, but unlike many an Alsace white, the wine

still tastes elegant and well-balanced. Restrained spice and a hint of liquorice.

1992 Vouvray, Domaine la Sabotière, Christian Chaussard
££ / 3 / ➡   16/20
Soft baked-apple sweetness balanced by crunchy, refreshingly zippy acidity. Classic Vouvray.

1989 Vouvray, Moelleux, Domaine la Sabotière, Christian Chaussard
£ / 6 / ▌   14/20
1989 was a great year for sweet wines in the Loire. This has plenty of honeycomb sweetness, but we found the acidity a little rasping.

Over 50FF

FRANCE

1992 Saint Romain, Bernard Fèvre
0 / 2 / ▌   12/20
Traditional, rustic white Burgundy. One of the few duffers at Bar à Vins.

Red

20–30FF

FRANCE

1993 Domaine de Tarrit, Vin de Pays des Côtes de Gascogne
£ / LB / ▌   13/20
A light, rhubarb crumble-style Gascon red with sharp acidity.

30–50FF

FRANCE

1992 Domaine Barreau-la-Grave, Premières Côtes de Blaye
£££ / MB / ▮   16/20
This organic red is an unusual claret. Its soft, cherryish fruitiness reminded us of a cross between a red Burgundy and a good Chinon from the Loire.

1990 Domaine Barreau-la-Grave, Premières Côtes de Blaye, Vieilli en Fûts de Chêne
£ / MB / ▮   14/20
Same producer, different vintage and tons of tannic oak. We preferred the younger, unoaked version.

1990 Château de Villepreux, Bordeaux Supérieur
£££ / MB / ▮   16/20
Fine-grained tannins, coffee bean oak and supple Merlot-derived fruitiness. A very appealing modern claret outperforming its humble *appellation*.

1992 Domaine St Julien-les-Vignes, Coteaux d'Aix-en-Provence
££ / FB / ▮   16/20
This takes farmyardy character to extremes, but don't be put off by the cowpats. A densely flavoured, fruity Provençal red from Luc Gille's home patch.

1991 Mâcon Rouge, Claudius Rongier
££ / MB / ▮   15/20
True to the rustic Rongier style, this is a juicy, chocolatey, oaked red, which neatly straddles Beaujolais and Burgundy in style.

1991 Bourgogne Passetoutgrains, Michel Goubard
££ / MB / ▮   16/20
A horrendous label is the worst possible introduction to this sweet and savoury Pinot Noir/Gamay blend. Buy blindfolded and get someone to decant it for you.

1992 La Vieille Jasso, Côtes du Rhône, Château de Husson
££ / MB / ♪   15/20
Made by a brilliant Châteauneuf-du-Pape producer, this is a
powerfully sweet, heady blend of Grenache and Syrah.

Over 50FF

FRANCE

1990 Château de Villepreux, Vieilli en Fûts de Chêne
0 / FB / ♪   14/20
Robust oak and a dry finish make this slightly less attractive than
the basic Château de Villepreux red. A wine that needs some time.

1990 Château de Husson, Châteauneuf-du-Pape, Granget
£££ / FB / ➴   18/20
An outstanding Châteauneuf-du-Pape from André and
Bernard Granget. Aromatic, spicy and powerful with
massive concentration of chocolatey, chunky fruit. Worth
buying a few bottles to lay down for special occasions.

1990 Bourgogne Côte Chalonnaise, Mont-Avril
£ / MB / ♪   15/20
Attractive raspberry Pinot Noir from the good value (for Burgundy)
area between the Côte d'Or and the Mâconnais. The oak is elegantly
handled.

Rosé

20–30FF

FRANCE

**1992 Domaine de St Julien-les-Vignes, Coteaux d'Aix-en-
Provence**
£££ / 2 / ♪   16/20
Attractive pale bronze rosé with strawberry fruit and a bit of tannic
grip. A good food rosé.

30–50FF

FRANCE

1993 Château de Villepreux, Bordeaux
££ / 2 / ▌   16/20
We thought we detected some stylish oaking here, although mine
host at the bar, Luc Gille, says the character of the wine comes
entirely from its strawberry and green pepper fruit. A dry rosé
with some elegance.

Sparkling

Over 50FF

FRANCE

Champagne François Heucq, Brut Réserve, Fleury la Rivière
££ / 2 / ▌   16/20
A grower's Champagne showing nice chocolatey fruit that could
do with a bit more bottle age.

Fortified

30–50FF

FRANCE

Muscat de Rivesaltes, Cave d'Opoul
£ / 7 / ▌   14/20
Luc Gille sells this one by the litre. A grapey, orange peel fortified
Muscat with plenty of sweetness and a spirity bite.

CALAIS WINE & BEER COMPANY **(*)

Address: Rue de Judée, Zone Marcel Doret, 62100 Calais

Telephone: 010 33 21 97 63 00 (or London 081 875 1900)

Hours of opening: 7am to 10pm seven days a week

Manager: Jerôme Castledine

Payment methods: Access, Visa; sterling, French francs

Discounts: Pallet and half-pallet discounts

English spoken: Yes

In-store tastings: Yes

The sign outside the door is brashly unequivocal: 'The Best British Wine Merchant'. Cynics might argue that, in Calais at least, there isn't much competition, but Calais Wine & Beer is certainly one of the better cross-Channel operations. It's a bright, modern warehouse on the outskirts of town with enthusiastic young staff, jokey murals and the sort of service you'd find in a Majestic or Oddbins back home.

The warehouse is the sole French outpost of Marco Attard's British retail operation, Marco's. Calais Wine & Beer opened in May 1993 and has deliberately opted for a mainstream, stack-it-high approach. The range is not as interesting as those in the six Marco's stores in Britain, but is very much aimed at the day tripper and bargain-conscious cross-Channel buyer. 'We didn't see the point of stocking anything over £8,' says marketing director Neil Cotton, 'because you can buy those wines just as cheaply in the UK. This game only really works up to £6.99.'

Still, there are plenty of wines (400 at present) to choose from with lots of stuff from the New World, Spain and Italy as well as France. Attard says he intends to add another 200 wines over the next 12 months now that he's happy with the way things are going.

The wines here are still on the safe side, with the emphasis on brands, basic blends and big names. All the New Zealand wines come from Cooks, all the Chilean wines from Santa Rita. This is a shame given the obvious knowledge of the two bilingual members of staff, Jerôme Castledine and Simon Delannoy. Given a better range to sell, they could turn this place into a goldmine.

White

Under 20FF

AUSTRALIA

1993 Denham Estate Semillon/Chardonnay
£ / 2 / ₤   14/20
Restrained by Australian standards, this is a soft, fruity blend of Semillon and Chardonnay with a few oak splinters for good measure.

FRANCE

Notre Cellier Blanc Vin de Table
£ / 3 / ₤   13/20
Made in Spain, bottled in Paris, sold in Calais and drunk all over the South of England. A basic, clean, appley dry quaffer.

1992 Gascogne Blanc, Marquise de Lassime
£ / 2 / ₤   13/20
Fine in a boiled-sweets sort of way, but the 1993 ought to be livelier.

GERMANY

1992 Binger St Rochuskapelle, Riesling Spätlese
££ / 5 / ₤   14/20
Sweet, but nicely balanced Rheinhessen Riesling, showing good richness and cassis fruit.

20–30FF

CHILE

1992 Santa Rita 120 Riesling
££ / 2 / ▪   15/20
Chile tends to be Chardonnay and Sauvignon Blanc country, so
let's hear it for this unoaked, citrus-crisp Riesling from one of the
New World's most reliable producers.

FRANCE

1992 Muscadet de Sèvre-et-Maine Sur Lie, La Sablière
0 / 2 / ▪   12/20
A case of the disappearing sur lie character, officer. Dull and flat
with a salty finish, like Margate on a typical summer's day.

ITALY

1992 Bianco di Toscana, Villa Antinori, Vino da Tavola
£ / 2 / ▪   14/20
Piero 'never knowingly undercharged' Antinori has produced this
oak-aged table wine from a blend of Trebbiano and Chardonnay.
A word of warning: we had to work our way through two corked
bottles to get to a drinkable one.

NEW ZEALAND

1992 Cooks Gisborne Chardonnay Chenin Blanc
0 / 2 / ▪   12/20
The basic Cooks range is a decent if dilute introduction to New
Zealand wines. Fine if you like watered down pineapple juice.

30–50FF

AUSTRALIA

1993 Richmond Grove Cowra Verdelho
£££ / 3 / ▪   16/20
The star buy at Calais Wine & Beer, surfing Australia's exciting
new wave. An unusual Australian white from the Cowra district

of New South Wales with tropical sweetness and a touch of smoky oak balanced by fresh acidity.

CHILE

1993 Santa Rita Chardonnay Reserve
££ / 2 / 🍷   15/20

Santa Rita is consistently among the best Chardonnay producers in Chile, combining New World style fruit with some European elegance. This fresh, grapefruity wine with its well-handled American oak char is a good example.

ENGLAND

1991 Denbies Surrey Gold
£ / 4 / 🍷   14/20

Possibly the only English wine available on French soil. Not the best way to resurrect the entente cordiale.

FRANCE

1992 Mâcon Blanc Villages, Antonin Rodet
£ / 2 / 🍷   13/20

Full, ripe unoaked white Burgundy in an old-fashioned *négociant* style. A bit so-what.

1991 Riesling, Turckheim, Alsace
££ / 1 / 🍷   15/20

Following a trio of excellent vintages, 1991 was a cooler year in Alsace producing leaner, atypical wines. For people who find Alsace wines a little fat and cloying, this bone-dry, lime-like Riesling will come as a refreshing change of style.

Red

Under 20FF

FRANCE

Notre Cellier Rouge, Vin de Table
0 / LB / 🎫   11/20
You can put this in your cellier, but we'd rather not have it in
ours.

1991 Bordeaux Supérieur, Pierre Jean
£ / MB / 🎫   14/20
Pierre Jean is none other than the ubiquitous Bordeaux merchant,
Yvon Mau, best known for producing innocuous red and white
blends. This soft, juicy tobaccoey Merlot is some way above
average.

1993 Côtes du Rhône, Domaine de la Rompe, Mousset
£ / MB / 🎫   13/20
Coarseness and high acidity undermine the promising Syrah
pepperiness of this straightforward southern Rhône red.

ROMANIA

1988 Classic Pinot Noir, Dealul Mare
££ / LB / 🎫   14/20
The French have a term for describing Pinot Noir which is *sous-
bois*, or undergrowth. This value for money Romanian red
demonstrates the leafy sweetness of mature Pinot Noir to good
effect. One for impoverished fans of old-fashioned red Burgundy.

20–30FF

AUSTRALIA

1991 Lindemans Bin 45, Cabernet Sauvignon
££ / FB / 🎫   15/20
The reds made at Lindemans tend to be more European in style
than those from stablemate Penfolds. This soft, vanilla and

blackcurrant scented red shows why Australian wines are so popular in Britain. Even the French are catching on to this one.

1992 Penfolds Bin 35 Shiraz/Cabernet, South Australia
££ / FB / ↦   15/20
A wine that never lets you down. Sweet American oak and lashings of toffee, blackcurrant and spice make for a consistently enjoyable style. Corked hats off to winemaker John Duval of London Transport tube poster fame for producing the goods with commendable regularity.

FRANCE
1993 Beaujolais-Villages, Jean Baptiste, Toussaint
0 / LB / ♪   11/20
Beaujolais-Villages should be a step up from basic Beaujolais, so we wonder how this dilute, tart number slipped past the tasting panel.

1992 Château Laurençon, Bordeaux Supérieur
£ / MB / ♪   14/20
Made by the mayor of St Pierre-de-Bat, wherever that might be, this is an attractive, easy-drinking claret with cherried Merlot ripeness. Allez, citoyens, keep the mayor in the Mairie.

1992 Château Vincy, Bordeaux Supérieur
££ / MB / ↦   15/20
You only have to pay an extra franc or so for this well-crafted, modern claret, whose firmer backbone and green pepper fruit make it a wine to tuck away or enjoy now. Another candidate for low office.

ITALY
1992 Chianti la Vigna, Botter
0 / LB / ♪   12/20
Light, inoffensive Sangiovese-based red, barely worthy of Italy's supposedly exalted DOCG (Denominazione di Origine Controllata e Garantita) status.

SOUTH AFRICA

1991 Sable View Pinotage
£ / FB / ▋   13/20
Pinotage, a cross between Pinot Noir and Cinsault, is South Africa's claim to an indigenous wine style. At its best, its earthy sweet fruit bite can be delicious. The dry rusticity of this one takes it over the top. Drink with barbecued impala.

SPAIN

1989 Señorio de Los Llanos Reserva
££ / MB / ▋   15/20
A gamey, good-value red with a bit of age from Valdepeñas, a sub-region of Spain's vast, central La Mancha plateau. An appealing Rioja substitute.

30–50FF

FRANCE

1989 Château Sigognac, Cru Bourgeois Médoc
££ / FB / ➥   16/20
Sweet vanilla and coconutty new oak are the hallmarks of this well-made, tight-grained modern Médoc. A chewy red that needs two to four years to soften.

1990 Château La Rose Chevrol, Fronsac
££ / MB / ▋   15/20
A soft, tealeaf-like Right Bank Merlot from one of the most consistent Bordeaux vintages in recent years. Already close to its peak.

1991 Crozes-Hermitage, Louis Mousset
££ / FB / ▋   15/20
From a merchant based in Châteauneuf-du-Pape at the southern end of the Rhône Valley, a wine with the characteristic liquorice and black olive flavours of northern Rhône Syrah. Gluggable stuff.

ITALY

1992 Santa Cristina, Antinori, Vino da Tavola
£ / MB / ▐   14/20

A reasonable, if slightly overpriced, Antinori red blend showing lively acidity and some, but not a vast amount of, bitter cherry Sangiovese fruitiness.

SPAIN

1990 Principe de Viana, Cabernet Sauvignon, Crianza
££ / MB / ▐   15/20

It's only in the 1990s that Navarra has begun to emerge from the shadow of its more famous neighbour, Rioja. Until recently, most of the region was planted with Garnacha, and was best known outside Spain for its pink rosados. This raisiny, broad-shouldered, oaky Cabernet Sauvignon shows how rapidly its reds are changing for the better.

Over 50FF

FRANCE

1989 Château Ramage la Batisse, Cru Bourgeois, Haut-Médoc
££ / FB / ➥   16/20

A *Grapevine* favourite. Lots of classy new oak on show, but more than enough concentrated, savoury fruit to compensate for the splinters. Just goes to show that oak barrels don't have to be clumsily handled.

Sparkling

20–30FF

AUSTRALIA

Killawarra Brut NV
££ / 3 / ▌   14/20
Brilliant wedding or party fizz from the Australian Penfolds group.
A creamy, sherbetty, tank-method sparkler with a touch of
sweetness. Thanks to the extra tax on sparkling wines, the price
differential makes this just the sort of wine to bring back by the
caseload.

30–50FF

AUSTRALIA

Seppelt Pinot Noir Rosé Cuvée Brut NV
£££ / 2 / ▌   16/20
A bronze-pink rosé from another Penfolds outpost. Elegant,
mouthfilling mousse with a refreshingly dry aftertaste. Hard to
beat under 50 francs.

1990 Seaview Pinot Noir Chardonnay Brut
££ / 2 / ▌   16/20
A toasty, bottle-aged bouquet and classic fudge-like blend of the
Champagne grapes, Pinot Noir and Chardonnay, make this an
interesting contrast in style. Even at a pound more it's still very
good value.

Over 50FF

FRANCE

Jacquesson Brut NV Champagne
£ / 2 / ▌   15/20
A young appley Champagne with the emphasis on fruit flavours
rather than bottle-aged complexity.

LE CHAIS ***

Address: Quartier Brequerecque, Rue des Deux Ponts, 62200 Boulogne

Telephone: 010 33 21 31 65 42

Hours of opening: 9am to 12 midday and 2pm to 7pm Tuesday to Saturday

Manager: Vincent Théret

Payment methods: Access, Visa; sterling and French francs

Discounts: Regular case promotions, with one free bottle for every 12 bought

English spoken: Yes

In-store tastings: Yes

The closest the French come to Majestic Wine Warehouses is Le Chais, which piles it high and sells it cheapish in a cool, efficient cellar underneath the arches of Boulogne railway station.

Offering wines by the dozen or in handy cases of six, with discounts for bulk purchases, Vincent Théret knows his wines and his customers' tastes. He buys cannily, mainly for French shoppers, who comprise 70 per cent of his customers as against a mere one per cent in the case of The Grape Shop. But he knows how to look after Brits, too.

The Boulogne branch of Le Chais is the oldest of the company's four stores – the other three are in Calais and Le Touquet – and Monsieur Théret and his Terry-Thomas moustache are major attractions here. Nevertheless, the other stores stock a lot of the same wines.

When Vincent Théret buys from *négociants*, he tends to use respectable names such as Jaboulet, Chapoutier and Louis Jadot – *négociants* who see no need to masquerade under brand names on supermarket shelves.

Good-value Champagne and other sparkling wines are a Le Chais speciality, so anyone looking for good wedding or party fizz will find plenty of choice here. There is a mouth-watering choice of classified clarets and crus bourgeois, available by the bottle or in wooden cases. Readers keen to shell out for a case of Château Margaux or Lynch Bages should carry a good UK wine list to compare prices.

Our only real gripe here was the absence of a retail list. Otherwise, there's plenty to recommend at Le Chais: good parking facilities, a knowledgeable and charming owner and some very enjoyable French wines.

White

Under 20FF

FRANCE

1993 Muscadet, Jacques Fontaine
£ / 1 / ▮   13/20
Jacques Fontaine is another label for the ubiquitous Loire merchant house of Donatien Bahuaud. This is very basic Muscadet with clean, appley fruit, but no real concentration.

1993 Chardonnay Jean Delataille, Vin de Pays du Jardin de la France
££ / 2 / ▮   14/20
Another Donatien Bahuaud label, this time wrapped around a floral, easy-drinking unoaked Chardonnay from the Loire's largest vin de pays.

1992 Touraine Blanc, Oisly et Thésée, Cuvée des Gourmets
££ / 2 / ▮   14/20
Modern, nettley Sauvignon Blanc from the consistent Oisly et Thésée co-operative. By the time you read this, Le Chais will probably have moved on to the next vintage.

20–30FF

FRANCE

1992 Pineau de la Loire, Oisly et Thésée
££ / 2 / 🌓   14/20
Pineau de la Loire is another name for the Chenin Blanc grape,
and this Loire white has all the green apple hallmarks of the variety.
Clean, quaffable and crisp

1992 Mâcon-Villages, Domaine Mathias, Chaintré
£££ / 2 / 🌓   16/20
Attractively unoaked Chardonnay with some grapefruit and peachy
complexity. A very good cross-Channel buy at under 30 francs.

30–50FF

FRANCE

1993 Pouilly-Fumé, Coteaux du Petit Boisgibault
££ / 1 / 🌓   15/20
Le Chais have been buying their Pouilly-Fumé from Denis Gaudry
for more than a decade now. Good, grassy fruit intensity with a
nip of austerity.

1992 Chablis, Jean-Pierre Grossot
££ / 2 / 🌓   15/20
Fattish, fruity almost New World Chardonnay with upfront flavours
of peach and honey. Traditionalists may find this Chablis a little
shocking.

1989 Château de Chantegrive, Graves
£ / 2 / 🌓   14/20
This is the estate wine of Henri Lévêque, the Bordeaux white wine
négociant. Marked by oak, it's an attractive, modern baked apple
style Graves.

1992 Bourgogne Aligoté, Louis Jadot
££ / 2 / 🌓   15/20
An Aligoté with some welcome flesh and rounded fruit from one
of Beaune's best-known *négociants*.

Over 50FF

FRANCE

1989 Gewürztraminer Clos Zisser, Domaines Klipfel, Alsace Grand Cru
££ / 3 / 🍾   16/20
Surprisingly elegant considering its Mike Tyson alcoholic punch, this is an intense, deeply flavoured Gewürztraminer with spicy fruit intensity. A special occasion white.

Red

Under 20FF

FRANCE

1993 Beaujolais Domaine du Clos St Paul
££ / MB / 🍾   14/20
Good, peasant Clochemerle Gamay with light, cherryish fruit.

1992 Touraine Rouge, Cuvée des Gourmets, Oisly et Thésée
£££ / MB / 🍾   15/20
A typical Loire blend of Gamay and Cabernet Franc, this is a refreshing summer red with green pepper tannins and oodles of juicy fruit.

1992 Château Miot, Bordeaux, J. P. Moueix
££ / MB / 🍾   15/20
A forward, palatable Merlot from Right Bank *négociant*, Jean-Pierre Moueix.

1993 Les Gazels, Vin de Pays de l'Aude, Domaine de Boëde
££ / MB / 🍾   14/20
A chunky, organic blend of Syrah and Mourvèdre, made without benefit of pesticides or insecticides by winemaker Juliette Arnaud. At this price, maybe she couldn't afford them. Gazelle-like it isn't.

1992 Cahors Côtes d'Olt
£ / FB / ♪   13/20
A rather unyielding tar and tealeaf style red from the home of the
Black Wine of Cahors. This isn't black, but it will leave treadmarks
on your teeth.

20–30FF

FRANCE

1992 Beaujolais-Villages, Cellier des Samsons
0 / MB / ♪   12/20
Dull, raspberryish Gamay from one of Beaujolais' biggest umbrella
wine groups. This really ought to have more concentration.

1991 Bordeaux Supérieur La Galante
££ / FB / ♪   15/20
Perfumed, grassy claret with a bit of oak. The slight greenness
reminded us of New Zealand's South Island.

1990 Château les Tonnelles du Roy, Fronsac, J. P. Moueix
££ / MB / ♪   15/20
Chunky, chocolatey Right Bank Merlot from Jean-Pierre Moueix.
A wine with lots of fruit and backbone.

1992 Belleruche, Côtes du Rhône, Chapoutier
££ / MB / ♪   15/20
An unusual Côtes du Rhône made entirely from the Grenache
grape, showing sweet ripe fruit and more than a hint of pepper.

1992 Côtes du Rhône, Parallèle 45, Jaboulet
£££ / FB / ♪   16/20
A contrast in style from rival Tain l'Hermitage *négociant* Paul
Jaboulet, with the accent on juicy, blackberryish Syrah fruit.

30–50FF

FRANCE

1992 Bourgueil Vieilles Vignes, Nau Frères
££ / MB / ❚   15/20
Bourgueil is often the most elegant of the top Loire reds, and this
one is true to form with its perfumed and appealingly rounded
fruit shot through with fresh acidity.

1992 Bourgogne Passetoutgrains, Louis Jadot
0 / MB / ❚   12/20
Louis Jadot usually make better whites than reds. This clumsy,
rooty Burgundy blend proves the point.

1992 Bourgogne, Couvent des Jacobins
£ / MB / ❚   13/20
Overoaked Pinot Noir with too many splinters for the weight of fruit.

1988 Château Roudier, Montagne St Emilion
££ / FB / ⬌   15/20
Meaty, concentrated, serious Merlot with backbone. A grand vin
at a petit price.

1990 Château Dasvin Bel-Air, Haut-Médoc, Cru Bourgeois
£ / FB / ⬌   14/20
Toffee and vanilla oak obscure a core of sweet fruit. Almost too
modern for its own good.

1990 Château Puygueraud, Côtes de Francs
£££ / MB / ⬌   16/20
A classy Right Bank claret with fine-grained tannins. It's a little
closed at the moment, but a year or two under the stairs should
see you right.

1990 L'Oustau Fauquet, Gigondas, Roger Combe
£££ / FB / ⬌   17/20
**A blend of 70 per cent Syrah and 30 per cent Grenache, this
is a big, sweet garrigue-infused southern French red that
could easily be mistaken for an expensive Châteauneuf-du-
Pape.**

Sparkling

Over 50FF

FRANCE

Champagne de Monbelian
££ / 2 / ⅃   16/20
Young, creamy, Marmitey Champagne blend of mainly Pinot Noir
and Pinot Meunier from a small grower in Venteuil.

Champagne Veuve Maurice Lepitre Brut Premier Cru
£££ / 2 / ⅃   17/20
Even on a sun-drenched ferry, it's worth crossing the
Channel to get your hands on a case of this rich, malty,
mouth-filling grower's Champagne. At just over 80 francs,
this is something of a bargain.

CONTINENT *

Address: Quai de l'Entrepôt, 5010 Cherbourg

Telephone: 010 33 33 43 14 11

Hours of opening: Monday to Saturday 8.30am to 9.30pm. Open till 10pm Friday

Managers: Olivier Beaufils and Pascal Pilon

Payment methods: Access, Visa; French francs

Discounts: No

English spoken: No

In-store tastings: No

When the French consumer wine magazine *La Revue du Vin de France* held an epoch-making tasting of hypermarket wines recently (Gallic wine writers rarely sully their palates with such lowly things), it gave high marks and considerable praise to Continent.

Encouraged by all the nice things they'd said, we fixed up a tasting at one of the Bayeux-based supermarket's largest Channel port stores, braving the rain, the bad roads and the D-Day celebrations to find out what all the fuss was about.

The convenient thing about Continent is that most of its wines are purchased through a centralised buying operation called Prodis Boissons, which sells 16 million bottles under its Les Maîtres Goustiers label. This means that nearly all the Continent range is available in the company's 70-odd stores. Some of the same wines also crop up in subsidiaries Shopi, Champion and Huit à Huit.

The bad news is that the 500-strong wine range shows all the traditional faults of French hypermarket buying: reliance on *négociant* blends, too much respect for *appellation contrôlée* and no more than a smattering of non-French wines. Continent's own-label brand, Les Maîtres Goustiers, which accounts for 50 per cent of sales, is particularly dull.

The interesting part of the range, as so often in France, is red Bordeaux. There is a handful of age-worthy Right Bank clarets with plenty of weight and concentration (these are reduced in price at the store's twice-yearly wine fairs). Burgundy and Beaujolais aren't bad either. But this is hardly worth a cross-Channel detour. If it is to live up to the praise given by *La Revue du Vin de France*, Continent needs a few more vins de pays and regional French wines. It could also do worse than fire a few of its 'maîtres goustiers'. Master tasters they are not.

White

Under 20FF

FRANCE

1993 Muscadet de Sèvre-et-Maine Sur Lie, Cave de Val et Mont
££ / 1 / ▌   14/20
Not much happening in the aroma department, but the tangy, fresh fruit comes through well on the palate.

1992 Château Monplaisir, Entre-Deux-Mers, Les Caves de Saint-Romain
£ / 2 / ▌   13/20
Sharp, green apple fruit and some Sauvignon bite make this cheap Bordeaux white a reasonable buy.

20–30FF

FRANCE

1992 Bourgogne Aligoté, Labouré-Roi
£ / 2 / ▌   14/20
Like several of Continent's white Burgundies, this comes from Nuits-St-Georges' reliable Labouré-Roi. Aligoté can be a fairly bracing experience, so this softer example comes as a pleasant surprise.

1992 Riesling, Eguisheim

£ / 2 / ❚   14/20

Aromatic lime-like, commercial Alsace Riesling. Approachable
stuff.

30–50FF

FRANCE

1993 Sancerre Blanc, Les Maîtres Goustiers

£ / 2 / ❚   14/20

Quaffable, bog-standard Sancerre, which could come from almost
anywhere in Touraine, but at least it's relatively cheap.

1993 Pouilly-Fumé, Fouassier Père et Fils

££ / 1 / ❚   15/20

Considerably more interesting than the Sancerre, this estate wine
from Fouassier is nicely dry with some of the flinty character for
which the *appellation* is famous.

1993 Pouilly-Fuissé, Domaine des Préauds

£ / 2 / ❚   14/20

From an estate based in the Beaujolais cru of St Amour, this wine
comes from the white side of the Beaujolais–Mâconnais border. A
rounded, slightly spicy white Burgundy with a touch of oak.

1992 Monbazillac

£ / 5 / ❚   13/20

Waxy, sweet Semillon-style dessert wine from the Bergerac region.
Lacks a bit of oomph.

Red

Under 20FF

FRANCE

Bordeaux Rouge, Les Celliers de Champs Billoux, Les Maîtres Goustiers
£ / MB / 🍷   12/20
Very cheap, basic claret with typically tough tannins.

1993 Mâcon Rouge, Les Maîtres Goustiers
£ / MB / 🍷   13/20
Pleasantly fruity Gamay-based red Mâcon with a drying aftertaste.

1993 Côtes du Rhône, Les Maîtres Goustiers
0 / MB / 🍷   11/20
An off-day for the maîtres goustiers, or master tasters. A soupy,
sweetened-up southern red.

1992 Côtes du Roussillon-Villages, Les Maîtres Goustiers
££ / FB / 🍷   14/20
Chunky, peppery red from the Catalan region of Roussillon down
on the border with Spain. Lots of Mediterranean character on show
here.

1992 Madiran, Cave de Crouseilles, Carte d'Or
££ / FB / 🥄   15/20
Characteristically robust, Tannat-based red from one of south-west
France's lesser known *appellations*. A red for those glowing ember
moments.

Minervois, Les Maîtres Goustiers
0 / MB / 🍷   11/20
Another off-day for the maîtres goustiers.

20–30FF

FRANCE

1993 Brouilly, Les Maîtres Goustiers
££ / MB / 〗   14/20
The maîtres goustiers were on better form when they chose this
cru Beaujolais. Soft, fresh, enjoyable Gamay with cherry-fruit
sweetness. A good price too.

1993 Bourgogne Pinot Noir
£ / MB / 〗   14/20
A wine with good, supple fruit and a fair whack of underlying
tannin. A little too serious for its own good?

1993 St Nicolas de Bourgueil, Domaine Gardière
£ / LB / 〗   13/20
Grassy, light Loire Valley Cabernet Franc with firm acidity.

1990 Valréas, Côtes du Rhône Villages, Cave La Gaillarde
££ / FB / 〗   15/20
Good, typical southern Rhône red from one of the lesser known
villages in this vast *appellation*. A bit of Rhône pepper and raisiny
Grenache sweetness.

30–50FF

FRANCE

1990 Bourgogne, Hautes Côtes de Beaune, Labouré-Roi
££ / MB / 〗   15/20
Appealing, sweet Pinot Noir fruit, a kiss of oak and some gamey
maturity make this a good-value red Burgundy from the Labouré-Roi
stable.

1993 Moulin-à-Vent, Domaine des Fontaines
££ / MB / ━   15/20
Moulin-à-Vent is the Beaujolais cru which ages best. This
well-textured, gently oaked Gamay is tight at the moment, but
should open out with age.

1989 Château Tayac, Margaux
££ / MB / 🍶   15/20
Elegant, seductive, modern-style Margaux with new oak to the fore.

1991 Château Artigues Arnaud, Pauillac
£££ / MB / 👞   16/20
The second wine of Pauillac Fifth Growth Château Grand Puy Ducasse. Surprisingly full and concentrated for a 1991.

1989 Château Lartigue, St Estèphe
££ / MB / 👞   15/20
Structured, sturdy, meaty St Estèphe that needs robust food and some time to show at its best.

Rosé

Under 20FF

FRANCE

1993 Côtes de Provence, Les Maîtres Goustiers
0 / 2 / 🍶   11/20
Light, fat, basic Provençal rosé with stewed-apple and cherryskin bitterness. You can do better than this almost anywhere.

1993 Cabernet d'Anjou, Château d'Avrillé, Les Maîtres Goustiers
£ / 3 / 🍶   13/20
Sweetish, soupy green pepper and apple style rosé bottled under Continent's ubiquitous own-label.

EASTENDERS **

Address: 110-112 Rue Mollien, 62100 Calais

Telephone: 010 33 21 34 55 33

Hours of opening: Monday to Friday

Manager: Dave West

Payment methods: Access, Visa; sterling and French francs

Discounts: On six or more bottles

English spoken: Sort of

In-store tastings: Yes

Dave West is wider than the Thames estuary. Inventor of Lovely Bubbly, Maquis de Calais and Vinocalapso, West and his EastEnders have brought a touch of Romford market to the Channel ports. If you want humour, Essex patter and sharp deals, this is the place to park your transit van.

EastEnders is the most demonstrably British of the Calais operations, right down to the Union Jacks fluttering outside and the British Bulldog cartoon of West himself on the wall. Cosmopolitan it isn't. As West himself puts it: 'Speak French, me? I can't even speak English properly.'

West caters unashamedly for the lower end of the market, with an emphasis on beer, Liebfraumilch (three sizes) and 'kill the competition prices'. Three-quarters of West's sales are beer but, encouraged by the interest of his customers, he has recently decided to 'go for wine in a big way'.

He has been operating from a variety of venues for nearly six years – first a warehouse, then a former dosshouse and now, finally, in his own enlarged premises near the docks. The local authorities have been trying to get rid of West for some time – using the French riot squad to evict him on one occasion – but he insists that he's in Calais for keeps.

By his own admission, West, charisma in a cardigan and carpet slippers, takes a keen interest in sampling his own wines. Surrounded by half-open bottles of anything from South African Chardonnay to grand cru Burgundy, he is one of Calais' more loveable rogues, with cigarette glued to his lips and two-day anti-designer stubble.

West's customers love him. Some of them might be selling the stuff back in Britain in a manner not altogether in keeping with the law, but a lot more are buying it for themselves. 'If they weren't buying beer from me, they'd be out on the streets mugging people,' claims West. West gives them what they want – and at very competitive prices. How does he do it? 'I specialise in buying wine from suppliers who have cash flow problems.'

What they get at EastEnders is a mixture of the good, the ordinary and, occasionally, the rather unsavoury. 'I am no wine expert,' says West, 'but I know what's drinkable, especially at the cheap end of the market.' His wines, it is true, go as low as 5.70 francs a bottle, but the list includes more enjoyable stuff too. The focus is on France and Germany, with the odd incursion into Australia, South Africa and Italy.

West has a nose for a bargain. There are some horrors on offer at EastEnders (Crustacés is X-certificate stuff), but there are a number of surprisingly decent wines too, especially from Bordeaux, the Rhône and Beaujolais. Cheap prices are a West speciality. 'I wouldn't be true to my costermonger instincts,' he tells you between puffs on a cigarette, 'if I weren't offering the best deals in Calais.'

White

Under 20FF

FRANCE

1993 Domaine de Papolle, Vin de Pays des Côtes de Gascogne
£ / 2 / 1   13/20
This domaine has received rave reviews on this side of the Channel for its inexpensive Gascon white. Although we found the peardrop-like 1993 marginally more interesting than the 1992, we still couldn't see what all the fuss was about.

1993 Domaine de Maubet, Vin de Pays des Côtes de Gascogne
££ / 2 / ▮   15/20

A grapefruity, boiled-sweets style Colombard-based blend with a refreshing tang. The best of Dave West's Côtes de Gascogne whites.

1993 Château Haut-Gaillard, Entre-Deux-Mers
£ / 2 / ▮   13/20

A light, fruity white Bordeaux with Granny Smith acidity.

1992 Château des Plantes, Graves
£ / 2 / ▮   14/20

A fat, rounded Semillon-based white Graves in an old-fashioned style.

1991 Domaine de Diana, Vin de Pays de l'Ile de Beauté, Chardonnay
£ / 2 / ▮   12/20

The Ile de Beauté in question is Corsica. This blowsy, fat Chardonnay with its baked banana fruit wine is starting to show a few unlovely wrinkles.

EastEnders Vinocalapso, Vin de Table, Moelleux
£ / 4 / ▮   11/20

Dave West's praiseworthy attempt to reduce the level of the European wine lake. A sweet and rather dull quaffer, popular with EastEnders' customers. Nothing to do with the fact that the label looks like Romford nick, of course.

1993 Château Tour de Peyraney, Moelleux, Bordeaux
££ / 5 / ▮   14/20

If you want a basic, sweet white Bordeaux, this slightly confected example is pleasant enough at the price.

Blanc Sec Crustacés, Vin de Table
0 / 2 / ▮   10/20

The best-selling white at EastEnders. More to do with the price than the baked, fruitless liquid in the bottle. Still, at under six francs . . .

GERMANY

Hock, Ernst Jungken, Deutscher Tafelwein, 1 Litre
£ / 4 / 🍷   12/20
Light, sweet, floral Müller-Thurgau-based German white.

1992 Karl Meister Liebfraumilch, Nahe
£ / 5 / 🍷   13/20
For the same price, this grapey, medium-sweet and richer German
quaffer is a better bet.

1991 Niersteiner Gutes Domtal, Jakob Demmer
££ / 4 / 🍷   14/20
The best of EastEnders' extensive range of cheap German whites,
showing more concentration and fresh floral appeal.

20–30FF

AUSTRALIA

1993 Dry Creek Estate, Semillon/Chardonnay
£ / 2 / 🍷   14/20
A good introduction to the fruity delights of Australian whites.
Restrained sweetness and smoky oak character.

FRANCE

1992 Vouvray Les Prateaux, Jean Sablenay
£ / 4 / 🍷   14/20
A medium-sweet, appley Chenin Blanc quaffer. A bit souped up,
but sold at a fair price.

SOUTH AFRICA

1993 Sable View Sauvignon Blanc
£ / 2 / 🍷   14/20
Green bean aromas and lemony fruit make this Cape white a good
party bet.

1993 Sable View Chardonnay
£ / 2 / ▌   14/20
A simple, commercial Chardonnay with a few splinters to add some character.

30–50FF

FRANCE

1992 Sancerre, Les Hauts Fourchaux, Jean Sablenay
£ / 2 / ▌   14/20
Cassis and elderflower aromas are the strong points of this rather one-dimensional Sancerre.

1992 Pouilly-Fumé, Domaine des Gominets
£ / 2 / ▌   14/20
Rich, grassy, old-style Sauvignon Blanc. A little long in the molar department.

1991 Chablis, Eugène Lebreton
££ / 2 / ▌   15/20
Commercial, rounded up-front Chablis from the reliable Nuits-Saint-Georges merchant, Labouré-Roi.

Red

Under 20FF

FRANCE

Vin de Pays de l'Aude, Cellier de l'Echanson
£ / LB / ▌   11/20
Cheap, faintly peppery southern red. Rotgut carafe rouge.

1992 Fitou, Seigneurie de Donneuve, Mont Tauch
££ / MB / ▌   14/20
Lightish for Fitou, this spicy red has had its rough edges softened by carbonic maceration.

20–30FF

FRANCE

1991 Mâcon Supérieur Rouge, Eugène Lebreton
£ / MB / ▌   13/20
A sweet and soupy Beaujolais lookalike from Labouré-Roi.

1991 Bourgogne Passetoutgrains, Eugène Brocard
££ / MB / ▌   15/20
Soft, easy-drinking blend of Gamay and Pinot Noir with some
attractive strawberry fruit character.

1992 Brouilly, Armand Dartois
£ / MB / ▌   14/20
A juicy, carbonic maceration Gamay from the largest of the ten
Beaujolais crus.

1989 Château Les Graves, Médoc, Marc Raymond
££ / MB / ▌   14/20
Nice, ripe blackcurrant fruit and enough tannin to provide
backbone.

1991 Côtes du Ventoux, Eugène Lebreton
£ / FB / ▌   14/20
Sweet, raisin and raspberry Grenache-style red from Provence.
Another example of consistent quality from Burgundy merchant,
Labouré-Roi.

1991 Château la Clede, Bordeaux Supérieur
££ / MB / ▌   15/20
Soft, good-value claret with plenty of grassy fruit and supple,
mouth-filling flavours.

1991 Château de Ségure, Fitou
£££ / FB / ▌   16/20
Aromatic, angostura bitters bouquet and punchy, peppery southern
fruit from the flagship estate of the Mont Tauch co-operative, which
dominates the Fitou *appellation*.

SOUTH AFRICA

1991 Sable View Pinotage
£ / FB / 🍷   13/20
Pinotage, a cross between Pinot Noir and Cinsault, is South Africa's
claim to an indigenous wine style. At its best, its earthy sweet fruit
bite can be delicious. The dry rusticity of this one takes it over the
top. Drink with barbecued impala.

30–50FF

FRANCE

1990 Bourgogne Rouge, Domaine Lorenzon
£ / MB / 🍷   15/20
A seductive, if straightforward, red Burgundy from the Côte
Chalonnaise-based merchant Antonin Rodet. Sweet Pinot Noir fruit
and a touch of oak.

1989 Domaine de Paradis, St Amour, Marc Dudet
£££ / MB / 🍷   17/20
**A wine selected by Georges Duboeuf, the self-styled king of
the Beaujolais. Exciting and refreshing Gamay fruit with a
fruit salad bowl of cherries and strawberries. If you're going
to buy just one at EastEnders, this is the one to choose.**

1990 Château Haut-Bertinerie, Premières Côtes de Blaye
££ / MB / ▬   16/20
This stylishly oaked blackcurrant and tobacco-like claret, from the
opposite bank of the Gironde to the Médoc, is beautifully balanced.
Drinkable now, but should keep happily for another two to five
years.

1991 Côtes du Rhône Guigal
£ / FB / 🍷   14/20
An easy-drinking, southern red with some pepper and oak. Fair
enough, but this is a let down after the excellent Côtes du Rhônes
Guigal made in 1988, 1989 and 1990.

1991 Château de Lardiley, Marthe Lataste, Premières Côtes de Bordeaux
££ / MB / ▌   15/20
It's a pleasure to come across a basic Bordeaux with well-judged vanilla oak character, ripe fruit and tannic grip.

1993 Vacquéyras, Paul Jaboulet Aîné
££ / FB / ▌   15/20
The best of a bewildering range of Jaboulet wines on offer at EastEnders. Dry, peppery tannins and attractive raspberry fruit make this a youthful southern Rhône red with plenty of character.

Over 50FF

FRANCE

1989 Château Hanteillan, Cru Bourgeois, Haut-Médoc
££ / MB / ▌   15/20
A seductive, fleshy Haut-Médoc, made by one of France's leading female winemakers, Catherine Blasco. Lashings of toasty new oak are currently rather marked in this good-value red Bordeaux.

Sparkling

Over 50FF

FRANCE

Champagne Lelarge-Ducrocq
£££ / 2 / ▌   16/20
A grower's Champagne from Le Mesnil le Huttier, which illustrates Dave West's well-honed nose for a bargain. At just over 50 francs, this fruity, tangy Champagne is one of the best-value fizzes available in the Channel ports.

Champagne Maurice Lassalle, Premier Cru, Demi-Sec
£ / 2 / ▌   14/20
If you like your Champagne on the sweet side, as Queen Victoria used to do, this rich, off-dry style should appeal. We found it a little gawky.

THE GRAPE SHOP ****

Address: 85-86 Rue Victor Hugo, 62200 Boulogne

Telephone: 010 33 21 31 28 28

Hours of opening: Monday to Friday 10am to 7.30pm

Also at: Gare Maritime, 62200 Boulogne

Telephone: 010 33 21 30 16 17

Hours of opening: Seven days a week 8.30am to 9.30pm

Managers: Martin Brown and Katrina Thom

Payment methods: Access, Visa; sterling cheques and cash; French francs

Discounts: Quantity discounts by negotiation

In-store tastings: Yes

English spoken: Yes

After the overstacked shopping trolleys of Calais, Boulogne is a walled haven of tranquillity full of charm and character. If you like food and wine, the place is a treat. There's a good market, plenty of fresh fish, decent restaurants and Philippe Olivier, one of the finest cheese shops in France.

There's also The Grape Shop, the best wine merchant in the Channel ports. Set up by Englishman Martin Brown on the site of a former car hire office in central Boulogne, the business did so well in its first year that it recently spawned a much larger, cash-and-carry style operation a few yards away from the Seacat dock.

Brown's new shop gives him ten times the floor space he has in the cramped premises of the Rue Victor Hugo, something he has used to good effect. The wooden shelves of this large green portakabin are crammed with well-chosen wines from the Old and New Worlds.

Indeed, The Grape Shop has one of the few cross-Channel ranges which really caters for the eclectic tastes of the British wine drinker. Not that this is a New World shop. Two-thirds of the 750-odd lines are French, many from individual growers.

This doesn't bring in much local trade, however, 'Only one per cent of our turnover comes from French consumers,' says Brown. 'There's a bit of snobbery involved, but the French also buy their wines in a different way. Rather than go to a wine merchant, they tend to buy direct from the grower. This isn't the sort of outlet they appreciate.'

Well, stuff them is all we can say. Martin Brown has made a conscious choice 'to attack the Oddbins/ABC1 end of the market' rather than go the cash-and-carry route. And he's succeeded in spades. With the backing of Hoverspeed, The Grape Shop has 'the marketing clout to tackle anyone here', according to Brown. It also has good staff, an enviable catch-the-tourists location and a super range of wines. Worth a detour on its own, but don't miss those cheeses.

White

Under 20FF

FRANCE

Vin de Pays du Var
£ / 2 / 🍶   12/20
Basic fat, southern white for less than the cost of British duty.

1992 Château Le Grange, Bordeaux Blanc
££ / 2 / 🍶   14/20
A pleasant grapefruity Sauvignon Blanc. Dry and fresh with a slightly sour aftertaste.

1993 Domaine de Papolle, Vin de Pays des Côtes de Gascogne
£ / 2 / 🍶   13/20
This domaine has received rave reviews on this side of the Channel for its inexpensive Gascon white. Although we found the peardrop-like 1993 marginally more interesting than the 1992, we still couldn't see what all the fuss was about.

1992 Domaine du Pigeonnier, Bergerac Sec
£ / 2 / ▮   14/20
Stylish, zippy Sauvignon Blanc from a good value area to the east
of Bordeaux.

20–30FF

FRANCE

1993 Château de Brussac Sauvignon Blanc, Bordeaux
££ / 2 / ▮   15/20
Smoky, grassy Sauvignon Blanc with good nettley concentration
and a fleck of gooseberry fruit.

1993 Château de Briacé Muscadet Tiré Sur Lie
£££ / 1 / ▮   16/20
Evidence of a return to form in the western Loire. This is Muscadet
sur lie at its best, with rich, appley fruit, good acidity and a typical
gassy prickle.

**1992 Chardonnay Treize Vents, Vin de Pays du Jardin de la
France**
£ / 2 / ▮   13/20
Unoaked, innocuous Chardonnay from the Loire Valley. The South
of France does this sort of thing a lot better.

**1993 Domaine de Montmarin, Marsanne, Vin de Pays des
Côtes de Thongue**
£ / 2 / ▮   14/20
Marsanne, a Rhône Valley white grape variety, is growing in
importance in the Languedoc. If you've ever tasted traditional white
wines from this area, you can see why. Peachy, full fruit with
some clove spice and a rustic edge.

**1993 Domaine de Montmarin, Sauvignon Blanc, Vin de Pays
des Côtes de Thongue**
££ / 2 / ▮   15/20
No mistaking the grape variety here. A grassy, floral, New World
style wine with a pleasing aftertaste.

1992 La Vieille Ferme, Côtes du Lubéron
££ / 2 / 🄳   15/20
A *négociant* wine made by François Perrin of Château de
Beaucastel, one of the great estates in Châteauneuf-du-Pape. Three
months' barrel-ageing has given this waxy, herbal white an extra
dimension.

1993 Château Tour des Gendres, Bergerac Blanc
££ / 2 / 🄳   16/20
A good-value white Graves tastealike, with grassy Sauvignon Blanc
and softer Semillon combining to produce an intensely flavoured,
modern dry white.

1993 Chais Baumière Sauvignon Blanc.
£ / 3 / 🄳   14/20
Chais Baumière is the southern French outpost of BRL-Hardy, one
of Australia's major producers. There's plenty of Sauvignon Blanc
fruit here, but a cloying sweetness make this a one-glass drink.

1992 Philippe de Baudin Chardonnay
££ / 2 / 🄳   15/20
Another Hardy annual from the South of France, also showing a
New World thumbprint or two. Melon and pineapple fruit with
overt smoky oak.

30–50FF

FRANCE

1993 Côtes du Rhône, Guigal
£££ / 2 / 🄳   17/20
Etienne Guigal is one of the stars of the Rhône, much
lionised by French *sommeliers* and sycophantic Americans.
His merchant wines don't always live up to the hype
surrounding his estate production, but this blend of
Bourboulenc and perfumed Viognier is fresh, ripe and
beautifully balanced. Needs food.

1992 Chinon Blanc, J. M. Raffault
££ / 1 / 🍷   15/20

Chinon is best known for its Cabernet Franc based red wines, but
it also produces a tiny amount of Chenin Blanc white. This
honeyed, dry white is worth a punt as a curiosity alone.

1993 Menetou-Salon, Morogues
£ / 1 / 🍷   15/20

Henry Pellé, the Mayor of Morogues, consistently produces fine,
flinty Sauvignon Blanc in the mould of Pouilly-Fumé. This is a bit
austere at the moment, but may improve with a few months' bottle
age.

1993 Chardonnay Vin de Pays d'Oc, Hugh Ryman
£££ / 2 / 🍷   17/20

**The 1992 Ryman Chardonnay was one of our wines of the
year in *Grapevine 1994* and this elegant southern white,
with its tropical fruit and nicely judged oak intensity,
maintains the tradition.**

1992 Mâcon-Villages, Raphaël Sallet
£££ / 2 / 🍷   17/20

**Wow! It's a while since we tasted a Mâcon-Villages as good
as this. Rich, super-ripe, honeyed flavours with a touch of
botrytis character make for an old-fashioned but extremely
characterful Chardonnay.**

1993 Mâcon-Fuissé, Le Moulin du Pont
££ / 2 / 🍷   16/20

From Auvigue, Bourrier, Revel, producers who sound like a firm
of undertakers, this is a vibrant, grapefruity village Mâcon from
Burgundy's southern hills.

1992 Bourgogne Chardonnay, Sylvain Dussort
££ / 2 / 🍷   16/20

Sylvain Dussort makes this basic, supposedly humble white
Burgundy from a vineyard just outside the Meursault *appellation*.
Like many a good Meursault, it shows the complexity of barrel-
fermentation and prolonged lees contact.

1992 Bourgogne Chardonnay, Mestre-Michelot
£££ / 2 / ⤙   17/20
Further confirmation that 1992 is one of the best white
Burgundy vintages of the last two decades. Toasty cinnamon
oak, fresh citrus fruit and remarkable depth of flavour for a
basic white Burgundy. Beaune *négociants*, take note.

50–80FF

FRANCE

1992 Pouilly-Fumé, Jean-Claude Chatelain
£££ / 2 / ⫷   17/20
With wines like this, the Loire Valley need not worry too much
about competition from New Zealand for the Sauvignon Blanc
crown. A concentrated, old-fashioned classic.

1993 Sancerre Les Baronnes, Henri Bourgeois
£££ / 2 / ⫷   17/20
Henri Bourgeois is one of Sancerre's top producers, travelling
the world to promote the wines of his native region. This is a
ripe, appealing style of Sancerre, but it's none the worse for
that. Go on, give him a few more air miles!

1990 Chablis, Domaine Etienne Defaix
£££ / 2 / ⫷   17/20
A year in barrel on its fermentation lees has given Etienne
Defaix' notable Chablis a buttery richness and aromatic
power to complement the wine's lime and grapefruit
intensity.

**1992 Ladoix, Les Clous, Côte de Beaune, Domaine de la
Galopière**
£ / 2 / ⤙   15/20
An unusual *appellation* in Burgundy's Côte d'Or. Heavy on the
oak, although, touch wood, it may blend in with time.

1992 Bourgogne Blanc, Les Setilles, Olivier Leflaive
££ / 2 / ⤙   16/20
Former theatrical impresario, Olivier Leflaive, has made a

remarkable success of his *négociant* business since he returned from treading the boards of Paris to his family's home village of Puligny-Montrachet. Leflaive and his winemaker, Franck Grux, are at their best in lesser *appellations*, and this elegantly oaked white Burgundy has capitalised on an excellent vintage.

1992 Pouilly-Fuissé, Les Bouthières, Auvigue, Bourrier, Revel
£ / 2 / 🕯   14/20
It's the part-time undertakers again, this time with a grown-up Pouilly-Fuissé as opposed to a junior Mâcon-Fuissé. A slight mustiness worried us here.

1992 Riesling, Coteau du Haut Königsbourg, Claude Bléger
£ / 1 / ▬   15/20
Riesling is Alsace's most elegant and least appreciated grape variety, but it's the one that often goes best with food. This bone-dry white has some of the typical kerosene-like character of the Riesling grape and pure minerally flavours.

1992 Tokay Pinot Gris, Coteau du Haut Königsbourg, Claude Bléger
£ / 3 / 🕯   15/20
Weighing in at a Cyril Smith-like 14.5 per cent alcohol, this is an exotic, blockbusting spicy white with more than a hint of sweetness. Another one-glass wonder.

Red

Under 20FF

FRANCE

1993 Château de Brau, Cabardès, VDQS
£ / MB / 🕯   13/20
An organic red from the South of France with no shortage of tannin and more oak than you'd expect on a wine at this price. Perhaps they saved some money on the chemicals.

20–30FF

FRANCE

1993 Domaine de Terre Mégère, Merlot, Vin de Pays d'Oc
££ / MB / ▌   15/20
A fresh, juicy, modern Merlot with a herbal undertone. A style which is better appreciated by the British than the French.

1992 La Vieille Ferme, Côtes du Ventoux
£ / FB / ▌   14/20
Not as good as the same merchant's white brand, but still proud of its southern French origins. There's some grip and a bit of spice to the fruit, but a touch of the old farmyard mars the finish.

1992 Cabernet Sauvignon, Vin de Pays d'Oc, Hugh Ryman
££ / MB / ▌   15/20
Classic, supple-textured capsicum and blackcurrant Cabernet Sauvignon from 'Hugh the Guru', as his marketing set-up would have it. It would be nice to see a few more clarets offering this sort of value for money.

1992 Domaine de Terre Mégère, Les Dolomies, Coteaux du Languedoc
££ / FB / ▌   15/20
Juicy southern red with a high dose of the increasingly popular Syrah grape. A dry aftertaste cries out for a plate of full-throated food.

1991 Château du Seuil, Coteaux d'Aix-en-Provence
£ / FB / �탁   14/20
A firmer, more tannic proposition with a hard but sweet fruit core that needs time to soften.

30–50FF

FRANCE

1989 Chinon Clos d'Isoré, Jean-Maurice Raffault
£ / MB / ▌   14/20
Nice wine, shame about the oak

1990 Domaine Ogereau, Anjou-Villages
£££ / MB / ⊷   17/20
**Another wine with a lot of oak, but this time the intensity
and richness of the Cabernet Franc has absorbed the barrel
tannins. A star domaine on top form**.

1991 Chénas, Domaine des Ducs
££ / MB / ⫿   15/20
Beaujolais was one of the few regions in France to escape the
difficult weather conditions in 1991. This lightly oaked wine from
one of the region's ten crus is textbook cherryish Gamay.

1992 St Amour, Domaine des Ducs
£££ / MB / ⫿   16/20
St Amour, the northernmost and often the most charming of the
ten Beaujolais crus, is popular with romantic Frenchmen. This
fresh and exuberant red is fittingly seductive.

1993 Menetou-Salon, Henri Pellé
££ / LB / ⫿   15/20
Characteristically light Loire Valley Pinot Noir with the emphasis
on charm rather than power.

1992 Bourgogne, Les Maisons-Dieu, Thierry Violot-Guillemard
£ / MB / ⫿   14/20
An oak-dominated red Burgundy declassified from Pommard to
the more simple Bourgogne Rouge. The transition doesn't quite
come off.

1992 Château Barreyre, Bordeaux Supérieur
£ / MB / ⊷   15/20
Stalky lead-pencil fruit and masses of new oak. Come back in two
years' time.

1989 Château Labarde, Haut-Médoc
££ / MB / ⫿   15/20
One for Snoopy's mate, Pigpen. An old-fashioned claret with a
composty finish, but plenty of good, honest fruit.

1992 Château Bonnet Réserve, André Lurton
£ / MB / ◗━ 13/20

A modern, aggressively oaked claret from a property in the vast Entre-Deux-Mers region of Bordeaux. Lurton is an old hand whose whites are generally better than his reds.

1989 Château Hanteillan, Cru Bourgeois, Haut-Médoc
££ / MB / ◗ 15/20

A seductive, fleshy Haut-Médoc made by one of France's leading female winemakers, Catherine Blasco. Lashings of toasty new oak are currently rather marked in this good-value red Bordeaux.

1990 Château Ramage la Batisse, Cru Bourgeois, Haut-Médoc
££ / MB / ◗━ 16/20

A consistent *Grapevine* favourite. Lots of classy new oak on show, but more than enough concentrated, chocolatey fruit to compensate. A splendid sequel to the equally enjoyable 1989.

1989 Château Roland Maillet, St Emilion Grand Cru
££ / MB / ◗━ 16/20

Soft Merlot and lots of new oak make this a balanced, stylish red that will repay a few years' wait.

1990 Domaine de Martialis, St Emilion Grand Cru
£££ / MB / ◗━ 17/20

A toasty, seductively sexy wine with plump, fleshy Merlot fruit and well-integrated new oak. One sip of this and you'll drop your boxer shorts.

1991 Côtes du Rhône Guigal
£ / FB / ◗ 14/20

An easy-drinking, southern red with some pepper and oak. Fair enough, but this is a let-down after the excellent Côtes du Rhônes Guigal made in 1988, 1989 and 1990.

1990 Vacquéyras, Delas Frères
£££ / FB / ◗━ 16/20

A strong, sweet, oaky red which reeks of plum, cherry and Provençal spices. Châteauneuf-du-Pape and Gigondas apart, Vacquéyras makes the best reds in the southern Rhône.

Over 50FF

FRANCE

1991 Côtes de Nuits Villages, Henri Naudin-Ferrand
£ / MB / ▮   14/20
An oddball red Burgundy showing some Pinot Noir character but
an almost Australian mintiness and hefty caramel oak.

1991 Gevrey-Chambertin, Michel Magnien
££ / MB / ▮   16/20
A forward and appealing Côtes de Nuits village Burgundy with
aromatic, wild strawberry fruitiness. Deceptively light, as elegant
red Burgundy often is.

1988 Beaune Cent Vignes, Besancenot-Mathouillet
0 / MB / ▮   15/20
Mature, gamey Pinot Noir with well-handled oak and soft, raspberry
fruit. Shame about the price.

Rosé

Under 20FF

FRANCE

Vin de Pays du Var Rosé
£ / 3 / ▮   12/20
Fine on a beach in the South of France, but don't expect this decent,
off-dry rosé to cross the Channel without a struggle.

1993 Domaine de Montmarin, Cabernet Sauvignon Rosé, Vin de Pays des Côtes de Thongue
£ / 3 / ▮   14/20
The Cabernet Sauvignon grape provides welcome backbone here.
But after a nice blackberry and apple start, the wine pulls up short.

20–30FF

FRANCE

1993 Château Tour des Gendres, Bergerac Rosé
£££ / 2 / ⌐   16/20
It's day-glo time. Aromatic, grassy blackcurrant fruit with a full-bodied richness that works well with food. A rosé of the modern school.

Sparkling

Under 30FF

FRANCE

Opéra Blanc de Blancs Brut
££ / 3 / ⌐   14/20
A basic, tangy, party fizz with a bit of sweetness for those aria moments.

Opéra Rosé Sec
£ / 3 / ⌐   13/20
For a fraction of the price of a Glyndebourne ticket, your chance to sample confected strawberry marshmallows with bubbles.

30–50FF

FRANCE

Pol Acker Chardonnay Brut, Méthode Traditionnelle
£ / 3 / ⌐   13/20
Pol Roger's long-lost relation, we presume. Not that the Epernay-based company would be too thrilled at the discovery. An off-dry Loire sparkler, which tastes more like Chenin Blanc than Chardonnay.

Louis de Grenelle Saumur, Méthode Traditionnelle
££ / 2 / 🍾   15/20
An altogether superior fizz with nicely balanced Chenin Blanc
character and creamy, almost crunchy, apple and pear fruitiness.

Louis de Grenelle, Crémant de Loire
£££ / 2 / 🍾   16/20
The Chenin character in this wine is more subdued, thanks no
doubt to the presence of some Chardonnay in the blend. Lively,
youthful stuff with a degree of finesse. A good Champagne
substitute.

Crémant de Bourgogne, Henri Naudin Ferrand
£££ / 2 / 🍾   16/20
Toasty, Champagne-like fizz from Burgundy. Some of the base wine
is fermented in oak barrels for extra complexity.

Crémant d'Alsace, Claude Bleger, Orschwiller
£££ / 2 / 🍾   16/20
A dry, all-Riesling sparkler showing some petrolly bottle-age and
good bracing acidity.

50–80FF

FRANCE

Maurice Lassalle Réserve, Chigny-lès-Roses
££ / 2 / 🍾   15/20
The Grape Shop's basic Champagne is a best seller. It's young and
pleasantly fruity, but we found the acidity rather aggressive.

Over 80FF

FRANCE

Michel Genet Blanc de Blancs Brut, Chouilly
£££ / 2 / 🍾   17/20
A 100 per cent Chardonnay fizz with a malty, Ovaltine-like
bouquet and considerable finesse. A bargain at under 100
francs.

Henri Goutorbe, Aÿ, Cuvée Traditionelle
££ / 2 / ▮   15/20
A fruity, drink-me Champagne with soft, strawberry jam Pinot Noir fruit.

Serge Mathieu, Cuvée Prestige, Avirey, Lingey
££ / 2 / ▮   16/20
Soft mouth-filling mousse and delicate red fruit aromas make this well balanced, grower's Champagne a good buy at under 100 francs.

Michel Genet Rosé Brut
£££ / 2 / ▮   17/20
A big, ripe, bronzed rosé showing considerable maturity for a non-vintage wine. The best of The Grape Shop's pink fizzes.

Vilmart et Cie Grande Réserve
££ / 2 / ▮   16/20
Vilmart is one of the few growers to ferment his base wine in oak barrels. The resulting traditional style is not everyone's flute of Champagne, but this is a complex, powerful fizz with some bottle-age.

Vilmart et Cie Grand Cellier d'Or Brut
£££ / 2 / ▸   17/20
This is Vilmart's top cuvée made in a rich oxidative style, not a million kilometres away from Krug. Not cheap, but then neither is Krug.

Henri Goutorbe 1986 Brut
£ / 2 / ▮   15/20
A mature, if idiosyncratic, vintage Champagne. What's this doing in a Perrier bottle?

LA MAISON DU VIN ***(*)

Address: 71 Avenue Carnot, 50100 Cherbourg

Telephone: 010 33 33 43 39 79

Hours of opening: Monday to Saturday 9am to 7pm. Sunday 11am to 6pm (but may vary)

Manager: Chris Bullimore

Payment methods: Access, Visa; Eurocheques; sterling and French francs

English spoken: Yes

In-store tastings: Yes

After a series of bureaucratic dead ends, Dorset wine merchant and Master of Wine Richard Harvey finally established La Maison du Vin in June 1993. The site is a former tool-hire warehouse more or less opposite the neo-Stalinist breeze-block building which houses the supermarket Continent.

Only five minutes away from the port, heralded by the noisy squawk of seagulls overhead, La Maison du Vin is popular with the Cowes Regatta brigade down in the marina, who call into port to load up with as many cases of 'cockpit wines' as their boats will carry. A dry dock it ain't.

Harvey, who stocks 130 wines and a handful of beers, prides himself on his selection. 'If you can't decide between five Sancerres, you're not really a wine merchant,' he says. 'We don't want to go above the number of wines we've got now.'

The list is 75 per cent French, mostly from single domaines, with a handful of New World wines. Some of his prices are excellent. Customers, 90 per cent of whom are British, include tourists returning to the UK or venturing into Brittany for their holidays. They are well served by La Maison du Vin – which is the best operation in Cherbourg and one of the three best we came across in the Channel ports.

Customers can also taste before they buy. 'We deliberately set out to make this place different,' says Harvey. 'There are always at least 12 bottles open for people to try and we also offer the service of delivering wine to the marina.' Perfect for the Cowes brigade – they don't even have to stir from their sun decks.

White

Under 20FF

FRANCE

Blanc de Blancs Dry, Donatien Bahuaud
££ / 3 / 🍾   13/20
A dryish, unusual blend of the Loire grapes, Chenin Blanc and Gros Plant. Muscadet producer Donatien Bahuaud has to find somewhere to put its Gros Plant. Pleasant, grapefruity stuff at an affordable price.

1993 Domaine de Papolle, Vin de Pays des Côtes de Gascogne
£ / 2 / 🍾   13/20
This domaine has received rave reviews on this side of the Channel for its inexpensive Gascon white. Although we found the peardrop-like 1993 marginally more interesting than the 1992, we still couldn't see what all the fuss was about.

1993 Domaine de Barroque, Vin de Pays des Côtes de Gascogne
££ / 3 / 🍾   14/20
Made, like Domaine de Papolle, by the English engineer, Peter Hawkins, this is sweeter and better balanced than its stablemate.

1993 Domaine de Lacquy, Vin de Pays des Terroirs Landais
£££ /2 / 🍾   15/20
A wine produced from the usually snoozeworthy Ugni Blanc grape, but the zest and refreshing fruit on show here should raise you from slumber.

20–30FF

FRANCE

1993 Domaine du Vieux Chai, Muscadet de Sèvre-et-Maine Sur Lie
£££ / 1 / ❧   16/20

A faith-restoring Muscadet sur lie with the genuine fresh spritz of the *appellation* backed up by concentration of rounded fruit.

1992 Château Richard, Bergerac Sec, Cuvée Spéciale
£££ / 2 / ❧   16/20

A large proportion of Richard Harvey's wines seem, for reasons obscure to us, to be made by Brits. Step forward Richard Doughty of Bergeracshire and take a bow for this ripe, honeyed, lees-aged blend. Tasty stuff.

1993 Château Bauduc, Bordeaux Blanc Sec
££ / 2 / ❧   15/20

Another Brit, this time in the shape of Welshman, David Thomas, and another very good wine in a grassy, grapefruity mould.

1993 Château Gabaron, Bordeaux Blanc Sec
£ / 2 / ❧   14/20

Softer than the Château Bauduc, with Semillon apparently to the fore. A pleasant, modern white Bordeaux, lacking that vital British ingredient perhaps.

1993 Chardonnay, Domaine de la Ferrandière, Vin de Pays d'Oc
£ / 2 / ❧   14/20

A technology-inspired Chardonnay from Languedoc producer, Yves Gau. Fine in a banana and peardrop sort of way.

30–50FF

FRANCE

1993 Lirac, Domaine Duseigneur, Cru Racé
££ / 1 / ❧   16/20

A southern Rhône blend of mainly Bourboulenc and Clairette,

which combines a ripe, warm climate weight of fruit with a herbal twist.

1993 Touraine Sauvignon, Domaine de la Charmoise
£ / 1 / 🖐   13/20

Henry (sic) Marionnet is the darling of the Parisian chattering classes. This rather tart Sauvignon Blanc would be fine at the Folies Bergères.

1992 Domaine Guy Roulot, Bourgogne Aligoté
££ / 1 / 🖐   15/20

You'd be more likely to find classical actor Jean-Marc Roulot at the Comédie Française than the Folies Bergères. His is one of the top domaines in Meursault, and this smoky, barrel-aged Aligoté has more richness than most. Encore!

1992 Chardonnay, Domaine de l'Aigle 'Classique', Vin de Pays de la Haute Vallée de l'Aude
££ / 2 / 🖐   15/20

From a coolish climate in the southerly Aude *département*, this is a barrel-fermented Chardonnay with plenty of toffeed oak, which may age well.

1993 Chardonnay, James Herrick, Vin de Pays d'Oc
££ / 1 / 🖐   15/20

The second vintage from Englishman James Herrick's impressive New World style vineyards near Narbonne. This is more elegant and restrained than the 1992 with deftly handled oak and a lime-like streak of acidity.

1991 Bourgogne Blanc, Henri Prudhon
££ / 2 / 🖐   16/20

This highly crafted, toast and grilled almond style, old-fashioned white Burgundy is an acquired taste, but it didn't take us long to acquire it.

1992 Chablis, Jean-Paul Droin
£££ / 2 / 🖐   16/20

Jean-Paul Droin is one of Chablis' most passionate young growers, famous for his restless quest for the perfect white Burgundy. This is his basic Chablis, with wonderful, minerally fruit and elegant acidity. Unusually for Droin, the wine is unoaked.

1992 Gewürztraminer, Vin d'Alsace, Nicolas Zusslin
£££ / 2 / ▮   16/20
If you can get past the awful headbanger label, there's an elegantly aromatic Gewürztraminer lurking in the bottle. The best thing here is an unusually sophisticated dry finish.

1992 Riesling Vin d'Alsace, Nicolas Zusslin
££ / 1 / ▮   15/20
It's headbanger time again, and once more the quality of the contents belies the naff label. A case for decanting this fresh, crisp and dry, burnt toasty Riesling.

1989 Château Richard, Saussignac
££ / 5 / ▮   15/20
Another wine from Richard Doughty, this time a sweet Sauternes lookalike. Rich flavours of barley sugar and honey and a dose of new oak make this an enjoyable, well-priced dessert wine.

GERMANY

1986 Mönchhof, Erdener Treppchen Riesling Kabinett, Robert Eymael
£££ / 2 / ▮   16/20
Robert Eymael seems to have made a lot of wine in 1986, as we have been enjoying his excellent 1986 Spätlese for some time now. This still lively cassis-scented, off-dry kabinett is drinking beautifully at the moment.

Red

Under 20FF

FRANCE

Club d'Or, Vin de Table de France, Donatien Bahuaud
££ / LB / ▮   14/20
Gluggable and suitably cheap banana and bubblegum style red from the Loire. A good party red for *Grapevine* readers on their uppers.

1992 Cabernet Sauvignon, Domaine de la Ferrandière, Vin de Pays d'Oc

££ / MB / 🍷   **15/20**

This is La Maison du Vin's best-selling red wine, which proves that Richard Harvey's customers have taste. It's a grassy, cool climate New Zealand style Cabernet Sauvignon with plenty of colour and fruit.

1990 Château de Donjon, Cuvée Tradition

£ / MB / 🍷   **13/20**

An eggy note on the nose didn't endear us to this rustic, southern red. Perhaps it's spent too much time down in the dungeon.

20–30FF

AUSTRALIA

1992 Penfolds Bin 35 Shiraz/Cabernet, South Australia

££ / FB / 🍷   **15/20**

A wine that never lets you down. Sweet American oak and lashings of toffee, blackcurrant and spice make for a consistently enjoyable style. Corked hats off to winemaker John Duval of London Transport tube poster fame for producing the goods with commendable regularity.

FRANCE

1991 Château Hélène, Cuvée Tradition, Corbières

£ / FB / 🍷   **14/20**

Hélène Gau makes surprisingly chunky wines, often with lots of oak and extract. This one is unoaked, but still punches you in the mouth with its firm tannins. A wine that needs robust southern French food.

1990 Domaine de Ribonnet Cabernet Sauvignon, Vin de Pays du Comté Tolosan

££ / MB / 🍷   **15/20**

A wine made in the Languedoc by Swiss producer, Christian Gerber, this is a forward New World influenced red with lots of blackcurrant pastille fruit and backbone.

1989 Domaine de Ribonnet Merlot, Vin de Pays du Comté Tolosan
£ / MB / 🍷   14/20
You'd expect the Merlot to be softer than the Cabernet Sauvignon, but this older vintage is beginning to dry out. Drink up.

30–50FF

FRANCE

1992 Beaujolais-Villages, Joel Rochette
£ / MB / 🍷   14/20
Light, honest wine bar Gamay. The sort of thing that first made Beaujolais famous in the cafés of Lyon.

1993 Brouilly, Pisse-Vieille, Joel Rochette
££ / MB / 🍷   15/20
Same producer, and an equally honest thirstquenching red with a bit more depth of fruit. Highly quaffable.

1991 Bourgogne Rouge, Henri Prudhon
£ / MB / 🍷   14/20
Dry, slightly rooty Pinot Noir from an average vintage. The same producer's white wine is a better bet.

1990 Château Lamartine, Cahors
£ / FB / 🍷   14/20
A meaty, tarry Cahors with broad-shouldered tannins and some soft, underlying fruit. Needs food unless you've got false teeth.

1990 Château Rozier, Côte de Francs
££ / MB / ➥   15/20
The second wine of Château de Francs, produced in a soft, green pepper style by a partnership of Château Cheval Blanc's Dominique Hébrard and Château L'Angélus' Hubert de Bouard.

1990 Château Grand Moulin, Haut-Médoc
££ / MB / ➥   15/20
Classic, well made, if oaky, claret at a good price. Should improve over the next two to three years.

1991 Côtes du Rhône, Guigal
£ / FB / 🕯   14/20
An easy-drinking, southern red with some pepper and oak. Fair enough, but this is a let-down after the excellent Côtes du Rhônes Guigal made in 1988, 1989 and 1990.

1991 Lirac, Domaine Duseigneur
££ / FB / 🕯   15/20
Hefty, bramble jam and chocolate, mini-Châteauneuf-du-Pape style red with a hint of mint.

Over 50FF

FRANCE

1992 Châteauneuf-du-Pape, Domaine St Benoît
£ / FB / ➽   15/20
A serious Châteauneuf-du-Pape with little or none of the Grenache softness and alcohol traditionally associated with the *appellation*. Needs time, but we'd like to reserve judgement on its future prospects.

Rosé

20–30FF

FRANCE

1993 Domaine de l'Aigle, Pinot Noir Rosé, Vin de Pays de l'Aude
£££ / 2 / 🕯   15/20
Pale, elegant pink Pinot Noir with a lively, slightly toasty bite and a beguiling wild strawberry fragrance. It's unusual to find Pinot Noir in the Aude.

Sparkling

30–50FF

FRANCE

Gratien et Meyer Saumur Soleil Brut
£ / 2 / ᎓   14/20
Young, sherbet and apple Chenin Blanc based fizz from the cool,
dark cellars of one of the Loire's most consistent sparkling
winemakers.

Over 50FF

FRANCE

Alexandre Bonnet Brut Champagne, Cuvée Prestige Brut
£££ / 2 / ᎓   17/20
Bonnet was one of *Grapevine*'s star winemakers last year.
This Aube-derived blend of 20 per cent Chardonnay and 80
per cent Pinot Noir with its strawberry jam elegance, fine
mousse and savoury fruitiness is a real treat.

MAMMOUTH **

Address: Route de Boulogne, 62100 Calais

Telephone: 010 33 21 34 04 44

Hours of opening: Monday to Saturday 9am to 9pm. Closed Sunday except for Christmas shopping

Wine manager: Patrick Novak

Payment methods: Visa, Access; sterling and French francs

Discounts: No

English spoken: Yes

In-store tastings: Yes

With a name like Mammouth, it's not entirely surprising that this lumbering set-up seems to have taken few steps (beyond allowing Sainsbury's to open a wine store nearby) to cater for the post-January 1993 invasion.

We all know what happened to mammoths, but in this case extinction seems highly unlikely. Over the last year, business has increased fivefold on a number of wines and tenfold on the cheapest lines. Mammouth is a very popular stop for British travellers, many of whom prefer to buy wine here rather than at Sainsbury's next door. Price apart, it's not always easy to see why.

The range on the shelves in Calais is common to several Mammouth hypermarkets. While spirits are bought centrally, the chain has a regional wine buying policy for northern France. The wine range is short on surprises and long on conservatism: 227 *appellation contrôlée* (AC) wines and 39 vins de pays with an additional 45 ACs and 22 vins de pays bought specially for Calais. There is also a handful of foreign wines.

The tendency chez Mammouth is to rely on large-scale *négociants* to pad out the range. Nevertheless, there are occasional bursts of excitement, especially from Bordeaux. Promotions, such as Château Hanteillan at only 29 francs, are worth keeping an eye out for. All the same, there's a lot of dross around.

We understand that changes are in the offing. As a reaction to competition from Sainsbury's, which has affected sales, Mammouth plans to introduce 50 to 60 new wines early in 1995. These might be just what Mammouth needs, but don't bet on it. Come on guys, surprise us.

White

Under 20FF

FRANCE

Casteret Blanc Sec, Vin de Table
£ / 3 / ▌   12/20
Cheapo baked-apple Euroblend, best drunk from a brown paper bag.

1993 Château du Coureau, Bordeaux Sauvignon Blanc
££ / 2 / ▌   15/20
A refreshing gooseberry and grapefruit-like Sauvignon Blanc at a price reflecting Bordeaux' desperation to shift a few bottles.

20–30FF

FRANCE

1993 Muscadet de Sèvre-et-Maine Sur Lie, Domaine de la Barillère, Michel et Pascal Cheneau
£ / 2 / ▌   13/20
Pleasant, reasonably well-made Muscadet which lacks a bit of oomph and genuine sur lie freshness.

1993 Chardonnay, Vin de Pays de la Haute Vallée de l'Aude, SICA des Coteaux Limousins
££ / 2 / ▌   14/20
Soft, rounded, fruity Languedoc Chardonnay with a bit of cool

climate lemon zest. You'll only find this one in the Calais branch of Mammouth.

1991 Riesling Alsace, Ernest Wein, Cave de Pfaffenheim
££ / 1 / ▮   15/20
If you tasted this wine blindfolded, you could almost mistake it for an Australian Rhine Riesling. Lemony, juicy, fresh and dry with abundant aromas.

1991 Sylvaner Alsace, Ernest Wein, Cave de Pfaffenheim
£ / 2 / ▮   14/20
Not as intense as the Riesling, but still drinkably elegant with food.

30–50FF

FRANCE

1992 Pouilly-Fumé, Domaine Les Chaumes, Jean-Jacques Bardin
££ / 2 / ▮   15/20
On the plump side for a Pouilly-Fumé, but this Sauvignon Blanc from the eastern end of the Loire Valley displays good concentration and nettley, smoky flavours.

1993 Sancerre Les Champlins, Jean Beauquin
£ / 2 / ▮   14/20
Solid *négociant* Sancerre with a flicker of Sauvignon Blanc grassiness.

1991 Loupiac, Château des Roches
££ / 5 / ▮   15/20
From the opposite side of the Garonne to Sauternes and Barsac, this is a poor person's Sauternes. We enjoyed the elegant flavours of lemon meringue and honey.

Red

Under 20FF

FRANCE

1992 Château Saint-Saturnin, Coteaux du Languedoc
££ / MB / **3**   14/20
Southern French *négociant* Jeanjean is at its best in Languedoc *appellations*. This typical Grenache/Carignan/Cinsault/Syrah blend has masses of sweet, plummy Mediterranean fruit vinified using the carbonic maceration technique.

Vin de Pays de la Cité de Carcassonne, Les Producteurs Foncalieu
£ / MB / **3**   11/20
Incongruously for a vin de pays, this *appellation* includes the name of a city. Apart from price, it's the only interesting thing we could find to say about this light, overcropped red.

Médoc, Les Chais de Montières
££ / MB / **3**   14/20
A wine bottled in Amiens and bearing Mammouth's own label. Good, juicy, basic claret with a nip of tannin.

Cahors Carte Noire, Les Chais de Montières
£ / FB / **3**   14/20
Another Amiens special. Tiptoe past the awful label, and you'll find a chunky, tannic wine with the bubblegum and pepper character of carbonic maceration vinification.

Fitou, Les Chais de Montières
£ / FB / **3**   13/20
Standard issue southern fare with robust fruit and rosemary seasoning. Drink with wild boar.

Côtes du Rhône, Cuvée Spéciale, Honoré Lavigne
£ / MB / **3**   13/20
Nice label and a decent honest Rhône Valley blend from the expanding empire of Burgundy merchant Jean-Claude Boisset.

20–30FF

FRANCE

1992 Beaujolais, Le Grand Chêne, Moillard
££ / MB / 🍷   15/20
Lots of colour and sweet red fruits aroma with a touch of banana for good measure. A good-value basic Beaujolais.

30–50FF

FRANCE

1990 Brouilly, Château de la Perrière, Moillard
£ / MB / 🍷   14/20
A nicely balanced Beaujolais cru showing a bit of oak and dry, leafy flavours. We felt it was getting on a bit. Needs drinking up.

1992 Bourgogne, Clos de Chenôves, Moillard
0 / MB / 🍷   12/20
Charmless red Burgundy from the Côte Chalonnaise. Overoaked, overpriced, and, fortunately, over there.

1991 Savigny-lès-Beaune, Vaucher
£ / MB / 🍷   15/20
From one of the Côte d'Or's lesser *appellations*, this is an honest, easy-drinking Pinot Noir with a faintly rustic, dry finish.

1990 Château La Fleur Plaisance, Montagne-St-Emilion
£££ / MB / 🍷   15/20
Soft, ripe mini St Emilion showing classic fruitcake Merlot characters and a whiff of the farmyard. A bargain.

1989 Château Pontoise Cabarrus, Haut-Médoc
££ / MB / ➡   16/20
Traditional, tannic, concentrated Médoc with excellent depth and plenty of blackcurrant fruit.

1993 Châteauneuf-du-Pape, Quinson
0 / FB / 🍾   12/20
Bottled in the Beaujolais village of Fleurie apparently. We're not convinced it was worth taking the wine all that way.

Sparkling

30–50FF

FRANCE

Champagne Jean Richecourt
£ / 3 / 🍾   13/20
The sort of tarted-up, very cheap Champagne that rarely makes its way to England. Ideal for label lovers and Bucks Fizz drinkers.

PERARDEL ***

Address: Zone Industrielle Marcel Doret, 190 Rue Marcel Dassault, 62100 Calais

Telephone: 010 33 21 97 21 22

Hours of opening: Monday to Saturday 8am to 8pm

Managers: Franck Broutard and Monique Janot

Payment methods: Access, Visa; sterling and French francs

Discounts: Negotiable

English spoken: Yes

In-store tastings: Yes

Monique Janot and Franck Broutard are the friendly faces that greet you when you step through the portals of Perardel, the closest thing to a French fine wine merchant in the Channel ports. Perardel is one of four outlets in France owned by the eponymous Châlons-sur-Marne-based gourmet, whose family manages the Aux Armes de Champagne Hotel in L'Epine near Châlons. If the other three are as good as this one, then visitors are in for a vinous treat or two.

Situated among a host of cash-and-carry warehouses, the surprising thing about Perardel is its Aladdin's Cave selection of fine wines, which range from good middle-ranking clarets to luxury, second-mortgage items such as Châteaux Lafite and Latour, Guigal's Côte Rôtie La Mouline and La Landonne and Domaine Leflaive white Burgundies.

There is a single nod in the direction of the New World with Cloudy Bay Sauvignon Blanc – now owned by French Champagne house Veuve Clicquot. Champagne starts at around 79 francs, while top Grandes Marques such as Bollinger and Taittinger are roughly £5 cheaper than their counterparts in the UK. It's worth looking out for special deals on individual Champagnes. When we visited, Pol Roger White Foil was going for a chanson.

Given that 80 to 90 per cent of Perardel's customers are British and don't exactly rush to fill their trolleys with expensive clarets and Burgundies, Perardel is taking the downmarket route to be more competitive. This is all very well if it means encouraging customers to trade up to better wines, but we hope the newly arrived pallets of Liebfraumilch, Lambrusco and spumante don't compromise Perardel's laudable venture. Perhaps he ought to move to Boulogne.

White

Under 20FF

FRANCE

1992 Château Gazeau, Bordeaux Blanc
£ / 2 / ❶   12/20
Almond and beeswax Semillon characters on the palate, but little else to commend this cheap white Bordeaux blend.

1992 Chardonnay, Vin de Pays du Jardin de la France, Pierre Brevin
£ / 2 / ❶   12/20
Cool-fermented butter and banana fruitiness with a slightly bitter finish. Acceptable at the price.

1990 Château Le Reyssac, Bergerac Blanc
£ / 2 / ❶   13/20
Another Semillon-based Bordeaux-style white, marginally better than Perardel's other two cheap whites, but running out of steam.

20–30FF

FRANCE

1993 Château Peyrat, Graves Blanc, J. M. Cambillau
££ / 2 / ❶   15/20
Clean, zingy Sauvignon-dominated white Graves blend with attractive, grapefruity flavours.

1993 Bourgogne Aligoté, Domaine Belleville
£ / 2 / ▌   14/20
Hints of liquorice and angelica spice add to the interest of this
honeyed, characterful Côte Chalonnaise white. As usual,
Burgundy's Aligoté grape doesn't stint on acidity.

1993 Mâcon-Solutré-Pouilly, Pascal Rollet
£££ / 2 / ▌   16/20
A rare southern Burgundian *appellation*, blending wines from the
Mâcon-Village communes of Solutré and Pouilly. Full, lemony,
cinnamon freshness and a touch of spicy oak make this full-bodied
white Burgundy a real treat.

1992 Muscadet de Sèvre-et-Maine Sur Lie, Domaine de la Muraille, Couillaud-Brunelière
£££ / 2 / ▌   17/20
Classic Muscadet Sur Lie, with a richness that reminded us
of a top Chardonnay. Yeasty freshness with good sur lie
zip. Worth a trip to Calais on its own.

30–50FF

FRANCE

1992 Bourgogne Chardonnay Moreau
££ / 2 / ▌   15/20
A basic white Burgundy with some fruit sweetness and old-style
wet wool character.

1991 Montagny Premier Cru, Domaine Maurice Bertrand
£ / 2 / ▌   15/20
A very individual Côte Chalonnaise white Burgundy with good
potential and a herbal, aniseedy note.

Red

20–30FF

FRANCE

1993 Beaujolais Perardel, Cave de Beau Vallon
£ / MB / ▌   14/20
Beaujolais Nouveau-style red with soft, charming, banana and
bubblegum fruit.

1992 Chinon, Moulin de Beaupuy, Domaine Jacques Morin
££ / LB / ▌   15/20
Very light in colour, almost a rosé, in fact. The washed-out colour
of a watery vintage is deceptive, because the underlying, grassy
fruit is ripe and nicely balanced.

1989 Bourgogne Pinot Noir, Domaine Louis Violland
££ / LB / ▌   15/20
A basic Pinot Noir with some evolution, a bit of oak and an
attractive core of sweet fruit. Drink up.

1991 Fitou, Sélection des Vignerons, Mont Tauch
££ / FB / ▌   15/20
Tarry, peppery southern French red from an excellent co-operative
in the Languedoc hills. Showing the maturity Fitou needs to soften
its naturally robust tannins.

1990 Château Dubois Claverie, Bordeaux
£ / FB / ▌   14/20
Honest treacle-toffee Merlot with a rustic dry finish. Attractively
priced for a Right Bank claret.

30–50FF

FRANCE

1989 Château La Rose Chevrol, Fronsac
££ / MB / 🍾   15/20

For an extra five or so francs, it's worth pulling this smooth, savoury sweet Merlot-based Bordeaux off the shelf.

Over 50FF

FRANCE

1991 Châteauneuf-du-Pape, Cuvée du Vatican, Diffonty Felicien & Fils
£ / FB / 🍾   13/20

The Pope wouldn't be too chuffed with this one. It's rich, peppery and alcoholic, but we'd like to have seen a bit more fruit on the altar.

Rosé

Under 20FF

FRANCE

1990 Bourgogne Rosé, Domaine Jean Gros
££ / 2 / 🍾   15/20

A dry made-for-food rosé with soft, rich textured fruit and delicate, savoury flavours.

Sparkling

20–30FF

FRANCE

Brut 1415, Moingeon, Méthode Traditionnelle
££ / 3 / ▌ ·   **15/20**
Clean, toasty Chardonnay-based fizz made using the Champagne method by a Burgundy *négociant*. Better than it looks and a good buy at under 30 francs.

Over 50FF

FRANCE

Champagne Gustave Léon, Carte d'Or
0 / 2 / ▌   **13/20**
This premier prix Champagne has a curious unripe malt character and rather simple, unbalanced fruit.

Champagne D. Perardel, Brut Réserve
£ / 2 / ▌   **14/20**
The owner of Perardel is a Champenois, so a wine that bears his name ought to be a bit better than this. Pleasant enough with a touch of toastiness.

PIDOU (*)

Address: Zone Industrielle Marcel Doret, 190 Rue Marcel Dassault, 62100 Calais

Telephone: 010 33 21 96 78 10

Hours of opening: Daily 9am to 8pm except Wednesday

Manager: Francis Pille

Payment methods: Access, Visa; sterling and French francs

Discounts: No

English spoken: Yes

In-store tastings: No

Dave West of EastEnders gets on with the owners of Pidou about as well as he gets on with the French riot squad. Pidou is known chez West as 'Dick Turpin' – something to do with its skill at luring coachloads of Brits in off the nearby motorway and then vacuuming up the contents of their wallets perhaps. Is it more than a coincidence that one of Pidou's red vins de table is called 'Grand Dick'?

Pidou receives as many as 120 beer-and-wine-thirsty coachloads a day, most of them from Britain. Heaven knows why they come here. A good deal of the 300-strong (if that's the right word) range of wines consists of drab stuff from yawn-inducing French *négociants* and overpriced clarets in wooden bins. A handful of moderate Argentinian, Californian and Chilean wines pay lip service to the New World. But that's about it.

The same suppliers crop up again and again. Almost the entire Rhône and Burgundy range comes from Reine Pédauque, while the Ingersheim co-op cleans up in Alsace. The exception is Bordeaux, where Pidou makes a bit more effort. Otherwise, it's wall-to-wall Mateus Rosé, Mouton Cadet, Veuve du Vernay and Piat d'Or.

Nearly two-thirds of Pidou's sales are beer, rather than wine – a tribute to the quality of the range as much as the tastes of Pidou's customers. As well as Duvel, Leffe, Chimay and Greuze, there's the wonderful Bishop's Finger (known in parts of Kent as Nun's Delight), Jeanlain and Trompe La Mort. The 100 beers are outnumbered by the 300 wines, but if you find your coach driver heading for Pidou next time you're in Calais, you know what to do.

White

Under 20FF

FRANCE

Sylvette Vin de Table
0 / 3 / 1   10/20
Pink-tinged sweetish white. The sort of wine you wouldn't find in a British supermarket. Glory be.

Bergerac Sec
£ / 2 / 1   12/20
Fresh, drinkable basic quaffing white that could come from almost anywhere.

1993 Vin de Pays des Côtes de Gascogne, Carval
0 / 2 / 1   11/20
An appley sourness put us off this Gascon country blend.

La Chanterelle Bordeaux Blanc Moelleux
0 / 5 / 1   12/20
This is one of a number of Pidou own-labels, which in theory means it comes with the stamp of Pidou's wine buyer, Denis Letailleur. Perhaps sweet wines are not his strong suit.

Côtes de Bergerac, Moelleux
£ / 5 / 1   13/20
If you want a basic sweet white, this toffee apple, caramelised number should be up your rue.

20–30FF

FRANCE

1992 Muscadet Sur Lie, Château Plessis, Brézot
££ / 2 / ⚑   14/20
By Pidou's standards, this is a drinkable, reasonably priced white wine, with some genuine tangy sur lie character and length.

1992 Chardonnay Vin de Pays du Jardin de la France, Drouet Frères
££ / 3 / ⚑   14/20
Unoaked, sweet banana style Chardonnay from one of France's four major regional vins de pays.

1992 Gewürztraminer, Alsace, Jean Geiler
££ / 3 / ⚑   15/20
Lanolin and lychee perfume and typical Gewürztraminer floral spice make this a pleasantly balanced white.

1993 Vouvray Medium Dry, Comte de la Boisserie, Drouet Frères
££ / 4 / ⚑   14/20
Typically appley Chenin Blanc with medium sweetness and bracing acidity.

30–50FF

FRANCE

1992 Mâcon-Villages, Gauthey-Cadet Frères
£ / 2 / ⚑   14/20
Light, spicy, unoaked Chardonnay which should be more exciting at this price.

1993 Chablis, Domaine Vocoret
£ / 2 / ⚑   14/20
Still rather closed when we tasted it, but it may come round with a few months' bottle age. A steely, minerally Chablis that could do with a bit more flesh on the bones.

1993 Pouilly-Fuissé, Gauthey-Cadet Frères
£ / 2 / ▮   14/20
For nearly 60 francs, you'd expect some Pouilly-Fuissé character.
But it isn't immediately obvious in this fruity, cool-fermentation
Chardonnay.

Red

Under 20FF

FRANCE

Adeline, Vin de Pays de l'Aude
£ / MB / ▮   12/20
A southern French red made in the soft, juicy carbonic maceration
style for easy quaffing. Good cheap plonk.

Cuvée du Patron
£ / FB / ▮   13/20
We suspect this EU blend originated somewhere in the Italian
South, judging by its baked, raisiny spice. We quite enjoyed it at
the price, but weren't convinced that the cuvée would prove
consistent.

Les Sarmentières, Côtes du Roussillon
££ / MB / ▮   14/20
Attractive angostura aromatics with plenty of robust, rustic fruit.
If you want a cheap, basic *appellation* red, this is the kind of
thing to look for.

Vin de Pays des Bouches du Rhône
£££ / MB / ▮   14/20
Another juicy quaffing red with plum and violet character. A
bargain at under 10 francs.

20–30FF

FRANCE

1992 Château Gabachot, Roger Fernandez, Bordeaux
£ / MB / 🍷   14/20
Light, charming Merlot-dominated claret. Soft textured, simple flavours and some vanilla oak.

1992 Château du Moulin, Corbières, Cave de Limoux
££ / MB / 🍷   14/20
The Cave de Limoux is one of the best co-operatives in the Languedoc. This is a well-made, milk chocolatey, spicy, Corbières with supple fruit sweetness.

30–50FF

FRANCE

1993 Chinon, Domaine des Champs Vignons, Drouet Frères
££ / MB / 🍷   14/20
There's plenty of Cabernet Franc character on this unusually young (for Chinon) Loire red. With its serious dry finish, it could do with a bit more time.

1992 Fleurie, Gauthey-Cadet Frères
0 / MB / 🍷   11/20
Did someone steal the Gamay? If so, we'd like it back, please.

1990 Château La Boutisse, St Emilion Grand Cru
££ / MB / 🍷   16/20
One of the best reds at Pidou. Gamay, liquorice and blackcurrant style Right Bank claret with a nice brushstroke of vanilla oak.

Over 50FF

FRANCE

1992 Nuits-St-Georges, Gauthey-Cadet Frères
0 / MB / ❚   **12/20**
At over 80 francs a bottle, this is indicative of the poor value so
often offered by supposedly swanky red Burgundy. Oaky, souped-
up, rooty stuff from Beaune *négociant* Reine Pédauque.

1989 Château Tour de Laroze, Margaux
0 / MB / ❚   **14/20**
This is the second wine of Château Labégorce-Zédé, an estate in
Margaux. It's a light minty claret, but barely worthy of a second
label. Why not just declassify it?

Rosé

Under 20FF

FRANCE

Rosé Prestige Monchatour
£ / 2 / ❚   **12/20**
A clean, cheap Loire-style rosé with some strawberry and rose
petal aromas and a suggestion of the Cabernet Franc grape. A bit
thin, but at under 10 francs, what do you expect?

Sparkling

Over 50FF

FRANCE

Champagne Veuve Lorinet, de Castelnau
0 / 2 / ❚   **13/20**
Young, tart, basic premier prix Champagne with none of the yeast
autolysis character which makes méthode champenoise fizz
interesting.

J. SAINSBURY BIÈRES VINS ET SPIRITUEUX **(*)

Address: Mammouth Centre, Route de Boulogne, 62100 Calais

Telephone: 010 33 21 34 04 44 (Mammouth, ask for Sainsbury's)

Hours of opening: Monday to Saturday 9am to 8pm

Manager: Christophe Delamaere

Payment methods: Access, Visa; sterling and French francs

Discounts: No, but special offers on selected wines and beers

English spoken: Yes

In-store tastings: No

Sainsbury's created a small piece of retailing history on 27 April 1994, by becoming the first British supermarket to set up shop on the other side of the Channel. The 3,000 square foot store, called J. Sainsbury Vins, Bières et Spiritueux, is the smallest JS has opened since the 1930s, but is still a significant toe in the water. Rival Tesco is expected to follow soon and, if cross-Channel shopping continues to expand, other major multiples will surely join the French exiles.

J. Sainsbury Vins, Bières et Spiritueux is effectively a store within a store. Tucked away at one end of a Calais hypermarket, it is, appropriately, dwarfed by Mammouth next door. Although the two are theoretically in competition, JS and Mammouth are now business partners in a pan-European buying group called SEDD.

The French group was instrumental in Sainsbury's move to Calais. Mammouth oiled the bureaucratic wheels and provided the six 'bilingual' staff. Fortunately, it had nothing to do with the wines. The range runs to 280 well-loved beer, wine and spirits lines from JS stores back in Britain, with the emphasis on bulk sales and fairly safe choices. The selection is cosmopolitan, if restricted by space.

British food is not on the menu. Selling pork pies and jelly in France would be 'like pushing water uphill', according to Mike Connolly, Sainsbury's director of off-licence buying. Initial reports suggest that selling JS wines might prove similarly difficult. The French are largely uninterested and the Brits we spoke to didn't see the point of going to France to buy something they could buy back home, even at French prices. In most cases, the savings barely cover the difference in duty.

There are some very good wines here – far better than most of what turns up in French hypermarkets – but the store is hardly a revelation. Apart from the French staff, it looks like a modest supermarket off-licence in Britain. If the venture is to prosper, JS may have to offer its British customers a little more in the way of temptation.

For tasting notes, see under Sainsbury's, page 244–73.

THE WINE SOCIETY ***

Address: Rue Fressin, 62140 Hesdin

Telephone: 010 33 21 81 61 70

Hours of opening: Monday to Saturday 8am to 6pm (closed for lunch 12.30-1.45pm, Sundays and French public holidays)

Manager: Frédéric Picavet

Payment methods: Visa, Access; French cheques or banker's draft

Discounts: No

English spoken: Yes

In-store tastings: Yes

The Wine Society's brand new premises are situated on a corner of the charming cobbled square of Hesdin, opposite a chemist promoting cures for incontinence. Since opening up in 1993, the French-run wine shop has been enlarged to take over a former estate agent's next door. Clearly, somebody is doing something right.

The Wine Society sold roughly 12,000 cases in the first year of business, both to customers dropping in for their wines and via mail order inside France. 1994 has been even more successful.

There's only one problem, or rather two, with all this. To buy from The Wine Society, you have to be a member. And you have to motor inland the necessary distance from Boulogne or Calais to collect your wines. There are worse places to stop: Hesdin is pretty enough to be worth a detour on its own, and there are plenty of good hotels in the vicinity.

With around 100 wines and spirits to choose from, The Wine Society's Hesdin range is considerably more limited than in the UK, but it is growing. Last year there were only 60 things on the list.

With a decent New World section and some enjoyable Wine

Society stalwarts, the list is sufficiently extensive to make bringing wine back from France, especially fizz for parties and weddings, an interesting proposition. The range is far better than anything you're likely to encounter in a French supermarket.

White

20–30FF

ENGLAND

1992 Midsummer Hill
££ / 3 / ▮   15/20
Quintessential, good-value English white from Three Choirs vineyard in Gloucestershire. Floral, hedgerow fragrance and nettley, summery fruit. A blend of Müller-Thurgau, Seyval Blanc, Reichensteiner, Madeleine Angevine and Schönburger, in case dinner party guests are still listening.

FRANCE

1993 Le Prada, Vin de Pays des Côtes de Gascogne
££ / 2 / ▮   14/20
Made by the densely bearded, leather-jacketed Yves Grassa, this is a clean, grassy, modern white from three musketeer country in the south-west of France.

1993 Domaine de Lahitte, Vin de Pays des Côtes de Gascogne
£££ / 2 / ▮   15/20
A step up in intensity from the slightly less expensive Le Prada, Alain Lalanne's blend of Ugni Blanc and the superior Colombard is well worth the extra few francs.

1993 The Society's French Country White, Corbières
0 / 2 / ▮   12/20
Corbières is not best known for its white wines. This earthy, lumpen white shows you why.

1993 The Society's French Dry White, Vin de Pays d'Oc
£ / 2 / 🍾   14/20

A clean, basic white from the sweep of coastline between Montpellier and the Pyrenees. Aromatic Sauvignon Blanc and Muscat have been added to the blend, but even a Master of Wine would have trouble spotting them.

1993 The Society's White Bordeaux
0 / 2 / 🍾   12/20

Surely Peter Sichel of Châteaux Palmer and d'Angludet fame can come up with something better than this ordinary blend.

The Society's Bordeaux Sauvignon
£ / 2 / 🍾   14/20

Thank you Peter, you just did.

1993 The Society's Muscadet de Sèvre-et-Maine
£££ / 2 / 🍾   15/20

One of a series of hearteningly good Muscadets tasted on the other side of the Channel. This is fresh, dry and appley with uncharacteristic length for a straightforward dry white.

ITALY

1993 Soave Via Nova
££ / 2 / 🍾   15/20

Made by the Cantine Sociale di Soave, which controls most of the region's production, this is a modern style Soave with good citrus fruit and a typical almondy bite.

30–50FF

FRANCE

1992 The Society's Sauvignon, Touraine
0 / 2 / 🍾   12/20

Oisly et Thésée is normally one of the best co-operatives in France, so we wonder what happened here. Wait for the fresher 1993.

1993 The Society's Vin d'Alsace
£ / 2 / 🍾   13/20

A simple, peachy blend of Alsatian grape varieties, made by the respected Hugel merchant family of Riquewihr.

1993 The Society's Chardonnay, Vin de Pays de l'Hérault
£ / 2 / 🍾   14/20
Fruity, unoaked, no-frills Chardonnay from white wine specialist Pierre Bésinet in the Midi. Expect more of this sort of thing from the South of France.

1992 The Society's White Burgundy, Mâcon-Villages
£ / 2 / 🍾   14/20
Clean, appley, straightforward Mâcon-Villages with a faintly bitter finish.

SPAIN

1993 Marqués de Alella Clásico
£ / 3 / 🍾   13/20
An unusual blend of Macabeo, Pansa Blanca and Chenin Blanc from the smallest *appellation* in Spain near Barcelona. Refreshing sweet and sour fruit.

Over 50FF

AUSTRALIA

1991 Wirra Wirra Chardonnay
££ / 2 / 🍾   15/20
Ben Riggs is one of Australia's finest red winemakers, but his whites come close to the same high standards. This is a rich but elegant South Australian Chardonnay with plenty of oak and a green olive aftertaste.

FRANCE

1990 The Society's Gewürztraminer
££ / 3 / 🍾   15/20
When it comes to Gewürztraminer, the Hugel family pulls out the big one, as the athletics commentator David Coleman used to put it. A richly upholstered, exotically perfumed example of a take it or leave it grape.

1985 The Society's Celebration White Burgundy
££ / 2 / ▮   16/20
Raise your glass to the normally uninspired Burgundian house of
Remoissenet who, on this special occasion, have come up with a
toasty, complex white Burgundy worth celebrating.

1992 The Society's Chablis, Moreau
£ / 2 / ▮   15/20
A forward, fruity Chablis from a large *négociant*. The cool
temperature derived flavours of banana are complemented by
minerally undertones.

1992 Pouilly-Fumé, Bailly
£££ / 1 / ⌐   17/20
Michel Bailly is a consistently excellent grower with whom
The Wine Society has established a long-standing
relationship. This is a dry, typically flinty Sauvignon Blanc
with fresh acidity and depth of flavour.

1992 Sancerre, La Reine Blanche
£££ / 2 / ⌐   17/20
Made by Vacheron, one of the leading families in Sancerre,
this is the sort of thing the Loire needs to produce to stand
up to the challenge of New Zealand. Soft, supple and grassy
with fine fruit intensity. A classic.

NEW ZEALAND

1993 Selaks Marlborough Sauvignon Blanc
££ / 2 / ▮   16/20
Selaks are based in the Auckland region, but the grapes for this
elderflower and asparagus scented Sauvignon Blanc come from
Marlborough in New Zealand's more temperate South Island.
Zingy, bracing stuff.

Red

20–30FF

FRANCE

The Society's Claret
0 / MB / ◗   12/20
By some distance, this is The Wine Society's most popular red
wine. Perhaps the name counts for more than the stuff in the bottle.

The Society's Merlot, Vin de Pays de l'Hérault
£ / MB / ◗   13/20
Yet another Pierre Bésinet wine, this soft blackcurrant pastille style
red is a better bet than the claret.

The Society's French Full Red
£ / MB / ◗   13/20
Supple, Beaujolais-style fruit with a tannic edge. The thinking
person's Piat d'Or.

1992 Minervois, Domaine du Moulin Rigaud
££ / MB / ◗   14/20
Attractive, juicy southern red with a touch of pepper and
Mediterranean herb, finishing rather dry.

Domaine de Limbardie, Vin de Pays des Coteaux de Murviel
££ / MB / ◗   15/20
Made by charming pied noir Henri Boukandoura, using the
carbonic maceration technique to soften the wine's hard edges,
this is a juicy upfront quaffer from a small vin de pays
dénomination in the Languedoc.

The Society's Côtes du Rhône
0 / MB / ◗   12/20
A rather soupy merchant blend, shy about its origins.

SPAIN

1990 The Society's Rioja
£ / MB / ❫   14/20

A good introduction to Rioja showing well-integrated fruit and
sweet American vanilla oakiness.

30–50FF

AUSTRALIA

1990 Basedow Barossa Valley Shiraz
££ / FB / ➦   15/20

No mistaking the origin of this wine or the grape variety from
which it was made. Sweet toffee and blackberry fruit, a touch of
mint and just the right amount of oak make this a winner, sport.

CHILE

1990 Concha y Toro Cabernet Sauvignon
££ / MB / ❫   15/20

Perfumed, well-balanced southern hemisphere red with a strong
emphasis on ripe blackcurrant fruit and none of the bitterness
often associated with Chilean Cabernet Sauvignon.

FRANCE

1990 The Society's Crozes-Hermitage
££ / MB / ❫   16/20

The Cave de Tain makes two-thirds of the entire production of
Crozes-Hermitage, and to a generally high standard. This juicy
blackberry and cherry style red shows plenty of the exuberant
spiciness of the Syrah grape.

1990 Côtes de Saint-Mont Collection
£ / MB / ➦   14/20

A savoury Tannat-based red from south-west France with oak-ageing
contributing to the wine's robust, unyielding tannins.

1992 The Society's Beaujolais-Villages
£ / MB / 🍷   **13/20**

A slight jamminess put us off here, but the wine shows some of the sweet, simple fruit of the Gamay grape.

The Society's Médoc
£ / MB / 🍷   **14/20**

A step up from the Society's Claret, this has a bit more weight, punch and length on the palate. Worth the extra dosh.

The Society's St Emilion
££ / MB / 🍷   **15/20**

From the specialist Right Bank merchant, Jean-Pierre Moueix, a rounder, sweeter claret with classic aromatic Merlot character and a well-judged kiss of oak.

The Society's Red Burgundy
£ / MB / 🍷   **14/20**

A pleasantly fruity, if basic, raspberryish Pinot Noir with marginally obtrusive tannins.

ITALY

1990 Chianti Rufina, Villa di Vetrice
££ / MB / 👉   **15/20**

Made by the value-conscious Grati family in the Rufina hills east of Florence, this is a typically savoury, almost rustic Chianti from one of the best vintages in recent years. Characterful stuff, which has improved with age.

1989 Rosso Cent'are Duca del Castelmonte
£ / MB / 🍷   **14/20**

A surprisingly modern red from the island of Sicily, using the obscure local Nero d'Avola and Nerello Mascalese grapes to good effect. Sweet smooth, raisiny fruit overlaid with hefty oak.

1991 Barbera d'Asti Superiore
££ / MB / 🍷   **14/20**

From the Araldica co-operative in Italy's hilly north-west, this is a reliable red for drinking with basic Italian food. Savoury fruit and a zip of acidity make this an enjoyable drop.

1990 The Society's Chianti Classico, Capelli
££ / MB / ▌   15/20
Made in the largest and most famous of Chianti's seven DOCG
zones at the Montagliari estate in Panzano, this is a characterful
Tuscan red from the excellent 1990 vintage.

SPAIN

1989 Rioja Crianza Navajas
£ / MB / ▌   14/20
Commercial Spanish red with lashings of coconutty American oak
character. Like a grown-up Don Darias.

1984 Valdepeñas Gran Reserva, Bodegas Los Llanos
££ / MB / ▌   15/20
A treat to come across a wine with ten years' cask- and bottle-age
behind it. This gamey, almost red Burgundy-like Spanish red is a
real bargain, but needs drinking up.

Over 50FF

FRANCE

1989 Château Beaumont, Haut-Médoc
££ / MB / ━   16/20
Situated between the villages of Margaux and St Julien in the heart
of the Haut Médoc, this large and dependable cru bourgeois estate
is one of Bordeaux's better buys. Green pepper and pencil shavings
characterise this coffee-ish, modern claret.

1989 The Society's Celebration Pomerol
££ / MB / ▌   16/20
A ripe, toffee-like Pomerol from the merchant firm of Jean-Pierre
Moueix in Libourne. There's a powerful, almost Californian
richness to the fruit. Celebrate in style.

1990 Sancerre Rouge, Les Cailleries, Vacheron
£ / MB / ⸙ 15/20
Pinot Noir from the cool Loire Valley is never going to achieve the same complexity or depth of flavour as the best wines from Burgundy's Côte d'Or, but the simple, honest fruit of this pleasant, slightly leafy red will do nicely on a warm summer's day.

Rosé

20–30FF

FRANCE

1993 The Society's Rosé, Vin de Pays de l'Hérault
£ / 3 / ⸙ 13/20
A pleasant strawberry-cup rosé from the southern French Pierre Bésinet stable. A trifle sweet perhaps.

Sparkling

30–50FF

SPAIN

Conde de Caralt Brut Cava
££ / 2 / ⸙ 15/20
A traditional blend of Xarel-lo, Parellada and Macabeo, this buttery, modern cava is a welcome new addition to The Wine Society's range. Very good basic fizz.

Over 50FF

FRANCE

The Society's Sparkling Saumur
££ / 2 / 🍾   15/20
The Chenin Blanc character, which can be off-putting in Loire whites, is nicely muted in this elegant, well-balanced fizz from Gratien et Mayer.

The Society's Champagne Brut
££ / 2 / 🍾   17/20
The Wine Society has been buying English favourite, Alfred Gratien Champagne, since 1907, so they are clearly doing something right. Chocolatey, tangy fizz, which, unusually for Champagne, is fermented in oak rather than stainless steel.

INDEX